On This Date:

A Day-By-Day
Guide to History

by Brian Merrill

Orginally published under the title On This Date: A Day-by-Day
Look at Historical Events.

ISBN   1440487979
EAN-13   9781440487972

I would like to dedicate this book to my wife, Cara, who makes my life complete, and to my students, past and present, which have laughed at my silly jokes and listened to my stories with enthusiasm.

This book has been compiled through years of research of sources way too numerous to list. I began what I call "On This Date" many years ago as a way to grab my students' attention in order to begin classes. It was just an interesting way to pass on some of my trivial knowledge to the kids. Along the way, it has turned into a love of knowledge, not just for me, but for the middle school students whom I have the honor of teaching.

This book is organized by date, starting with January 1st at the front and ending with December 31st at the end. Each page starts with famous birthdays listed with the person's birth year beside the name. Below that are the events that happened on that date, listed chronologically. This book is not intended to be read cover to cover, but to be used as a reference book.

I know full well that this second edition, although heavily edited, may still contain mistakes (hopefully not as many as the first edition) and I welcome feedback from my readers. If you see anything that is in error, please email me your corrections to **coachb_merr@yahoo.com**. I would also welcome comments.

Enjoy.

January

January 1: Paul Revere 1735, Betsy Ross 1752, J. Edgar Hoover 1895, Dana Andrews 1909, Barry Goldwater 1909, Hank Greenberg 1911, J. D. Salinger 1919, Rocky Graziano 1922, Matthew "Stymie" Beard 1925, Frank Langella 1940, Jimmy Hart 1943, Verne Troyer 1969

45 BC – The Julian calendar took effect
404 – The last gladiator competition was held in Rome
630 – The Prophet Muhammed set out on his journey to conquer Mecca
1600 – Scotland began using the Julian calendar
1700 – Russia began using the Julian calendar
1788 – The first edition of "The Times" of London was published
1797 – Albany became the capital of New York State, replacing New York City
1801 – Italian astronomer Giuseppe Piazzi became the first person to discover an asteroid, naming it Ceres
1808 – The United States prohibited the import of slaves from Africa
1818 – *Frankenstein* by Mary Shelley was published
1863 – President Abraham Lincoln signed the Emancipation Proclamation, which declared that all slaves in the rebel states were free (see picture on next page)
1892 – Ellis Island was opened in New York City, and began accepting immigrants
1893 – Japan began using the Gregorian calendar
1899 – Spanish rule of Cuba ended
1901 – The Commonwealth of Australia was formed
1902 – In the first Rose Bowl football game, Michigan defeated Stanford, 49-0
1908 – A ball was dropped in Times Square in New York City for the first time to signify the New Year
1934 – Alcatraz Island officially became a Federal Prison
1937 – The first Cotton Bowl was played in Dallas, Texas
1953 – Hank Williams died of drug and alcohol overdose at the age of 29

1959 – Fidel Castro overthrew the government of Fulgencio Batista, and seized power in Cuba

1971 – Cigarette ads on American television were banned

1985 – The Internet's Domain Name System was begun

1990 – David Dinkins was sworn in as New York City's first black mayor

1990 – The British television comedy *Mr. Bean* debuted

1993 – Czechoslovakia was split into two separate states, the Czech Republic and Slovakia

1999 – The Euro currency was introduced

2008 – A law went into effect in New Hampshire, allowing for civil unions of same-sex couples

January 2: Nathaniel Bacon 1647, James Wolfe 1727, Anna Lee 1913, Isaac Asimov 1920, Roger Miller 1936, Jim Bakker 1940, Jack Hanna 1947, Wendy Phillips 1952, Gabrielle Carteris 1961, David Cone 1963, Edgar Martinez 1963, Greg Swindell 1965, Cuba Gooding, Jr. 1968, Christy Turlington 1969, Lisa Harrison 1971, Tricia Helfer 1974, Jeff Suppan 1975, Paz Vega 1976, Kate Bosworth 1983, Heather O'Reilly 1985, Syesha Mercado 1987

1788 – Georgia became the 4th U.S. state

1860 – It was announced that a new planet, named Vulcan, had been discovered orbiting between Mercury and the Sun, although later evidence disproved this discovery

1870 – Construction on the Brooklyn Bridge began

1872 – Brigham Young, the 71-year-old leader of the Mormon Church, was arrested on charges of bigamy, for having 25 wives

1900 – The Chicago Canal opened

1929 – The United States and Canada agreed on a plan to preserve Niagara Falls

1942 – Manila, the capital of the Philippines, was captured by Japanese forces during World War II

1955 – President Jose Antonio Remon of Panama was assassinated

1959 – Luna-1, the first artificial satellite to orbit the sun and the first to fly past the Moon, was launched by the Soviet Union

1960 – Senator John F. Kennedy of Massachusetts announced his candidacy for the Democratic presidential nomination

1965 – University of Alabama quarterback Joe Namath was signed by the New York Jets football team

1968 – Dr. Christian Barnard performed the first successful heart transplant

1971 – In the United States, a federally imposed ban on television cigarette advertisements went into effect

1974 – President Richard Nixon signed a bill requiring all states to lower the maximum speed limit to 55 MPH

2001 – Sila Calderon became the first female governor of Puerto Rico

2006 – Twelve coal miners died as a result of an explosion at the Sago Mine in West Virginia

2008 – The price for a barrel of oil reached over $100 for the first time

January 3: Marcus Tillius Cicero 106 BC, Grace Coolidge 1879, J.R.R. Tolkien 1892, Ray Milland 1905, Victor Borge 1909, Hank Stram 1924, Robert Loggia 1930, Dabney Coleman 1932, Bobby Hull 1939, Stephen Stills 1945, John Paul Jones 1946, Betty Rollin 1946, Victoria Principal 1950, Mel Gibson 1956, Danica McKellar 1975, A.J. Burnett 1977, Kimberly Locke 1978, Eli Manning 1981, Lloyd 1986

1431 – Joan of Arc was turned over to Bishop Pierre Cauchon

1521 – Martin Luther was excommunicated by Pope Leo X

1777 – George Washington defeated the British forces, led by General Charles Cornwallis at the Battle of Princeton (see picture to the right)

1833 – Great Britain seized control of the Falkland Islands

1861 – Delaware voted not to secede from the United States

1920 – The New York Yankees bought Babe Ruth from the Boston Red Sox for $125,000

1924 – English explorer Howard Carter discovered the sarcophagus of Tutankhamen in the Valley of the Kings, near Luxor, Egypt

1938 – Franklin D. Roosevelt established the March of Dimes

1951 – *Dragnet* was first broadcast on NBC-TV

1953 – Frances Bolton and Oliver Bolton became the first mother-son combination to serve simultaneously in the United States Congress

1959 – Alaska became the 49th state

1961 – The United States cut diplomatic relations with Cuba

1962 – Pope John XXIII excommunicated Cuban leader Fidel Castro

1967 – Jack Ruby died in a Dallas, Texas hospital

1973 – CBS sold the New York Yankees to a 12-man syndicate headed by George Steinbrenner for $10 million

1980 – Conservationist Joy Adamson, author of *Born Free*, was killed in northern Kenya by a servant

1987 – Aretha Franklin became the first woman inducted into the Rock-and-Roll Hall of Fame

1993 – *Star Trek: Deep Space Nine* made its television debut

1993 – United States President George H. W. Bush and Russian President Boris Yeltsin signed the Strategic Arms Reduction Treaty (START) in Moscow

1997 – Bryant Gumbel signed off for the last time as host of NBC's Today Show

1999 – The Mars Polar Lander was launched

2000 – Charles M. Schulz's final original daily comic strip appeared in newspapers

January 4: Jacob Grimm 1785, Louis Braille 1809, Charles "Tom Thumb" Stratton 1838, James Bond 1900, Sterling Holloway 1905, Jane Wyman 1914, William Colby 1920, Sorrell Booke 1930, Don Shula 1930, Floyd Patterson 1935, Dyan Cannon 1937, Maureen Reagan 1941, Doris Kearns Goodwin 1943, Patty Loveless 1957, Matt Frewer 1958, Patrick Cassidy 1961, Dave Foley 1963, Julia Ormond 1965, Deana Carter 1966, Jeremy Licht 1971, Ted Lilly 1976

871 – Ethelred of Wessex was defeated by an invading Danish army at the Battle of Reading

1493 – Christopher Columbus left for his return trip to Europe after his first trip to the New World

1698 – The Palace of Whitehall, long-time home to English monarchs, was mostly destroyed by fire

1717 – England, France and the Netherlands signed the Triple Alliance, allying against Spain
1762 – England declared war on Spain and Naples
1847 – Samuel Colt sold his first revolver to the United States government
1885 – The first successful appendectomy was performed by Dr. William Grant
1896 – Utah became the 45th U.S. state
1936 – *Billboard Magazine* published its first pop music charts
1951 – Seoul was captured by North Korean and Chinese forces during the Korean War
1958 – Sputnik I fell to Earth after just 3 months in orbit
1965 – Poet T.S. Eliot died at age 76
1974 – President Richard Nixon refused to hand over tape recordings and documents subpoenaed by the Senate Watergate Committee
1980 – President Carter announced the United States would boycott the Olympics in Moscow
1982 – Bryant Gumbel moved from NBC Sports to the anchor desk where he joined Jane Pauley as co-host of the *Today* show on NBC
1984 – The first episode of *Night Court* aired
1987 – An Amtrak train bound from Washington to Boston collided with Conrail engines approaching from a side track killing 16 people
1999 – Former professional wrestler Jesse "The Body" Ventura was sworn in as Minnesota's 37th governor
2004 – NASA's Spirit rover landed on Mars and began sending back black and white images three hours after landing
2007 – Nancy Pelosi became the first woman elected as the Speaker of the House in the U.S. House of Representatives

January 5: King Camp Gillette 1855, Jeane Dixon 1904, Hugh Brannum 1910, George Reeves 1914, Walter Mondale 1928, Robert Duvall 1930, Chuck Noll 1932, Juan Carlos I of Spain 1938, Charlie Rose 1942, Diane Keaton 1946, Ted Lange 1947, Pamela Sue Martin 1953, Alex English 1954, Clancy Brown 1959, Jeff Fassero 1963, Marilyn Manson 1969, Warrick Dunn 1975

1781 – Richmond, Virginia was burned by a British naval expedition led by former American general Benedict Arnold
1896 – It was reported by *The Austrian* newspaper that Wilhelm Roentgen had discovered the type of radiation that became known as X-rays
1925 – Mrs. Nellie Taylor Ross was sworn in as the governor of Wyoming, the first female governor in the United States
1933 – Construction of the Golden Gate Bridge began
1934 – Fenway Park caught on fire

1945 – Pepe LePew made his debut
1956 – In the Peanuts comic strip, Snoopy walked on two legs for the first time
1957 – Jackie Robinson retired from Major League Baseball
1961 – The TV show *Mr. Ed* debuted
1970 – *All My Children* first appeared on ABC
1971 – The Harlem Globetrotters lost to the New Jersey Reds, 100-99, ending a 2,495 game win streak
1972 - President Richard Nixon ordered the development of the space shuttle
1998 - U.S. Representative and former entertainer Sonny Bono died in a skiing accident
1998 – The Ice Storm of '98 began in Maine and other parts of the Northeast
2005 – Eris, the largest dwarf-planet in the Solar System and just slightly larger than the more famous Pluto, was discovered

January 6: Richard II of England 1367, Joan of Arc 1412, Carl Sandburg 1878, Tom Mix 1880, Sam Rayburn 1882, Loretta Young 1910, Danny Thomas 1912, Sun Myung Moon 1920, Early Wynn 1920, Earl Scruggs 1924, John De Lorean 1925, Kim Dae-jung 1926, Vic Tayback 1930, Lou Holtz 1937, Bonnie Franklin 1944, Rowan Atkinson 1957, Nancy Lopez Knight 1957, Howie Long 1960, Gabrielle Reece 1970, Danny Pintauro 1976, Richard Zednik 1976, Asante Samuel 1981, Gilbert Arenis 1982

871 – England's King Alfred defeated the Danes at the Battle of Ashdown
1540 – King Henry VIII of England was married to Anne of Cleves, his fourth wife (see image to the left)
1759 – George Washington and Martha Dandridge Custis were married
1838 – Samuel Morse demonstrated the telegraph for the first time
1853 – Ben Pierce, the eleven-year-old son of President-elect Franklin Pierce, was killed in a train wreck in Massachusetts, while riding with his parents
1912 – New Mexico became the 47th U.S. state

1919 – Former President Theodore Roosevelt died in his sleep at the age of 60

1929 – Mother Theresa arrived in Calcutta to begin her life-long work to help the poor of India

1931 – Thomas Edison submitted his final patent application

1945 – The Battle of the Bulge ended with 130,000 German and 77,000 Allied casualties

1952 – *Peanuts* debuted in Sunday papers across the United States

1975 – *Wheel of Fortune* made its debut

1994 – Figure skater Nancy Kerrigan was clubbed on the right leg by an assailant at Cobo Arena in Detroit

January 7: Joseph Bonaparte 1768, Millard Fillmore 1800, Emile Borel 1871, Alan Napier 1903, Butterfly McQueen 1911, Charles Addams 1912, Maury Povich 1939, Tony Conigliaro 1945, Kenny Loggins 1948, Erin Gray 1952, David Caruso 1956, Katie Couric 1957, Nicholas Cage 1964, Doug E. Doug 1970, Eric Gagne 1976, Alfonso Soriano 1976, Dustin Diamond 1977, Jon Lester 1984

1536 – Catherine of Aragon, first wife of Henry VIII of England, died at the age of 50

1608 – Fire destroyed Jamestown, Virginia

1610 – Galileo Galilei was the first to see four of Jupiter's moons and named them Io, Europa, Ganymede, and Callisto

1782 – The Bank of North America, the first American commercial bank, opened

1785 – Frenchman Jean-Pierre Blanchard and American John Jeffries successfully made the first balloon crossing of the English Channel

1926 – George Burns and Gracie Allen were married

1927 – The Harlem Globetrotters played their first game

1947 – *It's a Wonderful Life* was released

1953 – President Harry Truman announced that the United States had developed the hydrogen bomb

1989 – Crown Prince Akihito became the emperor of Japan following the death of his father, Emperor Hirohito

1990 – The Leaning Tower of Pisa was closed to the public for safety concerns

1999 – President Bill Clinton went on trial before the Senate

January 8: James Longstreet 1821, William Hartnell 1908, Jose Ferrer 1909, Soupy Sales 1926, Charles Osgood 1933, Elvis Presley 1935, Shirley Bassey 1937, Bob Eubanks 1938, Christy Lane 1940, Stephen Hawking 1942, Terry Brooks 1944, David Bowie 1947, Bruce Sutter 1953,

Michelle Forbes 1967, R. Kelly 1969, Ami Dolenz 1969, Jason Giambi 1971, Rachel Nichols 1980, Gaby Hoffman 1982, Chris Masters 1983

1642 – Astronomer Galileo Galilei died in Arcetri, Italy
1790 – In the United States, George Washington delivered the first State of the Union address
1815 – The Battle of New Orleans began
1877 – Crazy Horse and his warriors fought their final battle against the U.S. Cavalry in Montana
1900 – President William McKinley placed Alaska under military rule
1918 – President Woodrow Wilson announced his Fourteen Points as the basis for peace upon the end of World War I
1958 – Bobby Fisher won the United States Chess Championship for the first time, at the age of 14
1959 – The conquest of Cuba by Fidel Castro was completed
1962 – Leonardo DaVinci's *Mona Lisa* was exhibited in the United States for the first time
1973 – The trial began in Washington of seven men accused of bugging the Democratic Party headquarters in the Watergate apartment complex in Washington, DC
1999 – The top two executives of Salt Lake City's Olympic Organizing Committee resigned amid disclosures that civic boosters had given money to members of the International Olympic Committee
2004 – *The Apprentice* first aired on NBC-TV

January 9: Pope Gregory XV 1554, Chic Young 1901, Richard M. Nixon 1913, Fernando Lamas 1915, Judith Krantz 1928, Bart Starr 1934, Bob Denver 1935, Dick Enberg 1935, Joan Baez 1941, Jimmy Page 1944, David "Buster Poindexter" Johansen 1950, M.L. Carr 1951, Crystal Gayle 1951, J.K. Simmons 1955, Mark Martin 1959, Otis Nixon, 1959, Joely Richardson 1965, Dave Mathews 1967, Jay Powell 1972, A.J. McLean 1978, Sergio Garcia 1980

1788 – Connecticut became the 5th state
1793 – Jean-Pierre Blanchard made the first successful balloon flight in the United States
1858 – Anson Jones, the last President of the Republic of Texas, committed suicide
1861 – Mississippi became the second state to secede from the United States
1902 – New York State introduced a bill to outlaw flirting in public
1951 – The United Nations headquarters officially opened in New York City

1972 – The ocean liner *Queen Elizabeth* was destroyed by fire in Hong Kong harbor
1984 – Clara Peller was first seen by TV viewers in the "Where's the Beef?" commercial campaign for Wendy's
1995 – Russian cosmonaut Valeri Poliakov, age 51, completed his 366th day in outer space aboard the Mir space station, breaking the record for the longest continuous time spent in outer space
2006 – *The Phantom of the Opera* surpassed *Cats* as the longest running show on Broadway

January 10: Charles Ingalls 1836, Frank James 1843, Mary Ingalls 1865, Grigori Rasputin 1869, Ray Bolger 1904, Paul Henried 1908, Bernard Lee 1908, Max Roach 1925, Roy Edward Disney 1930, Willie McCovey 1938, Frank Mahovlich 1938, Sal Mineo 1939, Jim Croce 1943, Rod Stewart 1945, William Sanderson 1948, George Foreman 1949, Pat Benatar 1953, Evan Handler 1961, Janet Jones 1961, Glenn Robinson 1973, Jake Delhomme 1975, Adam Kennedy 1976, Josh Ryan Evans 1982

1776 – Thomas Paine published his pamphlet *Common Sense*
1810 – The marriage of Napoleon and Josephine was annulled
1861 – Florida seceded from the United States
1870 – John D. Rockefeller incorporated Standard Oil
1901 – Oil was discovered at Spindletop in Beaumont, Texas
1920 – In its first meeting, the League of Nations ratified the Treaty of Versailles, officially ending World War I
1946 – The first General Assembly of the United Nations was held in London
1951 – The first jet passenger trip was made
1957 – Harold Macmillan became Prime Minister of Britain, following the resignation Anthony Eden
1967 – PBS television began with 70 stations
1969 – The last issue of *The Saturday Evening Post* was published
1990 – Time Inc. and Warner Communications Inc. completed a $14 billion merger, forming Time Warner
1999 – *The Sopranos* debuted on HBO-TV
2003 – North Korea announced that it was withdrawing from the global nuclear arms control treaty and that it had no plans to develop nuclear weapons

January 11: Alexander Hamilton 1755, Ezra Cornell 1807, Sir John A. Macdonald 1815, Slim Harpo 1924, Grant Tinker 1925, Mitchell Ryan 1934, Jean Chretien 1934, Clarence Clemons 1942, Naomi Judd 1946,

Ben Crenshaw 1952, Kim Coles 1963, Jason Connery 1963, Mary J. Blige 1971, Amanda Peet 1972, Tony Allen 1982

1693 – Mount Etna erupted in Sicily
1787 – Two of Uranus' moons, Titania and Oberon, were discovered by William Herschel
1815 – General Andrew Jackson achieved victory at the Battle of New Orleans
1861 – Alabama seceded from the United States
1902 – *Popular Mechanics* magazine was published for the first time
1922 – Insulin was first used to treat diabetes in a human
1935 – Amelia Earhart became the first person to fly solo from Hawaii to California
1938 – In Limerick, Maine, Frances Moulton assumed her duties as the first woman bank president
1942 – Japan declared war against the Netherlands
1942 – Kuala Lumpur was captured by Japan
1943 – The United States and Great Britain gave up territorial rights to China
1949 – The first recorded case of snowfall in Los Angeles occurred
1963 – The first disco in the United States opened in Los Angeles
1964 – The American Surgeon General said that smoking may be hazardous to your health
1973 – Owners of American League baseball teams voted to adopt the designated-hitter rule on a trial basis
1973 – The Watergate trial began
1974 – The world's first surviving sextuplets were born in Cape Town, South Africa
1976 – *The Bionic Woman* debuted on ABC-TV
1986 – The Gateway Bridge in Brisbane, Australia was officially opened
1995 – The WB television network began broadcasting
1996 – Ryutaro Hashimoto become Japan's Prime Minister
2001 – The Federal Trade Commission approved the merger of AOL and Time Warner to form AOL Time Warner
2002 – Thomas Junta, age 44, was convicted of involuntary manslaughter for beating another man to death at their sons' hockey practice

January 12: John Singer Sargent 1856, Jack London 1876, Herman Goering 1893, Tex Ritter 1905, Henny Youngman 1906, Ron Harper 1936, Alfred Rosenberg 1893, King Saud of Saudi Arabia 1902, Sergei Korolev 1907, PW Botha 1916, Katherine MacGregor 1925, The Amazing Kreskin 1935, William Lee Golden 1939, Joe Frazier 1944, Rush Limbaugh 1951, Ricky Van Shelton 1952, Howard Stern 1954, Kirstie Alley 1955, Oliver

Platt 1960, Dominique Wilkins 1960, Jeff Bezos 1964, Rob Zombie 1966, Vendela 1967, Bobby Crosby 1980, Dontrelle Willis 1982, Andrew Lawrence 1988

1915 – The Rocky Mountain National Park was founded
1915 – The United States House of Representatives rejected a proposal to give women the right to vote
1932 – Hattie W. Caraway became the first woman elected to the United States Senate
1945 – During World War II, Soviet forces began a huge offensive against the Germans in Eastern Europe
1966 – *Batman* debuted on ABC-TV
1969 – Led Zeppelin released their first album
1971 – *All in the Family* debuted on CBS-TV
1971 – The Harrisburg Six pled guilty to conspiring to kidnap Secretary of State Henry Kissinger and of plotting to blow up the heating tunnels of the federal buildings in Washington, DC
1976 – Prolific mystery writer Agatha Christie died at the age of 85
1981 – The ABC television show *Dynasty* debuted
1986 – The space shuttle Columbia blasted off with a crew that included the first Hispanic-American in space, Dr. Franklin R. Chang-Diaz
1991 – The U.S. Congress passed a resolution authorizing President George H. W. Bush to use military power to force Iraq out of Kuwait
1995 – The O.J. Simpson murder trail began, as he was accused of murdering his ex-wife and her friend
2000 – Charlotte Hornets guard Bobby Phills was killed in a crash during a drag race

January 13: Maria Anna of Austria 1610, Salmon P. Chase 1808, Sophie Tucker 1884, Robert Stack 1919, Johnny Haymer 1920, Gwen Verdon 1925, Frances Sternhagen 1930, Liz Anderson 1930, Charles Nelson Reilly 1931, Rip Taylor 1934, Richard Moll 1943, Brandon Tartikoff 1949, Bob Forsch 1950, Julia Louis-Dreyfus 1961, Trace Adkins 1962, Penelope Ann Miller 1964, Patrick Dempsey 1966, Traci Bingham 1968, Nicole Eggert 1972, Orlando Bloom 1977, James Posey 1977, Reggie Brown 1981

888 – Odo, Count of Paris, became King of the Franks
1610 – Galileo discovered the fourth Moon of Jupiter, Callisto
1840 – The steamship *Lexington* burned and sank off the coast of Long Island, New York resulting in the deaths of 139 people
1854 – Anthony Faas was granted a patent for the accordion
1893 – Britain's Independent Labor Party met for the first time

1915 – An earthquake in Italy killed almost 30,000 people
1928 – Ernst F. W. Alexanderson gave the first public demonstration of television
1929 – Wyatt Earp died at the age of 80
1930 – The Mickey Mouse comic strip first appeared in newspapers
1938 – The Church of England accepted the Theory of Evolution
1942 – The United States began Japanese American internment
1957 – Wham-O produced the first Frisbee
1962 – Ernie Kovacs died in a car crash in West Los Angeles
1966 – Robert C. Weaver became the first African-American Cabinet member when he was appointed Secretary of Housing and Urban Development by President Lyndon Johnson
1982 – An Air Florida 737 crashed into Washington DC's Potomac River after takeoff killing 78 people
1990 – L. Douglas Wilder was sworn in as America's first black governor when he became the Governor of Virginia
1990 – Disney's Swan resort hotel opened at Walt Disney World
2002 – President George W. Bush fainted after choking on a pretzel

January 14: Benedict Arnold 1741, Albert Schweitzer 1875, Hal Roach 1892, William Bendix 1906, Mark Goodson 1915, Andy Rooney 1919, Jack Jones 1938, Faye Dunaway 1941, Shannon Lucid 1943, Holland Taylor 1943, Carl Weathers 1948, Lawrence Kasdan 1948, "Hacksaw" Jim Duggan 1954, Steven Soderbergh 1963, Shepard Smith 1964, Dan Schneider 1966, L.L. Cool J 1968, Jason Bateman 1969, Kyle Brady 1972

1539 – Spain claimed Cuba
1690 – The clarinet was invented in Germany
1724 – King Philip V of Spain abdicated his throne
1784 – The United States ratified a peace treaty with England ending the Revolutionary War
1907 – An earthquake killed over 1,000 people in Kingston, Jamaica
1914 – Henry Ford introduced the assembly line
1943 – Franklin D. Roosevelt became the first United States President to travel by airplane while in office
1951 – The NFL played its first Pro Bowl
1952 – NBC's *Today* show premiered
1954 – The American Motors Company was formed after the merger of the Hudson Motor Car Company and Nash-Kelvinator Corporation
1955 – Marilyn Monroe and Joe DiMaggio were married
1972 – *Sanford & Son* debuted on NBC-TV
1973 – The Miami Dolphins defeated the Washington Redskins in Super Bowl VII and became the first NFL team to go undefeated in a season

1978 – *Fantasy Island* premiered on ABC-TV
1985 – Martina Navratilova won her 100th tennis tournament
1993 – Television talk show host David Letterman announced he was moving from NBC to CBS
1999 – The impeachment trial of President Bill Clinton began in Washington, DC
2004 – In St. Louis, a Lewis and Clark Exhibition opened at the Missouri History Museum
2005 – The space probe Huygens landed on Saturn's moon Titan and began sending back photos

January 15: Alfonso V of Portugal 1432, Moliere 1622, Philip Livingston 1716, Pierre S. DuPont 1870, King Saud of Saudi Arabia 1902, Aristotle Onassis 1906, Lloyd Bridges 1913, Robert Byrd 1917, Frank Thornton 1921, Norm Crosby 1927, Martin Luther King, Jr. 1929, Andrea Martin 1947, Charo 1951, Mario Van Peebles 1957, Lisa Lisa (Lisa Lisa and Cult Jam) 1967, Chad Lowe 1968, Shane McMahon 1970, Regina King 1971, Mary Pierce 1975, Eddie Cahill 1978, Drew Brees 1979, Matt Holiday 1980, Howie Day 1981

1559 – England's Queen Elizabeth I was crowned in Westminster Abbey (see picture to the right of Elizabeth in her coronation robes)
1844 – The University of Notre Dame was granted its charter from Indiana
1892 – James Naismith published the rules to basketball
1943 – The Pentagon was dedicated as the world's largest office building just outside Washington, DC, in Arlington, Virginia
1967 – The first National Football League Super Bowl was played, as the Green Bay Packers defeated the Kansas City Chiefs, 35-10

1974 – *Happy Days* first aired on ABC-TV
1975 – Angola was granted its independence from Portugal
1976 – Sara Jane Moore was sentenced to life in prison for attempting to assassinate President Gerald Ford in San Francisco
1981 – *Hill Street Blues* debuted on NBC-TV
1995 – *Star Trek: Voyager* debuted on UPN-TV
1999 – Disney's All-Star Movies opened at Walt Disney World

2001 – Wikipedia went online

January 16: John C. Breckinridge 1821, Andre Michelin 1853, Jimmy Collins 1870, Ethel Merman 1909, Dizzy Dean 1910, Dian Fossey 1932, A.J. Foyt 1935, Jim Stafford 1944, Ronnie Milsap 1944, John Carpenter 1948, Debbie Allen 1950, Sade 1959, Kate Moss 1974, Marlon Anderson 1974, Jeff Foster 1977, Aaliyah 1979, Brenden Morrow 1979, Albert Pujols 1980

1547 – Ivan the Terrible was crowned Czar of Russia
1581 – The English Parliament outlawed Catholicism
1777 – Vermont declared its independence from New York
1847 – John C. Fremont was appointed governor of the California territory
1919 – The 18th Amendment to the Constitution, which prohibited the sale or transportation of alcoholic beverages, was ratified
1920 – Prohibition went into effect in the United States
1945 – Adolf Hitler moved into an underground bunker called the Fuhrerbunker
1961 – Mickey Mantle signed a contract that made him the highest paid baseball player in the American League at $75,000 for the 1961 season
1976 – The TV variety show *Donny & Marie* premiered on ABC-TV
1979 – The Shah of Iran and his family fled Iran for Egypt
1991 – Operation Desert Storm began, designed to drive Iraq out of Kuwait
1997 – Bill Cosby's only son, Ennis, age 27, was shot to death while changing a flat tire on a dark road in Los Angeles
2003 – The space shuttle Columbia was launched on its final mission

January 17: Benjamin Franklin 1706, John Jacob Astor 1763, Anne Bronte 1820, Noah Beery 1883, Al Capone 1899, Betty White 1922, Eartha Kitt 1927, Vidal Sassoon 1928, Jacques Plante 1929, Don Zimmer 1931, James Earl Jones 1931, Sheree North 1932, Shari Lewis 1934, Troy Donahue 1937, Maury Povich 1939, Muhammad Ali 1942, Andy Kaufman 1949, Steve Earle 1955, Paul Young 1956, David Caruso 1956, Steve Harvey 1957, Jim Carrey 1962, Michelle Obama 1964, Joshua Malina 1966, Naveen Andrews 1969, Kid Rock 1971, Freddy Rodriguez 1975, Brad Fullmer 1977, Mark Malaska 1978, Dwayne Wade 1982

1806 – James Madison Randolph, grandson of Thomas Jefferson, became the first child born in the White House
1893 – Hawaii's monarchy was overthrown when a group of businessmen and sugar planters forced Queen Liliuokalani to abdicate

1900 – Mormon leader Brigham Young was denied a seat in Congress for practicing bigamy
1912 – Sir Robert Falcon Scott reached the South Pole one month after Roald Amundsen
1916 – The Professional Golfers Association, or PGA, was formed in New York City
1917 – The Virgin Island were bought by the United States from Denmark for $25 million
1929 – The first *Popeye the Sailor Man* comic strip appeared
1945 – Soviet and Polish forces liberated Warsaw during World War II
1946 – The United Nations Security Council held its first meeting
1949 – *The Goldbergs*, the first sitcom in America, aired its first episode
1991 – Coalition air strikes began against Iraq after negotiations failed to get Iraq to retreat from Kuwait
1995 – More than 6,000 people were killed when an earthquake with a magnitude of 7.2 struck the city of Kobe, Japan
1998 – President Bill Clinton was accused of sexual harassment by Paula Jones
2001 – Congo's President Laurent Kabila was shot and killed during a coup attempt

January 18: Peter Roget 1779, Daniel Webster 1782, Edmund Barton 1849, Thomas Watson 1854, A.A. Milne 1882, Thomas Spowith 1888, Oliver Hardy 1892, Cary Grant 1904, Danny Kaye 1913, William Stafford 1914, Kevin Costner 1955, Mike Michaud 1955, Mark Messier 1961, Alison Arngrim 1962, Jesse L. Martin 1969, Dave Batista 1969, Jonathan Davis 1971, Mike Lieberthal 1972, Kristy Lee Cook 1984

1486 – King Henry VII of England married Elizabeth, the daughter of Edward IV
1778 – English navigator Captain James Cook discovered the Hawaiian Islands, which he called the Sandwich Islands
1788 - The first English settlers, banished convicts, arrived in Australia's Botany Bay to establish a penal colony
1861 – Georgia seceded from the United States
1896 – The X-Ray machine was exhibited for the first time
1911 – Pilot Eugene B. Ely flew onto the deck of the *USS Pennsylvania* in San Francisco harbor, becoming the first person to land an aircraft on a ship
1919 – The Paris Peace Conference opened in Versailles, France
1939 – Louis Armstrong recorded the song "Jeepers Creepers"
1944 – The Siege of Leningrad ended when Russia liberated the city of the occupying Germans

1952 – Curly Howard of the Three Stooges died at the age of 48
1958 – Willie O'Ree made his debut with the Boston Bruins, becoming the first African American player to enter the NHL
1964 – Plans are unveiled for the World Trade Center in New York City
1967 – The Boston Strangler, Albert DeSalvo, was sentenced to life in prison
1974 – *The Six Million Dollar Man* debuted on ABC-TV
1975 – *The Jeffersons* debuted on CBS-TV
1976 – Super Bowl X was played in which the Pittsburgh Steelers beat the Dallas Cowboys, 21-17
1990 – Washington, DC Mayor Marion Barry was arrested for drug possession
1991 – Eastern Airlines closed its doors after operating for 62 years
1993 – The Martin Luther King Jr. holiday was observed in all 50 states for the first time

January 19: Francis II of France 1544, James Watt 1736, Robert E. Lee 1807, Edgar Allen Poe 1809, Paul Cezanne 1839, Minnesota Fats 1913, Jean Stapleton 1923, Nicholas Colasanto 1924, Tippi Hedren 1931, Michael Crawford 1942, Janis Joplin 1943, Shelley Fabares 1944, Dan Reeves 1944, Dolly Parton 1946, Robert Palmer 1949, Desi Arnaz Jr. 1953, Katey Sagal 1954, Paul Rodriguez 1955, Brad Mills 1957, Paul McCrane 1961, Stefan Edberg 1966, Junior Seau 1969, Shawn Wayans 1971, Jodie Sweetin 1982, Logan Lerman 1992

1419 – Rouen surrendered to Henry V, completing his conquest of Normandy
1793 – King Louis XVI was tried by the French Convention, found guilty of treason and sentenced to death at the guillotine
1840 – Antarctica was discovered
1861 – Georgia seceded from the Union
1870 – A political cartoon drawn by Thomas Nast first potrayed the Democratic Party as a donkey (see image to the right)

"A LIVE JACKASS KICKING A DEAD LION."
And such a Lion! and such a Jackass!

22

1901 – Queen Victoria of England suffered an apparent stroke, which would take her life 3 days later

1915 – More than 20 people were killed when German zeppelins bombed England for the first time

1929 – Acadia National Park in Maine was established

1942 – The Japanese invaded Burma

1953 – Sixty-eight percent of all TV sets in the U.S. were tuned the *I Love Lucy* show, as Lucy Ricardo gave birth to a baby boy

1966 – Indira Gandhi was elected Prime Minister of India

1977 – Snow fell in Miami, Florida for the first and only time on record

1978 – The last Volkswagon Beetle manufactured in Germany left the plant

1981 – The U.S. and Iran signed an agreement calling for the release of 52 Americans held hostage for more than 14 months

1983 – Nazi war criminal Klaus Barbi was arrested in Bolivia

1983 – Ham the Chimp, the first higher-primate launched into space, died at the age of 27 in retirement at the North Carolina Zoo

2006 – The New Horizons probe bound for Pluto was launched

January 20: Charles III of Spain 1716, George Burns 1896, Aristotle Onassis 1906, DeForest Kelley 1920, Slim Whitman 1924, Patricia Neal 1926, Edwin "Buzz" Aldrin 1930, Arte Johnson 1934, Tom Baker 1934, David Lynch 1946, Paul Stanley (KISS) 1952, Bill Maher 1956, Lorenzo Lamas 1958, James Denton 1963, John Michael Montgomery 1965, Melissa Rivers 1968, David Ekstein 1975

1265 – The first English Parliament met in Westminster Hall

1649 – Charles I of England went on trial for treason

1801 – John Marshall was appointed chief justice of the United States

1841 – The island of Hong Kong was ceded to Great Britain

1885 – L.A. Thompson received a patent for the roller coaster

1892 – The first official basketball game was played by students at the Springfield, Massachusetts YMCA Training School

1936 – Edward VIII became King of Great Britain, upon the death of George V

1937 – Franklin Delano Roosevelt became the first United States President to be inaugurated on January 20th

1969 – The first pulsar was discovered, in the Crab Nebula

1981 – Iran released 52 Americans that had been held hostage for 444 days, minutes after Ronald Reagan was sworn in as the new President of the United States

1986 – The United States observed the first federal holiday in honor of slain civil rights leader Martin Luther King Jr.

1994 – Shannon Faulkner became the first woman to attend classes at The Citadel in South Carolina

January 21: Ethan Allen 1738, Stonewall Jackson 1824, Oscar II of Sweden and Norway 1829, John Moses Browning 1855, Karl Wallenda 1905, Telly Savalas 1924, Benny Hill 1924, John Chaney 1932, Audrey Dalton 1934, Ann Wedgeworth 1935, Wolfman Jack 1939, Jack Nicklaus 1940, Placido Domingo 1941, Richie Havens 1841, Ivan Putski 1941, Mac Davis 1942, Johnny Oates 1946, Jill Eikenberry 1947, Billy Ocean 1950, Paul Allen 1953, Robby Benson 1956, Geena Davis 1956, Hakeem Olajuwon 1963, Detlef Schrempf 1963, Charlotte Ross 1968, Karina Lombard 1969, Brian Giles 1971, Byung-Hyun Kim 1979, Blake Lewis 1981, Jacob Roloff 1997

304 – Saint Agnes, the patron saint of young girls, was executed for refusing a marriage proposal
1189 – Philip II of France and Richard I of England began assembling troops for the Third Crusade
1643 – Tonga was discovered by Abel Tasman
1793 – During the French Revolution, King Louis XVI was executed at the guillotine
1799 – Edward Jenner's smallpox vaccine was introduced
1861 – The future president of the Confederacy, Jefferson Davis of Mississippi, resigned from the U.S. Senate
1900 – Canadian troops set sail from Halifax to fight in South Africa
1908 – New York City made it illegal for women to smoke in public
1915 – The first Kiwanis Club was formed in Detroit, Michigan
1924 – Soviet leader Vladimir Ilyich Lenin died
1944 – 447 German bombers attacked London
1954 – The *Nautilus*, the first atomic-powered submarine, was launched in Groton, Connecticut
1979 – Neptune temporarily became the outermost planet in the Solar System (Note: Now that Pluto is no longer classified as a planet, Neptune is once again the outermost planet)
1998 – Pope John Paul II visited Cuba

January 22: Ivan III of Russia 1440, Sir Francis Bacon 1561, Lord (George) Byron 1788, Nat Turner 1800, Grigori Rasputin 1889, David (D.W.) Griffith 1875, Sam Cooke 1931, Bill Bixby 1934, Jeff Smith 1939, John Hurt 1940, Steve Perry (Journey) 1953, John Wesley Shipp 1956, Linda Blair 1959, Diane Lane 1965, DJ Jazzy Jeff 1965, Olivia d'Abo 1967, Chone Figgins 1978, Christopher Masterson 1980

1840 – British colonists first reached New Zealand
1889 – Columbia Records, under their original name of Columbia Phonograph, was formed in Washington, DC
1901 – Queen Victoria of England died after reigning for nearly 64 years, and her son, Edward VII, became king
1905 – Bloody Sunday occurred, where peaceful demonstrators marching in St. Petersburg, Russia were gunned down
1946 – The Central Intelligence Group was formed as a forerunner to the Central Intelligence Agency
1952 – The first commercial jet plane was put into service
1957 – Israel withdrew from the Sinai Peninsula
1968 – *Rowan and Martin's Laugh-In* debuted on NBC-TV
1973 – Boxer Joe Frazier lost the first fight of his professional career to George Foreman
1973 – The U.S. Supreme Court's famous Roe v. Wade decision was handed down
1983 – Bjorn Borg retired from tennis
1992 – Dr. Roberta Bondar became the first Canadian woman in space, aboard the Space Shuttle Discovery on Flight STS-42
1997 – The U.S. Senate confirmed Madeleine Albright as the first female secretary of state
1998 – Theodore Kaczynski pled guilty to federal charges for his role as the Unabomber
2002 – K-Mart Corporation became the largest retailer in American history to file Chapter 11 bankruptcy
2006 – L.A. Lakers guard Kobe Bryant scored 81 points in a basketball game against the Toronto Raptors
2008 – Actor Heath Ledger died at the age of 28 due to an accidental prescription drug overdose

January 23: John Hancock 1737, Edouard Monet 1832, Randolph Scott 1903, Ernie Kovacs 1919, Jeanne Moreau 1928, Gil Gerard 1943, Rutger Hauer 1944, Anita Pointer 1948, Richard Dean Anderson 1950, Princess Caroline of Monaco 1957, Gail O'Grady 1963, Mariska Hargitay 1964, Lanei Chapman 1973, Tiffani Thiessen 1974, Larry Hughes 1979, Wily Mo Pena 1982

1556 – An earthquake in Shanxi Province, China, was thought to have killed about 830,000 people, the most ever killed by way of an earthquake
1570 – The assassination of James Stewart, 1st Earl of Moray, began a civil war in Scotland
1571 – The Royal Exchange opened in London
1719 – The Principality of Liechtenstein was created

1849 – Elizabeth Blackwell became the first woman doctor in the United States

1901 – A fire caused $2.5 million in damage in Montreal

1907 – Charles Curtis, of Kansas, began serving in the United States Senate, becoming the first Native American to become a U.S. Senator

1971 – In Prospect Creek Camp, Alaska, the lowest temperature ever recorded in the U.S. was reported as minus 80 degrees

1975 – *Barney Miller* made his debut on ABC-TV

1977 – The TV mini-series *Roots* began airing on ABC

1983 – *The A-Team* debuted on TV

1986 – The Rock and Roll Hall of Fame inducted its first members: Elvis Presley, Chuck Berry, James Brown, Ray Charles, Buddy Holly, Fats Domino, Jerry Lee Lewis and the Everly Brothers

2004 – Bob Keeshan, best known for his role of Captain Kangaroo, died a the age of 86

2005 – Johnny Carson died at the age of 77

January 24: Hadrian of the Roman Empire 76 AD, Frederick the Great of Prussia 1712, Mark Goodson 1915, Ernest Borgnine 1917, Oral Roberts 1918, John Romita Sr. 1930, Neil Diamond 1941, Aaron Neville 1941, John Belushi 1949, Yakov Smirnoff 1951, Nastassja Kinski 1961, Mary Lou Retton 1968, Alan Embree 1970, Matthew Lillard 1970, Chris Ferraro 1973, Peter Ferraro 1973, Tatyana Ali 1979, Scott Kazmir 1984, Mischa Barton 1986

41 AD – Roman Emperor Caligula was assassinated by his own Praetorian Guards and replaced by Claudius

1679 – King Charles II of England disbanded Parliament

1776 – Henry Knox arrived in Cambridge, Massachusetts with the artillery from conquered Fort Ticonderoga in New York

1848 – James W. Marshall discovered a gold nugget at Sutter's Mill in northern California, leading to the Gold Rush of '49

1924 – The Russian city of St. Petersburg was renamed Leningrad

1927 – Alfred Hitchcock released his first film, *The Pleasure Garden*

1943 – United States President Franklin D. Roosevelt and British Prime Minister Winston Churchill concluded a wartime conference in Casablanca, Morocco

1962 – Jackie Robinson became the first black person elected into the Baseball Hall of Fame

1965 – Winston Churchill died at the age of 90

1966 – An Air India Boeing 707 crashed on Mont Blanc on the French-Italian border, killing 117 people

1986 – Voyager 2 flew past Uranus

1989 – Ted Bundy, the convicted serial killer, was put to death in Florida's electric chair

1990 – Japan launched the first probe to be sent to the Moon since 1976

1995 – The prosecution gave its opening statement at the O.J. Simpson murder trial

2003 – The U.S. Department of Homeland Security began operations

2006 – Disney agreed to purchase Pixar, the deal to be completed on March 5, 2006

January 25: Robert Burns 1759, George Pickett 1825, Charles Curtis 1860, Virginia Woolf 1882, Ernie Harwell 1918, Edwin Newman 1919, Eduard Shevardnadze 1928, Dean Jones 1931, Corazon Aquino 1933, Gregory Sierra 1941, Dinah Manoff 1958, Chris Chelios 1962, Ana Ortiz 1971, Alicia Keys 1981

1327 – Edward III became King of England

1533 – England's King Henry VIII secretly married his second wife Anne Boleyn

1858 – Mendelssohn's Wedding March was played publicly for the first time, as the daughter of Queen Victoria married the Crown Prince of Prussia

1915 – In New York, Alexander Graham Bell spoke to his assistant in San Francisco, inaugurating the first transcontinental telephone service

1917 – The United States purchased the Danish West Indies (now the Virgin Islands) for $25 million

1924 – The first Winter Olympics began in Chamonix, France

1949 – The first Emmy Awards were given out

1953 – WABI-TV channel 5 began broadcasting in Bangor, Maine

1961 – John F. Kennedy presented the first live presidential news conference from Washington, DC

1971 – Charles Manson and three female members of his "family" were found guilty of one count of conspiracy to commit murder and seven counts of first degree murder

1971 – Major General Idi Amin led a coup that deposed Milton Obote and Amin became president of Uganda

1981 – The 52 Americans held hostage by Iran for 444 days arrived in the United States and were reunited with their families

1987 – The New York Giants defeated the Denver Broncos, 39-20, in Super Bowl XXI

1993 – A gunman shot and killed two CIA employees outside the agency's headquarters in Virginia

1998 – The Denver Broncos beat the Green Bay Packers 31-24 in Super Bowl XXXII

1999 – At least 1,000 people were killed when an earthquake hit western Columbia

2004 – *Opportunity* landed on the surface of Mars

January 26: Julia Grant 1826, Douglas MacArthur 1880, Zara Cully 1892, Maria Von Trapp 1905, Charles Lane 1905, Paul Newman 1925, Bob Uecker 1935, Scott Glenn 1942, Gene Siskel 1946, David Strathairn 1949, Eddie Van Halen 1957, Ellen DeGeneres 1958, Anita Baker 1958, Wayne Gretzky 1961, Dorian Gregory 1971, Vince Carter 1977, Emily Hughes 1989, Cameron Bright 1993, Kyle Chavarria 1995

1500 – Vicente Yáñez Pinzón of Spain became the first European to discover Brazil

1784 – In a letter to his daughter, Benjamin Franklin expressed unhappiness over the eagle as the symbol of America, instead wanting the symbol to be the turkey

1788 – British settlers in Australia, led by Captain Arthur Phillip, landed in what is now known as Sydney

1827 – Peru seceded from Colombia in protest against Simon Bolivar's alleged tyranny

1837 – Michigan became the 26th state

1838 – Tennessee became the first state with a prohibition law

1841 – The United Kingdom formally occupied Hong Kong

1861 – Louisiana seceded from the Union

1863 – General Ambrose Burnside was replaced as General of the Potomac by Joseph Hooker

1870 – Virginia rejoined the United States

1905 – The Cullinan diamond, weighing 114 lbs, was found at the Premier Mine near Pretoria, South Africa

1930 – January 26th was declared Independence Day in India

1934 – In Harlem, New York, the Apollo Theater opened

1942 – During World War II, the first American forced arrived in Europe, landing in Ireland

1950 - India officially proclaimed itself a republic as Rajendra Prasad took the oath of office as president

1961 – Janet G. Travell became the first female Presidential physician, to John F. Kennedy

1979 – CBS-TV debuted its newest show, *The Dukes of Hazzard*

1986 – The Chicago Bears won the Super Bowl

1986 – Halley's Comet was visible from Earth, for the first time in 76 years

1988 – *The Phantom of the Opera* opened on Broadway for the first time

1998 – President Bill Clinton denied having an affair with a former White House intern, saying "I did not have sexual relations with that woman, Miss Lewinsky."

1999 – Saddam Hussein vowed revenge against the U.S. in response to air-strikes

2001 – An earthquake in India resulted in 20,000 deaths

2003 – The Tampa Bay Buccaneers won the Super Bowl

2005 – Condoleezza Rice was sworn in as the first African-American woman Secretary of State

2005 – A helicopter crash in Iraq resulted in the deaths of 31 American soldiers

January 27: Wolfgang Amadeus Mozart 1756, Lewis Carroll 1832, Edward J. Smith 1850, Wilhelm II of Germany 1859, Art Rooney 1901, William Randolph Hearst Jr. 1908, Donna Reed 1921, Troy Donahue 1936, James Cromwell 1940, Mikhail Baryshnikov 1948, Peter Laird 1954, John Roberts Jr. 1954, Mimi Rogers 1956, Frank Miller 1957, Chris Collinsworth 1959, Keith Olbermann 1959, Bridget Fonda 1964, Tracy Lawrence 1968, Lil Jon 1971

1606 – The trial of Guy Fawkes and his fellow conspirators began

1825 – The United States Congress approved the formation of the Indian Territory, now Oklahoma

1870 – The first college sorority was formed, Kappa Alpha Theta, at DePauw University

1888 – The National Geographic Society was founded in Washington, DC

1926 – John Baird, a Scottish inventor, demonstrated a pictorial transmission machine called television

1945 – Soviet troops liberated the Nazi concentration camps Auschwitz and Birkenau in Poland

1951 – Nuclear testing began at the Nevada Test Site

1967 – At Cape Kennedy, Florida, astronauts Gus Grissom, Ed White and Roger Chaffee died in a flash fire during a test aboard their Apollo I spacecraft

1967 – More than 60 nations signed the Outer Space Treaty, which banned the orbiting of nuclear weapons and placing weapons on celestial bodies or space stations

1973 – The Vietnam peace accords were signed in Paris, officially ending the Vietnam War

1976 – *Laverne and Shirley* debuted on ABC-TV

1992 – Former world boxing champion Mike Tyson went on trial for raping an 18-year-old contestant in the 1991 Miss Black America Contest

1993 – Professional wrestler and actor Andre the Giant died at the age of 46

1996 – Mahamane Ousmane, the first democratically elected president of Niger, was overthrown by a military coup

1996 – Germany observed its first Holocaust Remembrance Day

2001 – Ten members of the Oklahoma State University's men's basketball team died in a plane crash in Colorado

January 28: Henry VII of England 1457, Pope Clement IX 1600, George Hamilton-Gordon 1784, Alexander Mackenzie 1822, Sir Henry M. Stanley 1841, John Banner 1910, Jackson Pollock 1912, Alan Alda 1936, Susan Howard 1943, Barbi Benton 1950, Sara McLachlan 1968, Rakim 1968, Magglio Ordonez 1974, Jermaine Dye 1974, Junior Spivey 1975, Joey Fatone 1977, Lyle Overbay 1977, Daunte Culpepper 1977, Nick Carter 1980, Elijah Wood 1981

814 – Charlemagne died

1547 – England's King Henry VIII died and his son, Edward VI, became king

1788 – The first British penal settlement was founded at Botany Bay, Australia

1813 – Jane Austen's *Pride and Prejudice* was first published

1820 – Antarctica was first spotted by Russians Fabian Gottlieb von Bellingshausen and Mikhail Petrovich Lazarev

1846 – At the Battle of Aliwal, India defeated the British

1871 – France surrendered in the Franco-Prussian War

1878 – The first daily college newspaper in America, *The Yale News*, was published

1902 – The Carnegie Institution was founded in Washington, DC

1915 – The United States Coast Guard was created by an act of Congress

1916 – Louis D. Brandeis was appointed by President Woodrow Wilson to the U.S. Supreme Court, becoming its first Jewish member

1921 – The Tomb of the Unknown Soldier was created beneath the Arc de Triomphe in Paris, France to honor the unknown dead of World War I

1935 – Iceland became the first country to legalize abortion

1938 – The first ski tow in the United States opened in Woodstock, Vermont

1956 – Elvis Presley made his first appearance on TV

1973 – *Barnaby Jones* debuted on NBC-TV

1986 – The United States Space Shuttle *Challenger* exploded just after takeoff, killing all seven of its crewmembers, including teacher Christa McAuliffe

1998 – Gunmen held over 400 children and teachers hostage for several hours at an elementary school in Manila, Philippines

January 29: Thomas Paine 1737, Christian VII of Denmark 1749, William McKinley 1843, Anton Chekhov 1860, John D. Rockefeller Jr. 1874, W.C. Fields 1880, Victor Mature 1916, John Forsythe 1918, Jean R. Yawkey 1929, Katherine Ross 1942, Tom Selleck 1945, Marc Singer 1948, Ann Jillian 1950, Oprah Winfrey 1954, Irlene Mandrell 1957, Judy Norton Taylor 1958, Greg Louganis 1960, Monica Horan 1963, Bob Holly 1963, Andre Reed 1964, Dominik Hasek 1965, Edward Burns 1968, Thomas Jane 1969, Heather Graham 1970, Jason Schmidt 1970, Sara Gilbert 1975, April Scott 1979

1595 – Shakespeare's play *Romeo and Juliet* was probably first performed
1814 – In the Battle of Brienne, France, under Napoleon, defeated Russia and Prussia
1820 – Britain's King George III died insane at Windsor Castle
1845 – Edgar Allan Poe's *The Raven* was published for the first time
1850 – Henry Clay introduced in the Senate a compromise bill on slavery, known as the Compromise of 1850, that included the admission of California into the Union as a free state
1861 – Kansas became the 34th state
1863 – The Bear River Massacre occurred
1886 – A patent for the first gasoline-powered automobile was issued to Karl Benz

1891 – Liliuokalani was proclaimed the last Queen of Hawaii (see photo at left)
1900 – The American Baseball League was organized in Philadelphia
1902 – It was announced that in less than a year, U.S. Steel, owned by J.P. Morgan, had made a profit of $174 million
1916 – During World War I, Paris was bombed for the first time by German zeppelins
1933 – Adolf Hitler was appointed Chancellor of Germany by President Paul von Hindenburg
1936 – The first members of major league baseball's Hall of Fame were named in Cooperstown, New York, including Babe Ruth, Ty Cobb, Honus Wagner, Christy Mathewson and Walter Johnson

1958 – Paul Newman and Joanne Woodward were married
1959 – Walt Disney released *Sleepy Beauty*
1963 – The first members to the NFL's Hall of Fame were named in Canton, Ohio
1977 – Actor Freddie Prinze died of a self-inflicted gunshot wound at the age of 22
1978 – Sweden became the first country to outlaw aerosol sprays, due to the harmful effects on the ozone layer
1990 – Joseph Hazelwood, the former skipper of the Exxon Valdez, went on trial in Anchorage, Alaska, on charges that stemmed from America's worst oil spill
1995 – The San Francisco 49ers became the first team in National Football League history to win five Super Bowl titles
1999 – Paris prosecutors announced the end of the investigation into the accident that killed Britain's Princess Diana

January 30: Franklin D. Roosevelt 1882, David Wayne 1914, John Ireland 1914, Dick Martin 1922, Barbara Hale 1922, Lloyd Alexander 1924, Dorothy Malone 1925, Gene Hackman 1930, Vanessa Redgrave 1937, Dick Cheney 1941, Charles Dutton 1951, Phil Collins 1951, John Baldacci 1955, Payne Stewart 1957, Brett Butler 1958, Jody Watley 1959, Julie McCullough 1965, Jalen Rose 1973, Christian Bale 1974, Wilmer Valderrama 1980, Josh Kelley 1980, Jorge Cantu 1982, Jake Thomas 1990

1648 – The Treaty of Munster was signed, ending the Eighty Years War between Spain and the Netherlands
1649 – England's King Charles I was beheaded
1835 – An assassination attempt against President Andrew Jackson, the first against any United States President, was unsuccessful, after both of Richard Lawrence's pistols misfired and President Jackson proceeded to beat Lawrence with his cane (see right)

1847 – The town of Yerba Buena was renamed San Francisco
1862 – The United States Navy's first ironclad warship, the Monitor, was launched
1900 – Kentucky Governor-elect William Goebel was fatally shot by a sniper, living a few days, long enough to be sworn in as governor
1933 – Adolf Hitler was sworn in as the German Chancellor
1948 – Indian political and spiritual leader Mahatma Gandhi was murdered by a Hindu extremist
1962 – Two of the Flying Wallendas were killed when their high-wire seven-person pyramid collapsed in Detroit, Michigan
1964 – The United States launched Ranger 6, an unmanned spacecraft carrying television cameras that was to crash-land on the moon
1968 – The Tet Offensive began as Communist forces launched surprise attacks against South Vietnamese provincial capitals
1969 – The Beatles performed together for the last time, in an impromptu performance from the roof of Apple Records in London
1994 – Peter Leko became the youngest grand master in chess at the age of 14
1996 – Magic Johnson played in his first basketball game after retiring in 1991 after testing HIV-positive
2000 – Kenyan Airways Flight 431 crashed off the coast of the Ivory Coast, killing 169 people
2003 – Belgium legally recognized same-sex marriage
2006 – Coretta Scott King, widow of Martin Luther King, died at the age of 88

January 31: Charles V of France 1338, King Henry of Portugal 1512, Zane Grey 1872, Anna Pavlova 1882, Eddie Cantor 1892, Jersey Joe Walcott 1914, Garry Moore 1915, Jackie Robinson 1919, Carol Channing 1923, Jean Simmons 1929, Norman Mailer 1929, Ernie Banks 1931, James Franciscus 1934, Suzanne Pleshette 1937, Queen Beatrix of the Netherlands 1938, Richard Gephardt 1941, Jessica Walter 1944, Nolan Ryan 1947, Jonathan Banks 1947, Harry Wayne Casey (KC and the Sunshine Band) 1951, Johnny Rotten 1956, Anthony LaPaglia 1959, Kelly Lynch 1959,

Grant Morrison 1960, John Dye 1963, Minnie Driver 1970, Portia de Rossi 1973, Justin Timberlake 1981

1504 – France ceded Naples to Aragon
1606 – Guy Fawkes was executed after being convicted for his role in the *Gunpowder Plot* against the English Parliament and King James I
1865 – General Robert E. Lee was named general-in-chief of the Confederate armies (see picture on previous page)
 1876 – All Native American were ordered by the U.S. government to move onto reservations
1915 – During World War I, Germany attempted to use poison gas against Russian troops during the Battle of Bolimov, but the chemical froze, having no impact
1929 – Leon Trotsky was exiled from the Soviet Union
1930 – Scotch Tape was first marketed by 3M
1936 – *The Green Hornet* debuted on the radio
1940 – The first Social Security check was issued by the United States Government
1944 – During World War II, U.S. forces invaded Kwajalein Atoll and other areas of the Japanese-held Marshall Islands
1950 – President Harry Truman announced a program to develop the hydrogen bomb
1956 – A.A. Milne, creator of the Winnie-the-Pooh books and characters, died at the age of 74
1958 – Explorer I was put into orbit around the earth, becoming the first U.S. Earth satellite
1958 – James Van Allen discovered the Van Allen radiation belt surrounding the Earth
1961 – Ham the Chimp became the first higher-primate launched into space aboard a Mercury capsule
1968 – The Viet Cong attacked the American embassy in Saigon
1971 – Astronauts Alan Shepard, Edgar Mitchell and Stuart Roosa blasted off aboard Apollo 14 on a mission to the moon
1990 – McDonald's opened its first fast-food restaurant in Moscow
1999 – In Super Bowl XXXIII, Denver beat Atlanta, and John Elway was chosen MVP
1999 – *Family Guy* debuted on FOX-TV
2000 – John Rocker of the Atlanta Braves was suspended from major league baseball for disparaging remarks against foreigners, homosexuals and minorities in an interview published by Sports Illustrated
2002 – A large section of the Antarctic Larsen Ice Shelf began to break apart, eventually consuming over 1,200 square miles
2005 – Michael Jackson went on trial on child molestation charges

February

February 1: John Ford 1895, Clark Gable 1901, Langston Hughes 1902, Boris Yeltsin 1931, Don Everly 1937, Garrett Morris 1937, Sherman Hemsley 1938, Bibi Besch 1940, Jessica Savitch 1947, Elisabeth Sladen 1948, Rick James 1952, Bill Mumy 1954, Princess Stephanie of Monaco 1965, Michelle Akers 1965, Brandon Lee 1965, Meg Cabot 1967, Lisa Marie Presley 1968, Pauly Shore 1968, Kent Mercker 1968, Brian Krause 1969, Big Boi 1975, Lauren Conrad 1986

1790 – The U.S. Supreme Court convened for the first time in New York City
1793 – France declared war on Britain and Holland
1814 – The Mayon Volcano in the Philippines erupted, killing about 1,200 people
1861 – Texas voted to secede from the United States
1862 – The *Battle Hymn of the Republic* by Julia Howe was published for the first time
1884 – The *Oxford English Dictionary* was first published
1893 – Thomas Edison completed his construction of the world's first motion picture studio in West Orange, New Jersey
1908 – King Carlos I of Portugal and his son were killed in Lisbon
1918 – Russia officially adopted the Gregorian calendar
1919 – The first Miss America was crowned in New York City
1920 – The Royal Canadian Mounted Police began operating
1960 – Four black students staged a sit-in at an all-white lunch counter in Greensboro, North Carolina
1974 – A fire in a 25-story building in Sao Paulo, Brazil resulted in the deaths of 189 people and injuring almost 300

1978 – Movie director Roman Polanski fled the United States after being convicted of having sex with a minor

1979 – Ayatollah Khomeini returned to Iran 15 years after he was exiled

1982 – *Late Night with David Letterman* debuted on NBC-TV

1994 – Jeff Gilooly, ex-husband of Tonya Harding, pled guilty for his role in the attack of figure skater (and rival of Harding) Nancy Kerrigan

2003 – NASA's space shuttle Columbia broke apart while re-entering the Earth's atmosphere, killing all seven astronauts

2004 – Singer Janet Jackson exposed her breast on live TV during the halftime show of the Super Bowl

2005 – Canada became the fourth country to legalize same-sex marriage

February 2: King John of Denmark 1455, Pope Benedict XIII 1649, Francois de Chavert 1695, Jacques Philippe Marie Binet 1786, James Joyce 1882, George Halas 1895, Howard Johnson 1897, Gale Gordon 1906, Robert Mandan 1932, Tom Smothers 1937, David Jason 1940, Graham Nash 1942, Geoffrey Hughes 1944, Farrah Fawcett 1947, Brent Spiner 1949, Christie Brinkley 1954, John Tudor 1954, Kim Zimmer 1955, Marc Price 1968, Melvin Mora 1972, Shakira 1977, Teddy Hart 1980, Martin Spanjers 1987

962 – Otto I was crowned Holy Roman Emperor by Pope John XII

1536 – Buenos Aires, Argentina was founded by Pedro de Mendoza of Spain

1653 – New Amsterdam, now known as New York City, was incorporated

1709 – Alexander Selkirk was rescued from a deserted island, the inspiration for the book *Robinson Crusoe*

1848 – The Mexican War was ended with the signing of the Treaty of Guadalupe Hidalgo, which gave the U.S. possession of Texas, New Mexico, Nevada, Utah, Arizona, California and parts of Colorado and Wyoming

1848 – The first shipload of Chinese emigrants arrived in San Francisco

1863 – Samuel Langhorne Clemens used the pseudonym Mark Twain for the first time

1876 – The National League of Professional Base Ball Clubs was formed in New York

1878 – Greece declared war on Turkey

1882 – The Knights of Columbus organization was formed in New Haven, Connecticut

1887 – Groundhog Day was celebrated for the first time, in Punxsutawney, Pennsylvania

1900 – Six U.S. cities, Boston, Detroit, Milwaukee, Baltimore, Chicago, and St. Louis, agreed to form baseball's American League

1925 – Dog sleds reached Nome, Alaska with serum for diphtheria, inspiring the Iditarod Race
1933 – Adolf Hitler dissolved the German Parliament
1940 – Frank Sinatra made his debut with the Tommy Dorsey Orchestra
1943 – In the Battle of Stalingrad, the last German forces surrendered to the Russians
1952 – A tropical storm formed off the coast of Cuba, eventually making landfall in Florida and becoming the earliest recorded tropical storm to form in a season
1962 – Neptune and Pluto aligned for the first time in 400 years
1967 – The American Basketball Association was formed, a league that eventually particially merged with the NBA
1969 – Horror movie legend Boris Karloff died at the age of 81
1971 – Idi Amin assumed power in Uganda after a coup that ousted President Milton Obote
1980 – Reported first surfaced about Abscam, in which members of the FBI were setting up stings against members of Congress
1982 – The Syrian government attacked the town of Hama, killing thousands of people in what was known as the Hama Massacre
1990 – South African President F.W. de Klerk lifted a ban on the African National Congress and promised to free Nelson Mandela
1992 – Port Orleans Riverside Resort opened at Walt Disney World under the original name Dixie Landings Resort
2006 – An Egyptian ferry sank in the Red Sea, killing 1,400 people

February 3: Samuel Osgood 1747, Felix Mendelssohn 1809, Horce Greeley 1811, Elizabeth Blackwell 1821, James Clark McReynolds 1862, Lou Criger 1872, Gertrude Stein 1874, Norman Rockwell 1894, Pretty Boy Floyd 1904, James A. Michener 1907, Robert Earl Jones 1911, Joey Bishop 1918, Henry Heimlich 1920, John Fielder 1925, Joan Lowery Nixon 1927, Fran Tarkenton 1940, Blythe Danner 1943, Bob Griese 1945, Morgan Fairchild 1950, Fred Lynn 1952, Nathan Lane 1956, Michele Greene 1962, Maura Tierney 1965, Warwick Davis 1970

1377 – In what is known as the Cesena Bloodbath, more than 2,000 people in Cesena, Italy were massacred by Papal troops
1690 – The first paper money was issued in America, in the Massachusetts Colony
1783 – Spain recognized American independence from England
1787 – Shay's Rebellion was thwarted
1809 – The Illinois Territory was formed
1870 – The 15th Amendment to the Constitution was ratified, giving voting rights regardless of race

1894 – The first steel sailing vessel in America was launched from Bath, Maine

1900 – Kentucky Democratic gubernatorial candidate William Goebels died as the result of gun wounds from an assassin

1913 – The 16th Amendment to the U.S. Constitution was ratified, authorizing the power to impose and collect income tax

1919 – The League of Nations held its first meeting in Paris

1924 – Former President of the United States Woodrow Wilson died at the age of 77

1944 – United States troops took the Marshall Islands during World War II

1945 – Russia agreed to enter World War II against Japan

1959 – Rock star Buddy Holly died in a plane crash at the age of 22, along with Richie Valens (age 17) and The Big Bopper (age 28)

1966 – The first weather satellite was launched

1966 – Russia made the first rocket-assisted landing on the Moon, with the unmanned Luna 9 spacecraft

1969 – At the Palestinian National Congress in Cairo, Yasser Arafat was appointed leader of the PLO

1984 - Space shuttle astronauts Bruce McCandless II and Robert L. Stewart made the first untethered space walk

1998 – In Italy, a U.S. Military plane hit a cable causing the death of 20 skiers on a ski lift

February 4: Johann Ludwig Bach 1677, Sir Hiram Maxim 1840, Charles Lindbergh 1902, Clyde Tombaugh 1906, Byron Nelson 1912, Rosa Parks 1913, Ida Lupino 1918, Conrad Bain 1923, Russell Hoban 1925, David Brenner 1936, John Schuck 1940, Dan Quayle 1947, Alice Cooper 1948, Patrick Bergin 1951, Don Davis 1957, Lawrence Taylor 1959, Jonathan Larson 1960, Stewart O'Nan 1961, Clint Black 1962, Sergei Grinkov 1967, Gabrielle Anwar 1970, Oscar de la Hoya 1973, Chris Sabin 1982, Bug Hall 1985, Carly Patterson 1988

1783 – Britain declared a formal cessation of hostilities with the United States of America, its former colonies

1789 – Electors unanimously chose George Washington to be the first President of the United States

1792 – Electors unanimously chose George Washington to a second term as President of the United States

1794 – The French government abolished slavery

1861 – Delegates from six southern breakaway states met in Montgomery, Alabama to form the Confederate States of America

1932 – The first Winter Olympics to be held in the United States, and the third ever, opened in Lake Placid, New York

1945 – During World War II, United States President Franklin D. Roosevelt, British Prime Minister Winston Churchill and Soviet leader Josef Stalin began a conference at Yalta to outline plans for Germany's defeat
1948 – Ceylon, later Sri Lanka, became independent from Great Britain
1974 – Patty Hearst was kidnapped in Berkeley, California, by the Symbionese Liberation Army
1976 – An earthquake in Guatemala and Honduras killed more than 22,000 people
1976 – The 12th Winter Olympic Games opened in Innsbruck, Austria
1983 – Karen Carpenter died of heart failure, brought on by anorexia nervosa
1987 – Entertainer Liberace died at the age 67 due to complications related to AIDS
1991 – The Baseball Hall of Fame voted to ban Pete Rose
1998 – In Afghanistan, at least 5,000 people were killed in an earthquake that measured 6.1 on the Richter scale
2003 – Yugoslavia was divided into the independent nations of Serbia and Montenegro

February 5: Emperor Sanjo of Japan 976, James Otis 1725, Robert Peel 1788, Belle Starr 1848, Adlai Stevenson 1900, John Carradine 1906, Daisy and Violet Hilton 1908, Red Buttons 1919, Andrew Greeley 1928, Henry "Hank" Aaron 1934, Stuart Damon 1937, Stephen Cannell 1940, David Selby 1941, Roger Staubach 1942, Nolan Bushnell 1943, Michael Mann 1943, Darrell Waltrip 1947, Barbara Hershey 1948, Christopher Guest 1948, Jennifer Jason Leigh 1962, Laura Linney 1964, Roberto Alomar 1968, Bobby Brown 1969, Sara Evans 1971, Devern Hansack 1978, Nora Zehetner 1981, Laurence Maroney 1985, Reed Sorenson 1986

1881 – The city of Phoenix, Arizona was incorporated
1901 – J.P. Morgan formed the U.S. Steel Corporation
1917 – Mexico's current constitution was adopted
1919 – United Artists film studio was founded by Charlie Chaplin, Mary Pickford, Douglas Fairbanks and D.W. Griffith
1922 – *Readers' Digest* was first published, although some claim it was February 7th
1936 – *Modern Times* starring Charlie Chaplin, considered the last of the last movie of the silent film era, was released
1945 – General Douglas MacArthur returned to the Philippines
1953 – The Walt Disney's film *Peter Pan* opened
1958 – A hydrogen bomb known as the Tybee Bomb was lost off the coast of Savannah, Georgia by the U.S. Air Force

1971 – *Apollo 14* with astronauts Alan Shepard and Edgar Mitchell landed on the Moon at Fra Mauro

1972 – Bob Douglas became the first black man elected to the Basketball Hall of Fame

1988 – General Manuel Noriega, former ruler of Panama, was indicted on charges of bribery and drug trafficking

1991 – A Michigan court barred Dr. Jack Kevorkian from performing doctor-assisted-suicides

2001 – It was announced the Kelly Ripa would be Regis Philbin's co-host and the show was renamed *to Live! With Regis and Kelly*

2001 – Tom Cruise and Nicole Kidman announced their separation

2003 – U.S. Secretary of State Colin Powell presented evidence to the United Nations Security Council concerning Iraq's material breach of U.N. Resolution 1441

2006 – The Pittsburgh Steelers won Super Bowl XL

February 6: Christopher Marlowe 1564, Queen Anne of England 1665, Nicolaus Bernoulli 1695, Charles Lee 1732, Aaron Burr 1756, Babe Ruth 1895, Ronald Reagan 1911, Eva Braun 1912, Thurl Ravenscroft 1914, Zsa Zsa Gabor 1919, Patrick Macnee 1922, Rip Torn 1931, Mamie Van Doran 1931, Mike Farrell 1939, Tom Brokaw 1940, Sarah Brady 1942, Fabian 1943, Michael Tucker 1944, Bob Marley 1945, Natalie Cole 1950, Jon Walmsley 1956, Kathy Najimy 1957, Robert Townsend 1957, Axl Rose 1962, Rick Astley 1966, Tanja Frieden 1976, Ty Warren 1981

1685 – James II of England became king upon the death of his brother, Charles II

1778 – The United States gained official recognition from France

1788 – Massachusetts became the sixth state when it voted to ratify the Constitution

1862 – In the Battle of Fort Henry, the North got their first victory in the American Civil War, under Ulysses Grant

1936 – The Fourth Winter Olympic Games opened in Germany

1952 – Britain's King George VI died, with his daughter, Elizabeth II, succeeding him

1968 – The Tenth Winter Olympic Games opened in Grenoble, France

1971 – NASA Astronaut Alan Shepard used a six-iron and hit three golf balls on the surface of the moon

1978 – The Blizzard of '78 hit New England, one of the worst Nor-Easters ever to hit the area

1994 – Legendary comic book artist and writer Jack Kirby died at the age of 78

1998 – Washington National Airport was renamed for former President Ronald Reagan
1999 – King Hussein of Jordan transferred full political power to his oldest son the Crown Prince Abdullah
2000 – In Finland, Foreign Minister Tarja Halonen became the first woman to be elected president

February 7: Sir Thomas Moore 1478, Anna of Russia 1693, John Deere 1804, Charles Dickens 1812, Laura Ingalls Wilder 1867, Sinclair Lewis 1885, Buster Crabbe 1908, Dan Quisenberry 1953, Miguel Ferrer 1954, Carney Lansford 1957, James Spader 1960, Garth Brooks 1962, Jason Gedrick 1965, Chris Rock 1966, Juwan Howard 1973, Steve Nash 1974, Ashton Kutcher 1978, Tina Majorino 1985

1900 – The British Labour Party was formed
1904 – In Baltimore, a fire raged for about 30 hours and destroyed over 1,500 buildings
1914 – Charlie Chaplin's first film, *Kid Auto Races at Venice*, was released
1948 – General Dwight D. Eisenhower resigned as Army chief of staff, to be replaced by General Omar Bradley
1964 – The Beatles arrived in the United States for the first time
1971 – Women were granted the right to vote in Switzerland
1974 – The nation of Grenada gained independence from Britain
1999 – King Hussein of Jordan died, one day after transferring power to his son

February 8: Alfonso IV of Portugal 1291, Jacques Cassini 1649, William Tecumseh Sherman 1820, Jules Verne 1828, Dame Edith Evans 1888, Fred Blassie 1918, Lana Turner 1921, Audrey Meadows 1924, Jack Lemmon 1925, James Dean 1931, Kenneth Curtis 1931, John Williams 1932, Ted Koppel 1940, Nick Nolte 1941, Robert Klein 1942, John Ford Coley 1948, Dan Seals 1948, Brooke Adams 1949, Cristina Ferrare 1950, Mary Steenburgen 1953, John Grisham 1955, Vince Neil 1961, Gary Coleman 1968, Mary McCormack 1969, Alonzo Mourning 1970, Seth Green 1974

1587 – Mary Queen of Scots, was executed
1693 – The College of William and Mary in Williamsburg, Virginia was granted a charter
1725 – Peter the Great, emperor of Russia, died at the age of 53 and was succeeded by his wife, Catherine
1837 – Richard Johnson became the first U.S. Vice-President chosen by the Senate

1861 – The Confederate States of America was formed
1900 – British troops were defeated by the Boers at Ladysmith, South Africa
1904 – The Russo-Japanese War began with Japan attacking Russian forces in Manchuria
1910 – The Boy Scouts of America was incorporated
1915 – The controversial film *Birth of a Nation* premiered
1918 – The first issue of the *Stars and Stripes* newspaper was published
1936 – The first National Football League draft was held
1943 – United States forces defeated the Japanese at the Battle of Guadalcanal
1952 – Queen Elizabeth II ascended to the British throne, following the death of her father, King George VI
1969 – The final weekly issue of the *Saturday Evening Post* was published
1971 – The NASDAQ stock market debuted
1974 – The three-man crew of the Skylab space station returned to Earth after 84 days
1985 – The final episode of *The Dukes of Hazzard* aired after a 6-1/2 year run on CBS-TV
1998 – The first female Olympic ice hockey game was held
2001 – Disneyland's California Adventure Park opened
2007 – Anna Nicole Smith died at the age of 39

February 9: Luther Martin 1748, William Henry Harrison 1773, Peggy Wood 1892, Bill Veeck 1914, Carmen Miranda 1914, Gypsy Rose Lee 1914, Roger Mudd 1928, Ronnie Claire Edwards 1933, Carole King 1942, Joe Pesci 1943, Alice Walker 1944, Mia Farrow 1945, Judith Light 1949, Danny White 1952, Mookie Wilson 1952, Ciaran Hinds 1953, Charles Shaughnessy 1955, JM J. Bullock 1955, John Kruk 1961, Travis Tritt 1963, Todd Pratt 1967, Jimmy Smith 1969, Vladimir Guerrero 1976, Irina Slutskaya 1979, David Gallagher 1985

1822 – Haiti invaded the Dominican Republic
1825 – The U.S. House of Representatives elected John Quincy Adams President, after no candidate had received a majority of the electoral votes
1861 – The Confederate States of America elected Jefferson Davis as its President
1870 – The United States Weather Bureau was authorized by Congress
1895 – Volley Ball was invented by W.G. Morgan
1895 – The first college basketball game was played as Minnesota State School of Agriculture defeated the Porkers of Hamline College, 9-3
1900 – Davis Cup tennis began

1943 – During World War II, the battle of Guadalcanal ended with an American victory over Japanese forces
1950 – Senator Joseph McCarthy declared that the United States State Department was full of Communists
1960 – Actress Joanne Woodward received the first star on the Hollywood Walk of Fame
1964 – The Beatles made their first appearance on *The Ed Sullivan Show*
1965 – The first United States combat troops were sent to South Vietnam
1971 – Satchel Paige became the first Negro League player voted into the Baseball Hall of Fame
1971 – *Apollo 14* returned to Earth after a trip to the Moon
1986 – Halley's Comet made its closest approach to the Sun, called perihelion
1997 – *The Simpsons* became the longest-running prime-time animated series
2001 – The *USS Greeneville*, an American submarine, accidentally sank a Japanese training vessel Uwajima Fishing High School

February 10: Alan Hale Sr. 1892, Jimmy Durante 1893, Bill Tilden 1893, Herb Pennock 1894, Harold Macmillan 1894, Dame Judith Anderson 1898, Lon Chaney, Jr. 1905, Neva Patterson 1922, Leontyne Price 1927, Jerry Goldsmith 1929, Robert Wagner 1930, Roberta Flack 1939, Mark Spitz 1950, Greg Norman 1955, Lionel Cartwright 1960, George Stephanopoulos 1961, Lenny Dykstra 1963, Glenn Beck 1964, Laura Dern 1967, Ty Law 1974, Lance Berkman 1976

1134 – Robert Curthose, former Duke of Normandy and son of William the Conqueror, died at the age of 80, after spending the last 28 years of his life as a prisoner to his younger brother, King Henry I of England

1258 – In the Battle of Baghdad, Mongols overran the city, killing thousands of people
1542 – Catherine Howard, fifth wife of King Henry VIII of England, was confined to the Tower of London, awaiting execution (see picture to the right)
1567 – Lord Darnley, husband of Mary, Queen of Scots, was found dead, likely assassinated
1763 – The Treaty of Paris ended the French and Indian War, giving control of Canada to England
1840 – Britain's Queen Victoria married Prince Albert of Saxe Coburg-Gotha

1863 – In New York City, two of the world's most famous dwarfs, General Tom Thumb and Lavinia Warren, were married

1870 – The YWCA was founded

1931 – New Delhi became the new capital of India

1933 – The first singing telegram was delivered

1949 – The play *Death of a Salesman* by Arthur Miller debuted in New York City

1957 – Children's author Laura Ingalls Wilder died at the age of 90

1981 – A fire at the Las Vegas Hilton Hotel and Casino resulted in the death of 8 people and injuries to nearly 200

1989 – Ron Brown became the first African-American elected chairman of a major American political party, when he became chairman of the Democratic Party

1990 – South African President F.W. de Klerk announced that black activist Nelson Mandela would be released the next day, after 27 years in captivity

1992 – Mike Tyson was convicted in Indianapolis of raping a Miss Black America contestant

1998 – Buddy the Wonder Dog, star of the movie Air Bud, died at the age of 9

1998 – Voters in Maine repealed a gay rights law passed the previous year, becoming the first state to abandon such a law

2005 – Maine received over a foot of snow, canceling school for much of the state

2005 – North Korea publicly announced for the first time that it had nuclear arms

2005 – Playwright Arthur Miller died at the age of 89

2006 – The 20th Winter Olympics opened in Turino, Italy

February 11: Elizabeth of York 1466, Pope Gregory XIV 1535, Alexander Hamilton Stevens 1812, Thomas Alva Edison 1847, Max Baer 1909, Sidney Sheldon 1917, Eva Gabor 1919, Farouk I of Egypt 1920, Lloyd Bentsen 1921, Kim Stanley 1925, Leslie Nielson 1926, Conrad Janis 1928, Tina Louise 1934, Sergio Mendes 1935, Burt Reynolds 1936, Manuel Noriega 1938, Jane Yolen 1939, Jeb Bush 1953, Sheryl Crow 1962, Hank Gathers 1967, Jennifer Aniston 1969, Brian Daubach 1972, Kelly Slater 1972, Brice Beckham 1976, Brandy 1979, Matthew Lawrence 1980, Kelly Rowland 1981

600 BC – Japan was first founded by Emperor Jimmu, according to tradition

1503 – Elizabeth of York, wife of King Henry VII of England, died on her 37th birthday

44

1531 – King Henry VIII of England was recognized as the head of the Church of England
1650 – French scientist, mathematician and philosopher Rene Descartes died in Sweden
1752 – The first hospital in America opened in Pennsylvania
1809 – Robert Fulton patented the steamboat
1943 – General Dwight David Eisenhower was chosen to command the Allied armies in Europe
1964 – The Beatles gave their first performance in America, in Washington, DC
1968 – The new 20,000 seat Madison Square Garden officially opened in New York
1979 – Nine days after the Ayatollah Khomeini returned to Iran after 15 years in exile, power was seized by his followers
1982 – ABC-TV's presentation of *The Winds of War* concluded, becoming the most watched television program in TV history
1990 – Nelson Mandela was freed after 27 years in captivity in South Africa
1993 – Janet Reno became the first woman to be Attorney General of the United States
1999 – Pluto again became the farthest planet from the Sun in the Solar System, although it was later declassified as a dwarf-planet
2005 – Maine received over a foot of snow, canceling school for the second day in a row for much of the state
2006 – Vice-President Dick Cheney accidentally shot his friend in the face with a shotgun while hunting

February 12: Cotton Mather 1663, Francis II of the Holy Roman Empire 1768, Louisa Adams 1775, Charles Darwin 1809, Abraham Lincoln 1809, Anna Pavlova 1881, Omar Bradley 1893, Lorne Greene 1915, Dom DiMaggio 1917, Forrest Tucker 1919, Joe Garagiola 1926, Arlen Specter 1930, Bill Russell 1934, Joe Don Baker 1936, Judy Blume 1938, Joe Lieberman 1942, Moe Bandy 1944, Maud Adams 1945, Cliff DeYoung 1945, Michael Ironside 1950, Michael McDonald 1952, Joanna Kerns 1953, Arsenio Hall 1955, Chet Lemon 1955, Josh Brolin 1968, Chynna Phillips 1968, Jesse Spencer 1979, Christina Ricci 1980

1541 – Santiago, Chile was founded
1554 – Lady Jane Grey was beheaded after being charged with treason for claiming the throne of England for nine days the previous year, as was her husband, Lord Guilford Dudley
1733 – The colony of Georgia in modern-day United States was founded, as was the city of Savannah

1771 – King Adolf Frederick of Sweden ate himself to death, having died after eating lobster, caviar, cabbage, smoked herring, and champagne, followed by 14 servings of his favorite dessert

1870 – In the Utah Territory, women gained the right to vote

1879 – North America's first artificial ice rink opened at Madison Square Garden in New York City

1892 – Abraham Lincoln's birthday was declared a national holiday

1909 – The National Association for the Advancement of Colored People (NAACP) was formed

1915 – The cornerstone of the Lincoln Memorial was laid in Washington, DC

1934 – The Austrian Civil War began

1971 – James Cash (J.C.) Penney died at the age of 95

1973 – The first American prisoners of war were released by the Viet Cong during the Vietnam War

1976 – Actor Sal Mineo was stabbed to death behind his West Hollywood Apartment at the age of 37

2000 – *Peanuts* comic strip creator Charles M. Schulz died at the age of 77

2001 – The space probe NEAR landed on the asteroid Eros

2004 – Mattel announced that Barbie and Ken were breaking up

2007 – A gunman opened fire at a mall in Salt Lake City, Utah, killing five people

February 13: Pope Alexander VII 1599, Almanzo Wilder 1857, Bess Truman 1885, Tennessee Ernie Ford 1919, Chuck Yeager 1923, Kim Novak 1933, George Segal 1934, Oliver Reed 1938, Jerry Springer 1944, Stockard Channing 1944, Peter Tork 1944, Peter Gabriel 1950, David Naughton 1951, Donnie Moore 1954, Neal McDonough 1966, Mats Sundin 1971, Randy Moss 1977

1429 – Joan of Arc, disguised as a man, began her journey through English-occupied France in order to reach the dauphin, Charles, and ask his permission for her to raise an army against English King Henry VI (see image to right)

1542 – Catherine Howard, the fifth wife of England's King Henry VIII, was executed for adultery

1633 – Galileo arrived in Rome for his trial

1635 – The first public school in the United States, the Boston Latin School, was founded

1668 – Spain officially recognized Portugal as an independent country

1692 – In what would become known as the Massacre at Glencoe, 78 members of the Macdonald clan were killed in Glen Coe, Scotland for not pledging allegiance to the new king, William of Orange, also known as William II of Scotland and William III of England

1920 – The National Negro Baseball League was organized

1935 – Bruno Hauptmann was found guilty of the kidnapping and murder of the infant son of Charles Lindbergh

1945 – Soviet forces captured Budapest, Hungary from Germany

1960 – France tested its first nuclear bomb

1965 – Sixteen-year-old Peggy Fleming won the ladies senior figure skating title at Lake Placid, New York

1984 – Konstantin Chernenko was chosen to be general secretary of the Soviet Communist Party's Central Committee, succeeding the late Yuri Andropov

1988 – The 15th Winter Olympic Games opened in Calgary, Alberta, Canada

1997 – Astronauts on the space shuttle Discovery brought the Hubble Space Telescope aboard for a tune up

2000 – Charles M. Schulz's last original Sunday *Peanuts* comic strip appeared in newspapers, the day after he died

2002 – Former New York mayor Rudolph Giuliani received an honorary knighthood from Queen Elizabeth II

2004 – The largest known diamond in the universe was discovered, the center of a white dwarf star about 2,500 miles across

February 14: Frederick Douglass 1818, Anna Howard Shaw 1847, Jack Benny 1894, Jimmy Hoffa 1913, Mel Allen 1913, Woody Hayes 1913, Edward Platt 1916, Hugh Downs 1921, Frank Borman 1928, Vic Morrow 1932, Florence Henderson 1934, Andrew Prine 1936, Michael Bloomberg 1942, Andrew Robinson 1942, Carl Bernstein 1944, Gregory Hines 1946, Pat O'Brien 1948, Teller (Pen and Teller) 1948, Jo Jo Starbuck 1951, Ken Wahl 1957, Jim Kelly 1960, Meg Tilly 1960, Manuela Maleeva 1967, Jules Asner 1968, Viscera 1968, Drew Bledsoe 1972, Rob Thomas 1972, Steve McNair 1973, Yul Kwon 1975, Richard Hamilton 1978, Freddie Highmore 1992

842 – Brothers Charles the Bald of France and Louis the German swore an oath to each other and in opposition to Holy Roman Emperor Lothair, their older brother, in what became known as the Oaths of Strasbourg

1014 – Henry II was crowned Holy Roman Emperor

1076 – Pope Gregory VII excommunicated Holy Roman Emperor Henry IV

1779 – English explorer James Cook was killed by Hawaiians during his third visit to the Hawaiian Islands

1849 – President James K. Polk became the first President to have his picture taken when he was photographed by Matthew Brady in New York City

1859 – Oregon became the 33rd state

1876 – Alexander Graham Bell filed a patent for the telephone

1912 – Arizona became the 48th U.S. state

1918 – *Tarzan of the Apes* became the first movie to feature the title character, created by Edgar Rice Burroughs

1918 – The Soviet Union adopted the Gregorian calendar

1920 – The League of Women Voters was founded in Chicago

1929 – The St. Valentine's Day Massacre took place in Chicago, when seven gangsters who were rivals of Al Capone were killed

1932 – The United States won the first bobsled competition at the Winter Olympic Games at Lake Placid

1952 – The 6th Winter Olympic Games opened in Oslo, Norway

1961 – Element 103, Lawrencium, was first synthesized at the University of California, Berkeley

1962 – First Lady Jacqueline Kennedy gave a tour of the White House on television

1980 – Walter Cronkite announced his retirement from the CBS Evening News

1980 – The 13th Winter Olympic Games opened in Lake Placid, New York

1981 – A fire in the Dublin night club, Stardust, left 48 people dead

1996 – China launched a Long March 3 rocket that blew off course 3 seconds after liftoff due to a gust of wind, hit a nearby village and killed 500 people

1997 – Astronauts on the space shuttle Discovery began a series of space walks designed to overhaul the Hubble Space Telescope

2000 – The *NEAR Shoemaker* became the first spacecraft to orbit an asteroid, when it went into orbit around Eros

2005 – The President of Lebanon, Rafik Hariri, was assassinated

February 15: Galileo Galilei 1564, Louis XV of France 1710, John Witherspoon 1723, Abraham Clark 1725, John Sutter 1803, Charles Lewis Tiffany 1812, Susan B. Anthony 1820, Sir Ernest Shackleton 1874, John Barrymore 1882, Cesar Romero 1907, Allan Arbus 1918, Harvey Korman 1927, Roger Chaffee 1935, Ron Cey 1948, Ken Anderson 1949, Jane Seymour 1951, Melissa Manchester 1951, Matt Groening 1954, Christopher McDonald 1955, Janice Dickinson 1955, Chris Farley 1964, Jaromir Jagr 1972, Amy Van Dyken 1973, Alex Borstein 1973, Ugueth Urbina 1974, Kaj-Erik Eriksen 1979, Jenna Morasca 1981

399 BC – Socrates was sentenced to death
1764 – The city of St. Louis was established

 1898 – The *USS Maine* sank when it exploded in Havana Harbor in Cuba for unknown reasons killing more than 260 crew members (see photo of *USS Maine* wreckage to left)

1903 – Morris and Rose Michtom, Russian immigrants living in Brooklyn, introduced the first teddy bear in America

1931 – The movie *Dracula* opened

1933 – President-elect Franklin Roosevelt escaped an assassination attempt in Miami, although Chicago Mayor Anton J. Cermak was mortally wounded in the attack

1942 – During World War II, Singapore surrendered to the Japanese

1952 – King George VI was buried at Windsor Castle in St. George's Chapel

1953 – 17-year old Tenley Albright became the first American to win a World Figure Skating Championship

1961 – The entire U.S. figure skating team, as well as coaches and family, was killed in a plane crash in Belgium

1965 – Canada unveiled its new red and white maple leaf flag

1965 – Singer Nat King Cole died

1989 – The Soviet Union announced that all of its troops had now left Afghanistan

1996 – A mortar attack was perpetrated against the U.S. embassy in Athens, Greece

2005 – You Tube was launched

February 16: Henry Wilson 1812, Julia Grant 1926, Edgar Bergen 1903, Vera-Ellen 1921, Tom Kennedy 1927, Sonny Bono 1935, Jeremy Bulloch 1945, William Katt 1951, Margaux Hemingway 1954, James Ingram 1956, LeVar Burton 1957, Ice-T 1958, John McEnroe 1959, John Valentin 1967, Jerome Bettis 1972, Mahershalalhashbaz Ali 1974, Eric Byrnes 1976, Ahman Green 1977, John Tartaglia 1978, Manny Delcarmen 1982

1568 – The Entire population of the Netherlands was sentenced to death by the Roman Catholic Church for heresy

1862 – During the American Civil War, Union General Ulysses S. Grant captured Fort Donelson, Tennessee

1883 – *Ladies Home Journal* began publication

1899 – French President Felix Faure died in office

1918 – Lithuania declared its independence from both Russia and Germany
1923 – Howard Carter unsealed the burial chamber of Egyptian Pharaoh Tutankhamen
1934 – The Austrian Civil War came to an end
1937 – Wallace C. Carothers received a patent for nylon
1950 – *What's My Line* debuted on CBS television
1959 – Fidel Castro was sworn in as Prime Minister of Cuba
1968 – The first 9-1-1 emergency service in the United States goes into effect in Haleyville, Alabama
1979 – The Bee Gees won a Grammy Award for their album, Saturday Night Fever
1997 – Jeff Gordon became the youngest person to win the Daytona 500, at age 25
2005 – The NHL announced the cancellation of the 2004-2005 season due to a labor dispute
2006 – The last Mobile Army Surgical Hospital (MASH) was decommissioned by the U.S. Army

February 17: William III of the Netherlands 1817, Montgomery Ward 1843, Red Barber 1908, Andre Norton 1912, Hal Holbrook 1925, Christina Pickles 1935, Jim Brown (NFL) 1936, Mary Ann Mobley 1939, Rene Russo 1954, Richard Karn 1956, Lou Diamond Phillips 1962, Michael Jordan 1963, Larry the Cable Guy 1963, Luc Robitaille 1966, Denise Richards 1971, Billie Joe Armstrong 1972, Jerry O'Connell 1974, Bryan White 1974, Scott Williamson 1976, Kelly Clarkson 1976, Joseph Gordon-Levitt 1981, Paris Hilton 1981, Bonnie Wright 1991

1600 – Philosopher Giordano Bruno was burned alive in Rome for heresy
1621 – Miles Standish was named the first commander of the Plymouth Colony
1801 – The U.S. House of Representatives broke an electoral tie between Thomas Jefferson and Aaron Burr where Jefferson was elected President and Burr became Vice-President
1819 – The United States House of Representatives passed the Missouri Compromise
1864 – The *H. L. Hunley* became the first submarine to sink a ship, when it sunk the *USS Housatonic*
1867 – The first ship passed through the Suez Canal
1908 – Apache Chief Geronimo died at the age of 79
1911 – Cadillac introduced the first self-starting automobile, which was an improvement on Ford's hand-cranked version
1933 - *Newsweek* was first published

1933 – Blondie Boopadoop married Dagwood Bumstead three years after Chic Young's popular comic strip first debuted
1933 – The Blaine Act was approved, ending prohibition in the United States
1934 – The first drivers' education course was offered
1974 – Robert K. Preston, a disgruntled army private, buzzed the White House in a stolen helicopter
1968 – The Naismith Memorial Basketball Hall of Fame opened in Springfield, Massachusetts
1992 – In Milwaukee, serial killer Jeffrey Dahmer was sentenced to life in prison
2000 – Microsoft released Windows 2000

February 18: Mary I of England 1516, Enzo Ferrari 1898, Hans Asperger 1906, Bill Cullen 1920, Jack Palance 1919, Helen Gurley Brown 1922, George Kennedy 1925, John Warner 1927, Toni Morrison 1931, Johnny Hart 1931, Yoko Ono 1933, Jean M. Auel 1936, Pat Bowlen 1944, Dennis DeYoung 1947, Princess Christina of the Netherlands 1947, John Hughes 1950, Cybil Sheppard 1950, Juice Newton 1952, John Travolta 1954, Vanna White 1957, Matt Dillon 1964, Dr. Dre 1965, Molly Ringwald 1968

1478 – George, Duke of Clarence, was executed after being convicted of treason against his brother King Edward IV of England
1564 – Michelangelo died in Rome
1735 – The first opera was performed in the America
1804 – Ohio University was founded in Athens, Ohio
1861 – Jefferson Davis was inaugurated as President of the Confederate States of America
1885 – Mark Twain's *Adventures of Huckleberry Finn* was published for the first time
1902 – 2,000 people died in an earthquake in Baku, Russia
1929 – The first Academy Awards were given out
1930 – The planet Pluto was discovered by Clyde Tombaugh, although it was later re-classified as a dwarf planet
1930 – Elm Farm Ollie became the first cow to fly in an airplane
1953 – Lucille Ball and Desi Arnaz signed an eight million dollar contract to continue the *I Love Lucy* show through 1955
1965 – The Gambia gained its independence from Great Britain
1977 – The space shuttle Enterprise went on its maiden flight sitting on top of a Boeing 747
2001 – NASCAR driver Dale Earnhardt, Sr., was killed in a crash during the Daytona 500 race
2003 – Almost 200 people were killed in a subway fire in South Korea

2008 – Fidel Castro stepped down as President of Cuba, due to poor health

February 19: Nicolas Copernicus 1473, Sir Cedric Hardwicke 1893, Merle Oberon 1911, Lee Marvin 1924, Smokey Robinson 1940, Homer Hickam 1943, Amy Tan 1952, Jeff Daniels 1955, Margaux Hemingway 1955, Prince Andrew of Britain 1960, Hana Mandlikova 1962, Seal 1963, Justine Bateman 1966, Haylie Duff 1985

197 – In the bloodiest battle between Roman armies, Emperor Septimius Severus defeated Clodius Albinus at the Battle of Lugdunum
1674 – England and the Netherlands sign the Peace of Westminster ending the Third Anglo-Dutch War, one of the agreements being the transfer of New Amsterdam to the English, who renamed it New York City
1807 – Former Vice-President of the United States Aaron Burr was arrested for treason
1846 – The Republic of Texas officially became the State of Texas
1847 – The Donner Party was rescued
1878 – Thomas Edison patented the phonograph
1913 – Prizes are included in Cracker Jack boxes for the first time
1945 – During World War II, about 30,000 U.S. Marines landed on Iwo Jima
1959 – Cyprus was granted its independence with the signing of an agreement with Britain, Turkey and Greece

1968 – *Mister Rogers' Neighborhood* debuted (see photo to left)
1980 – Bon Scott, the lead singer of AC/DC, died at the age of 33 after a night of heavy drinking
1986 – The Soviet Union launched the Mir space station
1999 – The world's tallest snowman, Angus, King of the Mountain, was completed, standing at 113 feet 7 inches tall in Bethel, Maine, and it did not melt until June 10th
2002 – NASA's Mars Odyssey spacecraft began mapping Mars

February 20: Cornelius Vanderbilt Whitney 1898, Ansel Adams 1902, Gloria Vanderbilt 1924, Robert Altman 1925, Sidney Poitier 1927, Amanda Blake 1929, Bobby Unser 1934, Marj Dusay 1936, Larry Hovis 1936, Nancy Wilson 1937, Phil Esposito 1942, Sandy Duncan 1946, Peter Strauss 1947, Jennifer O'Neill 1948, Ivana Trump 1949, Patty Hearst 1954, Charles Barkley 1963, French Stewart 1964, Cindy Crawford 1966, Andrew Shue 1967, Kurt Cobain 1967, Brian Littrell 1975, Livan Hernandez 1975, Rihanna 1988

1547 – 3 weeks after the death of his father Henry VIII, Edward VI was crowned King of England at the age of 9 (see image to right)

1792 – The U.S. Postal Service was created

1872 – The Metropolitan Museum of Art opened in New York City

1952 – The movie *African Queen*, starring Humphrey Bogart and Katharine Hepburn, opened

1962 – John Glenn became the first American to orbit the Earth

1987 – A bomb exploded in a computer store in Salt Lake City, which would eventually be linked to the Unibomber

1992 – Ross Perot announced his intention to run for President of the United States on CNN's *Larry King Live*

1993 – Two ten-year-old boys were charged by police in Liverpool, England, in the abduction and death of a toddler

1998 – American Tara Lipinski, at age 15, became the youngest gold medalist in Winter Olympics history when she won the ladies' figure skating title at Nagano, Japan

2003 – A fire at a nightclub in Rhode Island resulted in the death of about 100 people

2006 – Sports broadcaster Curt Gowdy died at the age of 86

February 21: Peter III of Russia 1728, Jeanne Calment 1875, Tom Yawkey 1903, Erma Bombeck 1927, Rue McClanahan 1935, Gary Lockwood 1937, Tyne Daly 1946, Alan Rickman 1946, Anthony Daniels 1946, Bob Ryan 1946, Olympia Snowe 1947, Larry Drake 1950, William L. Peterson 1953, Kelsey Grammer 1955, Alan Trammell 1958, Mary Chapin

Carpenter 1958, Jack Coleman 1958, Christopher Atkins 1961, Martha Hackett 1961, William Baldwin 1963, Steve Francis 1977, Charlotte Church 1979, Jennifer Love Hewitt 1979, Corbin Bleau 1989

1842 – John J. Greenough patented the sewing machine
1848 – Karl Marx and Friedrich published the *Communist Manifesto*
1885 – The Washington Monument was officially dedicated in Washington, DC
1925 – *The New Yorker* was first published
1947 – The first instant camera was demonstrated
1948 – NASCAR was incorporated
1965 – Malcolm X was assassinated in New York City at the age of 39 by members of the Nation of Islam
1972 – President Richard Nixon of the United States visited China
1972 – The Soviet unmanned spacecraft *Luna 20* landed on the Moon
1975 – Former U.S. Attorney General John N. Mitchell and former White House aides H.R. Haldeman and John D. Ehrlichman were sentenced to 2 ½ to 8 years in prison for their roles in the Watergate cover-up
1995 – Chicago stockbroker Steve Fossett became the first person to fly solo across the Pacific Ocean in a balloon
2000 – David Letterman returned to his Late Night show about five weeks after having an emergency quintuple heart bypass operation

February 22: Charles VII of France 1403, George Washington 1732, Frederic-Francois Chopin 1810, Edna St. Vincent Millay 1892, Robert Young 1907, John Mills 1908, Charlie Finley 1918, Robert Wadlow 1918, James Hong 1929, Rebecaa Schull 1929, Edward M. Kennedy 1932, Sparky Anderson 1934, Julius "Dr. J" Erving 1950, Julie Walters 1950, Bill Frist 1952, Kyle MacLachlan 1959, Steve "The Crocodile Hunter" Irwin 1962, Vijay Singh 1963, Jeri Ryan 1968, Michael Chang 1972, Drew Barrymore 1975, Rajon Rondo 1986

1295 BC – Ramses II was coronated
1630 – Quadequine introduced popcorn to English colonists at their first Thanksgiving dinner
1819 – Spain ceded Florida to the United States
1860 – Organized baseball's first game was played in San Francisco
1876 – John Hopkins University was founded in Baltimore
1879 – In Utica, New York, Frank W. Woolworth opened his first 5- and 10-cent store
1902 – A fistfight erupted in the Senate between Senators Benjamin Tillman and John McLaurin

1902 – It was announced that Major Walter Reed and Dr. James Carroll had discovered that yellow fever was carried by mosquitoes
1924 – President Calvin Coolidge delivered the first presidential radio broadcast from the White House
1956 – Elvis Presley first ranked on the music charts, with *Heartbreak Hotel*
1959 – Lee Petty won the first Daytona 500
1974 – Samuel Byck tried and failed in his attempt to assassinate President Richard Nixon
1980 – The "Miracle on Ice" happened when the U.S. ice hockey team defeated the Soviet Union to win the Olympic gold metal
1997 – It was announced that an adult sheep named Dolly had been successfully cloned in Scotland

February 23: Pope Paul II 1417, George Frederic Handel 1685, George Watts 1817, Victor Fleming 1883, Majel Barrett 1932, Peter Fonda 1940, Ed "Too Tall" Jones 1951, Patricia Richardson 1951, Bobby Bonilla 1963, Kristin Davis 1965, Dakota Fanning 1994

1455 – The Gutenberg Bible was first published
1660 – Charles XI became the king of Sweden
1778 – Baron von Steuben, a Prussian army officer, arrived at Valley Forge to help train the American forces
1822 – Boston was incorporated as a city
1836 – The Siege of the Alamo began
1848 – Former President John Quincy Adams died at the age of 80
1861 – President-elect Abraham Lincoln arrived secretly in Washington, DC to take his oath of office after an assassination attempt in Baltimore
1861 – Texas became the 7th state to secede from the Union
1870 – The state of Mississippi was readmitted to the Union
1887 – The French/Italian Riviera was hit by an earthquake that killed about 2,000 people
1896 – The Tootsie Roll was introduced by Leo Hirshfield
1904 – The United States acquired control of the Panama Canal Zone for $10 million
1927 – The Federal Radio Commission began assigning frequencies, hours of operation and power allocations for radio broadcasters
1940 – Walt Disney's animated movie *Pinocchio* was released
1941 – Plutonium was first produced and isolated by Dr. Glenn T. Seaborg
1954 – The first mass vaccination against polio began in Pittsburgh
1968 – Wilt Chamberlain of the Philadelphia 76ers became the first player to score 25,000 career points in the NBA

1993 – Child actor Gary Coleman won a $1,280,000 lawsuit against his parents
1997 – A large fire broke out on the Russian space station *Mir*
2006 – The one billionth song was downloaded from the i-Tunes Music Store

February 24: Emperor Toba of Japan 1103, Charles V of the Holy Roman Empire 1500, Mathias of the Holy Roman Empire 1587, John Burgoyne 1723, Winslow Homer 1836, Honus Wagner 1874, Chester Nimitz 1885, Abe Vigoda 1921, James Farentino 1938, Joe Lieberman 1942, Barry Bostwick 1945, Edward James Olmos 1947, Debra Jo Rupp 1951, Paula Zahn 1956, Eddie Murray 1956, Sammy Kershaw 1958, Billy Zane 1966, Jeff Garcia 1970, Alexei Kovalev 1973, Mike Lowell 1974, Bronson Arroyo 1977

616 – King Ethelbert of Kent died
1387 – King Charles III of Naples was assassinated
1582 – Pope Gregory XIII announced the new Gregorian calendar
1848 – The Communist Manifesto was published
1848 – French King Louis Philippe was overthrown by revolutionary citizens
1863 – Arizona became a U.S. territory
1868 – The first parade to use floats occurred in New Orleans at Mardi Gras
1868 – The U.S. House of Representatives impeached President Andrew Johnson due to his attempt to dismiss Secretary of War Edwin M. Stanton
1909 – The Hudson Motor Car Company was founded
1918 – Estonia declared its independence from Russia
1920 – The Nazi Party was founded
1945 – During World War II, the Philippine capital of Manila was liberated by U.S. soldiers
1970 – National Public Radio began in the United States
1981 – Buckingham Palace announced the engagement of Britain's Prince Charles to Lady Diana Spencer
1989 – Author Salman Rushdie had a price put on his head
1989 – A jet bound for New Zealand from Hawaii had the side ripped open, sucking 9 passengers out
1992 – Singers Kurt Cobain and Courtney Love were married
2002 – The Winter Olympic Games in Salt Lake City, Utah ended
2006 – Actor Don Knotts, star of the Andy Griffith Show and Three's Company, died at the age of 81

February 25: Pierre Auguste Renoir 1841, Enrico Caruso 1873, John Foster Dulles 1888, Zeppo Marx 1909, Jim Backus 1913, Bobby Riggs 1918, Monte Irvin 1919, Larry Gelbart 1928, Bob Schieffer 1937, Karen Grassle 1942, Sally Jessy Raphael 1943, George Harrison 1943, Lee Evans 1947, Ric Flair 1949, James Brown (sportscaster) 1951, Kurt Rambis 1958, Davey Allison 1961, Carrot Top 1965, Tea Leoni 1966, Sean Astin 1971, Daniel Powter 1971, Justin Berfield 1986, James Phelps 1986, Oliver Phelps 1986, Brendon Baerg 1998

1570 – Pope Pius V excommunicated England's Queen Elizabeth I in response to her having Mary Queen of Scots executed
1793 – President George Washington held his first cabinet meeting
1836 – Samuel Colt received a patent for the Colt revolver
1870 – Hiram Rhoades became the first African-American to serve in the United States Senate
1913 – The 13th Amendment to the Constitution was ratified, allowing a graduated income tax
1925 – Glacier Bay National Monument, now Glacier Bay National Park and Reserve, was established
1933 – The first aircraft carrier, Ranger, was launched
1943 – 158 Norwegian Jews were transported from Norway, bound for Auschwitz
1945 – Turkey declared war on Germany
1951 – The first Pan-American Games were held, in Buenos Aires, Argentina
1964 –Cassius Clay defeated boxing heavyweight champion Sonny Liston in a seventh-round technical knockout
1986 – President Ferdinand Marcos fled the Philippines
1986 – Corazon Aquino became the first female president of the Philippines
1991 – During the Persian Gulf War, 28 Americans were killed when an Iraqi Scud missile hit a United States barracks in Dhahran, Saudi Arabia
2006 – The population of the Earth reached 6.5 billion

February 26: Wencaslaus of the Holy Roman Empire 1361, Victor Hugo 1802, Levi Strauss 1829, William "Buffalo Bill" Cody 1846, John Harvey Kellogg 1852, Grover Cleveland Alexander 1887, William Frawley 1887, Arthur Brough 1905, Dub Taylor 1907, Tex Avery 1908, Robert Alda 1914, Jackie Gleason 1916, Theodore Sturgeon 1918, Mason Adams 1919, Tony Randall 1920, Tom Kennedy 1927, Fats Domino 1928, Ariel Sharon 1928, Johnny Cash 1932, Robert Novak 1934, Helen Clark 1950, Lee Atwater 1951, Michael Bolton 1953, J.T. Snow 1968, Marshall Faulk 1973, Jenny Thompson 1973, Oksana Baiul 1977

1815 – Napoleon Bonaparte escaped from the Island of Elba
1919 – The Grand Canyon was established as a National Park
1929 – The Grand Teton National Park was created
1951 – The 22nd Amendment to the U.S. Constitution was ratified, limiting U.S. Presidents to two terms
1972 – A dam burst caused the Buffalo Creek flood that killed 125 people in West Virginia
1986 – Corazon Aquino was inaugurated president of the Philippines
1991 – The first Internet browser was introduced, Worldwide Web, later renamed Nexus
1991 – On Baghdad radio, Saddam Hussein announced that Iraq had withdrawn from Kuwait
1993 – Six people were killed and more than a thousand injured when a van exploded in the parking garage beneath the World Trade Center in New York City

February 27: Roman Emperor Constantine I 272, Henry Wadsworth Longfellow 1807, John Steinbeck 1902, Marian Anderson 1902, John Connally 1917, Joanne Woodward 1930, Elizabeth Taylor 1932, Ralph Nader 1934, Barbara Babcock 1937, Howard Hesseman 1940, Mary Frann 1943, Adam Baldwin 1962, Grant Show 1962, Chelsea Clinton 1980, Josh Groban 1981

1594 – Henry IV was crowned King of France
1703 – The first Mardi Gras celebration was held, in Mobile, Alabama
1827 – New Orleans held its first Mardi Gras celebration
1864 – During the American Civil War, the first northern prisoners arrived at Andersonville Prison
1900 – The Boers surrendered to the British in South Africa
1922 – The U.S. Supreme Court upheld the 19th Amendment that guaranteed women the right to vote
1942 – The U.S. aircraft carrier *Langley* was sunk by Japanese warplanes
1951 – The Twenty-second Amendment to the Constitution was ratified, limiting presidential terms to two terms
1974 – *People* magazine was first published
1990 – The Exxon Corporation and Exxon Shipping were indicted on five criminal counts because of the 1989 Exxon Valdez oil spill off the coast of Alaska
1991 – President George H. W. Bush announced live on television that Kuwait was liberated
2003 – Fred Rogers, long-time host of *Mister Rogers' Neighborhood*, died at the age of 74

February 28: Linus Pauling 1901, Vincente Minnelli 1903, Bugsy Siegel 1906, Billie Bird 1908, Zero Mostel 1915, Charles Durning 1923, Gavin MacLeod 1931, Dean Smith 1931, Tommy Tune 1940, Mario Andretti 1940, Frank Bonner 1942, Bubba Smith 1945, Stephanie Beacham 1947, Bernadette Peters 1948, Rick Steamboat 1953, Brian Billick 1954, Gilbert Gottfried 1955, John Turturro 1957, Dorothy Stratton 1960, Rae Dawn Chong 1961, Robert Sean Leonard 1969, Rory Cochrane 1972, Eric Lindros 1973, Ali Larter 1976

1784 – John Wesley chartered the Methodist Church

1844 – A gun on the USS *Princeton* exploded while on a Potomac River cruise with President John Tyler and his cabinet, killing the ship's captain Beverly Kennon, Secretary of State Abel Upshur, Secretary of the Navy Thomas Gilmer, President Tyler's future father-in-law David Gardiner, and several others (see lithograph image to left)

1850 – The University of Utah opened in Salt Lake City

1854 – The Republican Party was organized in Ripon, Wisconsin

1861 – Colorado was organized as a U.S. territory

1885 – The American Telephone and Telegraph company was incorporated

1900 – The Labor Party in England was created

1940 – The first televised basketball game occurred

1979 – Mr. Ed, the talking horse, died

1983 – *M*A*S*H* became the most watched television program in history when the final episode aired

1993 – A fifty-one day standoff began when federal agents failed in their attempt to raid the Branch Davidian compound in Waco, Texas

2002 – The Euro became the official currency in 10 European countries: Germany, France, Italy, Spain, Portugal, Belgium, Luxembourg, the Netherlands, Austria, Finland, Greece and Ireland

2005 – A suicide bombing in Al Hillah, Iraq killed 127 people

February 29: Pope Paul III 1468, Jimmy Dorsey 1904, Pepper Martin 1904, Dinah Shore 1916, James Mitchell 1920, Al Rosen 1924, Carlos Humberto Romero 1924, Alex Rocco 1936, Jack Lousma 1936, Dennis Farina 1944, Richard Ramirez 1960, Tony Robbins 1960, Chucky Brown

1968, Pete Fenson 1968, Antonio Sabato, Jr. 1972, Ja Rule 1976, Simon Gange 1980, Cam Ward 1984

1288 – Scotland established this day as one when a woman could propose marriage to a man
1704 – During Queen Anne's War, French forces and Native Americans attacked and destroyed Deerfield, Massachusetts, killing over 100 people
1940 – Hattie McDaniel became the first black person to win an Oscar, when she won Best Supporting Actress award for her role as Mammy in *Gone with the Wind*
1960 – An earthquake in Morocco killed about 3,000 people
2004 – *Lord of the Rings: The Return of the King* won an Academy Award for best picture

March 1: Caroline of Ansbach 1683, William Cushing 1732, Frederic Chopin 1810, Glenn Miller 1904, David Niven 1910, Yitzhak Rabin 1922, Deke Slayton 1924, Robert Clary 1926, Pete Rozelle 1926, Harry Belafonte 1927, Robert Conrad 1935, Jed Allan 1937, Richard Bowman Myers 1942, Roger Daltry 1944, Dirk Benedict 1945, Alan Thicke 1947, Ron Howard 1954, Catherine Bach 1954, Tim Daly 1956, Bertrand Piccard 1958, George Eads 1967, Chris Webber 1973, Mark-Paul Gosselaar 1974, Alicia Leigh Willis 1978, Adam LaVorgna 1981

1565 – The city of Rio de Janeiro was founded
1642 – Georgeana, Massachusetts (now York, Maine) became the first incorporated city in the United States
1692 – The Salem Witch Trials began
1781 – In America, the Continental Congress adopted the Articles of Confederation
1790 – The U.S. Congress authorized the first U.S. census
1803 – Ohio became the 17th state
1805 – Justice Samuel Chase was acquitted by the U.S. Senate after his impeachment trial
1815 – Napoleon returned to France from his exile on the island of Elba
1867 – Nebraska became the 37th state and the city of Lancaster was renamed Lincoln and became the capital
1872 – The U.S. Congress authorized the creation of Yellowstone National Park, the world's first national park
1912 – Captain Albert Berry made the first successful parachute jump from a moving airplane
1932 – The 22-month-old son of Charles and Anne Lindbergh was kidnapped

1936 – Hoover Dam was completed
1941 – W47NV (now WSM-FM) became the first FM radio station in the United States
1949 – *Ripley's Believe It Or Not* debuted on TV
1953 – Soviet leader Joseph Stalin collapsed from a stroke, dying four days later
1954 – Five U.S. congressmen were wounded when four Puerto Rican nationalists opened fire from the gallery of the U.S. House of Representatives
1961 – The Peace Corps was established by President John F. Kennedy
1966 – The Soviet probe, Venera 3, crashed on the planet Venus, the first spacecraft to land on another planet
1969 – Mickey Mantle announced his retirement from Major League Baseball
1974 – Seven people were indicted in connection with the Watergate break-in
2003 – In the United States, approximately 180,000 personnel from 22 different organizations around the government became part of the Department of Homeland Security

March 2: Robert II of Scotland 1316, Pope Adrian VI 1459, Sam Houston 1793, Pope Leo XIII 1810, Pope Pius XII 1876, Moe Berg 1902, Dr. Seuss 1904, Mel Ott 1909, Desi Arnaz 1917, Jennifer Jones 1919, Tom Wolfe 1931, Mikhail Gorbachev 1931, John Irving 1942, Eddie Money 1949, Gates McFadden 1949, Karen Carpenter 1950, Jay Osmond 1955, Jon Bon Jovi 1962, Ron Gant 1965, Daniel Craig 1968, Lisa Lackey 1971, Jay Gibbons 1977, Henrik Lundqvist 1982, Ben Roethlisberger 1982, Reggie Bush 1985

1807 – The United States Congress abolished the African slave trade
1836 – Texas declared its independence from Mexico
1855 – Alexander II became Tsar of Russia
1861 – The United States Congress created the Territory of Nevada
1877 – The United States Congress declared that Rutherford B. Hayes had won the presidential election, even though Samuel J. Tilden had won the popular vote
1899 – Mount Rainier National Park in Washington was established
1917 – The Russian Revolution began with Czar Nicholas II abdicating
1917 – Citizens of Puerto Rico were granted U.S. citizenship with the enactment of the Jones Act
1923 – TIME magazine appeared on newsstands for the first time
1927 – Babe Ruth signed a 3-year contract with the New York Yankees for $210,000, making him the highest paid player to that point in history

1933 – The movie *King Kong* opened in New York City
1940 – Elmer Fudd made his debut in cartoons
1943 – In the Battle of the Bismarck Sea, United States and Australian forces sunk Japanese convoy ships
1946 – Ho Chi Minh was elected President of North Vietnam
1949 – The first automatic street light was installed in New Milford, Connecticut
1953 – The Academy Awards was first broadcast on television
1962 – Wilt Chamberlain scored 100 points against the New York Knicks, in a game that had a final score of 169-147
1969 – In Toulouse, France, the supersonic transport Concorde made its first test flight
1972 – Pioneer 10 was launched toward Jupiter
1974 – Postage stamps jumped from 8 to 10 cents for first-class mail
1987 – Chrysler bought American Motors
1998 – Images from the American spacecraft Galileo indicated that the Jupiter moon Europa has a liquid ocean and a source of interior heat
2004 – Al Qaeda carried out the Ashoura Massacre in Iraq, resulting in the deaths of 170 people and wounding of over 500 others
2004 – NASA announced that the Mars rover Opportunity had discovered evidence that water had once existed on Mars in the past

March 3: John II of Portugal 1455, George Pullman 1831, Alexander Graham Bell 1847, Willie Keeler 1872, Jean Harlow 1911, James Doohan 1920, James Merrill 1926, Joe Conley 1928, Jennifer Warnes 1947, Marc Silvestri 1958, Miranda Richardson 1958, Herschel Walker 1962, Jackie Joyner-Kersee 1962, Tone Loc 1966, David Faustino 1974, L'il Flap 1981, Jessica Biel 1982, Stacie Orrico 1986

1791 – The U.S. Mint was created
1845 – Florida became the 27th U.S. state
1849 – The United States Congress created the territory of Minnesota
1849 – The United States Department of the Interior was established
1857 – Britain and France declared war on China
1875 – The U.S. Congress authorized a 20-cent coin, which was used for just three years
1923 – *Time Magazine* was published for the first time
1931 – The Star Spangled Banner, written by Francis Scott Key, was adopted as the American National Anthem
1933 – The Mount Rushmore Memorial was officially dedicated
1938 – Oil was discovered in Saudi Arabia
1945 – During World War II, Finland declared war on the Axis
1952 – Lucy made her first appearance in a *Peanuts* comic strip

1955 – Elvis Presley appeared on television for the first time
1959 – The San Francisco Giants had their new stadium officially named Candlestick Park
1969 – Apollo 9 was launched by NASA to test a lunar module
1969 – Sirhan Sirhan testified in a Los Angeles court that he killed Robert Kennedy
1985 – The TV show *Moonlighting* premiered
1987 – Actor and comedian Danny Kaye died at the age of 74
1991 – Rodney King was severely beaten by Los Angeles police officers, the whole thing caught on amateur home video
1999 – Bertrand Piccard and Brian Jones began their attempt to circumnavigate the Earth in a hot air balloon

March 4: Prince Henry the Navigator 1394, Antonio Vivaldi 1678, Knute Rockne 1888, Dazzy Vance 1891, Shemp Howard 1895, Anne Haney 1934, Adrian Lyne 1941, Susan Clark 1944, Emilio Estefan 1953, Adrian Zmed 1954, Catherine O'Hara 1954, Patricia Heaton 1958, Steven Weber 1961, Ray "Boom Boom" Mancini 1961, Stacy Edwards 1965, Kevin Johnson 1966, Chastity Bono 1969, Andrea Bowen 1990

1461 – England's King Henry VI was deposed and Edward IV took over
1634 – Samuel Cole opened the first tavern in Boston
1665 – England's King Charles II declared war on the Netherlands
1681 – England's King Charles II granted a charter to William Penn for an area that later became the state of Pennsylvania
1776 – During the American Revolution, The Americans captured Dorchester Heights near Boston
1789 – The first Congress of the United States met in New York and declared that the U.S. Constitution was in effect
1791 – Vermont became the 14th U.S. state
1814 – During the War of 1812, the Americans defeated the British at the Battle of Longwoods in Ontario
1861 – Abraham Lincoln was sworn in as the 16th President of the United States
1887 – William Randolph Hearst, at age 23, bought the *San Francisco Examiner*, beginning the Hearst newspaper empire
1894 – Over 1,000 buildings were destroyed in a fire in Shanghai
1901 – William McKinley was inaugurated as President for the second time, this time with Theodore Roosevelt as his Vice-President
1902 – The American Automobile Association was founded in Chicago
1908 – The New York board of education banned the act of whipping students in school

1913 – The U.S. Department of Commerce and Labor was split into two departments
1917 – Jeannette Rankin became the first female member of the U.S. House of Representatives
1950 – Walt Disney's *Cinderella* was released
1952 – Ronald Reagan and Nancy Davis were married
1954 – The first kidney transplant was performed
1975 – Queen Elizabeth knighted American actor Charlie Chaplin
1979 – The United States space probe *Voyager I* discovered Jupiter's rings
1989 – Time, Inc. and Warner Communications Inc. announced a plan to merge
1999 – Monica Lewinsky's book about her affair with President Bill Clinton went on sale

March 5: Henry II of England 1133, David II of Scotland 1324, Charles Goodnight 1836, Henry Travers 1874, Rex Harrison 1908, James Noble 1922, James B. Sikking 1934, Nicholas Smith 1934, Dean Stockwell 1936, Samantha Egger 1939, Marsha Warfield 1954, Penn Jillette 1955, Kent Tekulve 1957, Andy Gibb 1958, Michael Irvin 1966, Lisa Robin Kelly 1970, Niki Taylor 1975, Jolene Blalock 1975, Paul Konerko 1976, Jake Lloyd 1989

1590 – Danish astronomer Tycho Brahe discovered a comet in the constellation Pisces
1623 – The first alcohol temperance law in America went into effect in Virginia

1770 – The Boston Massacre took place when British troops fired on a crowd in Boston killing five people (see image to left)
1836 – Samuel Colt manufactured the first pistol
1918 – The Soviets moved the capital of Russia from Petrograd to Moscow
1933 – President Franklin D. Roosevelt

ordered a four-day bank holiday in order to stop large amounts of money from being withdrawn from banks
1953 – Soviet dictator Joseph Stalin died
1979 – Voyager 1 flew the closest it would to Jupiter
1982 – Actor John Belushi died in Los Angeles of a drug overdose at the age of 33
1991 – Iraq released all Gulf War prisoners
1998 – NASA announced that an orbiting craft had found enough water on the moon to support a human colony and rocket fueling station
2002 – MTV began airing *The Osbournes*
2004 – Martha Stewart was found guilty of lying about the reason for selling 3,298 shares of ImClone Systems stock, conspiracy, making a false statement and obstruction of justice
2006 – Disney bought Pixar Animation Studios

March 6: John II of Castille 1405, Michelangelo Buonarroti 1475, Cyrano De Bergerac 1619, Elizabeth Barrett Browning 1806, Oscar Straus 1870, Lefty Grove 1900, Lou Costello 1906, Will Eisner 1917, Ed McMahon 1923, Alan Greenspan 1926, Gordon Cooper 1927, Marion Barry 1936, Ivan Boesky 1937, Valentina Tereshkova 1937, Cookie Rojas 1939, Willie Stargell 1940, Robert DeNiro 1941, Ben Murphy 1942, Mary Wilson 1944, Rob Reiner 1947, Dick Fosbury 1947, Kiki Dee 1947, Tom Arnold 1959, Connie Britton 1968, Moira Kelly 1968, Shaquille O'Neal 1972, Ken "Mr. Kennedy" Anderson 1976

1521 – Ferdinand Magellan discovered Guam
1820 – The Missouri Compromise was enacted
1836 – The thirteen-day siege of the Alamo by Santa Anna and his army ended, as the Mexican army of three thousand men defeated the 189 Texas volunteers
1899 – Aspirin was patented by German researchers Felix Hoffman and Hermann Dreser
1900 – An explosion trapped fifty coal miners underground in West Virginia
1944 – During World War II, U.S. heavy bombers began the first American raid on Berlin
1960 – The United States announced that it would send 3,500 troops to Vietnam
1964 – American boxing heavyweight champion Cassius Clay changed his name to Muhammad Ali
1975 – Iran and Iraq announced that they had settled their border dispute
1981 – Walter Cronkite appeared on his last episode of CBS Evening News

1982 – The most points ever scored in an NBA game, as San Antonio beat Milwaukee, 171-166
1992 – The last episode of The Cosby Show aired
2006 – Baseball Hall of Fame member Kirby Puckett died of a stroke at the age of 45

March 7: Rob Roy 1671, Pope Clement XIII 1693, John Herschel 1792, Ben Ames Williams 1889, Willard Scott 1934, Daniel J. Travanti 1940, Michael York 1942, Michael Eisner 1942, Tammy Faye Bakker 1942, Franco Harris 1950, Lynn Swann 1952, Bryan Cranston 1956, Joe Carter 1960, Ivan Lendl 1960, Taylor Dayne 1962, Wanda Sykes 1964, Jesper Parnevik 1965, Jeff Kent 1968, Sam Gash 1969, Laura Prepon 1980

322 BC – Aristotle, the Greek philosopher, died
161 – Roman Emperor Antonius Pius died after ruling for 23 years
1774 – The British closed the port of Boston to all commerce
1854 – Charles Miller received a patent for the sewing machine
1876 – Alexander Graham Bell received a patent for the telephone (see image to right)
1906 – Finland became the first country to give women the right to vote
1933 – The board game Monopoly was invented
1936 – Hitler sent German troops into the Rhineland
1945 – During World War II, United States forces crossed the Rhine River at Remagen, Germany
1965 – State troopers and a sheriff's posse broke up a march by civil rights demonstrators in Selma, Alabama
1969 – Golda Meir was elected the first female prime minister of Israel
1999 – Motion picture director Stanley Kubrick died

March 8: Richard Howe 1726, Hannah Van Buren 1783, Oliver Wendell Holmes 1841, Claire Trevor 1909, Alan Hale, Jr. 1918, Susan Clark 1940, Lynn Redgrave 1943, Micky Dolenz 1945, Jim Rice 1953, Aidan Quinn

1959, Camryn Manheim 1961, Kathy Ireland 1963, Andrea Parker 1970, Jason Elam 1970, Hines Ward 1976, Freddie Prinze Jr. 1976, Juan Encarnacion 1976, James Van Der Beek 1977

1618 – Johann Kepler discovered the third Law of Planetary Motion
1702 – England's Queen Anne took the throne upon the death of King William III
1817 – The New York Stock Exchange began operations
1880 – President Rutherford B. Hays declared that the United States would have jurisdiction over any canal built across Panama
1921 – Spanish Premier Eduardo Dato was assassinated while leaving the Parliament in Madrid
1936 – The first stock car race was held in Daytona Beach, Florida
1959 – Groucho, Chico and Harpo Marx made their final TV appearance together
1979 – Volcanoes on Jupiter's moon Io were discovered
1983 – United States President Ronald Reagan called the Soviet Union an "evil empire"
1993 – *Beavis and Butthead* premiered on MTV as a series

March 9: Amerigo Vespucci 1454, Vyacheslav Molotov 1890, Will Geer 1902, Mickey Spillane 1918, Carl Betz 1921, Yuri Gagarin 1934, Marty Ingels 1936, Mickey Gilley 1936, Raul Julia 1940, Bobby Fischer 1943, Charles Gibson 1943, Jeffrey Osborne 1948, Doug Ault 1950, Danny Sullivan 1950, Faith Daniels 1957, Mary Murphy 1958, Benito Santiago 1965, Brian Bosworth 1965, Emmanuel Lewis 1971, Jean Louisa Kelly 1972, Aaron Boone 1973, Yamila Diaz 1976, Chingy 1980, Bow Wow 1987

1788 – Connecticut became the 5th state
1796 – Napoleon Bonaparte and Josephine de Beauharnais were married
1820 – The U.S. Congress passed the Land Act that paved the way for westward expansion in North America
1832 – Abraham Lincoln announced that he would run for a political office for the first time
1841 – A judge ruled that captured Africans who had seized the salve-trading ship the *Amistad* that had been carrying them, had been captured illegally
1862 – During the U.S. Civil War, the ironclads Monitor and Virginia fought to a draw in a five-hour battle at Hampton Roads, Virginia
1863 – General Ulysses Grant was appointed commander-in-chief of the Union forces by President Abraham Lincoln
1959 – The Barbie doll made its debut

1964 – The first Ford Mustang rolled off the Ford assembly line
1965 – The first U.S. combat troops arrived in South Vietnam
1975 – Work began on the Alaskan oil pipeline
1986 – Navy divers found the largely intact crew compartment of the space shuttle *Challenger* along with the remains of all seven astronauts
1996 – Actor and comedian George Burns died at the age of 100
1997 – Rapper Notorious B.I.G. was shot and killed in Los Angeles
2005 – Dan Rather retired from the *CBS Evening News*
2006 – Liquid water was discovered on Saturn's largest moon, Enceladus

March 10: Ferdinand II of Aragon 1452, Holy Roman Emperor Ferdinand I 1503, Thomas Howard 1536, Alexander III of Russia 1845, James Earl Ray 1928, Ralph Emery 1933, Chuck Norris 1940, Jim Valvano 1946, Kim Campbell 1947, Shannon Tweed 1957, Osama bin Laden 1957, Steve Howe 1957, Sharon Stone 1958, Mitch Gaylord 1961, Prince Edward of Britain 1964, Jasmine Guy 1964, Rod Woodson 1965, Christopher Titus 1966, Mike Timlin 1966, Matt Kenseth 1972, Eva Herzigova 1973, Shannon Miller 1977, Robin Thicke 1977, Carrie Underwood 1983, Emily Osment 1992

241 BC – In the Battle of the Aegates Islands, the Romans sank the Carthaginian fleet, ending the First Punic War
49 BC – Julius Caesar crossed the Rubicon and invaded Italy
1629 – England's King Charles I dissolved Parliament and did not call it back for 11 years
1776 – *Common Sense* by Thomas Paine was published
1785 – Thomas Jefferson was appointed minister to France
1801 – The first census in Great Britain was begun
1804 – The formal ceremonies transferring the Louisiana Purchase from France to the United States took place in St. Louis
1831 – The French Foreign Legion was established
1848 – The United States Senate ratified the Treaty of Guadalupe Hidalgo, which ended the war with Mexico
1876 – Alexander Graham Bell made the first successful call with a telephone, when he spoke the words, "Mr. Watson, come here, I want to see you"
1880 – The Salvation Army began operating in the United States
1893 – New Mexico State University canceled its first graduation ceremony because the only graduate was robbed and killed the night before
1893 – The Ivory Coast became a French colony
1902 – The entire town of Tochangri, Turkey was wiped out in an earthquake

1910 – Slavery was abolished in China

1933 – An earthquake in Long Beach, California resulted in the deaths of 120 people

1941 – The Brooklyn Dodgers announced that their players would begin wearing batting helmets during the 1941 season

1969 – James Earl Ray pled guilty to the assassination of Martin Luther King Jr.

1971 – The United States Senate approved an amendment to lower the voting age to 18

1977 – Scientists discovered rings around Uranus

1982 – All nine planets (at the time Pluto was still considered a planet) aligned on the same side of the Sun

1997 – *Buffy, the Vampire Slayer* debuted on the WB

2000 – Country singers Vince Gill and Amy Grant were married

March 11: John McLean 1785, Frederick IX of Denmark 1899, Lawrence Welk 1903, Harold Wilson 1916, Robert Mosbacher 1927, Rupert Murdoch 1931, Sam Donaldson 1934, Antonin Scalia 1936, Bobby McFerrin 1950, Jerry Zucker 1950, Douglas Adams 1952, Susan Richardson 1952, Alex Kingston 1963, Lisa Loeb 1968, Terrence Howard 1969, Jesse Jackson Jr. 1965, Johnny Knoxville 1971, Bobby Abreu 1974, Elton Brand 1979, Joel Madden 1979, Benji Madden 1979, Dan Uggla 1980, Thora Birch 1982, Anton Yelchin 1989

537 – The Goths began their siege on Rome

1801 – Paul I of Russia was assassinated

1824 – The Bureau of Indian Affairs was established as part of the U.S. Department of War, although later it switched to the Department of Interior

1847 – Johnny Appleseed died

1861 – A Confederate Convention was held in Montgomery, Alabama, where a new constitution was adopted

1864 – A flood in Sheffield, England led to the deaths of over 250 people

1867 – In Hawaii, the volcano Great Mauna Loa erupted

1888 – The Blizzard of '88 began along the United States Atlantic Seaboard shutting down communication and transportation lines, killing more than 400 people

1901 – U.S. Steel was formed when industrialist J.P. Morgan purchased Carnegie Steel Corp

1930 – Howard Taft became the first President to be buried in the National Cemetery in Arlington, Virginia

1941 – President Franklin D. Roosevelt authorized the Lend-Lease Act, which allowed the act of providing war supplies to the Allies

1966 – Three men were convicted of the murder of Malcolm X

1985 – Mikhail Gorbachev became the new Soviet leader
1986 – Popsicle announced its plan to end the traditional twin-stick frozen treat for a one-stick model
1998 – The International Astronomical Union issued an alert that said that a mile-wide asteroid could come very close to, and possibly hit, Earth on Oct. 26, 2028, although it was later revealed that they were in error

March 12: Jane Pierce 1806, Sir John Abbott 1821, Clement Studebaker 1831, Jack Kerouac 1922, Wally Schirra 1923, Andrew Young 1932, Barbara Feldon 1932, Al Jarreau 1940, Liza Minnelli 1946, Mitt Romney 1947, James Taylor 1948, Ron Jeremy 1953, Dale Murphy 1956, Marlon Jackson 1957, Darryl Strawberry 1962, John Andretti 1963, Steve Finley 1965, Casey Mears 1978, Samm Levine 1982

515 BC – The Second Temple in Jerusalem was completed
1609 – The Bermuda Islands became an English colony
1664 – New Jersey became a British colony
1755 – In North Arlington, New Jersey, the steam engine was used for the first time
1789 – The United States Post Office was established
1863 – President Jefferson Davis delivered his State of the Confederacy address
1894 – Coca-Cola was sold in bottles for the first time
1912 – The Girl Scouts organization was first organized, originally called the Girl Guides
1918 – Moscow once again became the capital of Russia
1930 – Gandhi began his 200-mile march to the sea that symbolized his defiance of British rule over India
1938 – Germany occupied Austria
1951 – The *Dennis the Menace* comic strip first appeared in newspapers
1985 – Larry Bird, of the NBA's Boston Celtics, scored a club-record 60 points against the Atlanta Hawks
1987 – *Les Miserables* opened on Broadway
1993 – Janet Reno was sworn in as the first female U.S. Attorney General
1994 – The Church of England ordained its first female priests
1998 – Astronomers canceled a warning that a mile-wide asteroid might collide with Earth saying that calculations had been off by 600,000 miles
2002 – Andrea Yates was found guilty of drowning her five children in a Texas courtroom
2003 – In Utah, Elizabeth Smart was reunited with her family nine months after she was abducted from her home

71

March 13: Pope Innocent XII 1615, Holy Roman Emperor Joseph II 1741, Earl Grey 1764, Abigail Filmore 1798, William Casey 1913, Edward O'Hare 1914, Neil Sedaka 1939, Michael Martin Murphy 1945, William H. Macy 1950, Fred Berry 1951, Dana Delany 1956, Glenne Headly 1957, Will Clark 1964, Trent Dilfer 1972, Danny Masterson 1976, Marco Andretti 1987, Harry Melling 1989

1519 – Cortez landed in Mexico
1781 – Sir William Herschel discovered the planet Uranus
1852 – The *New York Lantern* newspaper published the first Uncle Sam cartoon
1865 – The Confederate States of America agreed to allow African American troops
1868 – The U.S. Senate began the impeachment trial of President Andrew Johnson
1877 – Chester Greenwood of Farmington, Maine, patented the earmuffs
1881 – Tsar Alexander II of Russia was assassinated when a bomb was thrown at him near his palace
1897 – San Diego State University was founded
1901 – Multi-millionaire Andrew Carnegie announced he was retiring from business and was going to spend the rest of his life giving away his fortune
1901 – Former President Benjamin Harrison died at the age of 67
1930 – It was announced that the planet Pluto had been discovered by scientist Clyde Tombaugh at the Lowell Observatory
1957 – Jimmy Hoffa was arrested by the FBI on charges of bribery
1969 – The Apollo 9 astronauts returned to Earth after the conclusion of a mission that included the successful testing of the Lunar Module
1991 – Exxon paid $1 billion in fines and for the clean-up of the Alaskan oil spill
1992 – An earthquake in Turkey killed over 500 people
1993 – A blizzard hit the eastern United States, bringing record snowfall amounts from Florida to Maine

March 14: Thomas R. Marshall 1854, Albert Einstein 1879, Lee Petty 1914, Frank Borman 1928, Quincy Jones 1933, Michael Caine 1933, Gene Cernan 1934, Steve Kanaly 1946, Billy Crystal 1947, Rick Dees 1950, Jerry Greenfield 1951, Adrian Zmed 1954, Prince Albert II of Monaco 1958, Kirby Puckett 1960, Penny Johnson Jerald 1961, Kevin Brown 1965, Megan Follows 1968, James Frain 1968, Larry Johnson 1969, Bobby Jenks 1981, Taylor Hanson 1983

1629 – A Royal charter was granted to the Massachusetts Bay Colony
1743 – The first American town meeting was held at Boston's Faneuil Hall

1794 – Eli Whitney received a patent for his cotton gin
1906 – The island of Ustica was devastated by an earthquake
1932 – George Eastman, the founder of the Kodak Company, committed suicide
1938 – Germany invaded Austria
1951 – United Nations forces recaptured Seoul for the second time during the Korean War
1964 – A Dallas jury found Jack Ruby guilty of the murder of Lee Harvey Oswald
1967 – John F. Kennedy's body was moved from a temporary grave to a permanent one
1998 – An earthquake left 10,000 homeless in southeastern Iran

March 15: Andrew Jackson 1767, Lord Melbourne 1779, MacDonald Carey 1913, Alan Bean 1932, Ruth Bader Ginsberg 1933, Judd Hirsch 1935, Jimmy Swaggert 1935, Bobby Bonds 1946, Ry Cooder 1947, Dee Snider 1953, Park Overall 1957, Harold Baines 1959, Fabio 1961, Terence Trent D'Arby 1962, Jimmy Baio 1962, Derek Parra 1970, Robert Fick 1974, Eva Longoria 1975, Kevin Youkilis 1979, Caitlin Wachs 1989

44 BC – Roman Emperor Julius Caesar was assassinated by high ranking Roman Senators, and the day became known as the Ides of March
1493 – Christopher Columbus returned to Spain after his first New World voyage
1820 – Maine was admitted as the 23rd state of the Union
1902 – In the college hockey championship, Yale beat Harvard, 5-3
1938 – Oil was discovered in Saudi Arabia
1955 – The U.S. Air Force unveiled a self-guided missile
1972 – *The Godfather* was released in movie theaters
1977 – The first episode of *Eight is Enough* was aired on ABC-TV
1977 – *Three's Company* debuted on ABC-TV
1989 – The United States Department of Veterans Affairs was created
1990 – Mikhail Gorbachev was elected the first executive president of the Soviet Union
1990 – The Ford Explorer was introduced to the public
1991 – Four Los Angeles police officers were indicted in the beating of Rodney King on March 3, 1991
1998 – *Titanic* overtook *Star Wars* as the highest grossing film in North America all time

March 16: James Madison 1751, George S. Ohm 1787, Emperor Ninko of Japan 1800, Marlon Perkins 1905, Henny Youngman 1906, Pat Nixon 1912, Jerry Lewis 1926, Daniel Patrick Moynihan 1927, Walter

73

Cunningham 1932, Chuck Woolery 1941, Robin Williams 1947, Erik Estrada 1949, Flavor Flav 1959, Todd MacFarlane 1961, Curtis Granderson 1981

1621 – Samoset, a native from the Monhegan tribe in Maine who spoke English, walked into the settlement of Plymouth Colony and made friends
1802 – The U.S. Congress established the West Point Military Academy in New York
1850 – The novel *The Scarlet Letter*, by Nathaniel Hawthorne, was published for the first time
1855 – Bates College in Lewiston, Maine was established
1917 – Russian Czar Nicholas II abdicated his throne
1926 – Massachusetts physicist Robert Goddard launched the first liquid-fuel rocket
1942 – The first V-2 rocket was tested, although it exploded during liftoff
1945 – The Battle of Iwo Jima ended
1951 – *The Caine Mutiny* by Herman Woulk was first published
1968 – The My-Lai massacre took place, when United States troops in Vietnam destroyed a village consisting mostly of women and children
1985 – Terry Anderson, an Associated Press newsman, was taken hostage in Beirut, and was not released until December 4, 1991
1988 – Lt. Col. Oliver North and Vice Admiral John Poindexter were indicted on charges of conspiracy to defraud the federal government
1993 – A blizzard on the East Coast of the United States killed 184 people
1994 – Tonya Harding pled guilty to conspiracy to hinder prosecution for covering up the attack on her skating rival Nancy Kerrigan
1995 – NASA astronaut Norman Thagard became the first American to visit the Russian space station Mir

March 17: Emperor Shinjo of Japan 1231, James IV of Scotland 1473, Roger Brooke Taney 1777, Nat King Cole 1919, Dick Curless 1932, Ken Mattingly 1936, Rudolf Nureyev 1938, John Sebastian 1944, Patrick Duffy 1949, Kurt Russell 1951, Lesley-Anne Down 1954, Gary Sinise 1955, Danny Ainge 1959, Rob Lowe 1964, Billy Corgan 1967, Bill Mueller 1971, Mia Hamm 1972, Samoa Joe 1979

45 BC – Julius Caesar defeated the forces of Titus Labienus and Pompey the Younger in his last victory at the Battle of Munda
493 – Bishop Patrick, later to be known as St. Patrick, died
1756 – St. Patrick's Day was celebrated in New York City for the first time
1776 – British forces evacuated Boston to Nova Scotia during the Revolutionary War
1845 – The rubber band was first invented

1886 – 20 African Americans were killed in the Carrollton Massacre in Mississippi
1910 – The Camp Fire Girls was founded
1930 – Al Capone was released from jail
1942 – Douglas MacArthur became the Supreme Commander of the United Nations forces in the Southwestern Pacific
1958 – The United States launched their third satellite into space, Vanguard I
1969 – Golda Meir became the first female Prime Minister of Israel
1985 – Richard Ramirez, known as the Night Stalker, murdered his first two victims
1989 – A series of solar flares caused a violent magnetic storm that brought power outages to large regions of Canada
1992 – Blacks obtained equal rights in South Africa

March 18: Mary Tudor 1496, Simon Bradstreet 1603, John C. Calhoun 1782, Grover Cleveland 1837, Rudolph Diesel 1958, Neville Chamberlin 1869, Edward Everett Horton 1886, Ernest Gallo 1909, Peter Graves 1926, George Plimpton 1927, John Updike 1932, F. W. deKlerk 1936, Charlie Pride 1938, Wilson Pickett 1941, Brad Dourif 1950, Ben Cohen 1951, Ingemar Stenmark 1956, Irene Cara 1959, Vanessa Williams 1963, Bonnie Blair 1964, Queen Latifah 1970, Brian Griese 1975, Brian Scalabrine 1978, Chad Cordero 1982

1766 – The British Parliament repealed the unpopular Stamp Act
1865 – The Congress of the Confederate States of America adjourned for the last time
1905 – Franklin Roosevelt and Eleanor Roosevelt were married (see image to right)
1913 – Greek King George I was killed by an assassin
1917 – The Germans sank the U.S. ships, City of Memphis, Vigilante and the Illinois, without any warning
1922 – Mohandas Gandhi was sentenced to six years in prison for civil disobedience in India
1925 – Tornadoes hit Missouri, Indiana and Illinois, killing 695 people
1937 – More than 300 people, mostly children, were killed in a gas explosion at a school in New London, Texas

1940 – Adolf Hitler and Benito Mussolini held a meeting at the Brenner Pass in which the Italian dictator agreed to join in Germany's war against France and Britain

1942 – The third military draft began in the United States because of World War II

1945 – 1,250 U.S. bombers attacked Berlin

1949 – The North Atlantic Treaty Organization, or NATO, was ratified

1959 – President Eisenhower signed a bill allowing Hawaii to become a state, which would go into effect on August 21

1961 – The Poppin' Fresh Pillsbury Dough Boy was introduced

1965 – Cosmonaut Alexei Leonov became the first man to perform a spacewalk, or EVA

1980 – A Vostok rocket exploded on the launch pad in Russia while fueling, killing 50 people

1985 – The longest running series on Australian television, *Neighbours*, began airing

1986 – Buckingham Palace announced the engagement of Prince Andrew to Sarah Ferguson

1989 – A 4,400-year-old mummy was discovered at the Pyramid of Cheops in Egypt

1990 – In Tampa, Florida, a little league player was killed after being hit with a pitch

1992 – Leona Helmsley was sentenced to 4 years in prison for tax evasion

2003 – The United States entered the war in Iraq

March 19: William Bradford 1589, David Livingstone 1813, Wyatt Earp 1848, William Jennings Bryan 1860, Earl Warren 1891, Adolph Eichmann 1906, Patrick McGoohan 1928, Ursula Andress 1936, Sirhan Sirhan 1944, Ruth Pointer 1946, Glenn Close 1947, Bruce Willis 1955, Ivan Calderon 1962, Andre Miller 1976

1628 – The Massachusetts colony was founded by Englishmen

1687 – French explorer La Salle was murdered by his own men while searching for the mouth of the Mississippi River, in the Gulf of Mexico

1702 – Upon the death of William III of Orange, Anne Stuart succeeded to the throne of England, Scotland and Ireland

1822 – The city of Boston, Massachusetts, was incorporated

1831 – The first bank robbery in America was reported in which the City Bank of New York City had nearly a quarter of a million dollars stolen

1903 – The U.S. Senate ratified the Cuban treaty, gaining naval bases in Guantanamo and Bahia Honda

1915 – Pluto was photographed for the first time, although it was not known at the time

1918 – The U.S. Congress approved Daylight Savings Time, as well as established time zones
1931 – The state of Nevada legalized gambling
1945 – About 800 people were killed when a Japanese kamikaze plane attacked the U.S. aircraft carrier *Franklin* off the coast of Japan
1953 – The Academy Awards aired on television for the first time
1976 – Buckingham Palace announced the separation of Princess Margaret and her husband, the Earl of Snowdon, after 16 years of marriage
1977 – The final episode of *The Mary Tyler Moore Show* aired
1979 – The U.S. House of Representatives began broadcasting its daily business on TV
1981 – During a test of the space shuttle Columbia, two workers were injured and one was killed
1987 – Televangelist Jim Bakker resigned from the PTL due to a scandal involving Jessica Hahn
2002 – Operation Anaconda, the largest U.S.-led ground offensive since the Gulf War, ended in eastern Afghanistan
2002 – Actor Ben Kingsley was knighted by Queen Elizabeth II at Buckingham Palace

March 20: Napoleon II of France 1811, Henrik Ibsen 1828, B.F. Skinner 1904, Ozzie Nelson 1906, Michael Redgrave 1908, Jack Barry 1918, Carl Reiner 1922, Fred Rogers 1928, Hal Linden 1931, Jerry Reed 1937, Brian Mulroney 1939, Paul Junger Witt 1943, Pat Riley 1945, Rick Berman 1945, John de Lancie 1948, Bobby Orr 1948, William Hurt 1950, Carl Plamer 1950, Spike Lee 1957, Holly Hunter 1958, Sting (wrestler) 1959, Tracy Chapman 1964, Liza Snyder 1968, Alexander Chaplin 1971, Bianca Lawson 1979, Dennis Wideman 1983

1413 – Henry V took the throne of England upon the death of his father Henry IV
1602 – The Dutch East India Company was established
1616 – Walter Raleigh was released from Tower of London to seek gold in Guyana
1760 – The Great Fire of Boston destroyed 349 buildings
1792 – In Paris, the Legislative Assembly approved the use of the guillotine
1815 – Napoleon Bonaparte entered Paris after his escape from Elba and began his Hundred Days rule
1852 – Harriet Beecher Stowe's *Uncle Tom's Cabin* was published

1865 – A plan by John Wilkes Booth to abduct President Abraham Lincoln was ruined when Lincoln changed his plans and did not appear at the Soldier's Home near Washington, DC
1868 – Jesse James Gang robbed a bank in Russellville, Kentucky, of $14,000
1914 – The first international figure skating championship took place in New Haven, Connecticut
1916 – Albert Einstein's theory of relativity was published
1922 – The first U.S. aircraft carrier, the USS Langley, was commissioned
1933 – The first German concentration camp was completed at Dachau
1956 – Tunisia was granted independence from France
1969 – John Lennon and Yoko Ono were married in Gibraltar
1972 – 19 mountain climbers were killed on Japan's Mount Fuji during an avalanche
1976 – Patty Hearst was convicted of armed robbery for her role in the hold up of a San Francisco Bank
1989 – It was announced that Cincinnati Reds manager Pete Rose was under investigation
1990 – The Los Angeles Lakers retired Kareem Abdul-Jabbar's #33
1992 – Former Barker's Beauty Janice Pennington was awarded $1.3 million for an accident on the set of the Price is Right
1999 – Bertrand Piccard and Brian Jones became the first men to circumnavigate the Earth in a hot air balloon
2003 – The United States and three other countries began military operations in Iraq

March 21: Johann Sebastian Bach 1685, Francis Lewis 1713, Florenz Ziegfeld 1869, John D. Rockefeller III 1906, Julio Gallo 1910, Russ Meyer 1922, James Coco 1930, Al Williamson 1931, Timothy Dalton 1944, Gary Oldman 1958, Sabrina LeBeauf 1958, Rosie O'Donnell 1962, Matthew Broderick 1962, Shawon Dunston 1963, Cynthia Geary 1966, Ananda Lewis 1973, Laura Allen 1974, Kevin Federline 1978, Cristian Guzman 1978, Aaron Hill 1982, Adrian Peterson 1985

1413 – Henry V is crowned King of England
1617 – Rebecca Rolfe, better known as Pocahontas, died in England, while visiting there with her English husband, colonist John Rolfe
1788 – Almost the entire city of New Orleans was destroyed by fire
1790 – Thomas Jefferson reported to President George Washington as the new secretary of state
1857 – An earthquake hit Tokyo killing about 107,000 people
1871 – Journalist Henry M. Stanley began his famous expedition to Africa to find explorer David Livingstone

1871 – Otto von Bismarck was appointed Chancellor of the German Empire
1928 – Charles Lindbergh was presented the Congressional Medal of Honor for his solo trans-Atlantic flight
1933 – Dechau, the first German concentration camp, was completed
1943 – In Germany, a plot by German army officers to assassinate Adolf Hitler failed
1963 – Alcatraz Island, the federal penitentiary in San Francisco Bay, was closed
1965 – More than 3,000 civil rights demonstrators led by the Rev. Martin Luther King Jr. began a march from Selma to Montgomery, Alabama
1980 – President Jimmy Carter announced that the United States would be boycotting the 1980 Olympics being held in Moscow, protesting the Russian invasion of Afghanistan
1980 – On the TV show Dallas, J.R. Ewing was shot, leading to a well publicized cliffhanger
1989 – Allegations linking Pete Rose to baseball gambling were first brought to the surface in an article in *Sports Illustrated*
1990 – Namibia became independent from South Africa
1994 – Steven Spielberg won his first Oscar, as best director for Schindler's List
2001 – Nintendo released the Game Boy Advance

March 22: Thomas de Mowbray 1366, Wilhelm I of Germany 1797, Chico Marx 1887, Louis L'Amour 1908, Karl Malden 1913, Werner Klemperer 1920, Marcel Marceau 1923, Stephen Sondheim 1930, Pat Robertson 1930, William Shatner 1931, Orrin Hatch 1934, Glen Campbell 1936, Roger Whittaker 1936, James Patterson 1947, Wolf Blitzer 1948, Andrew Lloyd Webber 1948, Bob Costas 1952, Stephanie Mills 1957, Matthew Modine 1959, Shawn Bradley 1972, Elvis Stojko 1972, Marcus Camby 1974, Reese Witherspoon 1976, Justin Masterson 1985

1457 – The Gutenberg Bible became the world's first printed book
1621 – The Pilgrims of the Plymouth Colony signed a peace treaty with Massasoit and the Wampanoigs
1622 – 347 colonists, one third of their population, were killed when Algonquian Indians attacked Jamestown, Virginia
1765 – The Stamp Act was passed, the first direct British tax on the American colonists
1790 – Thomas Jefferson became the first U.S. Secretary of State
1871 – William Holden of North Carolina became the first governor to be removed by impeachment from any state
1873 – Spain abolished slavery

1895 – A motion picture was screened for the first time
1903 – Niagara Falls ran out of water due to a drought
1934 – The first Masters Golf Championship began in Augusta, Georgia
1935 – Persia was renamed Iran
1945 – The Arab League was formed
1946 – At White Sands, New Mexico, the first American-built rocket to reach the atmosphere was launched
1954 – The first shopping mall opened in Southfield, Michigan
1963 – The Beatles' first album, *Please Please Me*, was released in the United Kingdom
1975 – Walt Disney World Shopping Village opened
1977 – Indira Gandhi resigned as the Prime Minister of India
1978 – Karl Wallenda, of the Flying Wallendas, fell to his death while walking a cable strung between two hotels in San Juan, Puerto Rico
1989 – Oliver North began two days of testimony at his Iran-Contra trial in Washington, DC
1991 – Pamela Smart, a high school teacher, was found guilty in New Hampshire of manipulating her student-lover to kill her husband
1993 – Cleveland Indians pitchers Steve Olin and Tim Crews were killed, while pitcher Bob Ojeda was seriously injured, in a boating accident in Florida
1995 – Russian Cosmonaut Valeri Polyakov returned to Earth after setting a record of 438 days in space
1997 – Tara Lipinski became the youngest world figure skating champion at the age of 14 years and 10 months

March 23: Schuyler Colfax 1823, Joan Crawford 1904, Werner Von Braun 1912, Roger Bannister 1929, Ric Ocasek 1949, Ron Jaworski 1951, Kim Stanley Robinson 1952, Chaka Khan 1953, Moses Malone 1954, Richard Grieco 1965, Jason Kidd 1973, Keri Russell 1976, Michelle Monaghan 1976, Mark Buehrle 1979, Tony Pena Jr. 1981, Princess Eugenie of Great Britain 1990

1513 – Don Juan Ponce de Leon, a former governor of Puerto Rico, discovered Florida and claimed the land for Spain
1775 – American revolutionary Patrick Henry declared, "Give me liberty, or give me death!"
1806 – Explorers Lewis and Clark, reached the Pacific coast, and began their return journey to the east
1903 – The Wright Brothers obtained a patent for their airplane
1909 – Theodore Roosevelt began an African safari sponsored by the Smithsonian Institution and National Geographic Society
1912 – The Dixie Cup was invented

1919 – Benito Mussolini founded the Fascist Party in Milan, Italy
1929 – The first telephone was installed in the White House
1942 – During World War II, the United States government began evacuating Japanese-Americans from West Coast homes to detention centers
1965 – Gemini 3 was launched, the first U.S. 2-person mission into space
1972 – Evil Knievel broke 93 bones after successfully motorcycle jumping 35 cars
1989 – A 1,000-foot diameter asteroid missed Earth by 500,000 miles
1994 – Wayne Gretsky became the all-time leading scorer in the NHL
1998 – The movie *Titanic* won 11 Oscars at the Academy Awards
2001 – The Mir Space Station broke up in the atmosphere and fell into the Pacific Ocean

March 24: Harry Houdini 1874, Fatty Arbuckle 1887, George Sisler 1893, Ub Iwerks 1901, Thomas Dewey 1902, Clyde Barrow 1909, Joseph Barbera 1911, Gorgeous George 1915, Phil Foster 1932, Norman Fell 1924, Steve McQueen 1930, Bob Mackie 1940, Tommy Hilfiger 1951, Louie Anderson 1953, Donna Pescow 1954, Robert Carradine 1954, Kelly LeBrock 1960, Star Jones 1962, Annabella Sciorra 1964, The Undertaker 1965, Lara Flynn Boyle 1970, Steve Karsay 1972, Peyton Manning 1976, Olivia Burnette 1977, Keisha Castle-Hughes 1990

1603 – Queen Elizabeth I of England died
1603 – James VI of Scotland also became James I of England
1664 – A charter to colonize Rhode Island was granted to Roger Williams in London
1765 – Great Britain passed the quartering act that required American colonists to house British troops
1837 – Canada gave black men the right to vote
1882 – American author Henry Wadsworth Longfellow died at the age of 75
1898 – The first automobile was sold
1900 – In New Jersey, the Carnegie Steel Corporation was formed
1900 – New York City Mayor Van Wyck broke ground for the city's first subway
1905 – Author Jules Verne died at the age of 77 of complications from diabetes
1923 – Greece became a republic
1934 – President Franklin Roosevelt signed a bill granting future independence to the Philippines
1944 – Seventy-six prisoners began breaking out of German Stalag Luft III in Poland, an event later dramatized in the movie *The Great Escape*

1972 – Great Britain imposed direct rule over Northern Ireland
1981 – *Nightline* with Ted Koppel premiered
1989 – The Exxon Valdez spilled 11 million gallons of oil in Alaska's Prince William Sound after it ran aground
1998 – In Jonesboro, Arizona, two young boys, ages 11 and 13, opened fire at students from woods near a school, killing four students and a teacher

March 25: Henry II of England 1133, Jack Ruby 1911, Howard Cosell 1920, Jim Lovell 1928, Gene Shalit 1932, Gloria Steinem 1934, Hoyt Axton 1938, Anita Bryant 1940, Aretha Franklin 1942, Paul Michael Glaser 1943, Bonnie Bedelia 1948, Nick Lowe 1949, Elton John 1947, Brenda Strong 1960, Haywood Nelson 1960, John Stockwell 1961, Fred Goss 1961, Marcia Cross 1962, Sarah Jessica Parker 1965, Tom Glavine 1966, Jeff Healey 1966, Debi Thomas 1967, Sheryl Swoopes 1971, Juvenile 1975, Lee Pace 1979, Danica Patrick 1982, Katherine McPhee 1984, Jason Castro 1987

461 – The city of Venice was founded, according to tradition
1306 – Robert the Bruce was crowned king of Scotland
1616 – William Shakespeare signed his will, leaving his property to his elder daughter's male heirs, and to his wife he left his second-best bed
1634 – Lord Baltimore founded the colony of Maryland
1655 – Saturn's largest moon, Titan, was discovered by Dutch astronomer Christiaan Huygens
1668 – The first horse race in America took place
1865 – During the American Civil War, the Confederates captured Fort Stedman
1901 – The first Mercedes automobile was introduced
1947 – A coalmine explosion in Centralia, Illinois, killed 111 people
1947 – John D. Rockefeller III presented check for $8.5 million to the United Nations for the purchase of land for the site of the U.N. center
1954 – RCA manufactured its first color TV set and began mass production
1970 – The Concorde made its first supersonic flight
1971 – The Boston Patriots football team became the New England Patriots
1975 – King Faisal of Saudi Arabia was assassinated by his nephew
1979 – The Space Shuttle *Columbia* arrived in Florida to make ready for the first space shuttle launch
1982 – Wayne Gretzky became the first player in NHL history to score 200 points in a season

1991 – Iraqi President Saddam Hussein launched a major counter-offensive to recapture key towns from the Kurds in northern Iraq
1996 – The United States issued a newly redesigned $100 bill for circulation

March 26: King Fuad I of Egypt 1868, Robert Frost 1874, Duncan Hines 1880, Tennessee Williams 1911, William Westmoreland 1914, Sterling Hayden 1916, Sandra Day O'Connor 1930, Leonard Nimoy 1931, Alan Arkin 1934, James Caan 1939, Nancy Pelosi 1940, Bob Woodard 1943, Diana Ross 1944, Steven Tyler 1948, Vicki Lawrence 1949, Martin Short 1950, Ronnie McDowell 1950, Teddy Pendergrass 1950, Ernest Thomas 1950, Leeza Gibbons 1957, Marcus Allen 1960, Jennifer Grey 1960, John Stockton 1962, Kenny Chesney 1968, T.R. Knight 1973, Larry Pafe 1973, Amy Smart 1976, Keira Knightley 1985

1199 – Richard the Lionheart was fatally wounded by a crossbow bolt during a siege in France, although he would not die for another eleven days
1812 – The city of Caracas, Venezuela was destroyed by an earthquake
1827 – German composer Ludwig van Beethoven died in Vienna at the age of 56
1885 – Eastman Kodak produced the first motion picture film
1898 – In South Africa, the world's first game reserve, the Sabi Game Reserve, was designated
1938 – Herman Goering warned all Jews to leave Austria
1942 – The first female prisoners arrived in Auschwitz, Poland
1945 – The battle of Iwo Jima ended
1953 – Jonas Salk announced his vaccine for Polio
1958 – The U.S. Army launched America's third successful satellite, Explorer III
1973 – Linus and Lucy's baby brother Rerun made his first appearance in the *Peanuts* comic strip
1979 – At the White House, with aid from President Jimmy Carter, Egyptian President Anwar Sadat and Israeli Prime Minister Menachem Begin signed the Camp David Accords, ending 31 years of hostility between Egypt and Israel
1982 – Ground breaking ceremonies were held for the Vietnam Veterans Memorial in Washington, DC
1989 – The NBC-TV show *Quantum Leap* debuted
1989 – Boris Yeltsin was elected President in the first free elections ever held in the Soviet Union
1992 – In Indianapolis, heavyweight boxing champion Mike Tyson was found guilty of rape

1999 – A jury in Minnesota found Dr. Jack Kevorkian guilty of second-degree murder, for assisted in the suicide of a terminally ill patient
2000 – The Seattle Kingdome was imploded to make room for a new football arena

March 27: Robert II of France 972, Louis XVII of France 1785, Sir Henry Royce 1863, Miller Huggins 1879, Gloria Swanson 1899, Carl Barks 1901, Eisaku Sato 1901, James Callaghan 1912, Cyrus Vance 1917, David Janssen 1931, Julian Glover 1935, Cale Yarborough 1939, Michael York 1942, Tom Sullivan 1947, Brian Jones 1947, Lynn McGlothen 1950, Tom Andrews 1953, Kevin J. Anderson 1962, Randall Cunningham 1963, Quentin Tarantino 1963, Mariah Carey 1970, Elizabeth Mitchell 1970, Fergie 1975, Michael Cuddyer 1979, Brenda Song 1988, Taylor Atelian 1995

1350 – While besieging Gibraltar, Alfonso XI of Castile died of the Black Death
1513 – Spanish explorer Juan Ponce de Leon first sighted Florida, mistaking it for another island
1794 – The United States Congress and President George Washington authorized the creation of the U.S. Navy
1814 – During the War of 1812, General Andrew Jackson's forces defeated the Creek Indians in Alabama at the Battle of Horseshoe Bend
1834 – President Andrew Jackson is censured by the United States Senate for his actions regarding the U.S. National Bank
1854 – The United Kingdom declared war on Russia
1871 – The first international rugby match, England vs. Scotland, was played
1958 – Nikita Khrushchev became Premier of the Soviet Union
1964 – An earthquake in Alaska registering 9.2 on the Richter scale, the most powerful ever to strike the United States, killed 125 people
1968 – Yuri Gagarin, the first man in space, died in a plane crash
1976 – The Washington, DC subway system opened
1977 – Two jumbo jets collided on a foggy runway in Tenerife, Canary Islands, and killing 583 people
2002 – Hollywood legends Milton Berle and Dudley Moore both died on the same day, Berle at age 93 and Moore at age 66
2005 – *Grey's Anatomy* first aired on ABC-TV

March 28: Frederick III of Denmark 1609, Wade Hampton III 1818, Frederick Pabst 1836, William Harvey Carney 1842, Maxim Gorky 1868, August Anheuser Busch 1899, Dame Flora Robson 1902, Marlin Perkins 1905, Jimmie Dodd 1910, Queen Ingrid of Denmark 1910, Edmund Muskie

1914, Freddie Bartholomew 1924, Jerry Sloan 1942, Conchatta Ferrell 1943, Ken Howard 1944, Rick Berry 1944, Dianne Wiest 1948, Reba McEntire 1955, Chris Myers 1959, Byron Scott 1961, Vince Vaughn 1970, Shannon Mitchell 1972, Eddie "Umaga" Fatu 1973, Luke Walton 1980, Julia Stiles 1981

193 – Roman Emperor Pertinax was assassinated
845 – Paris was ransacked by the Vikings, who were paid a huge ransom to leave
1854 – France declared war on Russia
1885 – The Salvation Army was organized
1910 – Henri Fabri became the first person to fly a seaplane
1921 – President Warren G. Harding named former President William Howard Taft as Chief Justice of the United States Supreme Court
1933 – In Germany, the Nazis ordered a ban on all Jews in businesses, professions and schools
1945 – Germany launched the last of the V-2 rockets against England
1967 – Raymond Burr starred in a TV movie titled *Ironside*, which later became a television series
1969 – Former United States president Dwight D. Eisenhower died at the age of 78
1974 – A streaker ran onto the set of the Tonight Show
1979 – A major accident occurred at Pennsylvania's Three Mile Island nuclear power plant, resulting in a partial meltdown
1990 – President George H. W. Bush posthumously awarded Olympics star Jesse Owens the Congressional Gold Medal
1997 – Disney's Wide World of Sports Complex opened at Disney World
2000 – In Murray County, Georgia, a freight train collided with a school bus, killing three children

March 29: John Tyler 1790, Edward Smith-Stanley 1799, Cy Young 1867, Lou Hoover 1874, Ernst Junger 1895, John McEwen 1900, Man O' War 1917, Sam Walton 1918, Pearl Bailey 1918, John McLaughlin 1927, Billy Carter 1937, Eric Idle 1943, John Major 1943, Denny McLain 1944, Walt Frazier 1945, Earl Campbell 1955, Marina Sirtis 1955, Kurt Thomas 1956, Christopher Lambert 1957, M.C. Hammer 1963, Elle MacPherson 1964, Brian Jordan 1967, Lucy Lawless 1968, Jennifer Capriati 1976

1461 – Edward IV secured his claim to the English thrown by defeating Henry VI's Lancastrians at the Battle of Towdon
1638 – Dutch colonists established the first settlement in Delaware, called New Sweden

1792 – King Gustav III of Sweden died as the result of being shot in the back thirteen days before
1847 – During the Mexican-American War, the U.S. and General Winfield Scott seized Vera Cruz
1848 – Niagara Falls stopped flowing for one day due to an ice jam
1865 – During the American Civil War, the Battle of Appomattox Court House began
1882 – The Knights of Columbus was established
1901 – The first federal elections were held in Australia
1951 – Julius and Ethel Rosenberg were convicted of conspiracy to commit espionage against the United States
1962 – Jack Paar made his final appearance on the Tonight Show
1966 – Leonid Brezhnev became the First Secretary of the Soviet Communist Party
1973 – The last American soldiers left Vietnam
1974 – Mariner 10 became the first spacecraft to fly past the planet Mercury
1979 – The Committee on Assassinations Report issued by the United States House of Representatives stated that the assassination of President John F. Kennedy was the result of a conspiracy
1984 – The Baltimore Colts football team moved to Indianapolis
1987 – Hulk Hogan pinned Andre the Giant in Wrestlemania III
1993 – Clint Eastwood won his first Oscar
2004 – Bulgaria, Estonia, Latvia, Lithuania, Romania, Slovakia and Slovenia became members of NATO
2004 – Ireland became the first country to ban smoking in all work places, including bars and restaurants

March 30: Francisco Goya 1746, Vincent Van Gogh 1853, Marc Davis 1913, Richard Helms 1913, Richard Dysart 1929, John Astin 1930, Peter Marshall 1930, Warren Beatty 1937, Jerry Lucas 1940, Eric Clapton 1945, Robbie Coltrane 1950, Grady Little 1950, Paul Reiser 1957, Tracy Chapman 1964, Celine Dion 1968, Secretariat 1970, Norah Jones 1979, Zach Gowen 1983

1533 – Henry VIII divorced his first wife, Catherine of Aragon
1822 – Florida became a United States territory
1842 – Anesthesia was used in an operation for the first time
1856 – The Treaty of Paris was signed, ending the Crimean War
1858 – Hyman L. Lipman of Philadelphia patented the pencil with attached eraser
1867 – The United States purchased Alaska from Russia for $7.2 million dollars, or two cents per acre

1870 – The 15th Amendment to the Constitution, guaranteeing the right to vote regardless of race, was passed by the U.S. Congress
1870 – Texas was readmitted to the Union
1909 – The Queensboro Bridge in New York, the first double decker bridge, opened, linking Manhattan and Queens
1932 – Amelia Earhart became the first woman to make a solo flight across the Atlantic Ocean
1954 – The first subway in Canada opened in Toronto
1964 – *Jeopardy* debuted on NBC-TV
1970 – *Another World* debuted on NBC-TV
1972 – The British government assumed direct rule over Northern Ireland
1981 – President Ronald Reagan was shot and wounded in Washington, DC, by John Hinckley Jr.
1993 – In the *Peanuts* comic strip, Charlie Brown hit his first home run

March 31: Pope Pius IV 1499, Henry II of France 1519, Rene Descartes 1596, Pope Benedict XIV 1675, Frederick V of Denmark 1723, Joseph Haydn 1732, Mary Chestnut 1823, Cesar Chavez 1927, William Daniels 1927, Gordie Howe 1928, Liz Claiborne 1929, John Jakes 1932, Shirley Jones 1934, Richard Chamberlain 1934, Herb Alpert 1935, Patrick Leahy 1940, Barney Frank 1940, Christopher Walken 1943, Angus King 1944, Gabe Kaplan 1945, Al Gore 1948, Rhea Perlman 1948, Ed Marinaro 1950, Samantha Brown 1969, Ewen McGregor 1971, Josh Kinney 1979, Chien-Ming Wang 1980, Michael Ryder 1980

1774 – England ordered the port of Boston, Massachusetts closed
1831 – The Canadian cities of Montreal and Quebec were incorporated
1889 – In Paris, the Eiffel Tower officially opened
1917 – The United States purchased and took possession of the Virgin Islands from Denmark for $25 million
1918 – For the first time in the United States, Daylight Savings Time went into effect
1933 – The U.S. Congress authorized the Civilian Conservation Corps to relieve rampant unemployment
1939 – Britain and France agreed to support Poland if Germany threatened invasion
1940 – La Guardia Airport in New York officially opened to the public
1949 – Newfoundland became the 10th province of Canada
1968 – President Lyndon Johnson announced he will not seek re-election
1993 – Brandon Lee was killed accidentally while filming a movie
1999 – Fabio was hit in the face by a bird during a promotional ride of a new roller coaster at the Busch Gardens theme park in Williamsburg, Virginia

April 1: William Harvey 1578, Otto Von Bismarck 1815, Wallace Beery 1881, Lon Chaney 1883, Abraham Maslow 1908, Grace Lee Whitney 1930, Gordon Jump 1932, Debbie Reynolds 1932, Ali MacGraw 1938, Phil Niekro 1939, Rusty Staub 1944, Jimmy Cliff 1948, Annette O'Toole 1953, Magdalena Maleeva 1975

1621 – The Plymouth, Massachusetts, colonists created the first treaty with Native Americans
1865 – John Milton, the Governor of Florida, committed suicide at the age of 57
1873 – The British White Star steamship *Atlantic* sank off Nova Scotia killing 547
1876 – The first official National League baseball game took place as Boston defeated Philadelphia 6-5
1891 – The Wrigley Company was founded in Chicago
1924 – Adolf Hitler was sentenced to five years in prison for high treason as a result of the Beer Hall Putsch
1929 – Louie Marx introduced the Yo-Yo
1931 – Jackie Mitchell became the first female in professional baseball when she signed with the Chattanooga baseball club
1933 – Nazi Germany began the persecution of Jews by boycotting Jewish businesses

1934 – Bonnie and Clyde killed 2 police officers near Grapevine, Texas
1938 – The Baseball Hall of Fame opened in Cooperstown, New York
1946 – Weight Watchers was formed
1946 – A tidal wave (or tsunami) struck the Hawaiian Islands killing more than 170 people
1952 – The Big Bang Theory was first proposed
1960 – The United States launched TIROS-1, the first weather satellite
1963 – The soap operas *General Hospital* and *The Doctors* premiered on television
1976 – Apple Computer began operations
1980 – A failed assassination attempt against Iraqi vice-premier Tariq Aziz occurred
1982 – The United States transferred the Canal Zone to Panama
1984 – Singer Marvin Gaye was murdered by his father
1994 – Blizzard Beach opened at Walt Disney World
1999 – The Canadian territory of Nunavut was created
2001 – Former Yugoslav President Slobodan Milosevic was arrested on corruption charges after a 26-hour standoff with the police at his Belgrade villa

April 2: Charlemagne 742, Giacomo Casanova 1725, Hans Christian Andersen 1805, Emile Zola 1840, Walter Chrysler 1875, Luke Appling 1907, Buddy Ebsen 1908, Alec Guinness 1914, Dabbs Greer 1917, Jack Webb 1920, Dick Radatz 1937, Marvin Gaye 1939, Don Sutton 1945, Reggie Smith 1945, Emmylou Harris 1947, Pamela Reed 1949, Debralee Scott 1953, Ron Palillo 1954, Dana Carvey 1955, Rodney King 1965, Bill Romanowski 1966, Adam Rodriguez 1975, Curtis Leskanic 1968

1513 – Spanish explorer Juan Ponce de Leon set foot in Florida, the first European to do so
1865 – Confederate President Jefferson Davis and most of his Cabinet fled the Confederate capital of Richmond, Virginia
1877 – The first Easter Egg Roll was held on the grounds of the White House in Washington, DC
1917 – The United States declared war on Germany
1956 – *The Edge of Night* and *As the World Turns* debuted on CBS-TV
1958 – The National Advisory Council on Aeronautics was renamed NASA, the National Aeronautics and Space Administration
1975 – CN Tower in Toronto was completed, the world's tallest free-standing structure at 1815 feet tall
1978 – The first episode of *Dallas* aired on CBS-TV
1982 – Argentina invaded the British-owned Falkland Islands

1984 – John Thompson became the first black coach to lead his team to the NCAA college basketball championship

1987 – The speed limit on U.S. interstate highways was increased to 65 miles per hour in limited areas

1992 – Mob boss John Gotti was convicted in New York of murder and racketeering

2005 – Pope John Paul II died at the age of 84

2006 – Over sixty tornadoes broke out in the United States, with Tennessee hit the hardest, with twenty-nine people dead in that state

April 3: Philip III of France 1245, Henry IV of England 1367, Washington Irving 1783, William "Boss" Tweed 1823, Leslie Howard 1893, Doris Day 1924, Marlon Brando 1924, Gus Grissom 1926, Kevin Hagen 1928, Jane Goodall 1934, Marsha Mason 1942, Wayne Newton 1942, Tony Orlando 1944, Lyle Alzado 1949, Ray Combs 1946, Alec Baldwin 1958, David Hyde Pierce 1959, Eddie Murphy 1961, Sabastion Bach 1968, Lance Storm 1969, Picabo Street 1971, Jennie Garth 1972, Jamie Bamber 1973, Amanda Bynes 1986

1721 – Robert Walpole became Great Britain's first Prime Minister

1776 – Harvard College conferred the first honorary Doctor of Laws degree to George Washington

1860 – The Pony Express mail service began

1865 – Union forces occupied the Confederate capital of Richmond, Virginia

1882 – The American outlaw Jesse James was shot in the back and killed by Robert Ford for a $5,000 reward

1900 – The Vanderbilts took over 3 major railroads, the Reading, Lehigh Valley and Erie lines

1922 – Joseph Stalin became the first General Secretary of the Communist Party of the Soviet Union

1936 – Richard Bruno Hauptmann was executed for the kidnapping and death of the son of Charles and Anne Lindbergh

1953 – *TV Guide* was published for the first time

1968 – Martin Luther King Jr. delivered his "mountaintop" speech just 24 hours before he was assassinated

1972 – Charlie Chaplin returned to the United States after a twenty-year absence

1973 – The first cell phone call was made

1974 – The largest tornado outbreak ever occurred, covering 13 U.S. states and 1 Canadian province, resulting in 315 deaths

1982 – John Chancellor stepped down as anchor of the *The NBC Nightly News*

1993 – The Norman Rockwell Museum opened in Stockbridge, Massachusetts
1996 – An Air Force jetliner carrying U.S. Commerce Secretary Ron Brown crashed in Croatia, killing all 35 people aboard
1996 – Unibomber Theodore Kaczynski was arrested in Montana
2000 – Microsoft was found in court to have violated anti-trust laws

April 4: Dorothea Dix 1802, Maria II of Portugal 1819, Tris Speaker 1888, John Cameron Swayze 1906, Gil Hodges 1924, Maya Angelou 1928, Anthony Perkins 1932, Dick Lugar 1932, Craig T. Nelson 1944, Caroline McWilliams 1945, Christine Lahti 1950, Steve Gatlin 1951, David E. Kelley 1956, Phil Morris 1959, Anthony Clark 1964, Robert Downey, Jr. 1965, Nancy McKeon 1966, David Blaine 1973, Scott Rolen 1975, Heath Ledger 1979, Jamie Lynn Spears 1991

1581 – Francis Drake completed the circumnavigation of the world
1812 – Louisiana became the 18th state
1818 – The United States flag was declared to have 13 red and white stripes and 20 stars, and that a new star would be added for the each new state
1841 – President William Henry Harrison, at the age of 68, became the first president to die in office (see right)

1850 – The city of Los Angeles was incorporated
1865 – President Abraham Lincoln visited Confederate capital Richmond, Virginia, the day after it was captured
1905 – In Kangra, India, an earthquake killed 370,000 people
1917 – The United States Senate voted 90-6 to enter World War I on the Allied side
1949 – Twelve nations signed a treaty to create the North Atlantic Treaty Organization
1968 – Martin Luther King Jr. was assassinated at the age of 39 in Memphis, Tennessee
1973 – The World Trade Center in New York was officially dedicated
1974 – Hank Aaron tied Babe Ruth's major league baseball homerun record with 714
1975 – Microsoft was founded by Bill Gates and Paul Allen
1979 – Zulfikar Ali Bhutto, the president of Pakistan, was executed

1983 – The Space Shuttle *Challenger* made its maiden flight into space
1994 – Netscape Communications was founded
1999 – The Colorado Rockies and the San Diego Padres played the first Major League Baseball season opener to be held in Mexico

April 5: Thomas Hobbes 1588, Booker T. Washington 1856, Spencer Tracy 1900, Bette Davis 1908, Gregory Peck 1916, Christopher Hewett 1922, Nigel Hawthorne 1929, Frank Gorshin 1934, Colin Powell 1937, Michael Moriarty 1941, Max Gail 1943, Judith Resnik 1949, Paula Cole 1968, Stephen Jackson 1978

456 – St. Patrick returned to Ireland as a missionary bishop
1242 – Russian troops repelled an invasion attempt by the Teutonic Knights

1614 – American Indian Pocahontas married English colonist John Rolfe in Virginia (see above, Pocahontas being baptized, believe to have taken place just prior to her marriage)
1621 – The *Mayflower* set sail from Plymouth on its return trip to England
1792 – George Washington cast the first presidential veto
1843 – Queen Victoria declared Hong Kong to be a British crown colony
1869 – Daniel Bakeman, the last surviving solider of the American Revolutionary War, died at the age of 109
1951 – Americans Julius and Ethel Rosenberg were sentenced to death for committing espionage for the Soviet Union
1955 – Winston Churchill resigned as prime minister of Great Britain due to ill health
1984 – Kareem Abdul-Jabbar of the Los Angeles Lakers became the all-time NBA regular season scoring leader when he broke Wilt Chamberlain's record of 31,419 career points
1986 – A disco in Berlin was bombed by Libyans

1987 – The first two FOX-TV shows were launched, *Married With Children* and *The Tracey Ullman Show*
2005 – ABC News anchor Peter Jennings, in his final broadcast, informed his viewers that he had lung cancer

April 6: Raphael 1483, Walter Huston 1884, Mickey Cochrane 1903, Gil Kane 1926, James D. Watson 1928, Andre Privon 1929, Ivan Dixon 1931, Merle Haggard 1937, Billy Dee Williams 1937, Zamfir 1941, Barry Levinson 1941, Michelle Phillips 1944, John Ratzenberger 1947, Bert Blyleven 1951, Marilu Henner 1952, Bret Boone 1969, Lou Merloni 1971, Jason Hervey 1972, Candace Cameron 1976, Tim Hasselbeck 1978

648 BC – The first solar eclipse to be documented occurred
1199 – English King Richard I was killed by an arrow at the siege of the castle of Chaluz in France
1789 – The first United States Congress began regular sessions at the Federal Hall in New York City
1830 – The Church of Jesus Christ of Latter-day Saints was organized by Joseph Smith
1832 – The Black Hawk War began
1841 – John Tyler became the first vice-president to be sworn in as president upon the death of a president
1862 – The American Civil War Battle of Shiloh began
1896 – The first modern Olympic Games began in Athens, Greece
1917 – The United States Congress approved a declaration of war on Germany
1941 – German forces invaded Greece and Yugoslavia
2003 – NBC News journalist David Bloom died at the age of 39 while on assignment in Iraq as a result of a pulmonary embolism

April 7: William R. King 1786, W. K. Kellogg 1860, Jersey Joe Wolcott 1872, Walter Winchell 1897, Billie Holiday 1915, Bobby Doerr 1918, James Garner 1928, Wayne Rogers 1933, Francis Ford Coppola 1939, John Oats 1949, Jackie Chan 1954, Tony Dorsett 1954, James "Buster" Douglas 1960, Russell Crowe 1964, Hazel Mae 1970

1652 – The Dutch began a settlement at Cape Town, South Africa
1862 – General Ulysses S. Grant led the Union army in a victory at the Battle of Shiloh
1864 – The first camel race in America was held in Sacramento, California
1933 – Prohibition ended in the United States
1940 – Booker T. Washington became the first black person to appear on a U.S. postage stamp

1945 – The Japanese battleship *Yamato*, the world's largest battleship, was sunk during the battle for Okinawa

1963 – Jack Nicklaus became the youngest person to win the Masters Golf Tournament at the age of 23

1970 – John Wayne won his only Oscar, for his role as Rooster Cogburn in *True Grit*

1983 – Specialists Story Musgrave and Don Peterson made the first Space Shuttle spacewalk

April 8: Buddha 563 B.C., Philip IV of Spain and Portugal 1605, Mary Pickford 1893, Betty Ford 1918, Jim "Catfish" Hunter 1946, John Schneider 1954, Gary Carter 1954, Julian Lennon 1963, Robin Wright Penn 1966, Patricia Arquette 1968, Tawny Cypress 1976, Katee Sackhoff 1980, Grace Park 1980, Kason Gabbard 1982, Taran Noah Smith 1984

217 – Roman Emperor Caracalla was assassinated by Marcus Opellius Macrinus, who succeeded him

1513 – Explorer Juan Ponce de Leon claimed Florida for Spain

1789 – The U.S. House of Representatives held its first meeting

1893 – The first college basketball game was played in Beaver Falls, Pennsylvania

1900 – The Colorado River in Texas flooded, engulfing 80 people

1904 – Longacre Square in New York City was renamed Times Square, after *The New York Times* newspaper

1913 – The Seventeenth Amendment to the Constitution became law, requiring direct election of senators

1939 – Italy invaded Albania

1974 – Hank Aaron hit his 715th home run, breaking Babe Ruth's record

1975 – Frank Robinson of the Cleveland Indians became first black manager of a Major League Baseball team

1979 – The last episode *of All in the Fa*mily aired

1986 – Actor Clint Eastwood was elected mayor of Carmel, California

April 9: Leopold II of Belgium 1835, Ward Bond 1903, Hugh Hefner 1926, Carl Perkins 1932, Jim Fowler 1932, Cheeta 1932, Marty Kroft 1937, Michael Learned 1939, Peter Gammons 1945, Dennis Quaid 1954, Paulina Porizkova 1964, Margaret Peterson Haddix 1964, Jeff Zucker 1965, Cynthia Nixon 1969, Keshia Knight Pulliam 1979, Jesse McCartney 1985, Kristen Stewart 1990, Elle Fanning 1998

1865 – At Appomattox Court House, Virginia, General Robert E. Lee surrendered his Confederate Army to Union General Ulysses S. Grant

1900 – British forces routed the Boers at Kroonstadt, South Africa

1912 – The first exhibition baseball game was held at Fenway Park in Boston, between the Red Sox and Harvard College
1913 – The Brooklyn Dodgers' Ebbets Field opened
1939 – Marian Anderson sang at the Lincoln Memorial after having been having been refused the right to sing at the DAR's Constitution Hall
1940 – Germany invaded Norway and Denmark
1945 – National Football League officials decreed that it was mandatory for football players to wear socks in all league games
1947 – 169 people died in a series of tornadoes in Texas, Oklahoma and Kansas
1953 – Warner Brothers premiered the first 3D movie, *The House of Wax*
1959 – NASA announced the selection of America's first seven astronauts, the Mercury Seven
1963 – Winston Churchill became an honorary U.S. citizen
1965 – The first baseball game in the Houston Astrodome was held
1967 – The first Boeing 737 flew
1968 – Martin Luther King, Jr. was buried
1991 – Georgia declared its independence from the Soviet Union
2003 – Baghdad, Iraq fell to American forces
2005 – Great Britain's Prince Charles married Camilla Parker Bowles

April 10: James V of Scotland 1512, Commodore Matthew Perry 1794, William Booth 1829, Joseph Pulitzer 1847, Harry Morgan 1915, Sheb Wooley 1921, Chuck Connors 1921, Junior Samples 1926, Max Von Sydow 1929, Omar Sharif 1932, John Madden 1936, Don Merideth 1938, Ken Griffey Sr. 1950, Steven Seagal 1951, Peter MacNichol 1954, Brian Setzer 1959, Cathy Turner 1962, Orlando Jones 1968, Kasey Kahne 1980, Mandy Moore 1984, Haley Joel Osment 1988

1790 – The United States patent system was established
1814 – Napoleon was defeated at the Battle of Toulouse by the British and the Spanish
1825 – The first hotel opened in Hawaii
1865 – The last photograph of Abraham Lincoln was taken before he died
1866 – The American Society for the Prevention of Cruelty to Animals, ASPCA, was created
1902 – South African Boers accepted British terms of surrender
1912 – The *Titanic* set sail from Southampton, England on its first and only voyage
1916 – The PGA held its first championship tournament
1925 – F. Scott Fitzgerald published *The Great Gatsby*
1938 – Germany annexed Austria
1960 – The United States Senate passed the "Civil Rights Bill"

1963 – 129 people died when the nuclear-powered submarine *USS Thresher* failed to surface off Cape Cod
1970 – Paul McCartney announced that the Beatles had broken up
1972 – An earthquake in Iran killed 5,000 people
1992 – Comedian Sam Kinison was killed when a pickup truck slammed into his car on a desert road between Los Angeles and Las Vegas
2001 – Jane Swift took office as the first female governor of Massachusetts

April 11: John I of Portugal 1357, Cap Anson 1852, Charles Evans Hughes 1862, Ethel Kennedy 1928, Joel Grey 1932, Meshach Taylor 1947, Jason Varitek 1972, Jennifer Esposito 1973, Trot Nixon 1974, Tricia Helfer 1974, Mark Teixeira 1980, Joss Stone 1987

1689 – William III and Mary II were crowned as joint sovereigns of Britain
1814 – Napoleon was forced to abdicate his throne
1865 – Abraham Lincoln made his last public speech
1898 – President William McKinley asked Congress for a declaration of war with Spain, starting the Spanish-American War
1899 – The treaty ending the Spanish-American War was declared in effect
1905 – Albert Einstein revealed his Theory of Relativity
1915 – The movie *The Tramp*, starring Charlie Chaplin, was released
1945 – During World War II, American soldiers liberated the Nazi concentration camp of Buchenwald in Germany
1947 – Jackie Robinson became the first black player in Major League Baseball history
1951 – President Harry Truman fired General Douglas MacArthur as head of United Nations forces in Korea
1970 – *Apollo 13* blasted off on a mission to the moon that was disrupted when an explosion crippled the spacecraft
1979 – Idi Amin was deposed as president of Uganda as rebels and exiles backed by Tanzanian forces seized control
1981 – President Ronald Reagan returned to the White House from the hospital after recovering from an assassination attempt

April 12: Christian IV of Denmark 1577, Lyman Hall 1724, Henry Clay 1777, Beverly Cleary 1916, Ann Miller 1923, Tiny Tim 1930, Herbie Hancock 1940, Ed O'Neill 1946, Tom Clancy 1947, Dan Lauria 1947, David Letterman 1947, David Cassidy 1950, Tom Werner 1950, Andy Garcia 1956, Vince Gill 1957, Mike MacFarlane 1964, Shannen Doherty 1971, Paul Lo Duca 1972, Roman Hamrlik 1974, Brad Miller 1976, Claire Danes 1979

1606 – The Union Jack was adopted as the official flag of Great Britain
1861 – Fort Sumter was fired upon by the Confederacy, starting America's Civil War
1877 – A catcher's mask was used in a baseball game for the first time by James Alexander Tyng
1931 – The strongest winds ever recorded was measured at 231 mph at the top of Mount Washington
1945 – President Franklin D. Roosevelt died in Warm Springs, Georgia, of a cerebral hemorrhage at the age of 63
1945 – Harry Truman was sworn in as President, hours after FDR's death
1954 – Bill Haley and the Comets recorded the song *Rock Around the Clock*
1961 – Russian Yuri Gagarin became first man in space and the first to orbit the Earth
1966 – Emmett Ashford became the first African-American Major League Baseball umpire
1981 – The space shuttle Columbia blasted off from Cape Canaveral, Florida, on its first test flight
1985 – U.S. Senator Jake Garn of Utah became the first senator to fly in space, as the space shuttle Discovery lifted off from Cape Canaveral
1992 – Disneyland Paris opened in Marne-La-Vallee, France
1999 – President Bill Clinton was found in contempt of court for intentionally lying in court in the Paul Jones sexual harassment case against him

April 13: Guy Fawkes 1570, Thomas Jefferson 1743, F.W. Woolworth 1852, Butch Cassidy 1866, Howard Keel 1919, Don Adams 1926, Ben Nighthorse Campbell 1933, Lyle Waggoner 1935, Paul Sorvino 1939, Bill Conti 1943, Tony Dow 1945, Ron Perlman 1950, Terry Lester 1950, Peabo Bryson 1951, Peter Davison 1951, Max Weinberg 1951, Gary Kasparov 1963, Davis Love III 1964, Rick Schroeder 1970, Sergei Gonchar 1974, Baron Davis 1979, Quentin Richardson 1980

1111 – Henry V was crowned Holy Roman Emperor
1250 – The Seventh Crusade was defeated in Egypt and France's Louis IX was captured
1742 – Handel's *Messiah* made its world debut in Dublin, Ireland
1782 – Washington, North Carolina, was incorporated as the first town to be named for George Washington
1796 – The first elephant arrived in the United States from India
1861 – Union-held Fort Sumter surrendered to the Confederacy
1913 – James C. Penny opened his first store, in Kemmerer, Wyoming

1943 – The Jefferson Memorial was dedicated in Washington, DC, on the 200th anniversary of Thomas Jefferson's birth
1954 – Hank Aaron debuted with the Milwaukee Braves
1963 – Pete Rose got his first Major League hit for the Cincinnati Reds
1970 – An oxygen tank exploded on *Apollo 13*, preventing a planned moon landing
1972 – The first strike in the history of Major League Baseball ended after 13 days
1983 – Harold Washington was elected Chicago's first African-American mayor
1997 – Tiger Woods became the youngest person to win the Masters Golf Tournament at the age of 21

April 14: Philip III of Spain 1578, Christiaan Huygens 1629, Anne Sullivan 1866, John Gielgud 1904, Rod Steiger 1925, Loretta Lynn 1935, Kenneth Mars 1936, Pete Rose 1941, Brad Garrett 1960, Greg Maddux 1966, Anthony Michael Hall 1968, Brad Ausmus 1969, Gregg Zaun 1971, Da Brat 1974, Jason Weimer 1976, Kyle Farnsworth 1976, Sarah Michelle Geller Prinze 1977, Abigail Breslin 1996

69 – Vitellius, commander of the Rhine armies, overthrew Emperor Otho in the Battle of Bedriacum
1471 – In England, Edward IV and the Yorkists defeated the Lancastrians at the Battle of Barnet, allowing Edward IV to resume the throne
1775 – The first abolitionist society in the United States was organized in Philadelphia, with Ben Franklin as president
1828 – The first edition of Noah Webster's dictionary was published under the name *American Dictionary of the English Language*
1860 – The first Pony Express rider arrived in San Francisco with mail
1865 – President Abraham Lincoln was fatally shot in the head by John Wilkes Booth at Ford's Theater in Washington, DC, although he would not die until the following morning
1900 – The World Exposition opened in Paris
1910 – President William Howard Taft threw out the first pitch at a Major League Baseball game, starting a tradition
1912 – The *Titanic* struck an iceberg and began to sink
1927 – The first Volvo car premiered in Sweden
1939 – John Steinbeck's novel *The Grapes of Wrath* was first published
1981 – America's first space shuttle, Columbia, returned to Earth after a 3-day test flight

April 15: Leonardo Da Vinci 1452, Christian V of Denmark 1646, Catherine I of Russia 1684, Henry James 1843, Kim Il-sung 1912, Hans

Conreid 1917, Michael Ansara 1922, Roy Clark 1933, Elizabeth Montgomery 1933, Kenneth Lay 1942, Dodi Al-Fayed 1955, Evelyn Ashford 1957, Emma Thompson 1959, Thomas F. Wilson 1959, Samantha Fox 1966, Stacey Williams 1968, Jeromy Burnitz 1969, Milton Bradley 1969, Seth Rogan 1982, Emma Watson 1990

1817 – The first American school for the deaf was opened in Hartford, Connecticut
1850 – The city of San Francisco was incorporated
1865 – The 16th President of the United States, Abraham Lincoln, died from injuries inflicted by John Wilkes Booth the previous evening
1865 – Andrew Johnson was sworn in as the 17th President of the United States, following the death of Abraham Lincoln earlier that day
1892 – The General Electric Company was organized
1912 – The ocean liner *Titanic* sank at 2:27 a.m. in the North Atlantic after hitting an iceberg the evening before, causing over 1,500 deaths, although more than 700 people survived
1923 – Insulin became generally available for people suffering with diabetes
1924 – Rand McNally published its first road atlas
1927 – Douglas Fairbanks, Mary Pickford, and Norma and Constance Talmadge became the first people to leave their footprints in concrete outside Grauman's Chinese Theater in Hollywood
1934 – In the comic strip "Blondie," Dagwood and Blondie Bumstead welcomed a baby boy, Alexander, later nicknamed Baby Dumpling
1947 – Jackie Robinson played his first non-exhibition Major League Baseball game for the Brooklyn Dodgers
1955 – Ray Kroc started the McDonald's restaurant chain
1977 – The last original episode of *The Electric Company* aired on PBS
1983 – Tokyo Disneyland opened
1989 – The Tiananmen Square Protest of 1989 began in China

April 16: John II of France 1319, John Hadley 1682, Henry Clinton 1730, Wilbur Wright 1867, Paul Waner 1903, Charlie Chaplin 1889, Garth Williams 1912, Peter Ustinov 1921, Henri Mancini 1924, Pope Benedict XVI 1927, Edie Adams 1929, Bobby Vinton 1935, George "the Animal" Steele 1937, Dusty Springfield 1939, Jim Lonborg 1942, Bob Montgomery 1944, Tom Allen 1945, Kareem Abdul-Jabbar 1947, Gerry Rafferty 1947, Bill Belichick 1952, Jay O. Sanders 1953, Ellen Barkin 1954, Bruce Bochy 1955, Jimmy Osmond 1963, Jon Cryer 1965, Martin Lawrence 1965, Selina 1971, Peter Billingsley 1972, Lukas Haas 1976

1705 – Queen Anne of England knighted Isaac Newton

1746 – Bonnie Prince Charles was defeated at the Battle of Culloden, the last pitched battle fought in Britain

1900 – The first postage stamp booklet was released

1905 – Andrew Carnegie donated $10-million of personal money to set up the Carnegie Foundation for the Advancement of Teaching

1912 – Harriet Quimby became the first woman to fly an airplane across the English Channel

1940 – The first no-hit, no-run game to be thrown on an opening day of the Major League Baseball season was earned by Bob Feller, as the Cleveland Indians beat the Chicago White Sox 1-0

1947 – The Zoomar lens, invented by Dr. Frank Back, was demonstrated in New York City

1962 – Walter Cronkite began anchoring the CBS Evening News

1972 – *Apollo 16* blasted off on a voyage to the moon

1972 – Two giant pandas arrived in the United States from China

1977 – The ban on women attending West Point was lifted

1996 – Britain's Prince Andrew and his wife, Sarah, the Duchess of York, announced that they were in the process of getting a divorce

1999 – Wayne Gretzky announced his retirement from the National Hockey League

2001 – Animal Kingdom Lodge opened at Walt Disney World

2007 – A gunman shot and killed 32 people before killing himself on the campus of Virginia Polytechnic Institute and State University in Blacksburg, Virginia

April 17: Alexander II of Russia 1818, J.P. Morgan 1837, Nikita Khrushchev 1894, Senor Wences 1896, Thornton Wilder 1897, William Holden 1918, Harry Reasoner 1923, David Bradley 1942, L. Scott Caldwell 1944, Olivia Hussey 1951, Rowdy Roddy Piper 1954, Sean Bean 1959, Teri Austin 1959, Boomer Esiason 1961, William Mapother 1965, Marquis Grissom 1967, Henry Ian Cusick 1967, Jennifer Garner 1972, Victoria Beckham 1974, Chad Hedrick 1977, Jed Lowrie 1984

1397 – Geoffrey Chaucer told the Canterbury Tales for the first time in the court of Richard II

1492 – Christopher Columbus signed a contract with Spain to find a passage to Asia and the Indies

1521 – Martin Luther was excommunicated from the Roman Catholic Church

1524 – New York Harbor was discovered by Giovanni Verrazano

1861 – Virginia became the eighth state to secede from the Union

1865 – Mary Surratt was arrested as a conspirator in the Lincoln assassination

1924 – Metro-Goldwyn-Mayer studios was formed with the merger of Metro Pictures, Goldwyn Pictures and the Louis B. Mayer Company

1937 – Daffy Duck made his debut in the short *Porky's Duck Hunt*

1941 – Igor Sikorsky accomplished the first successful helicopter lift-off from water near Stratford, Connecticut

1947 – Jackie Robinson of the Brooklyn Dodgers performed a bunt for his first Major League hit

1961 – About 1,400 U.S.-supported Cuban exiles invaded Cuba at the Bay of Pigs in an unsuccessful attempt to overthrow Fidel Castro

1964 – Jerrie Mock became first woman to fly an airplane solo around the world

1967 – The United States Supreme Court barred Muhammad Ali's request to be blocked from induction into the U.S. Army

1969 – In Los Angeles, Sirhan Sirhan was convicted of assassinating U.S. Senator and Presidential candidate Robert F. Kennedy

1970 – *Apollo 13* returned safely to Earth after an on-board accident with an oxygen tank

1973 – Federal Express made its first delivery

1976 – President Gerald Ford appeared on *Saturday Night Live*

1993 – A federal jury in Los Angeles convicted two former police officers of violating the civil rights of beaten motorist Rodney King

1996 – Erik and Lyle Menendez were sentenced to life in prison without parole for killing their parents

April 18: Lucrezia Borgia 1480, Clarence Darrow 1857, Sam Crawford 1880, Duffy Lewis 1888, Barbara Hale 1922, Henry Hyde 1924, Clive Revill 1930, Hayley Mills 1946, James Woods 1947, Nate Archibald 1948, Rick Moranis 1954, Eric Roberts 1956, Melody Scott Thomas 1956, Jane Leeves 1961, Eric McCormack 1963, Conan O'Brien 1963, Maria Bello 1967, Melissa Joan Hart 1976, Miguel Cabrera 1983, America Ferrera 1984

1506 – The cornerstone of St. Peter's Basilica in Rome was laid

1676 – Sudbury, Massachusetts was attacked by Indians

1775 – American revolutionaries Paul Revere, William Dawes and Samuel Prescott rode though the towns of Massachusetts giving the warning that, "The British are coming"

1834 – William Lamb became Prime Minister of England

1853 – United States Vice-President William King died after serving just 45 days in office

1861 – Colonel Robert E. Lee turned down an offer to command the Union armies during the U.S. Civil War

1906 – About 700 people were killed and most of the city was destroyed when an earthquake rocked San Francisco
1923 – Yankee Stadium opened in the Bronx
1949 – The Republic of Ireland was established
1950 – The first transatlantic jet passenger trip was completed
1955 – Albert Einstein died at the age of 76
1980 – Rhodesia became the independent nation of Zimbabwe
1983 – The United States Embassy in Beirut was blown up by a suicide car-bomber, killing 63 people, including 17 Americans
1999 – Wayne Gretsky played his final game in the NHL and his number (99) was retired by the league

April 19: Peter I of Portugal 1320, Ferdinand II of Aragon 1452, Roger Sherman 1721, Ferdinand I of Austria 1793, Lucretia Garfield 1832, George O'Brien 1899, Eliot Ness 1903, Hugh O'Brien 1925, Dick Sargent 1930, Jayne Mansfield 1932, Dudley Moore 1935, Elinor Donahue 1937, Tim Curry 1946, Rick Miller 1948, Frank Viola 1960, Al Unser Jr. 1962, Ashley Judd 1968, James Franco 1978, Kate Hudson 1979, Hayden Christiensen 1981, Joe Mauer 1983, Maria Sharapova 1987

1775 – The American Revolution began as fighting broke out at the Battle of Lexington and Concord
1861 – Union President Abraham Lincoln ordered a blockade of Confederate ports
1892 – The Duryea gasoline buggy was introduced in the United States by Charles and Frank Duryea
1897 – The first Boston Marathon was held
1904 – Most of Toronto was destroyed by fire
1943 – The Warsaw Ghetto uprising against Nazi rule began
1956 – Actress Grace Kelly and Prince Rainier of Monaco were married
1958 – The San Francisco Giants and the Los Angeles Dodgers played the first Major League Baseball game on the West Coast
1960 – Baseball uniforms began displaying player's names on their backs
1961 – The Bay of Pigs invasion of Cuba ended in failure
1967 – *Surveyor 3* landed on the moon and began sending photos back to the United States
1971 – Russia launched Salyut I, the first space station
1977 – Alex Haley received a special Pulitzer Prize for his book *Roots*
1987 – The Simpsons made their television debut in a short that appeared on *The Tracey Ullman Show*
1989 – A giant asteroid passed within 500,000 miles of Earth
1993 – The Branch-Davidian's compound in Waco, Texas, burned to the ground after a 51-day standoff between the cult and U.S. federal agents -

86 people were killed including 17 children, although nine of the Branch Davidians escaped the fire
1995 – The Alfred P. Murrah Federal Building in Oklahoma City was destroyed by a bomb, killing 168 people and wounding over 500
2000 – A plane crashed in the Philippines, killing 131 people
2005 – Joseph Cardinal Ratzinger was elected Pope Benedict XVI

April 20: Napoleon III of France 1808, Adolf Hitler 1889, Harold Lloyd 1893, Lionel Hampton 1908, John Paul Stevens 1920, Nina Foch 1924, George Takei 1939, Ryan O'Neil 1941, Steve Spurrier 1975, Jessica Lange 1949, Veronica Cartwright 1950, Luther Vandross 1951, Dennis Leary 1958, Clint Howard 1959, Don Mattingly 1961, Crispin Glover 1964, Andy Serkis 1964, Rosalynn Sumners 1964, Lara Jill Miller 1967, Brian Merrill 1968, Allan Houston 1971, Carmen Electra 1972, Stephen Marley 1972, Joey Lawrence 1976

1653 – Oliver Cromwell dissolved Parliament
1775 – The British began the siege of Boston during the American Revolution
1812 – George Clinton, Vice-President of the United States, became the first vice-president to die in office
1832 – Hot Springs National Park was established by an act of the United States Congress, the first national park in the United States
1836 – The U.S. territory of Wisconsin was created by the U.S. Congress
1861 – Robert E. Lee resigned from U.S. Army
1902 – Scientists Marie and Pierre Curie isolated the radioactive element radium
1912 – Fenway Park opened as the home of the Boston Red Sox
1916 – Wrigley Field opened in Chicago
1939 – Ted Williams made his Major League Baseball debut
1940 – The first electron microscope was demonstrated by RCA
1945 – Soviet troops began their attack on Berlin
1945 – During World War II, Allied forces took control of the German cities of Nuremberg and Stuttgart
1968 – A South African Airways Boeing 707 crashed during takeoff at Windhoek, West-South Africa, killing 122
1972 – The manned lunar module from *Apollo 16* landed on the moon
1978 – The Korean Airliner 007 was shot down while in Russian airspace
1986 – Michael Jordan set a record by scoring 63 points in a play-off game in the NBA
1999 – Thirteen people were killed at Columbine High School in Littleton, Colorado, when two teenagers opened fire on them with shotguns and pipe bombs, and then the two gunmen killed themselves

2007 – A man at Johnson Space Center in Houston killed a hostage then himself
2008 – Danica Patrick won the Indy Japan 300, becoming the first woman to ever win an Indy car race

April 21: Philip II of France 1165, Charlotte Bronte 1816, Joe McCarthy 1887, Pat Brown 1905, Anthony Quinn 1915, Elizabeth II of England 1926, Charles Grodin 1935, Paul Davis 1948, Patti Lupone 1949, Tony Danza 1951, Andie MacDowell 1958, Ken Caminiti 1963, John Cameron Mitchell 1963, Nicole Sullivan 1970, Tony Romo 1980

753 BC – Rome was founded, according to legend
1689 – William III and Mary II were crowned joint King and Queen of England, Scotland and Ireland
1789 – John Adams was sworn in as the country's first Vice-President
1862 – The United States Mint in Denver was established
1865 – President Abraham Lincoln's funeral train left Washington, DC
1898 – The Spanish-American War began
1900 – Floods in Mississippi destroyed three million dollars worth of property
1918 – Baron Von Richthofen, the German Red Baron, was shot down and killed during World War I
1930 – A fire at a prison in Columbus, Ohio killed 320 people
1944 – Women in France received the right to vote
1952 – Secretary's Day was first celebrated
1962 – The Seattle's World Fair opened
1965 – *Hollywood Squares* first aired, starting on CBS-TV
1967 – The daughter of Joseph Stalin defected to the United States
1972 – Apollo 16 astronauts John Young and Charles Duke explored the surface of the Moon
1986 – Geraldo Rivera opened a vault on live TV that belonged to Al Capone, revealing nothing of importance
1994 – The discovery of extra-solar planets, or planets outside the Solar System, was announced
2007 – A Blue Angels jet crashed during an air show in South Carolina

April 22: Queen Isabella I of Spain 1451, Edward de Vere 1550, Pope Alexander VIII 1610, Immanuel Kant 1724, Vladimir Lenin 1870, J. Robert Oppenheimer 1904, Eddie Albert 1908, Aaron Spelling 1923, Jim Longley 1924, Charlotte Rae 1926, Glen Campbell 1936, Jack Nicholson 1937, Steve Fossett 1944, Steve Englehart 1947, Peter Frampton 1950, Ryan Stiles 1959, Terry Francona 1959, Byron Allen 1961, Sheryl Lee 1967

1509 – Henry VIII ascended to the throne of England upon the death of his father Henry VII
1876 – The National League began their first baseball season with eight teams
1889 – The Oklahoma land rush officially started at noon
1898 – The US Navy blockaded the ports of Cuba, in the first act of the Spanish-American War
1964 – New York's World Fair opened for its first season
1964 – "It's a Small World" ride opened at the New York World's Fair, running a year and a half and then becoming a permanent attraction at Disneyland
1970 – The first Earth Day was observed
1993 – The Holocaust Memorial Museum opened in Washington, DC
1998 – Walt Disney World's Animal Kingdom opened
2005 – Zacarias Moussaoui pled guilty to conspiring with hijackers in the September 11, 2001 plot to attack American buildings and citizens

April 23: Alfonso II of Portugal 1185, William Shakespeare 1564, Frederick I of Sweden 1676, James Buchanan 1791, Stephen Douglas 1813, Max Planck 1858, Allen Dulles 1893, Lester B. Pearson 1897, Warren Spahn 1921, Shirley Temple 1928, Roy Orbison 1936, David Birney 1939, Lee Majors 1939, Sandra Dee 1942, Herve Villechaize 1943, Joyce DeWitt 1949, Michael Moore 1954, Jan Hooks 1957, Valerie Bertinelli 1960, George Lopez 1961, Melina Kanakaredes 1967, Rheal Cormier 1967, Timothy McVeigh 1968, Andruw Jones 1977, Jaime King 1979, Aaron Hill 1983, Jessica Stam 1986

1597 – Shakespeare's *Merry Wives of Windsor* was first performed, with Queen Elizabeth I attending
1661 – Charles II was crowned King of England, Scotland and Ireland
1789 – George Washington moved into the first executive mansion, Franklin House in New York
1954 – Hank Aaron of the Milwaukee Braves hit his first Major League Baseball home run
1963 – Pete Rose of the Cincinnati Reds got his first Major League Baseball hit
1967 – Soyuz I was launched by the Soviet Union
1968 – The Methodist Church and the Evangelical United Brethren Church merged to form the United Methodist Church
1985 – Coca-Cola announced it was changing its 99-year old formula and coming out with New Coke
1989 – Kareem Abdul-Jabbar played his last regular season game in the NBA

105

1998 – James Earl Ray died in prison
2006 – Mount Merapi in Central Java erupted
2007 – Former Russian President Boris Yeltsin died

April 24: Richard Donner 1930, Shirley MacLaine 1934, Jill Ireland 1936, Barbra Streisand 1942, Richard M. Daley 1942, Cedric the Entertainer 1964, Djimon Hounsou 1964, Omar Visquel 1967, Stacy Haiduk 1968, Melinda Clarke 1969, Chipper Jones 1972, Carlos Beltran 1977, Eric Balfour 1978, Kelly Clarkson 1982

1704 – The first regular newspaper in the United States was first printed, the *Boston, Massachusetts New-Letter*
1800 – The Library of Congress was established
1877 – Russia declared war on the Ottoman Empire, starting the Russo-Turkish War
1898 – Spain declared war on the United States
1953 – Winston Churchill was knighted by Queen Elizabeth II
1965 – Civil War broke out in the Dominican Republic
1967 – Soviet astronaut Vladimir Komarov died when his spacecraft crashed with a tangled parachute
1981 – The IBM personal computer was introduced
1990 – The Space Shuttle Discovery blasted off carrying the Hubble Space Telescope
1994 – Disney's All-Star Sports Resort opened at Walt Disney World
2005 – Pope Benedict XVI was officially inaugurated

April 25: Louis IX (Saint Louis) of France 1215, Edward II of England 1284, Roger de Mortimer 1287, Oliver Cromwell 1599, Guglielmo Marconi 1874, John Henry "Pop" Lloyd 1884, Edward R. Murrow 1908, Ella Fitzgerald 1917, Meadowlark Lemon 1932, Al Pacino 1940, Talia Shire 1946, Hank Azaria 1964, Joe Buck 1969, Renee Zellweger 1969, Darren Woodson 1969, Jason Lee 1970, Tim Duncan 1976, Anja Parson 1981, Andre Woodson 1984, Sara Paxton 1988

1719 – *Robinson Crusoe* by Daniel Defoe was first published
1792 – The guillotine was first used in an execution
1846 – The Mexican-American War began
1859 – Work began in Egypt on the Suez Canal
1898 – The United States declared war on Spain
1901 – New York became the first state to require license plates for automobiles
1945 – Delegates from about 50 countries met in San Francisco to organize the United Nations

1980 – An attempt to free the American hostages being held at the American Embassy in Tehran, Iran, failed when a helicopter and a transport plane collided, killing 8 American servicemen
1983 – Soviet President Yuri Andropov invited American Samantha Smith (a child from Maine) to visit the Soviet Union after she wrote him a letter expressing her concerns over nuclear war
1983 – Pioneer 10 became the first space probe to travel beyond Pluto's orbit
1984 – David Anthony Kennedy, the son of Robert F. Kennedy, was found dead of a drug overdose in a hotel room
1990 – The Hubble Space Telescope was placed into Earth's orbit

April 26: Marcus Aurelius 121 AD, Peter II of Portugal 1648, John James Audubon 1785, Rudolf Hess 1895, Charles Richter 1900, I.M. Pei 1917, Carol Burnett 1933, Bobby Ridell 1942, Gary Wright 1943, Michael Damian 1962, Jet Li 1963, Kevin James 1965, Tom Welling 1977, Jessica Lynch 1983

1607 – Colonists that would settle Jamestown, Virginia, made landfall at what is now Cape Henry, Virginia
1865 – John Wilkes Booth was killed by the United States Federal Cavalry, despite orders to be taken alive
1900 – A raging fire destroyed parts of the Canadian cities of Ottawa and Hull, causing $15 million in damages and leaving 12,000 people homeless
1901 – The Boston Americans, later the Red Sox, played their first baseball game ever
1933 – The Gestapo was established in Germany
1941 – An organ was played at a baseball stadium for the first time in Chicago
1964 – The African nations of Tanganyika and Zanzibar merged to form Tanzania
1982 – Argentina surrendered to Britain over the Falkland Island crisis
1986 – The world's worst nuclear disaster to date occurred at Chernobyl, in the Ukraine, where 31 people died and thousands were exposed to deadly radiation
2005 – After 29 years of occupation, Syrian forces withdrew from Lebanon

April 27: Samuel F. B. Morse 1791, Ulysses S. Grant 1822, Rogers Hornsby 1896, Walter Lantz 1900, Enos Slaughter 1916, Jack Klugman 1922, Coretta Scott King 1927, Chuck Knox 1932, Casey Kasem 1932, Doug Sheehan 1949, Ace Frehley 1951, George Gervin 1952, Sheena Easton 1959, Jason Whitlock 1967, Chris Carpenter 1975, Runelvys Hernandez 1978, William Moseley 1987

1124 – David I became King of Scotland
1296 – The Scots were defeated by Edward I at the Battle of Dunbar
1521 – Portuguese explorer Ferdinand Magellan was killed by natives in the Philippines
1810 – Beethoven composed his most famous piece, Fur Elise
1861 – West Virginia seceded from Virginia after Virginia seceded from the Union during the American Civil War
1937 – The first Social Security checks were issued in the United States
1965 – Pampers were patented
1982 – The trial of John W. Hinckley Jr. began, having been accused of the attempted assassination of President Ronald Reagan
1983 – Nolan Ryan of the Houston Astros broke a 55-year-old Major League Baseball record when he struck out his 3,509th batter of his career
2006 – Construction began on Freedom Tower, which was replacing the fallen World Trade Center in New York City

April 28: Edward IV of England 1442, James Monroe 1758, Lionel Barrymore 1878, Jan Oort 1900, Dick Ayers 1924, Harper Lee 1926, James Baker 1930, Saddam Hussein 1937, Madge Sinclair 1938, Ann-Margaret 1941, Paul Guilfoyle 1949, Bruno Kirby 1949, Jay Leno 1950, Mary McDonnell 1952, Hal Sutton 1958, Barry Larkin 1964, John Daly 1966, Nicklas Lidstrom 1970, Jorge Garcia 1973, Penelope Cruz 1974, Josh Howard 1980, Jessica Alba 1981

1788 – Maryland became the seventh state
1789 – A mutiny on the British *Bounty* took place when a rebel crew took the ship and set sail to Pitcairn Island, leaving Captain W. Bligh and 18 sailors adrift
1862 – During the Civil War, Admiral David Farragut captured New Orleans, Louisiana for the Union
1930 – The first organized night baseball game was played in Independence, Kansas
1932 – A vaccine for Yellow Fever was announced
1945 – Benito Mussolini and his mistress Clara Petacci were executed by Italian partisans as they attempted to flee the country
1967 – Muhammad Ali refused induction into the United States Army and was stripped of boxing title
1967 – Expo 67 opened in Montreal
1969 – Charles de Gaulle resigned as President of France
1985 – The largest sand castle ever built was completed in St. Petersburg, Florida, measuring over four stories tall
2001 – Millionaire Dennis Tito became the world's first space tourist

2003 – Apple Computer's iTunes Music Store was launched, selling over a million songs in the first week

April 29: Oliver Ellsworth 1745, William Randolph Hearst 1863, Duke Ellington 1899, Hirohito 1901, George Allen 1918, Luis Aparicio 1934, Duane Allen 1943, Richard Kline 1944, Dale Earnhart Sr. 1951, Rick Burleson 1951, Nora Dunn 1952, Bob McClure 1952, Jerry Seinfeld 1954, Kate Mulgrew 1955, Daniel Day-Lewis 1957, Michelle Pfeiffer 1957, Eve Plumb 1958, Master P 1967, Carnie Wilson 1968, Uma Thurman 1970, Andre Agassi 1970, Tony Armas Jr. 1978

1429 – Joan of Arc led Orleans, France in a victory over England
1770 – Captain James Cook named Botany Bay, Australia after arriving there for the first time
1813 – Rubber was patented by J.F. Hummel
1852 – The first edition of Peter Roget's Thesaurus was published
1861 – Maryland decided not to secede from the Union
1910 – Andrew Fisher became Prime Minister of Australia for the second time
1945 – In a bunker in Berlin, Adolf Hitler and Eva Braun were married
1945 – The German Army in Italy surrendered unconditionally to the Allies
1945 – The Nazi death camp, Dachau, was liberated
1970 – The United States and South Vietnam invaded Cambodia
1975 – The U.S. involvement in the Vietnam War came to an end as the last U.S. citizens are pulled out of Saigon
1985 – Billy Martin was brought back, for the fourth time, to the position of manager for the New York Yankees
1986 – Roger Clemens of the Boston Red Sox set a new Major League Baseball record when he struck out 20 batters in one game
1990 – The destruction of the Berlin Wall began
1992 – Rioting began after a jury decision to acquit four Los Angeles policemen in the Rodney King beating trial

April 30: Philip III of France 1245, Mary II of England 1662, Eve Arden 1912, Al Lewis 1923, Cloris Leachman 1926, Willie Nelson 1933, Gary Collins 1938, Larry Niven 1938, Burt Young 1940, Bobby Vee 1943, Jill Clayburgh 1944, Perry King 1948, Phil Garner 1949, Merrill Osmond 1953, Isiah Thomas 1961, Michael Waltrip 1963, Adrian Pasdar 1965, Elliott Sadler 1975, Johnny Galecki 1975, Kirsten Dunst 1982, Lloyd Banks 1982

1006 – Supernova SN 1006 appeared in the constellation Lupus, the brightest in recorded history
1492 – Spain gave Christopher Columbus his commission to explore

1789 – George Washington took office as the first President of the United States

1803 – The United States purchased the Louisiana Territory from France for $15 million

1812 – Louisiana admitted as the 18th U.S. state

1900 – Hawaii was organized as an official United States territory

1939 – Lou Gehrig played his last game with the New York Yankees

1939 – The 1939 New York World's Fair opened

1939 – President Franklin Roosevelt became the first president to appear on television, during the World's Fair opening ceremonies broadcast

1945 – Adolf Hitler and Eva Braun committed suicide after being married one day

1947 – In Nevada, the Boulder Dam was renamed the Hoover Dam, as it was once called

1975 – Saigon fell to the Communists and the Vietnam War officially ended

1980 – Queen Beatrix ascended to the throne of the Netherlands

1991 – A cyclone hit Bangladesh, killing over 138,000 people

1993 – The World Wide Web was created

1993 – Monica Seles, ranked number one at the time, was stabbed in the back during a tennis match in Hamburg, Germany, causing her to miss two years of competition while she recovered

May 1: Calamity Jane 1852, Kate Smith 1909, Glen Ford 1916, Jack Paar 1918, Harry Carey 1919, Joseph Heller 1923, Art Fleming 1924, Scott Carpenter 1925, Harry Belafonte 1927, Judy Collins 1939, Rita Coolidge 1945, Joanna Lumley 1946, Douglas Barr 1949, Ray Parker Jr. 1954, Marilyn Milian 1961, Tim McGraw 1967, Curtis Martin 1963, Darius McCrary 1976, Wes Welker 1981

1707 – England, Wales and Scotland were united to form Great Britain
1751 – The first cricket match was played in America
1834 – Slavery was abolished in all British colonies
1863 – In Virginia, the Battle of Chancellorsville began
1867 – Reconstruction in the South began with black voter registration
1883 – Buffalo Bill Cody had his first Wild West Show
1893 – The World's Columbian Exposition opened in Chicago
1900 – An explosion in a Utah coal mine took the lives of 200 people
1901 – The Pan-America Exposition opened in New York
1930 – The dwarf planet Pluto got its official name
1931 – The Empire State Building in New York was dedicated and opened, and at 102 stories tall it was the tallest building in the world at that time
1956 – The polio vaccine discovered by Jonas Salk was made available to the public
1958 – James Van Allen reported that two radiation belts encircled Earth
1960 – Francis Gary Powers was shot down in his U-2 spyplane over the Soviet Union
1982 – The 1982 World's Fair opened in Knoxville, Tennessee
1989 – Disney-MGM Studios, later renamed Disney Hollywood Studios, opened at Walt Disney World

May 2: Catherine II (the Great) of Russia 1729, Eddie Collins 1887, Baron Manfred Von Richthofen (The Red Baron) 1892, Benjamin Spock 1903, Pinky Lee 1907, Roscoe Lee Browne 1925, Engelbert Humperdinck 1936, Lorenzo Music 1937, Bianca Jagger 1945, Larry Gatlin 19948, Christine Baranski 1952, The Rock 1972, Jenna Von Oy 1977, Sara Hughes 1985, Kyle Busch 1985

1519 – Leonardo da Vinci died at the age of 67
1568 – Mary, Queen of Scots, escaped from Loch Leven Castle where she had been imprisoned by Sir William Douglas
1670 – The Hudson Bay Company was founded by England's King Charles II
1776 – France and Spain agreed to donate arms to American rebels fighting the British
1863 – Confederate General Thomas "Stonewall" Jackson was wounded by his own men in the battle of Chancellorsville, Virginia, and died 8 days later
1885 – *Good Housekeeping* magazine was first published
1902 – The first science fiction film, *A Trip to the Moon*, was first released
1918 – General Motors acquired Chevrolet Motor Company
1919 – Air passenger service began in the United States
1920 – The first game of the Negro League was played in Indianapolis
1932 - Jack Benny's first radio show debuted on NBC Radio
1933 – The Loch Ness Monster was spotted for the first time
1939 – Lou Gehrig set a new Major League Baseball record when he played in his 2,130[th] consecutive game
1945 – Russians took Berlin after 12 days of fierce house-to-house fighting
1969 – The British ocean liner *Queen Elizabeth II* set sail on her maiden voyage
1974 – The filming of the movie Jaws began at Martha's Vineyard
2008 – Cyclone Nargis made landfall in Myanmar, killing over 130,000 people

May 3: Niccolo Machiavelli 1469, Beulah Bondi 1888, Golda Meir 1898, Bing Crosby 1903, Red Ruffing 1905, Sebastian Shaw 1905, Anna Roosevelt 1906, Mary Astor 1906, Pete Seeger 1919, Sugar Ray Robinson 1921, James Brown 1928, Frankie Valli 1934, Davey Lopes 1945, Greg Gumble 1946, Doug Henning 1947, Christopher Cross 1951, Dulé Hill 1974

1802 – Washington, D.C. was incorporated as a city
1901 – A fire in Jacksonville, Florida left over 10,000 people homeless

1937 – Margaret Mitchell won the Pulitzer Prize for the novel *Gone with the Wind*

1952 – The first airplane landed at the North Pole

1959 – The first Grammy Awards were given out

1971 – National Public Radio broadcasted for the first time

1973 – The Sears Tower in Chicago became the world's tallest building

1979 – Margaret Thatcher became the first woman to hold the office of Prime Minister of Great Britain

1988 – The White House acknowledged that first lady Nancy Reagan had used astrological advice to help schedule her husband's activities

2003 – New Hampshire's famous Old Man of the Mountain collapsed

May 4: Henry I of France 1008, Horace Mann 1796, Julia Tyler 1820, Raymond D. Mills 1916, Hosni Mubarak 1928, Audrey Hepburn 1929, George Will 1941, Roger Rees 1941, Jackie Jackson 1951, Pia Zadora 1954, Ken Oberkfell 1956, Randy Travis 1959, Mary McDonough 1961, Miguel Cairo 1974, Laci Peterson 1975, Ben Grieve 1976, Lance Bass 1979

1471 – In England, the Yorkists defeated the Lancastrians at the battle of Tewkesbury in the War of the Roses

1494 – Christopher Columbus landed in Jamaica

1715 – A French manufacturer introduced the first folding umbrella

1863 – The Battle of Chancellorsville ended when the Union Army retreated

1865 – Abraham Lincoln was buried in Springfield, Illinois, three weeks after he was assassinated

1904 – Construction began on the Panama Canal

1910 – The Royal Canadian Navy was created

1924 – The 1924 Summer Olympics began in Paris, France

1932 – Mobster Al Capone began serving an 11-month prison sentence for tax evasion

1953 – Ernest Hemingway was awarded a Pulitzer Prize for his book *Old Man and the Sea*

1964 – The soap opera *Another World* debuted on NBC-TV

1970 – Four students at Kent State University were killed when National Guardsman opened fire on student protesters

1979 – Margaret Thatcher became the first woman to serve as Prime Minister of the United Kingdom

1998 – Unabomber Theodore Kaczynski was given four life sentences plus 30 years by a federal judge in Sacramento

2007 – Greensburg, Kansas was almost completely destroyed by a tornado

May 5: Karl Marx 1818, Nellie Bly 1965, Charles Bender 1883, Rex Harrison 1908, Tyrone Power 1914, Anne B. Davis 1926, Lance Henriksen 1940, Tammy Wynette 1942, Marc Alaimo 1942, Michael Palin 1943, Roger Rees 1944, John Rhys-Davies 1944, Annette Bening 1959, Brian Williams 1959, Tina Yothers 1973, Santiago Cabrera 1978, Chris Brown 1989

1260 – Kublai Khan became ruler of the Mongol Empire
1821 – Napoleon Bonaparte died on the island of St. Helena, where he had been in exile
1862 – Mexican forces stopped a French invasion at the Battle of Puebla
1864 – In the American Civil War, the Battle of the Wilderness began
1865 – The 13th Amendment to the Constitution was ratified, abolishing slavery
1865 – The first train robbery in the United States occurred at North Bend, Ohio
1891 – Music Hall, later renamed Carnegie Hall, was dedicated in New York City
1904 – Cy Young of the Boston Red Sox threw a perfect game
1961 – Alan Shepard became the first American in space
2000 – The final episode of *Boy Meets World* aired on ABC-TV

May 6: Maximilien Robespierre 1758, Sigmund Freud 1856, Robert E. Peary 1856, Tsar Nicholas II of Russia 1868, Rudolph Valentino 1895, Orson Welles 1915, Willie Mays 1931, Bob Seger 1945, David Micheline 1948, Michael O'Hare 1952, Tony Blair 1953, Tom Bergeron 1955, Mare Winningham 1959, Roma Downey 1960, George Clooney 1961, Dana Hill 1964, Martin Brodeur 1972, Chris Paul 1985

1861 – Arkansas became the ninth state to secede from the Union
1863 – During the American Civil War, the Battle of Chancellorsville ended with a Confederate victory
1877 – Chief Crazy Horse of the Oglala Sioux surrendered to United States troops in Nebraska
1889 – The Eiffel Tower was officially opened to the public
1910 – Kind Edward VII of England died and was succeeded by his son, George V
1915 – Babe Ruth hit his first homerun in the Major Leagues, while he was playing for the Boston Red Sox
1937 – The German airship *Hindenburg* crashed and burned in Lakehurst, New Jersey, killing 36 of the 97 people on board

1940 – John Steinbeck was awarded the Pulitzer Prize for his novel *The Grapes of Wrath*
1941 – Bob Hope gave his first USO show at California's March Field
1942 – During World War II, Japan seized the Philippines
1954 – Roger Bannister became the first person to run a mile in under four minutes
1994 – The Channel Tunnel, nicknamed the Chunnel, opened, a tunnel under the English Channel linking England and France

May 7: Robert Browning 1812, Johannes Brahms 1833, Pyotr Ilyich Tchaikovsky 1840, Archibald Primrose 1847, Gabby Hayes 1885, Gary Cooper 1901, Eva Peron 1919, Darren McGavin 1922, Anne Baxter 1923, Dick Williams 1929, Johnny Unitas 1933, Tim Russert 1950, Amy Heckerling 1954, Owen Hart 1965, Traci Lords 1969, Shawn Marion 1978

1429 – The English siege of Orleans was pushed back by Joan of Arc, despite having to pull an arrow from her shoulder and fighting wounded
1763 – Indian chief Pontiac began all out war on the British in New York
1789 – The first U.S. Presidential Inaugural Ball was held in New York City
1847 – The American Medical Association was formed in Philadelphia
1915 – The *Lusitania*, a civilian ship, was sunk by a German submarine, killing 1,198 people
1939 – Germany and Italy announced a military and political alliance known as the Rome-Berlin Axis
1940 – Winston Churchill became British Prime Minister
1945 – Baseball owner Branch Rickey announced the organization of the United States Negro Baseball League
1945 – Germany signed an unconditional surrender ending World War II in Europe, taking effect the next day
1960 – Leonid Brezhnev became President of the Soviet Union
1975 – President Gerald Ford declared an end to the Vietnam War
1992 – The Space Shuttle *Endeavor* was launched on its maiden voyage
1998 – Mercedes-Benz bought Chrysler for $40 billion, forming DaimlerChrysler
2006 – *Rolling Stone* magazine published it 1000th issue
2007 – The tomb of Herod the Great was discovered

May 8: Harry Truman 1884, Don Rickles 1926, David Attenborough 1926, Sonny Liston 1932, Ricky Nelson 1940, Peter Benchley 1940, Toni Tennille 1943, Philip Bailey 1951, David Keith 1954, Steven Furst 1954, Alex Van Halen 1955, Bill Cowher 1957, Ronnie Lott 1959, Melissa Gilbert 1964, Bobby Labonte 1964, Enrique Iglesias 1975

1794 – Antoine Lavoisier was executed by guillotine; he was the French chemist that discovered oxygen

1794 – The U.S. Post Office was established

1846 – In the first major battle of the Mexican-American War, Zachary Taylor led the American forces in victory in the Battle of Palo Alto

1861 – Richmond, Virginia was named the capital of the Confederate States of America

1877 – The first Westminster Kennel Club Dog Show opened in New York City

1886 – Pharmacist Dr. John Styth Pemberton invented what would later be called Coca-Cola

1902 – Mount Pelee on Martinique erupted and killed over 30,000 people and destroyed the town of St. Pierre

1914 – The U.S. Congress passed a Joint Resolution that designated the second Sunday in May as Mother's Day

1914 – Paramount Pictures was formed

1933 – Gandhi began a hunger strike to protest British oppression in India

1945 – President Harry Truman announced that World War II had ended in Europe

1978 – David R. Berkowitz, known as the Son of Sam, pled guilty to six murder charges

1984 – The Soviet Union announced it would boycott the 1984 Olympics in Los Angeles

1994 – *The Stand* mini-series, based on the novel by Stephen King, debuted on ABC-TV

May 9: Pope Pius III 1439, John Brown 1800, James Barrie 1860, Howard Carter 1874, Mike Wallace 1918, Arthur English 1919, Albert Finney 1936, Glenda Jackson 1936, James L. Brooks 1940, John Ashcroft 1942, Candace Bergen 1946, Calvin Murphy 1948, Billy Joel 1949, Alley Mills 1951, Kermit the Frog 1955, Wendy Crewson 1956, Tony Gwynn 1960, Steve Yzerman 1965, Rosario Dawson 1979, Brandon Webb 1979, Prince Fielder 1984

1502 – Christopher Columbus left Spain on his fourth and final voyage to the New World

1671 – Thomas Blood, aka Captain Blood, stole the Crown Jewels from the Tower of London

1868 – The city of Reno, Nevada was founded

1887 – Buffalo Bill Cody's Wild West Show opened in London

1901 – The first Australian Parliament met in Melbourne

1945 – Hermann Goring was captured by the United States Army

1955 – *Sam and Friends* debuted on television, making the first appearance of Jim Henson, Kermit the Frog and the Muppets
1962 – A laser beam was successfully bounced off the moon for the first time
1994 – Nelson Mandela was chosen to be the first black President of South Africa

May 10: John Wilkes Booth 1838, Sir Thomas Lipton 1850, Fred Astaire 1899, David O. Selznick 1902, Mother Maybelle Carter 1909, Nancy Walker 1922, Fats Domino 1929, Pat Summerall 1930, Barbara Taylor Bradford 1933, Tito Santana 1953, Chris Berman 1955, Mark David Chapman 1955, Bono 1960, Victoria Rowell 1960, Linda Evangelista 1965, Young MC 1967, Kenan Thompson 1978, Zach Roloff 1990, Jeremy Roloff 1990

1773 – The English Parliament passed the Tea Act, which taxed all tea in the U.S. colonies
1774 – Louis XVI ascended to the throne of France
1775 – Ethan Allen and Benedict Arnold led an attack on the British Fort Ticonderoga and captured it from the British
1794 – Elizabeth, the sister of King Louis XVI, was beheaded
1801 – The Barbary Pirates of Tripoli declared war on the United States, leading to the First Barbary War
1865 – Jefferson Davis was captured by Union troops near Irvinville, Georgia
1869 – Central Pacific and Union Pacific Railroads meet in Promontory, Utah, where a golden spike was driven in at the celebration of the first transcontinental railroad in the United States
1972 – Victoria Woodhull became the first woman nominated for President of the United States
1900 – The Populist Party nominated William Jennings Bryan for President
1908 – The first Mothers' Day celebration took place
1924 – J. Edgar Hoover was sworn in as the head of the FBI, serving until 1972
1940 – Germany invaded Belgium, France, the Netherlands, and Luxembourg
1940 – Winston Churchill became Prime Minister of Great Britain
1941 – Great Britain's House of Commons was destroyed by a German air raid
1954 – Bill Haley and the Comets released "Rock Around the Clock", the first rock-and-roll song to reach number one on the charts
1960 – The nuclear submarine *USS Triton* became the first vessel to circumnavigate the globe under water

117

1978 – Britain's Princess Margaret and the Earl of Snowdon announced they were divorcing after 18 years of marriage
1994 – Nelson Mandela was sworn in as the first black President of South Africa
1996 – A storm near the summit of Mount Everest left eight climbers dead
2005 – An assassination attempt against U.S. President George W. Bush while he was visiting the country of Georgia failed when the thrown hand grenade failed to detonate

May 11: Chang and Eng Bunker 1811, Charles W. Fairbanks 1852, Irving Berlin 1888, Charlie Gehringer 1903, Salvador Dali 1904, Phil Silvers 1911, Denver Pyle 1920, Louis Farrakhan 1933, Doug McClure 1938, Mike Lupica 1952, Martha Quinn 1959, Natasha Richardson 1963, Laetitia Casta 1978, Jonathan Jackson 1982

1310 – Fifty-four members of the Knights Templar were burned at the stake for heresy
1573 – Henry of Anjou was the first elected king of Poland
1812 – British Prime Minister Spencer Perceval was assassinated
1858 – Minnesota became the 32nd state
1910 – Glacier National Park in Montana was established
1927 – The Academy of Motion Pictures Arts and Sciences was founded
1949 – Siam changed its name to Thailand
1949 – Israel joined the United Nations
1953 – A tornado struck Waco, Texas, resulting in the death of 114 people
1960 – Adolf Eichmann was captured in Argentina
1985 – In Bradford, England, more than 50 people died when a flash fire swept a soccer stadium
1996 – A ValuJet DC-9 crashed shortly after take-off in Miami Florida killing all 110 people on board

May 12: Florence Nightingale 1820, Henry Cabot Lodge 1850, Katharine Hepburn 1907, Mary Kay Ash 1915, Yogi Berra 1925, Burt Bacharach 1929, Felipe Alou 1935, Tom Snyder 1936, George Carlin 1937, Linda Dano 1943, Steve Winwood 1948, Gabriel Byrne 1950, Bruce Boxleitner 1950, Kix Brooks 1955, Lou Whitaker 1957, Ving Rhames 1959, Bruce McCulloch 1961, Emilio Estevez 1962, Stephen Baldwin 1966, Tony Hawk 1968, Kim Fields 1969, Samantha Mathis 1970, Jim Furyk 1970, Mike Weir 1970, Jamie Luner 1971, MacKenzie Astin 1973, Jason Biggs 1978, Josh Phelps 1978, Malcolm David Kelley 1992, Sawyer Sweetin 1995, Sullivan Sweetin 1995

1191 – Richard I of England married Berengaria of Navarre

1780 – During the American Revolution, British forces seized Charleston, South Carolina

1870 – Manitoba became a Canadian province

1932 – The infant body of Charles and Anna Lindbergh's son was found just a few miles from the Lindbergh home near Hopewell, New Jersey

1937 – Britain's King George VI was crowned

1942 – 1,500 Jews were sent to the gas chambers and their deaths at Auschwitz

1970 – Ernie Banks of the Chicago Cubs hit his 500th home run

1978 – It was announced that hurricanes would no longer be named just after women

1992 – Four suspects were arrested in the beating of trucker Reginald Denny at the start of the Los Angeles riots

May 13: Joe Louis 1914, Bea Arthur 1926, Jim Jones 1931, Harvey Keitel 1939, Richie Valens 1941, Mary Wells 1943, Marv Wolfman 1946, Stevie Wonder 1950, Bobby Valentine 1950, Dennis Rodman 1961, Sean McDonough 1962, Stephen Colbert 1964, Darius Ricker 1966, Barry Zito 1978

1515 – Mary Tudor, sister of England's Henry VIII and widow of France's Louis XII, married Charles Brandon, the Duke of Suffolk and close friend of Henry VIII

1846 – The United States declared war on Mexico

1865 – The last battle of the American Civil War was fought one month after the war officially ended

1867 – Jefferson Davis, the former Confederate President, was freed two years after being imprisoned for his role during the Civil War

1939 – The first FM radio station in the United States was launched in Bloomfield, Connecticut

1940 – Winston Churchill made his first speech as Prime Minister of Great Britain

1967 – Mickey Mantle hit his 500th home run

1981 – Pope John Paul II was shot in an unsuccessful assassination attempt

May 14: Otto Klemperer 1885, Hans Albert Einstein 1904, Bobby Darin 1936, Dick Howser 1936, Tony Perez 1942, George Lucas 1944, Robert Zemeckis 1951, Dennis Martinez 1955, Eoin Colfer 1965, Cate Blanchett 1969, Sofia Coppola 1971, Roy Halladay 1977, Eddie House 1978, Amber Tamblyn 1983

1607 – Jamestown, Virginia was settled

1643 – Louis XIV became King of France at age 4 upon the death of his father, Louis XIII

1787 – In Philadelphia, delegates began meeting to discuss and write a new American Constitution

1796 – The first smallpox vaccination was given by Edward Jenner

1897 – "The Stars and Stripe Forever" was first performed

1900 – The summer Olympics opened in Paris, France

1904 – The first Olympic Games were held in the United States, when they opened in St. Louis

1940 – The Netherlands surrendered to Nazi Germany

1973 – Skylab One, the first manned U.S. space station, was launched into Earth orbit (see photo at left)

1989 – The final episode of *Family Ties* aired

1998 – The final episode of *Seinfeld* aired

2006 – After 7 years on TV, *The West Wing* aired its final episode

May 15: L. Frank Baum 1856, Pierre Curie 1859, Ellen Louise Wilson 1860, Richard J. Daley 1902, Eddy Arnold 1918, Paul Zindel 1936, Madeleine Albright 1937, Don Nelson 1940, K.T. Oslin 1941, Nicholas Hammond 1950, George Brett 1953, Lee Horsley 1955, Dan Patrick 1956, John Smoltz 1967, Emmitt Smith 1969, Ray Lewis 1975, Richard Kahan 1980, Josh Beckett 1980, Jamie-Lynn Sigler 1981

1756 – The Sevens Years War began, when England declared war on France

1869 – Susan B. Anthony and Elizabeth Cady Stanton formed the National Woman Suffrage Association

1905 – Las Vegas was founded

1941 – Joe DiMaggio began his historic 56 game hitting streak

1963 – The last Project Mercury space flight was launched

1970 – The first two female generals were appointed in the United States

1972 – Alabama Governor George Wallace was shot by Arthur Bremer in Laurel, Maryland, while campaigning for the U.S. presidency, paralyzing him

1973 – Nolan Ryan threw his first no-hitter

1980 – The first transcontinental balloon crossing of the United States took place

2008 – California became the second state, after Massachusetts, to legalize same-sex marriages

May 16: William Henry Seward 1801, Elizabeth Palmer Peabody 1804, Levi P. Morton 1824, Henry Fonda 1905, Liberace 1909, Harry Carey Jr. 1921, Billy Martin 1928, Bill Smitrovich 1947, Pierce Brosnan 1953, Olga Korbet 1955, Jack Morris 1955, Debra Winger 1955, Mare Winningham 1959, Janet Jackson 1966, Tracey Gold 1969, Gabriella Sabatini 1970, Tori Spelling 1973, Laura Pausini 1974, Melanie Lynskey 1977, Jean-Sebastien Giguere 1977, George Kattaras 1983, Megan Fox 1986

1568 – Mary Queen of Scots fled to England
1770 – Marie Antoinette, at age 14, married the future King Louis XVI of France, who was 15
1836 – Edgar Allan Poe married his 13-year old cousin Virginia
1868 – President Andrew Johnson was acquitted during the Senate impeachment, by one vote
1869 – America's first professional baseball team, the Cincinnati Reds, played its first game
1929 – The first Academy Awards were held in Hollywood
1963 – After 22 Earth orbits Gordon Cooper returned to Earth, ending Project Mercury
1965 – Spaghetti-O's first went on sale
1971 – The cost of a stamp went from 6 cents to 8 cents
1985 – Michael Jordan was named Rookie of the Year in the NBA
1990 – Jim Henson, creator of the Muppets, died pneumonia at the age of 53
1991 – Queen Elizabeth II became the first British monarch to address the United States Congress
1992 – The space shuttle *Endeavour* landed safely after its maiden voyage
1999 – Daisuke Matsuzaka, in his rookie season in Japan at age 18, faced Ichiro Suzuki for the first time, striking him out three times

May 17: Edward Jenner 1749, Cool Papa Bell 1903, Maureen O'Sullivan 1911, Dennis Hopper 1936, Gary Paulson 1939, Bill Paxton 1955, Sugar Ray Leonard 1956, Bob Saget 1956, Jim Nantz 1959, Enya 1961, Craig Ferguson 1962, David Eigenberg 1964, Hill Harper 1966, Jordan Knight 1970, Sendhil Ramamurthy 1974, Jose Guillen 1976, Carlos Pena 1978, Tony Parker 1982, Tahj Mowry 1986

1756 – Britain declared war on France, beginning the French and Indian War
1792 – The New York Stock Exchange was founded

1846 – The saxophone was patented by Adolphe Sax
1875 – The first Kentucky Derby was run at Louisville, Kentucky
1940 – Germany began its invasion of France
1954 – The United States Supreme Court unanimously ruled for school integration in "Brown vs. Board of Education of Topeka"
1991 – Port Orleans French Quarter Resort opened at Walt Disney World
1998 – New York Yankees pitcher David Wells became the 13th player in modern Major League Baseball history to throw a perfect game
2004 – Saratoga Springs Resort opened at Walt Disney World
2006 – The *USS Oriskany* aircraft carrier was sunk in the Gulf of Mexico in order for it to become an artificial reef

May 18: Nicholas II of Russia 1868, Frank Capra 1897, Perry Como 1912, Pope John Paul II 1920, Bill Macy 1922, Pernell Roberts 1930, Don Martin 1931, Brooks Robinson 1937, Reggie Jackson 1946, Andreas Katsulas 1946, Joe Bonsall 1948, George Strait 1952, Vince Young 1983, Spencer Breslin 1992

1152 – King Henry II of England married Eleanor of Aquitaine
1631 – John Winthrop became the first governor of Massachusetts
1652 – Rhode Island passed the first law in North America making slavery illegal
1804 – Napoleon Bonaparte was proclaimed Emperor of France
1860 – In Chicago, the National Republican Convention nominated Abraham Lincoln of Illinois as its presidential candidate and Hannibal Hamlin of Maine as its vice-presidential candidate
1897 – The first public reading of Bram Stoker's novel "Dracula" occurred
1993 – President Franklin D. Roosevelt signed an act creating the Tennessee Valley Authority
1980 – Mount St. Helens in Washington State erupted, killing 57 people and causing $3 billion in damage

May 19: John Hopkins 1795, Ho Chi Minh 1890, Malcolm X 1925, Jim Lehrer 1934, David Hartman 1935, Peter Mayhew 1944, Pete Townsend 1945, Andre the Giant 1946, Grace Jones 1948, Dusty Hill 1949, Archie Manning 1949, Steven Ford 1956, Kevin Garnett 1976, Brandon Inge 1977, Eric Lloyd 1986, Jordan Pruitt 1991

1535 – French explorer Jacques Cartier set sail for North America
1536 – King Henry VIII had his second wife, Anne Boleyn, beheaded
1568 – Queen Elizabeth I of England had her cousin, Mary, Queen of Scots, imprisoned
1588 – The Spanish Armada set sail from Lisbon, bound for England

1604 – Montreal, Quebec, Canada was founded
1900 – Great Britain annexed the Tonga Islands
1935 – T.E. Lawrence, also known as Lawrence of Arabia, died in England from injuries sustained in a motorcycle crash
1962 – Marilyn Monroe performed a sexy rendition of "Happy Birthday" for President John F. Kennedy
1984 – The Edmonton Oilers won their first Stanley Cup
1992 – Vice-President Dan Quayle criticized the TV show *Murphy Brown* for having its main character have a child out of wedlock
1994 – Jacqueline Kennedy Onassis died at the age of 64
1999 – Rosie O'Donnell and Tom Selleck got into an argument concerning gun control on O'Donnell's talk show
1999 – *Star Wars: The Phantom Menace* opened in theaters across the country, setting a new record for opening day sales, at $28.5 million
2005 – *Star Wars: Revenge of the Sith* brought in $50 million on opening day

May 20: Dolley Madison 1768, Napoleon II of France 1811, Jimmy Stewart 1908, George Gobel 1919, Anthony Zerbe 1936, Joe Cocker 1944, Cher 1946, John McKernan 1948, Dave Thomas 1949, Dean Butler 1956, Ron Reagan Jr. 1958, Bronson Pinchot 1959, John Billingsley 1960, David Wells 1963, Mindy Cohn 1966, Tony Stewart 1971, Busta Rhymes 1972, Tahmoh Penikett 1975, Ramon Hernandez 1976, Kasey James 1982

325 – The First Council of Nicea was held
1506 – In Spain, Christopher Columbus died in poverty
1570 – Cartographer Abraham Ortelius published the first atlas
1861 – North Carolina became the last state to secede from the Union
1861 – During the American Civil War, the capital of the Confederacy was moved from Montgomery, Alabama, to Richmond, Virginia
1862 – President Abraham Lincoln signed the Homestead Act into law
1873 – Levi Strauss began marketing blue jeans with copper rivets
1916 – Norman Rockwell's first cover on "The Saturday Evening Post" appeared
1982 – ABC's *Barney Miller* aired its last episode
1990 – The Hubble Space Telescope sent back its first photographs
1993 – The final episode of *Cheers* aired on NBC-TV
2006 – Barry Bonds hit his 714th career home run, tying Babe Ruth for 2nd all-time

May 21: Plato 427 BC, Philip II of Spain 1527, Alexander Pope 1688, Henri Rousseau 1844, Armand Hammer 1898, Raymond Burr 1917, Dennis Day 1917, Andrei Sakharov 1921, Peggy Cass 1922, Ronald Isley

1941, Richard Hatch 1945, Jonathan Hyde 1947, Leo Sayer 1948, Al Franken 1951, Mr. T 1952, Judge Reinhold 1957, Jeffrey Dahmer 1960, Kent Hrbek 1960, Chris Benoit 1967, Notorious B.I.G. 1972, Laura Allen 1974, Ricky Williams 1977, Ashlie Brillault 1987

996 – Sixteen year-old Otto III was crowned Roman Emperor
1471 – Henry VI was killed in the Tower of London, as Edward IV took over
1832 – In the United States, the first Democratic National Convention was held
1881 – The American branch of the Red Cross was formed by Clara Barton
1927 – Charles Lindberg completed the first solo nonstop airplane flight across the Atlantic Ocean
1932 – Amelia Earhart became the first woman to fly solo across the Atlantic
1945 – Lauren Bacall and Humphrey Bogart were married
1980 – The movie *Star Wars: The Empire Strikes Back* was released

May 22: Sir Arthur Conan Doyle 1859, Al Simmons 1902, Sir Laurence Olivier 1907, Johnny Olson 1910, Paul Winfield 1939, Bernard Shaw 1940, Ted Kaczynski 1942, Tommy John 1943, Jose Mesa 1966, Naomi Campbell 1970, Julian Tavarez 1973, Apolo Anton Ohno 1982

1455 – King Henry VI was taken prisoner by the Yorkists at the Battle of St. Albans, during the War of the Roses
1807 – Former Vice-President of the United States Aaron Burr was indicted by a grand-jury for treason
1891 – The first public showing of a motion picture took place in Thomas Edison's lab
1939 – Adolf Hitler and Benito Mussolini signed a military alliance between Germany and Italy known as the Pact of Steel
1942 – Mexico entered World War II on the side of the Allies
1960 – An earthquake measuring 9.5 hit Chile, the most powerful ever recorded
1967 – *Mister Rogers' Neighborhood* debuted on PBS-TV
1972 – Richard Nixon became the first U.S. President to visit Russia
1992 – Johnny Carson hosted the *Tonight Show* for the final time
2003 – At the Colonial in Fort Worth, Texas, Annika Sorenstam became the first woman to play on the PGA tour in 58 years

May 23: Philip I of France 1052, Margaret Fuller 1810, Ambrose Burnside 1824, Grace Ingalls 1877, Douglas Fairbanks 1883, Scatman Crothers

124

1910, Betty Garrett 1919, Rosemary Clooney 1928, Nigel Davenport 1928, Barbara Barrie 1931, Joan Collins 1933, Seabiscuit 1933, Charles Kimbrough 1936, Anatoly Karpov 1951, Marvelous Marvin Hagler 1952, Buck Showalter 1956, Drew Carey 1958, Shelley West 1958, Mitch Album 1958, Ricky Gutierrez 1970, Jewel 1974, Ken Jennings 1974

1430 – Joan of Arc was captured by the Burgundians (and later sold to the English)
1533 – Henry VIII's marriage to Catherine of Aragon was declared null and void
1701 – Captain Kidd was hanged in London for murder and piracy
1788 – South Carolina became the eighth state when it voted to ratify the Constitution
1827 – The first nursery school in the United States was established in New York City
1846 – Mexico declared war on the United States
1876 – Boston's Joe Bordon pitched the first no-hitter in professional baseball history
1901 – Italy's King Humbert's assassin, Gaetano Bresci, committed suicide while awaiting execution in prison
1934 – Bonnie and Clyde were ambushed and killed by Texas Rangers
1937 – John D. Rockefeller died
1945 – Nazi Gestapo leader Heinrich Himmler committed suicide in an Allies prison
1949 – The Republic of West Germany was established
1994 – The final episode of *Star Trek: The Next Generation* aired, after 7 seasons
1999 – Owen Hart, also known as the Blue Blazer, fell 90 feet to his death during a WWF wrestling match while being lowered into the ring in Kansas City

May 24: Nicolaus Copernicus 1473, Gabriel Fahrenheit 1686, Queen Victoria 1819, H.B. Reese 1879, Timothy Brown 1937, Tommy Chong 1938, Bob Dylan 1941, Gary Burghoff 1943, Patti LaBelle 1944, Priscilla Presley 1945, Alfred Molina 1953, Rosanne Cash 1955, Kristin Scott Thomas 1960, Gene Anthony Ray 1963, Joe Dumars 1963, Ricky Craven 1966, Bartolo Colon 1973, Brad Penny 1978, Tracey McGrady 1979, Billy Gilman 1988

1738 – The Methodist Church was established
1830 – *Mary Had a Little Lamb* was published by Sarah Hale
1844 – Samuel F. B. Morse formally opened America's first telegraph line
1878 – America's first bicycle race was held in Boston

1881 – About 200 people died when the Canadian ferry *Princess Victoria* sank near London, Ontario

1883 – After 14 years of construction the Brooklyn Bridge was opened to traffic

1911 – The New York Public Library opened

1935 – The Cincinnati Reds played the Philadelphia Phillies in the first Major League Baseball game at night, with the switch to turn on the lights thrown by President Franklin Roosevelt

2001 – Temba Tsheri of Nepal became the youngest person to climb Mount Everest at the age of fifteen

May 25: Ralph Waldo Emerson 1803, Bill Bojangles Robinson 1878, Martin Dihigo 1906, Claude Akins 1918, Beverly Sills 1929, Tom T. Hall 1936, Dixie Carter 1939, Ian McKellen 1939, Leslie Uggams 1943, Frank Oz 1944, Karen Valentine 1947, Connie Sellecca 1955, Mike Myers 1963, Anne Heche 1969, Jamie Kennedy 1970, Lindsay Greenbush 1970, Sidney Greenbush 1970, Molly Sims 1973, Lauryn Hills 1975, Miguel Tejada 1976, Brian Urlacher 1978, Shawne Merriman 1984

1787 – The Constitutional Convention opened in Philadelphia with George Washington presiding

1927 – The Ford Motor Company announced that the Model A would replace the Model T

1935 – Babe Ruth hit his final home run, his 714th, setting a record that would hold for 39 years

1961 – John F. Kennedy declared that the United States would put a man on the moon before the end of the decade

1977 – The first *Star Wars* movie, now known as *Episode IV: A New Hope*, was released

1983 – *Star Wars Episode VI: Return of the Jedi* was released

1985 – Bangladesh was hit with a hurricane and tidal wave that killed more than 11,000 people

1992 – Jay Leno debuted as the new permanent host of NBC's Tonight Show

May 26: Pope Clement VII 1478, Al Jolson 1886, John Wayne 1907, Robert Morley 1908, Peter Cushing 1913, Jay Silverheels 1919, Peggy Lee 1920, James Arness 1923, Miles Davis 1926, Jack Kevorkian 1928, Brent Musburger 1939, Stevie Nicks 1948, Hank Williams Jr. 1949, Phillip Michael Thomas 1949, Sally Ride 1951, Kevin Kennedy 1954, Rob Murphy 1960, Genie Francis 1962, Bobcat Goldthwait 1962, Lenny Kravitz 1964, Helena Bonham-Carter 1966, Zola Budd 1966, Travis Lee 1975

1647 – Alse Young became the first person executed for being a witch in the American colonies when she is hanged in Hartford, Connecticut
1864 – The territory of Montana was established
1869 – Boston University was chartered
1896 – The last czar of Russia, Nicholas II, was crowned
1908 – In Persia, the first oil strike was made in the Middle East
1937 – San Francisco's Golden Gate Bridge opened
1969 – The *Apollo 10* astronauts returned to Earth after a successful eight-day dress rehearsal for the first manned moon landing
2005 – Actor Eddie Albert died at the age of 99

May 27: Cornelius Vanderbilt 1794, Julia Ward Howe 1819, Wild Bill Hickock 1837, Rachel Carson 1907, Vincent Price 1911, Hubert Humphrey 1911, Hermon Wouk 1915, Christopher Lee 1922, Henry Kissenger 1923, Harlan Ellison 1934, Lee Merriweather 1935, Lou Gossett Jr. 1936, Don Williams 1939, Bruce Weitz 1943, Christopher Dodd 1944, Richard Schiff 1955, Peri Gilpin 1961, Todd Bridges 1965, Jeff Bagwell 1968, Frank Thomas 1968, Andre 3000 1975

1703 – The Russian city of Saint Petersburg was founded
1896 – A tornado struck St. Louis killing 255 people
1927 – The Ford Motor Company stopped making the Model T and began retooling the factory in order to start making the Model A
1933 – The Walt Disney film *The Three Little Pigs* was released
1937 – The Golden Gate Bridge opened to pedestrian traffic
1939 – Batman made his debut in DC Comics *Detective Comics* issue number 27
1941 – The German battleship *Bismarck* was sunk by British naval and air forces
1969 – Construction of Walt Disney World began in Florida
1995 – Actor Christopher Reeve was paralyzed after being thrown from his horse

May 28: George I of England 1660, Dr. Joseph Ignace Guillotine 1738, Jim Thorpe 1888, Ian Fleming 1908, Beth Howland 1941, Gladys Knight 1944, Rudolph Giuliani 1944, John Fogerty 1945, Patch Adams 1945, Larry Gatlin 1948, Christa Miller 1964, Kylie Minogue 1968, Ekaterina Gordeeva 1971, Daniel Cabrera 1981, Jhonny Peralta 1982, Jaslene Gonzalez 1986

1774 – The First Continental Congress convened in Virginia
1900 – A solar eclipse was seen over much of the Northern Hemisphere
1902 – Thomas Edison announced his latest invention, the alkaline battery
1928 – The Chrysler Corporation merged with Dodge Brothers, Inc.

1934 – The Dionne Quintuplets were born, the first quints to survive infancy

1940 – Belgium surrendered to Germany during World War II

1957 – Club owners voted to allow the Brooklyn Dodgers to move to Los Angeles and the New York Giants to move to San Francisco

1994 – Wilderness Lodge Resort opened at Walt Disney World

1996 – President Bill Clinton's former business partners in the Whitewater land deal were convicted of fraud

1998 – Actor Phil Hartman was shot to death at his home by his wife, Brynn, who then killed herself

1999 – In Milan, Italy, Leonardo de Vinci's "The Last Supper" was put back on display after 22 years of restoration work

2006 – Barry Bonds hit his 715th career home run to pass Babe Ruth for second all-time

May 29: Charles II of England 1630, Patrick Henry 1736, Bob Hope 1903, T.H. White 1906, John F. Kennedy 1917, Fay Vincent 1938, Al Unser Sr. 1939, Stacy Keach Sr. 1941, Anthony Geary 1947, Danny Elfman 1953, John Hinckley Jr. 1955, LaToya Jackson 1956, Annette Bening 1958, Wayne Duvall 1958, Melissa Etheridge 1961, Eric Davis 1962, Lisa Whelchel 1963, Melanie Brown 1975, Jerry Hairston Jr. 1976, Brian Kendrick 1979, Carmelo Anthony 1984, Danielle Riley Keough 1989

1790 – Rhode Island became the thirteenth state when it ratified the Constitution

1848 – Wisconsin became the 30th state

1849 – A patent for lifting vessels was granted to Abraham Lincoln

1911 – The Indianapolis 500 was run for the first time

1935 – Construction of the Hoover Dam was completed

1953 – Edmund Hillary and Sherpa Tenzing Norgay became first men to reach the top of Mount Everest

1973 – Tom Bradley was elected the first black mayor of Los Angeles

1978 – The price of a postage stamp rose from 13 cents to 15 cents

1988 – President Ronald Reagan began his first visit to the Soviet Union

1999 – The space shuttle Discovery completed the first docking with the International Space Station

2004 – The World War II Memorial in Washington, DC was dedicated

May 30: Mel Blanc 1908, Benny Goodman 1909, Clint Walker 1927, Aleksei Leonov 1934, Michael J. Pollard 1939, Gale Sayers 1943, Michael Piller 1948, Colm Meaney 1953, Ted McGinley 1958, Kevin Eastman 1962, Wynonna Judd 1964, Manny Ramirez 1972

1431 – Joan of Arc was burned at the stake at the age of 19 in Rouen, France

1536 – Henry VIII married Jane Seymour, his third wife (see portrait to right)

1539 – Hernando de Sota landed in Florida, near present day Tampa Bay, with 600 men in search of gold

1806 – Andrew Jackson killed Charles Dickinson in a duel, after the man had made disparaging remarks about Jackson's wife

1868 – Memorial Day was observed for the first time

1889 – The brassiere was invented

1896 – The first automobile accident occurred in New York City

1911 – Ray Harroun won the first Indianapolis Sweepstakes, later to be called the Indianapolis 500

1922 – The Lincoln Memorial was dedicated in Washington, DC

1935 – Babe Ruth played in his last baseball game, playing for the Boston Braves

1951 – Schroeder made his first appearance in a *Peanuts* comic strip

1975 – Bob Watson of the Houston Astros scored the one millionth run in Major League Baseball history

1998 – An earthquake hit Afghanistan, leaving over 5,000 people dead

2003 – Peter Jennings was sworn in as an American citizen

May 31: Walt Whitman 1819, Norman Vincent Peale 1898, Don Ameche 1908, Denholm Elliot 1922, Prince Ranier III 1923, Clint Eastwood 1930, Peter Yarrow 1938, Johnny Paycheck 1938, Joe Namath 1943, Sharon Gless 1943, Tom Berenger 1949, Gregory Harrison 1950, Chris Elliot 1960, Lea Thompson 1961, Corey Hart 1962, Brooke Shields 1965, Kenny Lofton 1967, Dave Roberts 1972, Chad Campbell 1974, Colin Farrell 1976, Jake Peavy 1981, David Hernadez 1983, Nate Robinson 1984

1854 – The Kansas-Nebraska Act passed by the United States Congress

1879 – New York's Madison Square Garden opened

1884 – Dr. John Harvey Kellogg patented the corn flake

1889 – In Johnstown, Pennsylvania, more the 2,200 people died when a dam broke, wiping out the town

1902 – The Boer War came to an end

1910 – The Republic of South Africa was established

1977 – The trans-Alaska oil pipeline was finished after three years of construction

1988 – President Ronald Reagan visited Moscow while on his first trip to the Soviet Union

1990 – The TV show *Seinfeld* debuted on NBC-TV

1997 – The Confederation Bridge opened, linking New Brunswick with Prince Edward Island

2000 – Hit American reality show *Survivor* premiered on CBS-TV

2008 – Manny Ramirez of the Boston Red Sox hit his 500th career home run

June 1: Brigham Young 1801, Andy Griffith 1926, Marilyn Monroe 1926, Edward Woodard 1930, Pat Boone 1934, Morgan Freeman 1937, Cleavon Little 1939, Rene Auberjonois 1940, Graham Russell 1950, John M. Jackson 1950, Diana Canova 1953, Lisa Hartman Black 1956, Paul Coffey 1961, Mark Curry 1964, Derek Lowe 1973, Heidi Klum 1973, Alanis Morissette 1974, Brad Wilkerson 1977, Santana Moss 1979, Carlos Zambrano 1981, Jake Silbermann 1983

193 AD – Roman Emperor Marcus Didius was murdered in his palace
1533 – Anne Boleyn, Henry VIII's new queen, was crowned
1792 – Kentucky became the 15th state
1796 – Tennessee became the 16th state
1861 – The first battle of the Civil War took place at Fairfax Court House, Pennsylvania
1938 – Superman, the world's first super hero, debuted in *Action Comics*
1938 – Baseball helmets were worn for the first time
1954 – In the *Peanuts* comic strip, Linus' blanket made its first appearance
1958 – Charles De Gaulle became Prime Minister of France
1968 – Helen Keller died
1980 – CNN made its debut as the first all-news network
1989 – Typhoon Lagoon opened at Walt Disney World
1990 – Disney's Dolphin resort hotel opened at Walt Disney World
2007 – Smoking was banned in the United Kingdom in all public places
2008 – A fire on the backlot of Universal Studios Hollywood destroyed a number of famous movie icons, including the clock tower from the *Back to the Future* movies, Courthouse Square, and the King Kong exhibit

June 2: Martha Washington 1731, Nellie Taft 1861, Johnny Weissmuller 1904, Pete Conrad 1930, Barry Levinson 1933, Sally Kellerman 1937,

Stacy Keach 1941, Charles Haid 1943, Jerry Mathers 1948, Dana Carvey 1955, Kyle Petty 1960, Wayne Brady 1972, Neifi Perez 1973, Nikki Cox 1978, Justin Long 1978, Brooke White 1983

455 – The Vandals entered Rome and began two weeks of plundering
1835 – P.T. Barnum began his first circus tour of the United States
1851 – Maine became the first state to pass a law prohibiting alcohol
1883 - The first baseball game under electric lights was played in Fort Wayne, Indiana
1886 – Grover Cleveland became the first President to get married while in office
1896 - Guglielmo Marconi's radio was patented
1935 – Babe Ruth announced he was retiring from baseball
1941 – Lou Gehrig died
1953 – Elizabeth II was crowned Queen of Great Britain
1966 - *Surveyor 1*, the U.S. space probe, landed on the moon and started sending photographs back to Earth of the moon's surface
1997 - Timothy McVeigh was found guilty of the bombing of a federal building in Oklahoma City in which 168 people were killed
2004 – Ken Jennings began his 74-game winning streak on *Jeopardy*

June 3: Jefferson Davis 1808, Frederick VIII of Denmark 1843, Garret Hobart 1844, George V of England 1865, Maurice Evans 1901, Josephine Baker 1906, Paulette Goddard 1910, Ellen Corby 1911, Colleen Dewhurst 1924, Tony Curtis 1925, Allen Ginsburg 1926, Chuck Barris 1929, Larry McMurtry 1936, Edward Winter 1937, Loretta Long (Susan of Sesame Street) 1940, John Dykstra 1947, Melissa Mathison 1950, Suzi Quatro 1950, Scott Valentine 1958, Carl Everett 1971, Jose Molina 1975, Jamie McMurray 1976, Travis Hafner 1977

1098 – Christian Crusaders of the First Crusade seized Antioch, Turkey after an eight month siege
1539 – Hernando De Soto claimed Florida for Spain
1800 – John Adams moved to Washington, DC, becoming the first President to live there
1851 – The New York Knickerbockers became the first baseball team to wear uniforms
1888 – The poem "Casey at the Bat" by Ernest Lawrence Thayer was first published
1932 – Lou Gehrig set a Major League Baseball record when he hit 4 consecutive home runs
1937 – The Duke of Windsor, who had abdicated the British throne, married Wallis Warfield Simpson

1965 – Ed White became the first American to perform a space walk

1969 – The final episode of the original *Star Trek* aired on NBC-TV

2003 – Sammy Sosa broke a bat while batting in a baseball game, revealing that he was using a corked bat, which later resulted in a suspension

June 4: George III of England 1738, Robert Merrill 1919, Dennis Weaver 1924, Dr. Ruth Westheimer 1928, John Drew Barrymore 1932, John McNamara 1932, Bruce Dern 1936, Freddy Fender 1937, Joyce Meyer 1943, Michelle Phillips 1944, Parker Stevenson 1952, El De Barge 1961, Scott Wolf 1968, Rachel Griffiths 1968, Noah Wyle 1971, Angelina Jolie 1975, JC Romero 1976

1783 – The Montgolfier brothers publicly demonstrated their hot air balloon

1911 – Gold was discovered in Alaska's Indian Creek

1919 – The United States Senate passed the Women's Suffrage bill

1939 – The first shopping cart was introduced by Sylvan Goldman in Oklahoma City; it was actually a folding chair mounted on wheels

1942 – The Battle of Midway began during World War II

1970 – The island nation of Tonga gained its independence from Great Britain

1974 – The Cleveland Indians promoted ten-cent beer night, but ended up forfeiting the game after drunken fans became violent and the mayhem spread onto the field

2003 – Martha Stewart was indicted on federal charges of using illegal privileged information and then obstructing an investigation

June 5: Thomas Chippendale 1718, Pat Garrett 1850, Jack Chesbro 1874, Pancho Villa 1878, Richard Scarry 1919, Bill Hayes 1926, Bill Moyers 1934, Robert Kraft 1941, Gail Davies 1948, Suze Orman 1951, Kenny G 1956, Brian McKnight 1969, Mark Wahlberg 1971, Chad Allen 1974, Kevin Faulk 1976

1752 – Benjamin Franklin flew a kite in a thunderstorm, in order to demonstrate that lightning was a form of electricity

1837 – The city of Houston, Texas was incorporated

1851 – *Uncle Tom's Cabin* by Harriet Beecher Stowe was first published

1900 – Author Stephen Crane died at the age of 28

1956 – Elvis Presley made the first public performance of his new single, *Hound Dog*

1968 – Robert Kennedy, who was running for president, was fatally shot by Sirhan Sirhan in Los Angeles

1977 – The *Apple II*, the first home computer for practical use, was introduced to the public
2004 – Former President Ronald Reagan died

June 6: John III of Portugal 1502, Joseph I of Portugal 1714, Nathan Hale 1755, David Abercrombie 1867, Robert Falcon Scott 1868, Bill Dickey 1907, V.C. Andrews 1923, Gary U.S. Bonds 1939, Neal Adams 1941, David Dukes 1945, Robert Englund 1949, Harvey Firestein 1954, Sandra Bernhard 1955, Bjorn Borg 1956, Josie Lawrence 1959, Jason Isaacs 1963, Cam Neely 1965, Paul Giamatti 1967, Staci Keanan 1975

1833 – Andrew Jackson became the first U.S. president to ride in a train
1844 – The first YMCA opened in London, England
1925 – The Chrysler Corporation was founded
1930 – Frozen foods were sold for the first time
1933 – In Camden, New Jersey, the first drive-in movie theater opened
1936 – The first helicopter was tested
1944 – The D-Day invasion of Europe began in Normandy, France during World War II
1968 – Senator Robert Kennedy died after being shot by Sirhan Sirhan the day before
1971 – The final episode of *The Ed Sullivan Show* aired
1978 – The ABC-TV news show *20/20* first aired

June 7: Alois Hitler 1837, Paul Gauguin 1848, Jessica Tandy 1909, Dean Martin 1917, Rocky Graziano 1922, Tom Jones 1940, Jenny Jones 1946, Thurman Munson 1947, Liam Neeson 1952, Prince 1958, Mick Foley 1965, Andrei Kovalenko 1975, Karl Urban 1972, Allen Iverson 1975, Anna Kournikova 1981

1099 – The Siege of Jerusalem began during the First Crusade
1498 – Christopher Columbus left on his third trip to the New World
1654 – Louis XIV was crowned King of France
1775 – The United Colonies changed their name to the United States of America
1914 – The first vessel passed through the Panama Canal
1932 – Over 7,000 war veterans marched on Washington, DC demanding their bonuses
1939 – King George VI of England became the first British monarch to visit the United States
1942 – The Battle of Midway ended during World War II
1965 – Sony unveiled its first videotape recorder, which sold for $995

1966 – Ronald Reagan, a former actor and later President, became governor of California
1982 – Graceland, the former home of Elvis Presley, was opened to the public
2000 – A court order was issued ordering the break-up of the Microsoft Corporation

June 8: Giovanni Cassini 1625, Ida McKinley 1847, Frank Lloyd Wright 1867, Robert Preston 1918, Barbara Pierce Bush 1925, Jerry Stiller 1929, Joan Rivers 1930, James Darren 1936, Nancy Sinatra 1940, Boz Scaggs 1944, Alex Van Halen 1950, Kathy Baker 1950, Bonnie Tyler 1953, Scott Adams 1957, Keenan Ivory Wayans 1958, Robert Pilatus 1965, Julianna Margulies 1966, Lindsay Davenport 1976, Kanye West 1977

362 – The prophet Mohammed died
452 – Italy was invaded by Attila the Hun
1789 – The Bill of Rights was introduced in the U.S. House of Representatives by James Madison
1845 – Former President Andrew Jackson died at the age of 78
1861 – Tennessee seceded from the Union
1866 – The Canadian Parliament met for the first time in Ottawa
1912 – Universal Pictures was formed
1948 – *Texaco Star Theater* debuted on television, starring Milton Berle
1949 – George Orwell's *1984* was published
1968 – James Earl Ray was captured in a London airport, having been suspected of assassinating Martin Luther King, Jr.
1986 – The Boston Celtics won their sixteenth NBA championship
1995 – U.S. Air Force pilot Captain Scott O'Grady was rescued by U.S. Marines having survived alone in Bosnia after his F-16 fighter was shot down on June 2

June 9: Peter the Great 1672, Johann Gottfried Galle 1812, Cole Porter 1891, Les Paul 1915, Robert McNamara 1916, Jackie Mason 1931, Bill Virdon 1931, Donald Duck 1934, Dick Vitale 1939, Gary Thorne 1948, Dave Parker 1951, George Perez 1954, Patricia Cornwell 1956, Michael J. Fox 1961, Aaron Sorkin 1961, Johnny Depp 1963, Gloria Reuben 1964, Tedy Bruschi 1973, Natalie Portman 1981

69 AD – Roman Emperor Nero committed suicide
1534 – Jacques Cartier became the first person to sail into what he named the St. Lawrence River
1856 – 500 Mormons left Iowa City, Iowa bound for Salt Lake City, Utah carrying all their possessions in two-wheeled carts

1863 – During the American Civil War, the Battle of Brandy Station was fought in Virginia
1934 – Donald Duck made his debut in a movie short called *The Wise Little Hen*
1940 – Norway surrendered to Nazi Germany during World War II
1946 – Mel Ott became the first baseball manager to be ejected from both games of a double header
1973 – Secretariat won the Triple Crown of horse racing
1980 – Richard Pryor was severely burned
1985 – The Los Angeles Lakers won the NBA Championship by defeating the Boston Celtics

June 10: Hattie McDaniel 1889, Barry Morse 1918, Prince Philip of Great Britain 1921, Judy Garland 1922, Earl Hamner 1923, Maurice Sendak 1928, F. Lee Bailey 1933, Mickey Jones 1941, Ken Singleton 1947, Dan Fouts 1951, John Edwards 1953, Andrew Stevens 1955, Elisabeth Shue 1963, Jeanne Tripplehorn 1963, Elizabeth Hurley 1965, Doug McKeon 1966, Faith Evans 1973, Pokey Reese 1973, Freddy Garcia 1976, Shane West 1978, Tara Lipinsky 1982, Leelee Sobieski 1983

1854 – The first class of U.S. Naval Academy students graduated
1940 – Italy declared war on France and Great Britain
1940 – Canada declared war on Italy
1943 – Laszlo Biro patented his ballpoint pen
1944 – Joe Nuxall became the youngest person to play in the Major Leagues, at the age of 15 years, 10 months and 11 days
1947 – The first Saab automobile was manufactured
1948 – Chuck Yeager became the first person to fly faster than the speed of sound
1977 – James Earl Ray escaped from prison with 6 others
1983 – Johnny Bench announced his plans to retire at the end of the baseball season
1988 – Western author Louis L'Amour died at age 80

June 11: Joseph Warren 1741, Jacques Cousteau 1910, Vince Lombardi 1913, Nelson Mandela 1918, Gene Wilder 1935, Chad Everett 1936, Roscoe Orman (Gordon from Sesame Street) 1944, Adrienne Barbeau 1945, Frank Beard 1949, Graham Russell 1950, Bonnie Pointer 1951, Peter Bergman 1953, Joe Montana 1956, Hugh Laurie 1959, Joshua Jackson 1978, Shia LaBeouf 1986

1509 – Henry VIII married his first of six wives, Catherine of Aragon
1770 – Captain James Cook ran aground on the Great Barrier Reef

1776 – The Continental Congress appointed a committee to draft the Declaration of Independence, including Thomas Jefferson, John Adams, Ben Franklin, Roger Sherman and Robert Livingston
1935 – The first public demonstration of FM radio occurred
1942 – The United States and the Soviet Union signed a lend lease agreement
1977 – Seattle Slew won horse racing's Triple Crown
1981 – The first Major League Baseball Players' strike began
1982 – Steven Spielberg's movie *E.T.* opened
1993 – Steven Spielberg's movie *Jurassic Park* opened
2001 – Timothy McVeigh was executed by the U.S. federal government for his role in the bombing of a federal building in Oklahoma City
2004 – The funeral for former President Ronald Reagan was held
2007 – The Finding Nemo Submarine Voyage ride opened at Disneyland

June 12: David Rockefeller 1915, Irwin Allen 1916, George H. W. Bush 1924, Richard M. Sherman 1928, Anne Frank 1929, Jim Nabors 1930, Marv Albert 1941, Brad Delp 1951, Timothy Busfield 1957, Jenilee Harrison 1959, Ryan Klesko 1971, Hideki Matsui 1974, Antawn Jamison 1976, Dallas Clark 1979, Jason David 1982, Chris Young 1985

1429 – Joan of Arc led the French army in the capture of the English city of Jargeau
1667 – The first human blood transfusion was administered by Dr. Jean Baptiste
1812 – Napoleon's invasion of Russia began
1839 – Abner Doubleday created the game of baseball, according to legend
1939 – The Baseball Hall of Fame opened in Cooperstown, New York
1942 – Anne Frank received a diary for her thirteenth birthday
1963 – The epic movie *Cleopatra*, starring Elizabeth Taylor, opened
1964 – In South Africa, Nelson Mandela was sentenced to life in prison
1971 – President Nixon's daughter Patricia was married in the White House Rose Garden
1978 – David Berkowitz, also known as the Son of Sam, was sentenced to 365 years in prison for six murders
1981 – Major League Baseball players began a 49-day strike over the issue of free agency
1987 – President Ronald Reagan challenged Russian President Mikhail Gorbachev to tear down the Berlin Wall
1991 – The Chicago Bulls won their first NBA championship
1994 – Nicole Brown Simpson and Ronald Goldman were murdered outside her home in Los Angeles

1997 – Interleague play began in Major League Baseball
1998 – The newly designed fifty-dollar bill was unveiled in the United States
2007 – Don Herbert, known to millions as Mr. Wizard, died at the age of 89

June 13: Charles the Bald 823, King Charles the Fat of France 839, Winfield Scott 1786, William Butler Yeats 1865, Basil Rathbone 1892, Ralph Edwards 1913, Mary Wickes 1916, Paul Lynde 1926, Christo 1935, Malcolm McDowell 1943, Richard Thomas 1951, Tim Allen 1953, Ally Sheedy 1962, Sam Adams 1973, Chris Evans 1981, Ashley Olsen 1986, Mary-Kate Olsen 1986

1777 – Marquis de Lafayette arrived in the United States
1901 – A collision sunk the Staten Island Ferry
1912 – Captain Albert Berry made the first successful parachute jump from an airplane
1920 – It was ruled by the United States Postal Service that children may not be sent in the mail
1922 – Charlie Osborn got the hiccups, which lasted for 69 years
1943 – Some German spies came ashore in Long Island, New York
1966 – The Supreme Court ruled in *Miranda v. Arizona* that the police must inform suspects of their rights before questioning them
1967 – Thurgood Marshall was nominated by President Lyndon Johnson to be the first black member of the Supreme Court
1977 – James Earl Ray was recaptured, after escaping from prison 3 days earlier
1983 – The U.S. spacecraft Pioneer 10 became the first spacecraft to leave the Solar System
1989 – The Detroit Pistons won their first NBA championship
1991 – In the first round of the U.S. Open golf tournament, a spectator was killed when lightning struck
1994 – A jury in Anchorage, Alaska, found Exxon Corp. and Captain Joseph Hazelwood to be reckless in the *Exxon Valdez* oil spill
1994 – O.J. Simpson was questioned by Los Angeles police concerning the deaths of his ex-wife and her friend
2005 – A jury acquitted singer Michael Jackson of molesting a 13-year-old boy

June 14: Harriet Beecher Stowe 1811, Alois Alzheimer 1864, Burl Ives 1909, Dorothy McGuire 1914, Marla Gibbs 1931, Donald Trump 1946, Harry Turtledove 1949, Eddie Mekka 1952, Eric Heiden 1958, Boy George 1961, Sam Perkins 1961, Yasmine Bleeth 1968, Steffi Graff 1969, Traylor Howard 1971, Chris McAlister 1977

1775 – The United States Army was founded by the Continental Congress
1777 – The stars and stripes were officially adopted as the flag of the United States
1900 – Hawaii became a U.S. territory
1902 – In the college baseball championship, Yale beats Princeton, 5-4
1907 – Women in Norway gained the right to vote
1922 – President Warren G. Harding became the first President of the United States to be heard on the radio
1938 – *Action Comics* issued the first Superman comic
1940 – The Nazis opened their concentration camp at Auschwitz in German-occupied Poland
1940 – German troops entered Paris
1952 – The *Nautilus* was dedicated as the first nuclear powered submarine
1985 – The 17-day hijacking of TWA flight 847 by Muslim extremists began
1989 – Former United States President Ronald Reagan received an honorary knighthood from Britain's Queen Elizabeth II
1989 – Actress Zsa Zsa Gabor was arrested in Beverly Hills for slapping a motorcycle policeman

June 15: Edward the Black Prince 1330, William Butler Ogden 1805, Yuri Andropov 1914, Johnny Most 1923, Mario Cuomo 1932, Waylon Jennings 1937, Billy Williams 1938, Brian Jacques 1939, Jim Varney 1949, Dusty Baker 1949, Russell Hitchcock 1949, Steve Walsh 1951, Jim Belushi 1954, Julie Hagerty 1955, Brett Butler (MLB) 1957, Wade Boggs 1958, Eileen Davidson 1959, Helen Hunt 1963, Courtney Cox 1964, Ice Cube 1969, Leah Remini 1970, Ramiro Mendoza 1972, Andy Pettitte 1972, Justin Leonard 1972, Neil Patrick Harris 1973

1215 – King John of England put his seal on the Magna Carta (see image to left)
1775 – George Washington was appointed head of the Continental Army
1836 – Arkansas became the 25th state

1846 – The Oregon Treaty established the 39th parallel as the border between the United States and Canada in the western parts of the countries
1864 – Arlington National Cemetery was established
1924 – Native Americans were proclaimed United States citizens
1934 – The Great Smoky Mountains National Park was established
1995 – During the O.J. Simpson murder trail, Simpson was asked to try on a pair of gloves that did not appear to fit
2002 – An asteroid missed the Earth by 75,000 miles, or one-third the distance from the Earth to the Moon

June 16: Adam Smith 1723, Geronimo 1829, Stan Laurel 1890, Jack Albertson 1910, Joan Van Ark 1943, Roberto Duran 1951, Gino Vannelli 1952, Laurie Metcalf 1955, Wally Joyner 1962, Phil Mickelson 1970, Tupac Shakur 1971, Kerry Wood 1977, Olivia Hack 1983

1487 – The War of the Roses ended with the Battle of Stoke Field
1567 – Mary, Queen of Scots, was imprisoned in Lochleven Castle in Scotland
1858 – In a speech in Springfield, Illinois, Abraham Lincoln uttered the words: "A house divided against itself cannot stand"
1903 – Ford Motor Company was incorporated
1910 – The first Fathers Day was celebrated
1963 – Valentina Terishkova, a 26-year old Russian Cosmonaut, became the first woman to go to space
1977 – Leonid Brezhnev was named the first Soviet President of the USSR
1978 – The movie *Grease* premiered
1992 – President George H. W. Bush welcomed Russian President Boris Yeltsin to a meeting in Washington, DC

June 17: Edward I (Edward Longshanks) of England 1239, Charles XII of Sweden 1682, John Wesley 1703, William Hooper 1742, M.C. Escher 1898, Ralph Bellamy 1904, Newt Gingrich 1943, Barry Manilow 1946, Dave Concepcion 1948, Joe Piscapo 1951, Thomas Haden Church 1960, Greg Kinnear 1964, Dan Jansen 1965, Kami Cotler 1965, Venus Williams 1980, David Pauley 1983

1775 – The British took Bunker Hill outside Boston
1856 – The Republican Party opened its first national convention in Philadelphia
1861 – President Abraham Lincoln witnessed Dr. Thaddeus Lowe demonstrate the use of a hot-air balloon

1885 – The Statue of Liberty arrived in New York City aboard the French ship *Isere*
1928 – Amelia Earhart began the flight that made her the first woman to successfully fly across the Atlantic Ocean
1944 – The Republic of Iceland was established
1960 – Ted Williams of the Boston Red Sox became the fourth Major League Baseball player to hit 500 home runs
1972 – Five men were arrested for burglarizing the Democratic Party Headquarters in the Watergate complex in Washington, DC
1994 – O.J. Simpson drove his Ford Bronco across Los Angeles with police in pursuit and millions of people watching live on television

June 18: William Henry Seward 1839, Dick Foran 1910, E.G. Marshall 1910, John D. Rockefeller IV 1937, Lou Brock 1939, Paul McCartney 1942, Roger Ebert 1942, Carol Kane 1952, Isabella Rossellini 1952, Bruce Smith 1963, Kurt Browning 1966, Sandy Alomar Jr. 1966, Blake Shelton 1976

1429 – Joan of Arc led the French army in a victory over the British in the Battle of Patay, turning the tide of the Hundred Years War
1778 – Britain evacuated Philadelphia during the Revolutionary War
1812 – The War of 1812 began when the United States declared war on England
1873 – Susan B. Anthony was fined $100 for attempting to vote for president
1953 – Seventeen major league baseball records were tied or broken in a game between the Boston Red Sox and the Detroit Tigers
1953 – The monarchy of Egypt was abolished with the establishment of the Republic of Egypt
1975 – Fred Lynn of the Boston Red Sox hit three home runs, a triple and a single in a game against the Detroit Tigers
1983 – Sally Ride became the first American woman in space
1999 – Walt Disney's *Tarzan* opened

June 19: James I of England 1566, Blaise Pascal 1623, Wallis Simpson 1896, Moe Howard 1897, Guy Lombardo 1902, Lou Gehrig 1903, Julius Schwartz 1915, Gena Rowlands 1930, Salman Rushdie 1947, Phylicia Rashad 1948, Ann Wilson 1950, Mark Gruenwald 1953, Kathleen Turner 1954, Paula Abdul 1962, Mia Sara 1967, Bumper Robinson 1974, Doug Mienkiewicz 1974, Dirk Nowitzki 1978, *Garfield* 1978

240 BC – Eratosthenes estimated the circumference of the Earth using two sticks

1778 – U.S. General George Washington's troops finally left Valley Forge after a winter of training
1846 – The first baseball game to be played under modern rules was played in Hoboken, New Jersey
1862 – President Abraham Lincoln outlined his Emancipation Proclamation, which outlawed slavery in United States territories
1864 – The *USS Kearsarge* sank the *CSS Alabama* off Cherbourg, France
1910 – The first Father's Day celebration was held in Spokane, Washington
1912 – The eight-hour work day was established in the United States
1934 – The U.S. Congress established the FCC, Federal Communications Commission
1939 – Lou Gehrig was diagnosed with ALS on his 36th birthday
1942 – British Prime Minister Winston Churchill arrived in Washington, DC
1949 – The first NASCAR race was held
1953 – Julius and Ethel Rosenberg were executed at Sing Sing Prison in Ossining, New York after they had been convicted of conspiring to pass U.S. atomic secrets to the Soviet Union
1961 – Kuwait regained independence from Great Britain
1978 – The comic strip *Garfield* was first published
1986 – University of Maryland basketball star Len Bias died of a cocaine-induced seizure
1989 – The movie *Batman* premiered
1989 – Splash Mountain opened at Disneyland
1999 – Stephen King nearly died when he was struck from behind by a mini-van while walking along a country road in Maine

June 20: Lillian Hellman 1905, Errol Flynn 1909, Chet Atkins 1924, Audie Murphy 1924, Bonnie Bartlett 1929, Martin Landau 1931, Olympia Dukakis 1931, Danny Aiello 1933, John Mahoney 1940, Brian Wilson 1942, Anne Murray 1945, Bob Vila 1946, Dave Thomas (actor) 1949, Lionel Ritchie 1949, John Goodman 1952, Michael Landon Jr. 1964, Nicole Kidman 1967, Josh Lucas 1971, Paul Bako 1972, Carlos Lee 1976, Charles Howell III 1979

1214 – The University of Oxford in Oxford, England received its charter
1782 – The Great Seal of the United States was adopted by Congress
1837 – Queen Victoria ascended to the throne, following the death of her uncle, King William IV
1863 – West Virginia became the 35th state
1893 – Lizzie Borden was found not guilty of the ax murders of her parents by a jury in New Bedford, Massachusetts
1947 – Bugsy Siegel was murdered in Hollywood, California by the mob

1948 – *The Ed Sullivan Show* debuted on CBS-TV
1976 – Walt Disney World's River Country water park opened
1977 – The Trans-Alaska Pipeline began operation
1994 – O.J. Simpson pled not guilty to the killings of his ex-wife and her friend
2001 – Andrea Yates was arrested in Texas for drowning her five children in the bathtub

June 21: Pope Leo IX 1002, Daniel D. Tompkins 1774, Al Hirschfeld 1903, Jane Russell 1921, Maureen Stapleton 1925, Bernie Kopell 1933, Mariette Hartley 1940, Michael Gross 1947, Merideth Baxter 1947, Robert Pastorelli 1954, Kathy Mattea 1959, Doug Savant 1964, Juliette Lewis 1973, Chris Pratt 1979, Prince William of Wales 1982

1749 – Halifax, Nova Scotia was founded
1788 – The U.S. Constitution went into effect when New Hampshire became the 9th state to ratify it
1788 – New Hampshire became the 9th U.S. state
1939 – Lou Gehrig retired from baseball due to illness
1940 – Richard Nixon married Pat Ryan
1940 – During World War II, France surrendered to Germany
1981 – The movie *Raiders of the Lost Ark*, starring Harrison Ford, opened
1982 – A jury in Washington, DC found John Hinckley Jr. innocent by reason of insanity for the attempted assassination of President Ronald Reagan
1989 – The U.S. Supreme Court ruled that burning the American flag as a form of political protest was protected by the First Amendment
2003 – The fifth Harry Potter book, *Harry Potter and the Order of the Phoenix*, was released
2004 – *SpacePlaneOne* became the first privately funded spaceplane to achieve spaceflight
2006 – Pluto's newly discovered moons were officially named Nix and Hydra

June 22: George Vancouver 1757, Carl Hubbell 1903, John Dillinger 1903, Billy Wilder 1906, Paul Frees 1920, Ralph Waite 1928, Dianne Feinstein 1933, Kris Kristofferson 1936, Ed Bradley 1941, Michael Lerner 1941, Brit Hume 1943, David Lander 1947, Meryl Streep 1949, Lindsay Wagner 1949, Allen Osmond 1949, Graham Greene 1952, Cyndi Lauper 1953, Freddie Prinze 1954, Tim Russ 1956, Bruce Campbell 1958, Tracy Pollan 1960, Clyde Drexler 1962, Amy Brenneman 1964, Dan Brown 1964, Darrell Armstrong 1968, Kurt Warner 1971, Carson Daly 1973, Paul

Campbell 1979, Joey Cheek 1979, Ian Kinsler 1982, Lindsay Ridgeway 1985

1535 – John Fisher, the Bishop of Rochester, was beheaded by order of King Henry VIII
1611 – English explorer Henry Hudson, his son John and several other people were set adrift in present-day Hudson Bay by mutineers, never to be seen again
1633 – The Catholic Church forced Galileo to retract his statement that the Sun is the center of the Solar System, not the Earth
1772 – Slavery was outlawed in England
1911 – George V of England was crowned
1933 – Adolf Hitler banned all political parties except the Nazi Party
1941 – Germany invaded the Soviet Union
1945 – During World War II, the battle for Okinawa officially ended after 81 days
1969 – Judy Garland died at the age of 47 of an accidental overdose of prescription sleeping pills
1970 – The 26th Amendment was passed which lowered the voting age to 18
1973 – Skylab astronauts splashed down after a record 28 days in space
1978 – Pluto's moon, later named Charon, was discovered
1979 – *The Muppet Movie* was released
1981 – Mark David Chapman pled guilty to killing former Beetle John Lennon
1990 – Billy Joel became the first rock artist to perform at Yankee Stadium
2006 – Moose, the Jack Russell Terrier that played Eddie on *Frasier*, died at the age of 15 and a half

June 23: Johannes Gutenberg 1400, Edward VIII of Great Britain 1894, Bob Fosse 1927, June Carter Cash 1929, Wilma Rudolph 1940, Ted Shackleford 1946, Clarence Thomas 1948, Jim Metzler 1954, Randy Jackson 1956, Frances McDormand 1957, Colin Montgomerie 1963, Marty Klebba 1969, Selma Blair 1972, Brandon Stokley 1976, Matt Light 1978, LaDainian Tomlinson 1979

1532 – England's Henry VIII and France's Francois I signed a secret treaty against Holy Roman Emperor Charles V
1611 – Henry Hudson, his son, and several loyal crew members were set adrift in a small boat in the Atlantic Ocean by mutineers and never seen again
1683 – William Penn signed a friendship treaty with the Lenni Lenape Indians in Pennsylvania

1810 – John Jacob Astor formed the Pacific Fur Company
1860 – The U.S. Secret Service was created
1888 – Frederick Douglass became the first African-American nominated for President
1938 – Marineland, America's first aquarium, opened in Florida
1985 – A bomb aboard an Air India flights explodes in midair, killing all 329 people
1989 – The movie *Batman* was released nationwide
1990 – Moldavia declared its independence
1992 – John Gotti was sentenced to life in prison for racketeering
1993 – Lorena Bobbitt cut off her husband's penis
2006 – American television producer Aaron Spelling died at the age of 83

June 24: Ambrose Bierce 1842, Roy Oliver Disney 1893, Jack Dempsey 1895, Al Molinaro 1919, Mick Fleetwood 1942, Michelle Lee 1942, Georg Stanford Brown 1943, Peter Weller 1947, Joe Penny 1956, Danielle Spencer 1965, Sherry Stringfield 1967, Petra Nemcova 1979, Phil Hughes 1986

1314 – Scottish forces led by Robert the Bruce defeated Edward II of England at the Battle of Bannockburn in Scotland
1497 – Italian explorer John Cabot, sailing in the service of England, landed in North America on what is now Newfoundland
1509 – Henry VIII and Catherine of Aragon were crowned King and Queen of England
1664 – The colony of New Jersey was founded
1675 – King Philip's War began when Indians massacred colonists at Swansee, Plymouth colony
1812 – Napoleon invaded Russia
1692 – Kingston, Jamaica was founded
1794 – Bowdoin College was founded
1896 – Booker T. Washington became the first African American to receive an honorary master's degree from Howard University
1901 – Pablo Picasso's work was shown publicly for the first time in Paris
1916 – Mary Pickford became the first female film star to get a million dollar contract
1975 – 113 people were killed when an Eastern Airlines Boeing 727 crashed while attempting to land during a thunderstorm at New York's John F. Kennedy International Airport
1998 – Walt Disney World Resort admitted its 600-millionth guest

June 25: George Orwell 1903, June Lockhart 1925, Carly Simon 1945, Jimmy Walker 1947, Phyllis George 1949, George Michael 1963, Dikembe

Mutombo 1966, Aaron Sele 1970, Carlos Delgado 1972, Linda Cardellini 1975

1788 – Virginia became the 10th state
1844 – John Tyler married Julia Gardner, becoming the first president to marry while in office
1868 – Florida, Alabama, Louisiana, Georgia, North Carolina and South Carolina were readmitted to the Union
1870 – In Spain, Queen Isabella abdicated her throne in favor of Alfonso XII
1876 – Lt. Col. George Custer and the U.S. 7th Cavalry were wiped out by Sioux and Cheyenne Indians at Little Big Horn in Montana
1941 – Finland declared war on the Soviet Union
1947 – *The Diary of Anne Frank* was published
1950 – The Korean War began when North Korea invaded South Korea
1966 – *Dark Shadows* began airing on ABC-TV
1993 – Kim Campbell took office as Canada's first female prime minister
1997 – The Russian space station Mir was hit by an unmanned cargo vessel causing severe damage
1999 – After 35 years on the air, the NBC soap opera *Another World* aired for the last time

June 26: Abner Doubleday 1819, Pearl S. Buck 1892, Peter Lorre 1904, Col. Tom Parker 1909, Eleanor Parker 1922, Richard Bull 1924, Chris Isaak 1956, Greg LeMond 1961, Shannon Sharpe 1968, Mike Myers (MLB) 1969, Chris O'Donnell 1970, Sean Hayes 1970, Gretchen Wilson 1973, Derek Jeter 1974, Jason Kendall 1974, Chad Pennington 1976, Michael Vick 1980

363 – Roman Emperor Julian was killed while in retreat from the Sassanid Empire
1284 – According to legend, the Pied Piper lured 130 children from Hamelin away
1819 – A patent for the bicycle was granted
1870 – In the United States, Christmas became a federal holiday
1901 – The *Lusitania* sunk off the coast of Newfoundland, yet 350 people were rescued
1945 – The United Nations Charter was signed in San Francisco
1963 – U.S. President John F. Kennedy announced "Ich bin ein Berliner (I am a Berliner)" at the Berlin Wall
1976 – The CN Tower in Toronto, Canada opened, becoming the tallest free-standing structure in the world

2001 – Ray Bourque of the Colorado Avalanche announced his retirement just 17 days after winning his first Stanley Cup
2006 – The Republic of Montenegro joined the United Nations

June 27: Louis XII of France 1462, Charles IX of France 1550, Helen Keller 1880, Bob *Captain Kangaroo* Keeshan 1927, Ross Perot 1930, Rico Petrocelli 1943, Julia Duffy 1951, Lorrie Morgan 1959, Dan Jurgens 1959, Johnny Benson 1963, J.J. Abrams 1966, Jim Edmonds 1970, Tobey Maguire 1975, Drake Bell 1986, Matthew Lewis 1989, Madylin Sweeten 1991

1864 – During the American Civil War, the Battle of Kennesaw Mountain was fought
1940 – Robert Pershing Wadlow was measured by Dr. Cyril MacBryde and Dr. C. M. Charles, who recorded his height at 8 feet 11 inches, the tallest human ever
1942 – The FBI announced the capture of eight Nazi saboteurs who had been put ashore from a submarine on New York's Long Island
1955 – The state of Illinois enacted the first automobile seat belt legislation
1957 – More than 500 people were killed when Hurricane Audrey hit the coastal area of Louisiana and Texas
1966 – *Dark Shadows* debuted on ABC-TV
1967 – The world's first ATM opened in London
1979 – Muhammad Ali announced he was retiring from boxing
2007 – Gordon Brown took over as Prime Minister of the United Kingdom, after Tony Blair served in that role for more than 10 years
2008 – Bill Gates stepped down as the chairman of Microsoft

June 28: Pope Paul IV 1476, Henry VIII of England 1491, John Wesley 1703, Jean-Jacques Rousseau 1712, Pierre Laval 1883, Esther Forbes 1891, Richard Rogers 1902, Mel Brooks 1926, Pat Morita 1932, John Inman 1935, John Byner 1938, Leon Panetta 1938, Gilda Radner 1946, Kathy Bates 1948, Alice Krige 1955, John Elway 1960, Mark Grace 1964, Jessica Hecht 1965, John Cussack 1966, Mary Stuart Masterson 1966, Danielle Brisebois 1969, Seth Wescott 1976, Kellie Pickler 1986

1635 – The French colony of Guadeloupe was established in the Caribbean
1776 – Thomas Hinkey, one of George Washington's bodyguards, was hanged for plotting to kidnap Washington
1778 – Mary Hays McCauley, wife of an American artilleryman and better known as Molly Pitcher, carried water to the soldiers during the Battle of

Monmouth and, supposedly, took her husband's place at his gun after he was overcome with heat

1838 – The coronation of Queen Victoria of Great Britain was held

1894 – Labor Day became a national holiday in the United States

1902 – The United States Congress authorized the building of a canal across Panama

1914 – Archduke Francis Ferdinand and his wife were assassinated in what is now known as Sarajevo, Bosnia, launching World War I

1919 – The Treaty of Versailles was signed, ending World War I exactly five years after it began

1922 – The Irish Civil War began

1938 – A meteorite weighing over 500 tons crashed to Earth near Chicora, Pennsylvania

1976 – The first women entered the U.S. Air Force Academy

1988 – The Grand Floridian Resort opened at Walt Disney World

1997 – Evander Holyfield won the WBA heavyweight boxing title fight after his opponent, Mike Tyson, was disqualified for biting off part of Holyfield's ear

2000 – Six-year-old Elián González returned to Cuba from the United States with his father

2005 – Canada became the third country to legalize same-sex marriage

June 29: William Mayo 1861, Wilbert Robinson 1863, Harry Frazee 1881, Nelson Eddy 1901, Slim Pickens 1919, Harmon Killebrew 1936, Gary Busey 1944, Richard Lewis 1947, Fred Grandy 1948, Dan Dierdorf 1949, Rick Honeycutt 1954, Pedro Guerrero 1956, Sharon Lawrence 1961, Amanda Donohoe 1962, Kathleen Wilhoite 1964, Jeff Burton 1967, Samantha Smith 1972, Martin Truex 1980

1534 – Jacques Cartier became the first European to discover Prince Edward Island

1613 – The original Globe Theatre in London burned to the ground (see left)

1767 – The British Parliament approved the Townshend Revenue Acts, which imposed import duties on glass, lead, paint, paper and tea shipped to America

1776 – The Virginia Constitution was adopted and Patrick Henry was named governor
1897 – The Chicago Cubs scored 36 runs in a game against Louisville, setting a record for runs scored by a team in a single game
1956 – Marilyn Monroe and Arthur Miller were married
1957 – Buddy Holly recorded the song *Peggy Sue*
1978 – Bob Crane, star of the TV show *Hogan's Heroes*, was found bludgeoned to death
2000 – In Santa Rosa, California, the official groundbreaking ceremony took place for the Charles M. Schulz Museum
2002 – Vice President Dick Cheney served as Acting President for about two and a half hours while President Bush underwent a medical procedure
2007 – Apple Computer released the iPhone in the United States
2008 – Thomas Beatie, the world's first pregnant man, gave birth to a daughter

June 30: Charles VIII of France 1470, William Wheeler 1819, David Wayne 1916, Lena Horne 1917, Susan Hayward 1917, Harry Blackstone Jr. 1934, Nancy Dussault 1936, Terry Funk 1944, William Atherton 1947, David Alan Grier 1955, Sterling Marlin 1957, Tony Fernandez 1962, Mike Tyson 1966, Garret Anderson 1972, Chan-ho Park 1973, Travis Minor 1979, Fantasia Barrino 1984, Michael Phelps 1985

1882 – Charles Guiteau was hanged for the assassination of President James Garfield
1908 – An explosion in Siberia, which knocked down trees in a 40-mile radius and struck people unconscious some 40 miles away, was believed by some scientists to be caused by a falling fragment from a meteorite
1921 – The Radio Corporation of America, or RCA, was formed
1934 – Adolf Hitler purged the Nazi Party by destroying the SA and bringing to power the SS in the Night of the Long Knives
1936 – The book *Gone with the Wind*, by Margaret Mitchell, was published in New York City
1952 – *The Guiding Light* debuted on CBS-TV
1953 – The first Corvette rolled off the assembly lines for Chevrolet in Flint, Michigan
1962 – Los Angeles Dodger Sandy Koufax pitched his first no-hitter in a game with the New York Mets
1970 – The Cincinnati Reds moved to their new home at Riverfront Stadium
1971 – The Soviet space ship *Soyuz II* returned to Earth, where the 3 cosmonauts were found dead after all their oxygen was lost during re-entry

1985 – Thirty-nine American hostages were freed from a hijacked TWA jetliner in Beirut after being held for 17 days

1994 – The U.S. Figure Skating Association stripped Tonya Harding of the 1994 national championship and banned her from the organization for life for an attack on rival Nancy Kerrigan

1997 – *Harry Potter and the Philosopher's Stone* (retitled *Harry Potter and the Sorcerer's Stone* in the United States) was first published, the first in the Harry Potter series by J.K. Rowling

2005 – Spain legalized same-sex marriage

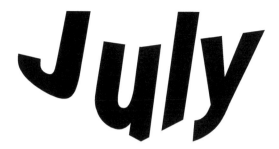

July 1: Christian II of Denmark 1481, Frederick II of Denmark 1534, Charles Laughton 1899, Estes Lauder 1908, Olivia DeHavilland 1916, Jamie Farr 1934, Jean Marsh 1934, Sydney Pollack 1934, Genevieve Bujold 1942, Debbie Harry 1945, Shirley Hemphill 1947, Dan Aykroyd 1952, Alan Ruck 1956, Carl Lewis 1961, Princess Diana of Wales 1961, Michelle Wright 1961, Pamela Anderson 1967, Missy Elliott 1971, Liv Tyler 1977, Jarome Iginla 1977

1543 – England and Scotland signed the peace of Greenwich
1798 – Napoleon Bonaparte conquered Alexandria, Egypt
1847 – The United States Post Office issued its first adhesive stamps
1863 – During the Civil War, the Battle of Gettysburg began
1867 – Canada gained its independence from Great Britain and John Macdonald was sworn in as Canada's first prime minister
1870 – The United States Department of Justice began operations
1873 – Prince Edward Island joined Canada
1874 – The first zoo in the United States opened in Philadelphia
1881 – The first international telephone call was made between St. Stephens, New Brunswick and Calais, Maine
1898 – During the Spanish-American War, Theodore Roosevelt and his Rough Riders charged up San Juan Hill in Cuba
1934 – The Federal Communications Commission replaced the Federal Radio Commission as the regulator of broadcasting in the United States
1941 – NBC debuted its first television broadcast
1941 – The first TV commercial was run, sponsored by Bulova Watch
1946 – The United States exploded a 20-ton atomic bomb near Bikini Atoll in the Pacific Ocean

1951 – Bob Feller set a new Major League Baseball record when he pitched his third no-hitter for the Cleveland Indians
1963 – The U.S. Post Office introduced the 5-digit zip code
1966 – The Medicare federal insurance program went into effect
1969 – Britain's Prince Charles officially became the Prince of Wales
1979 – Sony introduced the walkman
1980 – *O Canada* became the national anthem of Canada
1987 – John Kevin Hill became the youngest person to fly across the United States at the age of 11
1991 – Court TV began airing
1996 – Margaux Hemingway was found dead of an apparent suicide
1997 – The sovereignty of Hong Kong changed from Great Britain to China
2002 – Disney's Beach Club Villas opened at Walt Disney World
2005 – Sandra Day O-Connor, the first female justice on the U.S. Supreme Court, announced she would be retiring
2005 – Singer Luther Vandross died of a stroke at the age of 54
2007 – A ban on smoking in any indoor public place in England went into effect

July 2: Nicholas I of Russia 1796, King Olav V of Norway 1903, Thurgood Marshall 1908, Jean Craighead George 1919, Dan Rowan 1922, Brock Peters 1927, Imelda Marcos 1929, Dave Thomas of Wendy's 1932, Richard Petty 1937, Polly Holliday 1937, John Sununu 1939, Vicente Fox 1942, Ron Silver 1946, Larry David 1947, Saul Rubinek 1948, Tony Armas 1953, Jerry Hall 1956, Bret "Hitman" Hart 1957, Jimmy McNichol 1961, Jose Canseco 1964, Scotty 2 Hotty 1970, Troy Brown 1971, Sean Casey 1974, Joe Thornton 1979, Michelle Branch 1983, Lindsay Lohan 1986

1566 – Nostradamus died
1776 – The Continental Congress adopted a resolution breaking ties with Great Britain, although this declaration was not made public until the fourth of July
1776 – John Hancock became the first to sign the Declaration of Independence
1777 – Vermont became the first American territory to abolish slavery
1839 – The slave ship *Amistad* was taken over by rebelling slaves off the coast of Cuba
1853 – The Crimean War began when Russia invaded Turkey
1881 – President James A. Garfield was fatally wounded by Charles Guiteau in Washington, DC
1900 – The first zeppelin flight occurred
1937 – American aviation pioneer Amelia Earhart disappeared in the Central Pacific during an attempt to fly around the world at the equator

1939 – At Mount Rushmore, Theodore Roosevelt's face was officially dedicated
1947 – An object believed to be a UFO crashed near Roswell, New Mexico
1961 – Ernest Hemingway committed suicide
1962 – The first Wal-Mart store opened in Rogers, Arkansas
1964 – President Lyndon Johnson signed the Civil Rights Act of 1964, prohibiting segregation in public places
1979 – The Susan B. Anthony dollar coin was introduced
1998 – The second Harry Potter book, *Harry Potter and the Chamber of Secrets*, was released
2002 – Steve Fossett became the first person to fly solo around the world nonstop in a balloon

July 3: Louis XI of France 1423, Samuel de Champlain 1567, George M. Cohan 1878, Harrison Schmitt 1935, Kurtwood Smith 1943, Johnny Lee 1946, Betty Buckley 1947, Dave Barry 1947, Jan Smithers 1949, Montel Williams 1956, Laura Branigan 1957, Aaron Tippin 1958, Tom Cruise 1962, Hunter Tylo 1962, Yeardley Smith 1964, Moises Alou 1966, Sandra Lee 1966, Brian Cashman 1967, Shawnee Smith 1970, Teemu Selanne 1970, Patrick Wilson 1973, Andrea Barber 1976

987 – Hugh Capet was crowned King of France, the first of the Capetian Dynasty
1608 – Quebec City was founded by Samuel de Champlain
1754 – During the French and Indian War, George Washington surrendered Fort Necessity in Pennsylvania to the French
1775 – General George Washington took command of the Continental Army in Cambridge, Massachusetts
1778 – The British, aided by Iroquois raiders, massacred 360 men, women and children in Wyoming Valley, Pennsylvania, including torturing to death more than 30 people who had surrendered
1819 – The first bank in the United States, The Bank for Savings, opened in New York City
1852 – The United States established its second mint, in San Francisco, California
1863 – The Battle of Gettysburg ended, becoming the turning point in the American Civil War for the North
1884 – Dow Jones published its first stock average
1890 – Idaho became the 43rd state
1901 – The Wild Bunch, led by Butch Cassidy, committed its last American robbery near Wagner, Montana
1924 – Clarence Birdseye founded the General Seafood Corporation
1940 – Bud Abbott and Lew Costello debuted on NBC radio

1962 – Jackie Robinson became the first black person inducted into the National Baseball Hall of Fame
2005 – A national law legalizing same-sex marriage in Spain went into effect

July 4: Nathaniel Hawthorne 1804, Giuseppe Garibaldi 1807, Stephen Foster 1826, Calvin Coolidge 1872, Louis B. Mayer 1882, Rube Goldberg 1883, Louis Armstrong 1900, Gloria Stuart 1910, Mitch Miller 1911, Ann Landers 1918, Abigail Van Buren 1918, Leona Helmsley 1920, Eva Marie Saint 1924, Neil Simon 1927, Al Davis 1929, George Steinbrenner 1930, Geraldo Rivera 1943, Jim Beattie 1954, John Waite 1955, Pam Shriver 1962, Vinny Castilla 1967, Brendan Donnelly 1971, Koko the gorilla 1971

1054 – A supernova was first observed, lasting several days and bright enough to be seen during the day, the remnants of which formed the Crab Nebula
1636 – The city of Providence, Rhode Island was founded

1776 – The amended Declaration of Independence, prepared by Thomas Jefferson, was approved by the Continental Congress in America (above)
1802 – West Point Military Academy opened
1803 – The Louisiana Purchase was announced in newspapers in America
1817 – Construction began on the Erie Canal
1826 – Third U.S. President Thomas Jefferson died, followed by second U.S. President John Adams a few hours later

1827 – Slavery was abolished in New York

1838 – The Iowa Territory was organized

1845 – Henry David Thoreau began his two years of simple living at Walden Pond

1848 – The cornerstone of the Washington Monument was laid in Washington, DC

1865 – The first edition of Lewis Carroll's *Alice's Adventures in Wonderland* was published

1884 – France presented the Statue of Liberty to the United States

1934 – Boxer Joe Louis won his first professional fight

1934 – At Mount Rushmore, George Washington's face was dedicated

1939 – Lou Gehrig retired from baseball

1959 – The 49-star U.S. flag was introduced

1960 – The 50-star American flag made its debut

1970 – The *American Top 40* starring Casey Kasem made its debut on the radio

1976 – The United States celebrated its bicentennial

1995 – Bob Ross, the host of the PBS series *The Joy of Painting*, died of lymphoma at the age of 52

1997 – The Mars Pathfinder landed on Mars

2004 – In New York, the cornerstone of the Freedom Tower was laid on the former World Trade Center site

2005 – The *Deep Impact* collider hits the comet *Tempel 1*

2007 – The Zaca Fire starts in Santa Barbara, California, which would go on to become the second largest fire in California history

July 5: David Farragut 1801, P.T. Barnum 1810, Cecil Rhodes 1853, Robert Bacon 1860, Henry Cabot Lodge 1902, Katherine Helmond 1928, Huey Lewis 1951, Goose Gossage 1951, Bill Watterson 1958, Edie Falco 1963, Jason Dolley 1991

1811 – Venezuela became the first South American country to declare independence from Spain

1865 – William Booth started the Salvation Army in London

1937 – Spam luncheon meat was introduced to the public

1943 – The Battle of Kursk began, the tank and air battle in history

1946 – The bikini bathing suit, created by Louis Reard, made its debut during a fashion show in Paris

1950 – U.S. forces engaged the North Koreans for the first time at Osan, South Korea

1954 – Elvis Presley had his first commercial recording session

1971 – The 26th Amendment to the Constitution was passed, lowering the voting age from 21 to 18

1975 – Arthur Ashe became the first black man to win a Wimbledon singles tennis title when he defeated Jimmy Connors
1989 – The show *Seinfeld* first aired on NBC
1998 – Japan launched a space probe to Mars, becoming only the third country to send a probe to another planet
2002 – Hall of Fame baseball player Ted Williams died at the age of 83

July 6: John Paul Jones 1747, Czar Nicholas I of Russia 1796, Harold Vanderbilt 1884, Nancy Reagan 1921, William Schallert 1922, Merv Griffin 1925, Janet Leigh 1927, Bill Haley 1927, Della Reese 1931, Will McDonough 1935, Ned Beatty 1937, James Naughton 1945, Burt Ward 1946, Fred Dryer 1946, Jamie Wyeth 1946, Sylvester Stallone 1946, George W. Bush 1946, John Byrne 1950, Geoffrey Rush 1951, Shelly Hack 1952, Grant Goodeve 1952, Allyse Beasley 1954, 50 Cent 1976, Tia Mowry 1978, Tamera Mowry 1978, Pau Gasol 1980

1483 – King Richard III of England was crowned
1535 – Sir Thomas More was executed by King Henry VIII of England on charges of treason
1699 – Captain Kidd was captured in Boston
1785 – The dollar was chosen as the monetary unit of the United States
1885 – Louis Pasteur successfully tested his anti-rabies vaccine
1923 – The Union of Soviet Socialist Republic was established
1932 – The cost of a first-class stamp went from 2 cents to 3 cents
1933 – The first Major League Baseball All-Star game was held in Chicago
1942 – Diarist Anne Frank and her family took refuge from the Nazis in Amsterdam
1957 – Althea Gibson became the first black athlete to win at Wimbledon, when she won the women's singles tennis competition
1957 – John Lennon and Paul McCartney met for the first time
1983 – Fred Lynn of the California Angels became the first person to hit a grand slam in a Major League Baseball All-Star Game
1997 – The *Mars Pathfinder* released *Sojourner*, a robot rover, on the surface of Mars

July 7: Thomas Howard 1586, Satchel Paige 1907, Jon Pertwee 1919, Pierre Cardin 1922, Doc Severinsen 1927, David McCullough 1933, Ringo Starr 1940, Joel Siegel 1943, Joe Spano 1946, Shelley Duvall 1949, Bill Campbell 1959, Jessica Hahn 1959, Vonda Shepard 1963, Jorja Fox 1968, Joe Sakic 1969, Cree Summer 1970, Lisa Leslie 1972, Michelle Kwan 1980

1456 – Joan of Arc was acquitted of her crimes 25 years after her death

1863 – The first American military draft began
1865 – Four people were hanged in Washington, DC, after being convicted of conspiring with John Wilkes Booth to assassinate President Abraham Lincoln
1898 – The United States took possession of Hawaii
1930 – Construction began on Boulder Dam, later Hoover Dam, on the Colorado River
1981 – President Ronald Reagan announced the nomination of Sandra Day O'Connor to become the first female justice on the U.S. Supreme Court
1983 – Eleven-year-old Samantha Smith of Manchester, Maine, left for a visit to the Soviet Union at the personal invitation of Soviet leader Yuri Andropov
2005 – Four terrorist explosions occurred in the London subway system, killing 56 people

July 8: Frederick William Seward 1830, Joseph Chamberlain 1836, John D. Rockefeller 1839, Louis Jordan 1908, Nelson Rockefeller 1908, Jerry Vale 1932, Marty Feldman 1933, Steve Lawrence 1935, Phil Gramm 1942, Jeffrey Tambor 1944, Kim Darby 1947, Raffi 1948, Wolfgang Puck 1949, Anjelica Huston 1951, Jack Lambert 1952, Kevin Bacon 1958, Toby Keith 1961, Joan Osborne 1962, Beck 1970, Milo Ventimiglia 1977, Sophia Bush 1982, Joshua Alba 1982, Jaden Smith 1998

1099 – Christian soldiers on the First Crusade march around Jerusalem
1630 – The Massachusetts Bay Colony celebrated Thanksgiving Day
1680 – The first documented tornado in America killed a servant in Cambridge, Massachusetts
1776 – The Liberty Bell was rung in Philadelphia to summon people to a reading of the Declaration of Independence
1889 – *The Wall Street Journal* was first published
1898 – Crime boss Soapy Smith was shot to death in Skagway, Alaska, relieving the fears of Skagway citizens
1933 – The Pittsburgh Steelers football team was formed
1950 – General Douglas MacArthur was named commander-in-chief of United Nations forces in Korea
1982 – An assassination attempt was made on Saddam Hussein in Iraq
2000 – *Harry Potter and the Goblet of Fire*, the 4th in the book series, was released in the United States

July 9: Ferdinand II of the Holy Roman Empire 1578, Elias Howe 1819, Edward Heath 1916, Vince Edwards 1928, Donald Rumsfeld 1932, Brian Dennehy 1938, Richard Roundtree 1942, Dean Koontz 1945, O. J.

Simpson 1947, Chris Cooper 1951, John Tesh 1952, Willie Wilson 1955, Jimmy Smits 1955, Tom Hanks 1956, Kelly McGillis 1957, Tim Kring 1957, Courtney Love 1964, Trent Green 1970, Scott Grimes 1971, Kelly Holcomb 1973, Fred Savage 1976, Linda Park 1978, Georgie Henley 1995

1540 – England's King Henry VIII had his 6-month-old marriage to his fourth wife, Anne of Cleves, annulled
1816 – Argentina declared its independence from Spain
1850 – President Zachary Taylor died in office at the age of 55 and he was succeeded by Millard Fillmore
1868 – The 14th Amendment to the Constitution was ratified, granting all African-Americans full citizenship and full rights under the law
1877 – Alexander Graham Bell, Gardiner Greene Hubbard, Thomas Sanders and Thomas Watson formed the Bell Telephone Company
1900 – The Commonwealth of Australia was established by an act of the British Parliament, uniting the separate colonies under a federal government
1918 – Two trains collided in Nashville, Tennessee, killing 101 people and injuring 171
1922 – Johnny Weissmuller became the first person to swim the 100 meters freestyle in less than a minute
1947 – The engagement of Britain's Princess Elizabeth to Lt. Philip Mountbatten was announced
1951 – President Harry Truman asked Congress to end the state of war that existed with Germany
2002 – The 2002 Major League Baseball All-Star Game ended in a tie, after both teams exhausted their supply of pitchers
2006 – Roger Federer won his fourth straight Wimbledon men's singles championship

July 10: James III of Scotland 1452, John Calvin 1509, George M. Dallas 1792, James Whistler 1834, Adolphus Busch 1839, Nicola Tesla 1856, Joe Shuster 1914, Don "Mr. Wizard" Herbert 1917, David Brinkley 1920, Eunice Kennedy Shriver 1921, Earl Hamner Jr. 1923, Fred Gwynne 1926, Jerry Nelson 1934, Mills Watson 1940, Robert Pine 1941, Arthur Ashe 1943, Ron Glass 1945, Hal McRae 1946, Arlo Guthrie 1947, Andre Dawson 1954, Jonathan Gilbert 1968, Jessica Simpson 1980, Thomas Ian Nicholas 1980

988 – The city of Dublin, Ireland was founded
1553 – Lady Jane Grey took the throne of England
1778 – In support of the American Revolution, Louis XVI of France declared war on England

1821 – The United States took possession of Florida, after buying it from Spain

1890 – Wyoming became the 44th state

1913 – Death Valley, California rose to 134 degrees, the highest recorded temperature in the United States

1928 – George Eastman first demonstrated color motion pictures

1938 – Howard Hughes completed a 91-hour flight around the world

1962 – Telstar became the world's first communications satellite when it was launched into orbit

1973 – Britain granted the Bahamas their independence after three centuries of British colonial rule

1978 – *World News Tonight* debuted on ABC-TV

1985 – Coca Cola resumed selling the old formula Coke, calling it Classic Coke

1989 – Mel Blanc, the voice of Bugs Bunny, Daffy Duck, Porky Pig and the other Looney Tunes characters, died at the age of 81

1991 – Boris Yeltsin was sworn in as the first freely elected President of the Russian Republic

1992 – In Miami, a federal judge sentenced former Panamanian leader Manuel Noriega to 40 years in prison for drug and racketeering charges

1997 – Scientists in London said DNA from a Neanderthal skeleton supported a theory that all humanity descended from an African Eve 100,000 to 200,000 years ago

2005 – Hurricane Dennis hit Florida

July 11: Robert I (the Bruce) of Scotland 1274, John Quincy Adams 1767, E. B. White 1899, Yul Brynner 1915, Brett Somers 1924, Tab Hunter 1931, Bob McGrath (of Sesame Street) 1933, Beverly Todd 1946, Jay Johnson 1949, Bruce McGill 1950, Bonnie Pointer 1950, Leon Spinks 1953, Sela Ward 1956, Richie Sambora 1959, Debbe Dunning 1966, Greg Grunberg 1966, Jeff Corwin 1967, Justin Chambers 1970, Lil' Kim 1975, Javier Lopez 1977, Chris Cooley 1982, Rachael Taylor 1984

1346 – Charles IV of Luxembourg was elected Holy Roman Emperor in Germany

1750 – Halifax, Nova Scotia was almost completely destroyed by fire

1804 – The first secretary of the treasury, Alexander Hamilton, was killed by Vice President Aaron Burr in a pistol duel

1859 – *A Tale of Two Cities* by Charles Dickens was first published

1914 – Babe Ruth made his Major League Baseball debut with the Boston Red Sox

1921 – William Howard Taft became the first former President of the United States to also serve as Chief Justice of the Supreme Court

1934 – Franklin D. Roosevelt became the first United States President to travel through the Panama Canal while in office
1960 – Harper Lee's *To Kill a Mockingbird* was published
1977 – The Medal of Freedom was awarded posthumously to Reverend Martin Luther King Jr. in a White House ceremony
1979 – Skylab burned up in the atmosphere, showering debris over Australia and the Indian Ocean
1987 – The world population was estimated to have surpassed five billion
2004 – *The 4400* began broadcasting on the USA Network
2007 – Lady Bird Johnson, former U.S. First Lady, died at the age of 94

July 12: Julius Caesar 100 BC, Henry David Thoreau 1817, George Eastman 1854, George Washington Carver 1864, Oscar Hammerstein II 1895, Milton Berle 1908, Joe "Curly Joe" DeRita 1909, Andrew Wyeth 1917, Bill Cosby 1937, Christine McVie 1943, Richard Simmons 1948, Jay Thomas 1948, Cheryl Ladd 1951, Brian Grazer 1951, Jamey Sheridan 1951, Sandi Patti 1956, Mel Harris 1957, Jennifer Saunders 1958, Kristi Yamaguchi 1971, Anna Friel 1976, Topher Grace 1978, Michelle Rodriguez 1978, Erik Per Sullivan 1991

1543 – England's King Henry VIII married his sixth and final wife, Catherine Parr
1812 – During the War of 1812, the United States invaded Canada at Windsor, Ontario
1862 – The Medal of Honor was authorized by the U.S. Congress
1933 – A minimum wage of 40 cents per hour was established in the United States
1957 – The U.S. Surgeon General reported that there was a direct link between smoking and lung cancer
1960 – The first Etch-A-Sketch went on sale
1984 – Geraldine Ferraro was chosen as the first female Vice-Presidential candidate on a major party ticket by Presidential candidate Walter Mondale
2000 – The movie *X-Men* premiered
2005 – Prince Albert II was coronated as ruler of Monaco

July 13: Father Edward Joseph Flanagan 1886, Dave Garroway 1913, Bob Crane 1928, Jack Kemp 1935, Patrick Stewart 1940, Harrison Ford 1942, Cheech Marin 1946, Didi Conn 1951, Louise Mandrell 1954, Spud Webb 1963

1754 – At the beginning of the French and Indian War, George Washington surrendered Fort Necessity in southwestern Pennsylvania to the French

1793 – French revolutionary writer Jean Paul Marat was stabbed to death in his bath by Charlotte Corday, who was executed four days later (see image to left)

1837 – Queen Victoria became the first British monarch to live in Buckingham Palace

1908 – Women first competed in the modern Olympics

1923 – The Hollywood sign was dedicated, originally reading Hollywoodland

1954 – Pigpen made his first appearance in a *Peanuts* comic strip

1972 – Carroll Rosenbloom, owner of the Baltimore Colts, and Robert Irsay, owner of the Los Angeles Rams, traded teams

1978 – Lee Iacocca was fired as president of Ford Motor Company by Chairman Henry Ford II

1982 – The Major League Baseball All-Star Game was played outside the United States for the first time, in Montreal, Canada

July 14: William Hanna 1910, Terry-Thomas 1911, Woody Guthrie 1912, Gerald Ford 1913, Ingmar Bergman 1918, Harry Dean Stanton 1926, John Chancellor 1927, Polly Bergen 1930, Rosey Grier 1932, Jerry Houser 1952, Matthew Fox 1966, Robin Ventura 1967, Missy Gold 1970, Tim Hudson 1975, Chad Faust 1980

1223 – Louis VIII became King of France upon the death of his father, King Philip II

1789 – The French Revolution began when Parisians stormed the Bastille prison and released the seven prisoners inside

1914 – Robert Goddard received a patent for liquid rocket fuel

1933 – All political parties in Germany except the Nazi party were outlawed

1965 – The American space probe Mariner 4 flew past Mars and sent back photos, the first of any other planet

1969 – The $500, $1,000, $5,000, and $10,000 bills were officially withdrawn from circulation in the United States, due to lack of use, leaving the $100 bill as the largest

July 15: Rembrandt 1606, Clement Moore 1779, Alex Karras 1935, Ken Kercheval 1935, Patrick Wayne 1939, Jan-Michael Vincent 1944, Linda Ronstadt 1946, Richard Russo 1949, Jesse Ventura 1951, Terry O'Quinn 1952, Alicia Bridges 1953, Kim Alexis 1960, Willie Aames 1960, Forest Whitaker 1961, Lolita Davidovich 1961, Brigitte Nielsen 1963, Eddie Griffin 1968, Brian Austin Green 1973, Jim Jones 1976, Lana Parrilla 1977, Miguel Olivo 1978

1099 – Jerusalem fell to the Crusaders
1870 – Georgia became the last of the Confederate States to be re-admitted into the Union
1876 – George Washington Bradley of St. Louis pitched the first no-hitter in baseball in a 2-0 win over Hartford
1901 – 74,000 steel workers in Pittsburgh went out on strike
1934 – Continental Airlines began operations
1940 – Robert Wadlow, the tallest person in the world at 8 feet 11 inches tall, died at the age of 22
1995 – Amazon.com began operations
1997 – Italian fashion designer Gianni Versace was shot to death outside his home in Miami by serial killer Andrew Cunanan
2005 – Jack Nicklaus retired from Professional Golf

July 16: Roald Amundsen 1872, Shoeless Joe Jackson 1888, Barbara Stanwyck 1907, Orville Redenbacher 1907, Ginger Rogers 1911, Barnard Hughes 1915, Dick Thornburgh 1932, Katherine D. Ortega 1934, Jimmy Johnson (NFL) 1943, Dave Goelz 1946, Alexis Herman 1947, Ruben Blades 1948, Mickey Rourke 1953, Michael Flatley 1958, Gary Anderson 1959, DeMarlo Hale 1961, Phoebe Cates 1963, Will Ferrell 1967, Barry Sanders 1968, Rain Pryor 1969, Corey Feldman 1971, Adam Scott 1980

1429 – Joan of Arc led the French army to victory in the Battle of Orleans
1779 – During the American Revolution, American forces captured Stony Point, New York from the British
1790 – The District of Columbia, or Washington, DC, was established as the permanent seat of the United States Government
1791 – Louis XVI was suspended from office until he agreed to ratify the Constitution
1875 – The new French Constitution was finalized

162

1918 – Czar Nicholas II and his family were executed by Bolsheviks at Ekaterinburg, Russia

1935 – In Oklahoma City, parking meters were first used in the United States

1940 – Adolf Hitler ordered the start of Operation Sea Lion, the invasion of England

1941 – Joe DiMaggio of the New York Yankees hit in his record-setting 56th consecutive game

1945 – The United States detonated the first atomic bomb in a test in New Mexico

1951 – *The Catcher in the Rye* by J.D. Salinger was first published

1969 – Apollo 11 blasted off from Cape Kennedy on its way to becoming the first manned mission to land on the Moon

1979 – Saddam Hussein became President of Iraq after he forced Hasan al-Bakr to resign

1985 – The Major League Baseball All-Star Game, broadcast by NBC, became the first television show to be broadcast in stereo

1990 – An earthquake in the Philippines killed over 1600 people

1999 – John F. Kennedy Jr., his wife Carolyn, and her sister were killed when their plane crashed off the coast of Martha's Vineyard, Massachusetts

2004 – Martha Stewart was sentenced to five months in prison for lying about a stock sale

2005 – *Harry Potter and the Half-Blood Prince*, the sixth book in the Harry Potter series, was released

July 17: Elbridge Gerry 1744, John Jacob Astor 1763, James Cagney 1899, Art Linkletter 1912, Lou Boudreau 1917, Phyllis Diller 1917, Juan Antonio Samaranch 1920, Vince Guaraldi 1928, Pat McCormick 1934, Donald Sutherland 1935, Diahann Carroll 1935, Camilla Duchess of Cornwall 1947, Lucie Arnaz 1951, David Hasselhoff 1952, J. Michael Staczynski 1954, Bobby Thigpen 1963, M.I.A. 1977, Mike Vogel 1979, Ryan Miller 1980, Summer Bashil 1988

1212 – The Moslems were defeated in the Spanish Crusade

1453 – The 100 Years War ended when the French defeated the English at Castillon, France

1762 – Peter III of Russia and his wife were murdered

1815 – Napoleon Bonaparte surrendered to the British at Rocheforte, France

1821 – Spain ceded Florida to the United States

1897 – The Klondike Gold Rush began

1917 – The British Royal Family took the Windsor name

1941 – The longest hitting streak in baseball history ended when the Cleveland Indians held Joe DiMaggio hitless after 56 consecutive games with a hit

1945 – U.S. President Harry Truman, Soviet leader Josef Stalin and British Prime Minister Winston Churchill began meeting at Potsdam, Germany in the final Allied summit of World War II

1955 – Disneyland opened in Anaheim, California

1975 – An Apollo space capsule docked with a Russian Soyuz capsule, the first time 2 different countries docked in space

1987 – Oliver North and John Poindexter began testifying before Congress in the Iran-Contra hearings

1992 – Splash Mountain opened at Walt Disney World

July 18: George Machine Gun Kelly 1895, Harriet Nelson 1909, Hume Cronyn 1911, Red Skelton 1913, Nelson Mandela 1918, John Glenn 1921, Dick Button 1929, Paul Verhoeven 1938, James Brolin 1940, Joe Torre 1940, Martha Reeves 1941, Steve Forbes 1947, Richard Branson 1950, Ricky Skaggs 1954, Nick Faldo 1957, Audrey Landers 1959, Anne-Marie Johnson 1960, Elizabeth McGovern 1961, Lee Arenberg 1962, Mike Greenwell 1963, Vin Diesel 1967, Penny Hardaway 1971, Torii Hunter 1975, Adalius Thomas 1977, Ben Sheets 1978, Deion Branch 1979, Kristen Bell 1980

64 AD – The Great Fire of Rome began

1536 – The authority of the pope was declared void in England

1925 – Hitler published *Mein Kampf*

1936 – The Spanish Civil War began as General Francisco Franco led an uprising of army troops based in Spanish North Africa

1944 – Hideki Tojo was removed as Japanese premier and war minister due to setbacks suffered by his country in World War II

1954 – Construction began on Disneyland

1969 – After a party at Chappaquiddick Island, Massachusetts, Senator Edward Kennedy drove off a bridge into a pond, killing his female passenger

1976 – 14 year old Nadia Comaneci scored the first perfect 10 in gymnastics at the Olympics

1984 – At a McDonald's restaurant in San Ysidro, California, a gunman killed 21 people and wounded 19 others, before police shoot and kill him

1985 – Jack Nicklaus II, at age 23 years old, made his playing debut on the pro golf tour at the Quad Cities Open in Coal Valley, Illinois

1989 – Actress Rebecca Schaeffer was shot and killed by an obsessed fan, leading California to pass an anti-stalking law

July 19: Samuel Colt 1814, Lizzie Borden 1860, Charles Horace Mayo 1865, Max Fleischer 1883, George McGovern 1922, George Hamilton 1937, Anthony Edwards 1962, Garth Nix 1963, Rick Ankiel 1979

1553 – Fifteen-year-old Lady Jane Grey was deposed as Queen of England after claiming the crown for nine days
1692 – Five women in Salem, Massachusetts were hanged for witchcraft
1799 – The Rosetta Stone, a tablet with hieroglyphic translations into Greek, was found in Egypt
1984 – Geraldine Ferraro was nominated by the Democratic Party to become the first woman from a major political party to run for the office of U.S. Vice-President
1985 – Christa McAuliffe of New Hampshire was chosen to be the first schoolteacher to ride aboard the space shuttle
1989 – 112 people were killed when a United Airline DC-10 airplane crashed in Sioux City, Iowa, although 184 people survived
1995 – MTV's *Road Rules* began airing
1996 – The 1996 Olympic Games in Atlanta, Georgia, United States opened

July 20: Alexander the Great 356 BC, Gregor Mendel 1822, Sir Edmund Hillary 1919, Dick Giordano 1932, Chuck Daly 1933, Diana Rigg 1938, Natalie Wood 1938, Wendy Richard 1943, Kim Carnes 1946, Carlos Santana 1947, Donna Dixon 1957, Josh Holloway 1969, Vitamin C 1969, Sandra Oh 1971, Benjie Molina 1974, Ray Allen 1975, Elliott Yamin 1978, Pavel Datsyuk 1978

1861 – The Congress of the Confederate States began holding sessions in Richmond, Virginia
1871 – British Columbia officially joined the Confederation of Canada
1881 – Chief Sitting Bull surrendered the last of the Sioux people to U.S. troops at Fort Buford, North Dakota
1903 – Ford Motor Company shipped its first automobile
1921 – Air mail service began between New York and San Francisco
1944 – An attempt by a group of German officials to assassinate Adolf Hitler failed
1969 – *Apollo 11* astronauts Neil Armstrong and Buzz Aldrin became the first people to walk on the moon
1976 – America's *Viking I* robot spacecraft made a successful landing on Mars
1976 – Hank Aaron of the Milwaukee Brewers hit the last homerun of his career, number 755, setting a record that held for over 30 years

1977 – A flash flood hit Johnstown, Pennsylvania, killing 80 people and causing $350 million worth of damage
1984 – Vanessa Williams was asked to give up her Miss America crown after nude photos were published of her
1993 – White House deputy counsel Vincent Foster Jr. was found shot to death, a suicide, in a park near Washington, DC
2005 – Actor James Doohan, best known as Star Trek's Scotty, died at the age of 85

July 21: Frances Cleveland 1864, Johnny Evers 1881, Ernest Hemingway 1899, Isaac Stern 1920, Mollie Sugden 1922, Don Knotts 1924, Janet Reno 1938, Edward Herrmann 1943, Kenneth Starr 1946, Cat Stevens 1947, Garry Trudeau 1948, Al Hraboskey 1949, Robin Williams 1952, Jon Lovitz 1957, Mike Bordick 1965, Brandi Chastain 1968, Damian Marley 1978, Josh Hartnett 1978, C.C. Sabathia 1980, Blake Lewis 1981

1861 – The first major battle of the American Civil War began, the First Battle of Bull Run
1873 – Jesse James and his gang pulled off the first train robbery in the United States
1957 – Althea Gibson became the first black woman to win a major U.S. tennis title when she won the Women's National clay-court singles competition
1961 – Gus Grissom became the second American in space
1983 – The lowest temperature on Earth is recorded at Vostok Station, Antarctica at -129 degrees Fahrenheit
1984 – In Jackson, Michigan, a factory robot crushed a worker to death in the first ever robot-related death in the United States
2007 – *Harry Potter and the Deathly Hallows*, the 7th and final book in the series, was released

July 22: Edward Hopper 1882, James Whale 1889, Rose Kennedy 1890, Karl Menninger 1893, Amy Vanderbilt 1908, Bob Dole 1923, The Fabulous Moolah 1923, Orson Bean 1928, Terence Stamp 1939, Alex Trebek 1940, George Clinton 1940, Kay Bailey Hutchison 1943, Bobby Sherman 1943, Sparky Lyle 1944, Danny Glover 1946, Albert Brooks 1947, Don Henley 1947, S.E. Hinton 1948, Willem Dafoe 1955, Dave Steib 1957, David Von Erich 1958, David Spade 1964, Patrick Labyorteaux 1965, Shawn Michaels 1965, Tim Brown 1966, Keyshawn Johnson 1972, Mike Sweeney 1973

1298 – At the Battle of Falkirk, the British led by King Edward I defeated William Wallace and the Scots

166

1933 – Wiley Post became the first person to fly solo around the world, completing the flight in 7 days and 18 hours
1934 – John Dillinger was mortally wounded by FBI agents at the Biograph Theatre in Chicago
1991 – Police arrested Jeffrey Dahmer after finding the remains of 11 victims in his apartment in Milwaukee
2003 – In northern Iraq, Saddam Hussein's sons Odai and Qusai died after a gunfight with U.S. forces

July 23: Pope Clement XI 1649, Julia Gardiner Tyler 1820, Pee Wee Reese 1918, Bert Convey 1933, Don Drysdale 1936, Don Imus 1940, Larry Manetti 1947, Edie McClurg 1951, Woody Harrelson 1961, Eriq LaSalle 1962, Slash (Guns N' Roses) 1965, Philip Seymour Hoffman 1967, Gary Payton 1968, Stephanie Seymour 1968, Alison Krauss 1971, Marlon Wayans 1972, Nomar Garciaparra 1973, Monica Lewisnky 1973, Terry Glenn 1974, Maurice Greene 1974, Daniel Radcliffe 1989

1715 – The first lighthouse in America was authorized for construction at Little Brewster Island, Massachusetts
1862 – During the American Civil War, General Henry Hallack was put in charge of the Union Army
1904 – The ice cream cone was invented by Charles E. Menches during the Louisiana Purchase Exposition in St. Louis
1952 – Egyptian military officers led by Gamal Abdel Nasser overthrew King Farouk I
1982 – Actor Victor Morrow and two child actors were killed while filming *Twilight Zone: The Movie* when a stunt helicopter crashed into them
1984 – Miss America Vanessa Williams turned in her crown after it had been discovered that nude photos of her had appeared in *Penthouse* magazine
1985 – The final episode of *The Jeffersons* alred
1986 – Britain's Prince Andrew married Sarah Ferguson at Westminster Abbey in London
1995 – Comet Hale-Bopp was discovered

July 24: Simon Bolivar 1783, Alexander Dumas 1802, Amelia Earhart 1897, John Aniston 1933, Ruth Buzzi 1936, Dan Hedaya 1940, Chris Sarandon 1942, Robert Hays 1947, Michael Richards 1949, Lynda Carter 1951, Pam Tillis 1957, Karl Malone 1963, Barry Bonds 1964, Kadeem Hardison 1965, Kristin Chenoweth 1968, Rick Fox 1969, Jennifer Lopez 1970, Eric Szmanda 1975, Anna Paquin 1982, Patrice Bergeron 1985, Mara Wilson 1987, Daveigh Chase 1990

1567 – Mary Queen of Scots was deposed by the people of Scotland and replaced with her infant son, James VI
1823 – Chile abolished slavery
1847 – Mormon leader Brigham Young and his followers arrived in the valley of the Great Salt Lake in present-day Utah
1866 – Tennessee became the first state to be readmitted to the Union after the U.S. Civil War
1956 – Dean Martin and Jerry Lewis ended their comedy team
1966 – New Orleans Square at Disneyland opened
1969 – The *Apollo 11* astronauts splashed down safely in the Pacific Ocean
1974 – The U.S. Supreme Court unanimously ruled that President Richard Nixon had to turn over subpoenaed White House tape recordings to the Watergate special prosecutor
1978 – Billy Martin was fired for the first of three times as the manager of the New York Yankees baseball team
1979 – Carl Yastrzemski of the Boston Red Sox hit his 400th career homerun
1983 – George Brett of the Kansas City Royals had a home run nullified, when umpires decided he had gotten pine tar too far up his bat, although the ruling was later reversed and the game replayed from the moment of the home run on
1984 – Terry Bradshaw retired from the National Football League
1998 – A gunman, Russell Weston Jr., burst into the U.S. Capitol and opened fire, killing two police officers
2005 – Lance Armstrong won his seventh consecutive Tour de France

July 25: Henry Knox 1750, Walter Brennan 1894, Jack Gilford 1907, Estelle Getty 1924, Walter Payton 1954, Iman 1955, Matt LeBlanc 1967, Billy Wagner 1971, Javier Vasquez 1976, Michael Welch 1987, Rachel Mae Ewing Merrill 2006

1394 – King Charles VI ordered all Jews out of France
1564 – Maximillian II became the new emperor of the Holy Roman Empire
1603 – Scotland's King James VI was crowned James I of Great Britain, uniting England and Scotland
1844 – John Tyler took Julia Gardiner as his wife, thus becoming the first U.S. President to marry while in office
1897 – Author Jack London left to join the Klondike Gold Rush
1898 – The United States invaded Puerto Rico
1943 – Italian dictator Benito Mussolini was overthrown
1946 – Dean Martin and Jerry Lewis performed their first show together as a comedy team

168

1956 – The Italian passenger ship *Andrea Doria* sank
1978 – The first test tube baby, Louise Joy Brown, was born in England
1984 – Soviet cosmonaut Svetlana Savitskaya became the first woman to walk in space
1999 – Lance Armstrong won the Tour de France for the first time
2007 – Pratibha Patil was sworn in as the woman President of India

July 26: George Clinton 1739, George Bernard Shaw 1856, Carl Jung 1875, Gracie Allen 1906, Vivian Vance 1912, Ellis Kinder 1914, Blake Edwards 1922, Jason Robards, Jr. 1922, Hoyt Wilhelm 1922, James Best 1926, Stanley Kubrick 1928, Dobie Gray 1943, Mick Jagger 1943, Helen Mirren 1945, Susan George 1950, Dorothy Hamill 1956, Nana Visitor 1957, Kevin Spacey 1959, Sandra Bullock 1964, Jeremy Piven 1965, Taylor Momsen 1993

1775 – A postal system was established by the 2nd Continental Congress of the United States with Ben Franklin as the first Postmaster General
1788 – New York became the 11th state in the U.S.
1861 – General George McClellan assumed command of the Army of the Potomac
1944 – The first German V-2 rocket hit Great Britain
1945 – Winston Churchill resigned as Britain's Prime Minister
1947 – President Harry Truman signed The National Security Act, which created The National Security Council, the Department of Defense, the Central Intelligence Agency and the Joint Chiefs of Staff
1964 – Teamsters president Jimmy Hoffa and six others were convicted of fraud and conspiracy in the handling of a union pension fund
1971 – *Apollo 15* was launched from Cape Kennedy
1991 – Paul Reubens, also known as Peewee Herman, was arrested for exposing himself
2005 – The space shuttle Discovery returned to orbit after a two and a half year delay, following the Columbia disaster

July 27: Johann Bernoulli 1667, Leo Durocher 1905, Keenan Wynn 1916, Norman Lear 1922, Jack Higgins 1929, Jerry Van Dyke 1931, Peggy Fleming 1948, Bettty Thomas 1948, Maureen McGovern 1949, Bill Engvall 1957, Christopher Dean 1958, Julian McMahon 1968, Shea Hillenbrand 1975, Alex Rodriguez 1975, Jonathan Rhys Meyers 1977

1214 – At the Battle of Bouvines in France, King Philip Augustus of France defeated King John of England
1777 – The Marquis de Lafayette arrived in New England to help the American colonists fight the British

169

1940 – Bugs Bunny made his official debut in the Warner Bros. animated cartoon *A Wild Hare*
1953 – The armistice agreement that ended the Korean War was signed at Panmunjon, Korea
1974 – The U.S. Congress asked for impeachment procedures against President Richard Nixon
1980 – The deposed shah of Iran, Muhammad Riza Pahlavi, died in a hospital near Cairo, Egypt
1992 – Boston Celtics star Reggie Lewis died after collapsing on a Brandeis University basketball court during practice
1995 – The Korean War Veterans Memorial was dedicated in Washington, DC
1996 – At the Atlanta Olympics a pipe bomb exploded at the public Centennial Olympic Park killing one person and injuring more than 100
2007 – In Phoenix, Arizona, two media helicopters collide and crash while filming a high-speed chase, killing all four people on board

July 28: Thomas Heywood Jr. 1746, Beatrix Potter 1866, Rudy Vallee 1901, Jacqueline Kennedy Onassis 1929, Bill Bradley 1943, Jim Davis 1945, Sally Struthers 1948, Georgia Engel 1948, Vida Blue 1949, Terry Fox 1958, Lori Loughlin 1964, Garth Snow 1969, Elizabeth Berkley 1972

1540 – King Henry VIII of England married his fifth wife, Catherine Howard, on the same day he had Thomas Cromwell executed on charges of high treason
1609 – Bermuda was first settled
1750 – Johann Sebastian Bach died after an unsuccessful eye operation
1794 – Maximilien Robespierre was executed via guillotine
1896 – The city of Miami, Florida was incorporated
1914 – World War I officially began when Austria-Hungary declared war on Serbia
1945 – A U.S. Army bomber crashed into the 79th floor of New York City's Empire State Building, killing 14 people and injuring 26 others
1976 – An earthquake northern China, killed at least 242,000 people
2000 – Kathie Lee Gifford made her final appearance as co-host of the ABC talk show *Live with Regis and Kathie Lee*

July 29: Benito Mussolini 1883, Lloyd Bochner 1924, Lou Albano 1933, Elizabeth Dole 1936, Peter Jennings 1938, David Warner 1941, Ken Burns 1953, Luis Alicea 1965, Martina McBride 1966, Wil Wheaton 1972, Allison Mack 1982

1565 – Mary Queen of Scots married Henry Stuart

1567 – James VI was crowned King of Scotland
1890 – Artist Vincent van Gogh died of a self-inflicted gunshot wound in Auvers, France
1900 – King Humbert I of Italy was shot to death
1901 – A land lottery began in Oklahoma
1958 – The National Aeronautics and Space Administration (NASA) was authorized by the U.S. Congress
1981 – England's Prince Charles and Lady Diana Spencer were married
2005 – Astronomers announced the discovery of Eris, the largest of the dwarf planets

July 30: Emily Bronte 1818, Henry Ford 1863, Smedley Butler 1881, Casey Stengel 1890, Dick Wilson 1916, Sid Krofft 1929, Bud Selig 1934, Peter Bogdanovich 1939, Paul Anka 1941, Arnold Schwarzenegger 1947, Frank Stallone 1950, Ken Olin 1954, Delta Burke 1956, Clint Hurdle 1957, Laurence Fishburne 1961, Lisa Kudrow 1963, Chris Mullin 1963, Vivica A. Fox 1964, Tom Green 1971, Hillary Swank 1974, Jaime Pressly 1977

1619 – At Jamestown, Virginia, the House of Burgesses convened for the first time
1729 – The city of Baltimore was founded in Maryland
1932 – The Summer Olympics opened in Los Angeles
1932 – Walt Disney's *Flowers and Trees* premiered, which would become the first animated Oscar winner
1945 – During World War II, a Japanese submarine sank the *USS Indianapolis*, killing over 800 crew members
1954 – Elvis Presley made his first public performance
1956 – The phrase "In God We Trust" was adopted as the United States national motto
1965 – President Lyndon Johnson signed an act creating Medicare and Medicaid
1975 – Jimmy Hoffa, former Teamsters union president, disappeared in Michigan
1990 – The first Saturn automobile rolled off the assembly line
2000 – Jennifer Aniston and Brad Pitt were married

July 31: Bill Todman 1916, Curt Gowdy 1919, Hank Bauer 1922, Don Murray 1929, Geoffrey Lewis 1935, William Bennett 1943, Geraldine Chaplin 1944, Barry Van Dyke 1951, James Read 1953, Michael Biehn 1956, Wesley Snipes 1962, J. K. Rowling 1965, Dean Cain 1966, Gabe Kapler 1975, Tim Couch 1977, Evgeni Malkin 1986

1498 – Christopher Columbus, on his third voyage to the Western Hemisphere, arrived at the island of Trinidad

1790 – The first patent was issued in the United States

1948 – New York International Airport, later renamed John F. Kennedy International Airport, was dedicated

1961 – The first tie in All-Star Game major league baseball history was recorded when it was stopped in the 9th inning due to rain at Boston's Fenway Park

1964 – *Ranger 7* sent back the first close-up pictures of the Moon

1968 – Franklin made his first appearance in the *Peanuts* comic strip

1971 – Men rode in a vehicle on the moon for the first time, in a lunar rover

1981 – The seven-week baseball players' strike came to an end when the players and owners agreed on the issue of free agent compensation

1995 – The Walt Disney Company agreed to acquire Capital Cities/ABC in a $19 billion deal

2004 – Nomar Garciaparra was traded from the Boston Red Sox to the Chicago Cubs

August

August 1: Roman Emperor Claudius 10 BC, William Clark 1770, Francis Scott Key 1779, Herman Melville 1819, Robert Todd Lincoln 1843, Alexander I of Greece 1893, Dom DeLuise 1933, Yves Saint-Laurent 1936, Al D'Amato 1937, Ron Brown 1941, Jerry Garcia 1942, Coolio 1963, Tempestt Bledsoe 1973

1461 – Edward IV was crowned King of England
1619 – The first African slaves (twenty) arrived at Jamestown
1790 – The first U.S. census was completed
1831 – London Bridge opened
1876 – Colorado became the 38th United State
1902 – The United States bought the rights to the Panama Canal
1914 – Germany declared war on Russia at the beginning of World War I
1936 – Adolf Hitler presided over the Olympic Games as they opened in Berlin
1944 – Anne Frank made the last entry in her diary
1945 – Mel Ott hit his 500th career homerun, the third person to do so
1966 – Charles Joseph Whitman opened fire from a tower at the University of Texas at Austin, killing 15 people and wounding 31 others
1981 – MTV began broadcasting
1993 – Reggie Jackson was admitted into the Baseball Hall of Fame
1997 – Coronado Springs Resort opened at Walt Disney World
2007 – The Interstate-35 West Mississippi River Bridge in Minneapolis, Minnesota collapsed during rush hour traffic

August 2: Pierre Charles L'Enfant 1754, Constantine I of Greece 1868, Jack Warner 1892, Myrna Loy 1905, Gary Merrill 1915, Shimon Peres 1923, Carroll O'Connor 1924, Peter O'Toole 1932, Wes Craven 1939, Max Wright 1943, Tom Burgmeier 1943, Joanna Cassidy 1945, Lance Ito 1950,

173

Butch Patrick 1953, Victoria Jackson 1959, Cynthia Stevenson 1963, Mary-Louise Parker 1964, Tim Wakefield 1966, Kevin Smith 1970

1100 – King William II of England was killed by an arrow in New Forest (right), near Winchester, England, although it was never determined if this was the result of a hunting accident or murder

1610 – Henry Hudson first sailed into what today is known as Hudson Bay
1776 – Members of the Continental Congress began adding their signatures to the Declaration of Independence
1870 – The world's first subway opened in London
1876 – Wild Bill Hickok was shot from behind and killed while playing poker in Deadwood, South Dakota
1921 – Eight White Sox players were acquitted of throwing the 1919 World Series
1922 – Alexander Graham Bell died
1934 – Adolf Hitler became Fuhrer of Germany
1985 – 137 people were killed when a jumbo jet crashed at Dallas-Fort Worth International Airport
1990 – Iraq invaded the neighboring country of Kuwait
1999 – In eastern India, at least 278 people were killed when two trains collided

August 3: Carrie Ingalls 1870, Harry Heilmann 1894, Marv Levy 1925, Tony Bennett 1926, Haystacks Calhoun 1934, Stephen Berkoff 1937, Martin Sheen 1940, Martha Stewart 1941, JoMarie Payton 1950, John Landis 1950, Jay North 1951, Isaiah Washington 1963, Rod Beck 1968, Troy Glaus 1976, Tom Brady 1977, Evangeline Lilly 1979, Jon Foster 1984

1492 – Christopher Columbus left Spain with three ships in an attempt to circle the globe
1678 – Robert LaSalle built *Le Griffon*, the first ship built in America
1783 – 35,000 people were killed in Japan when Mt. Asama erupted
1852 – The first intercollegiate event was held when Yale and Harvard had a boat race
1900 – Firestone Tire & Rubber Co. was founded
1914 – Germany declared war on France
1923 – Calvin Coolidge was sworn in as the 30th President of the United States after the sudden death of President Warren G. Harding
1933 – The Mickey Mouse watch was first sold at a price of $2.75
1936 – Jesse Owens won the first of his four Olympic gold medals
1949 – The National Basketball Association (NBA) was formed
1958 – The *Nautilus* became the first vessel to cross the North Pole underwater
1981 – Air traffic controllers in the United States began to strike
1990 – Thousands of Iraqi troops pushed within a few miles of the border of Saudi Arabia
2004 – In New York, the Statue of Liberty re-opened to the public, having been closed since the terrorist attacks on the United States on September 11, 2001

August 4: Percy Bysshe Shelley 1792, John Venn 1834, Elizabeth Bowes-Lyon (the Queen Mother) 1900, Louis Armstrong 1901, Helen Thomas 1920, Dallas Green 1934, John Riggins 1949, Billy Bob Thornton 1955, Mary Decker Slaney 1958, Kym Karath 1958, Barack Obama 1961, Roger Clemens 1962, John Farrell 1962, Daniel Dae Kim 1968, Troy O'Leary 1969, Michael DeLuise 1970, Jeff Gordon 1971, Kurt Busch 1978, Tiffany Evans 1992, Dylan Sprouse 1992, Cole Sprouse 1992

1821 – The *Saturday Evening Post* was first published
1892 – The family of Lizzie Borden was found murdered in their Fall River, Massachusetts home
1914 – Germany invaded Belgium
1914 – Britain declared war on Germany during World War I
1916 – The United States purchased the Danish Virgin Islands
1944 – Nazi police raided a house in Amsterdam and arrested eight people, including teenager Anne Frank
1977 – The Department of Energy was formed in the United States
1983 – New York Yankee outfielder Dave Winfield threw a baseball during warm-ups and accidentally killed a seagull
2007 – NASA's *Phoenix* space craft was launched toward Mars

August 5: John Huston 1906, Les Paul 1915, Neil Armstrong 1930, Loni Anderson 1946, Bernie Carbo 1947, Maureen McCormick 1956, Tawny Kitaen 1961, Patrick Ewing 1962, Jonathan Silverman 1966, John Olerud 1968, Terri Clark 1968, Mark Mulder 1977, Eric Hinske 1977, Carl Crawford 1981

1305 – William Wallace was captured by the English near Glasgow
1620 – The *Mayflower* departed Southampton, England
1833 – The village of Chicago was incorporated
1861 – The first income tax was issued in the United States
1884 – On Bedloe's Island in New York Harbor, later Liberty Island, the cornerstone for the Statue of Liberty was laid
1940 – Latvia was annexed by the Soviet Union
1957 – *American Bandstand* made its national debut on ABC-TV
1962 – Marilyn Monroe was found dead in her home at the age of 36 of an apparent suicide
1962 – Nelson Mandela was jailed in South Africa, and not released until 1992
1969 – *Mariner 7*, a U.S. space probe, passed by Mars
1981 – President Ronald Reagan fired over 11,000 striking air traffic controllers
1991 – Iraq admitted to misleading United Nations inspectors about secret biological weapons
1998 – The America version of *Whose Line Is It Anyway?* debuted on ABC-TV
1999 – Mark McGwire hit his 500th home run

August 6: Louis XIX of France 1775, Alfred Lord Tennyson 1809, Edith Roosevelt 1861, Alexander Fleming 1881, Will Lee (Mr. Hooper of Sesame Street) 1908, Lucille Ball 1911, Robert Mitchum 1917, Andy Warhol 1928, Piers Anthony 1934, Peter Bonerz 1938, Ray Buktenica 1942, Dorian Harewood 1950, Catherine Hicks 1951, David Robinson 1965, M. Night Shyamalan 1970, Victor Zambrano 1975, Soleil Moon Frye 1976, Adrienne Curry 1982, JonBenet Ramsey 1990

1787 – The Constitutional Convention began in Philadelphia
1806 – The Holy Roman Empire went out of existence as Emperor Francis I abdicated
1890 – William Kemmler became the first person executed by electric chair
1914 – Austria-Hungary declared war against Russia.
1914 – Serbia declared war against Germany
1926 – Gertrude Ederle became the first woman to swim the English Channel

1945 – The United States dropped an atomic bomb on Hiroshima, Japan, killing 140,000 people
1952 – Satchel Paige, at age 46, became the oldest pitcher to complete a Major League Baseball game
1962 – Jamaica gained its independence

August 7: James Bowdoin 1726, Nathaniel Greene 1742, Mata Hari 1876, Billie Burke 1884, Louis Leakey 1903, Carl Switzer 1927, Romeo Muller 1928, Don Larsen 1929, B.J. Thomas 1942, Garrison Keillor 1942, John Glover 1944, Rodney Crowell 1950, Wayne Knight 1955, Alberto Salazar 1958, David Duchovny 1960, Maggie Wheeler 1961, Harold Perrineau 1963, Charlize Theron 1975, Edgar Renteria 1975, Cirroc Lofton 1978

1789 – The United States War Department was established by the U.S. Congress
1794 – The Whiskey Rebellion began
1914 – Germany invaded France
1942 – During World War II, the Battle of Guadalcanal began
1976 – *Viking II* entered Mars orbit
1997 – Garth Brooks gave a concert in Central Park, New York in front of 750,000 people
1998 – The U.S. embassies in Nairobi, Kenya and Dar es Salaam, Tanzania were bombed killing 224 people and injuring over 5,500
2003 – In California, Arnold Schwarzenegger announced that he would run for the office of governor
2005 – News anchor Peter Jennings died at the age of 67
2007 – Barry Bonds of the San Francisco Giants broke Hank Aaron's record when he hit his 756th career home run
2008 – The brief South Ossetia War between Georgia and Russia began

August 8: Bob Smith 1879, Rory Calhoun 1922, Esther Williams 1922, Richard Anderson 1926, Mel Tillis 1932, Frank Howard 1936, Dustin Hoffman 1937, Connie Stevens 1938, Dennis Tito 1940, Peter Weir 1944, Jose Cruz 1947, Larry Wilcox 1948, Svetlana Savitskaya 1948, Keith Carradine 1949, Donny Most 1953, Deborah Norville 1958, Tawny Cypress 1976, Odie (from the "Garfield" comic) 1978, Rashard Lewis 1979, Roger Federer 1981, Katie Leung 1987, Princess Beatrice of York 1988

1588 – The Spanish Armada was defeated by the English fleet, ending an invasion attempt
1942 – In Washington, DC, six Germans convicted of attempted sabotage were executed

1945 – During World War II, the Soviet Union declared war on Japan

1963 – In England, the Great Train Robbery takes place

1974 – President Richard Nixon announced that he would resign his office the following day

1988 – Wrigley Field in Chicago became the last Major League Baseball field to play a game using lights

August 9: Ralph Houk 1919, Ernest Angley 1921, Robert Shaw 1927, Bob Cousy 1928, Ken Norton 1943, Sam Elliott 1944, Melanie Griffith 1957, Whitney Houston 1963, Karyn Parsons 1966, Deion Sanders 1967, Gillian Anderson 1968, Eric Bana 1968, Troy Percival 1969, Matt Morris 1974, Derek Fisher 1974, Jessica Capshaw 1976, Audrey Tautou 1978, Ashley Johnson 1983

1173 – Construction began on what would become known as the Leaning Tower of Pisa

1483 – The Sistine Chapel opened

1678 – American Indians sold the Bronx to Jonas Bronck for 400 beads

1862 – During the American Civil War, the Confederates under General Stonewall Jackson defeated the Union under General John Pope

1901 – Troops from Columbia invaded Venezuela

1902 – After the death of Queen Victoria, Edward VII was crowned King of England

1930 – Betty Boop appeared in her first cartoon, *Dizzy Dishes*

1936 – Jesse Owens won his fourth gold medal at the Berlin Olympics, the first American ever to do so

1945 – The United States dropped an atomic bomb on Nagasaki, Japan killing over 70,000 people

1965 – A fire at a Titan missile base in Little Rock killed 53 workers

1969 – In Disneyland, the Haunted Mansion opened

1974 – President Richard M. Nixon formally resigned and Gerald Ford was sworn in as the 38th President

1981 – Major League Baseball teams resumed play at the conclusion of the first mid-season players' strike

1983 – Peter Jennings became the solo anchor of *ABC's World News Tonight*

1986 – The musical group Queen gave their final performance with lead singer Freddie Mercury

1988 – The Chicago Cubs became the last Major League Baseball team to play a night game at home

1988 – In the NHL, Wayne Gretsky was traded from the Edmonton Oilers to the Los Angeles Kings

1995 – Jerry Garcia, lead singer of the Grateful Dead, died at the age of 53

August 10: Herbert Hoover 1874, Jack Haley 1898, Noah Berry 1913, Jeff Corey 1914, Rhonda Fleming 1923, Claus Von Bulow 1926, Jimmy Dean 1928, Eddie Fisher 1928, Rocky Colavito 1933, Bobby Hatfield 1940, Daniel Hugh Kelly 1952, Rosanna Arquette 1959, Antonio Banderas 1960, Claudia Christian 1965, John Starks 1965, Riddick Bowe 1967

1776 – Word of America's Declaration of Independence reached London
1792 – French King Louis XVI was arrested and taken into custody
1821 – Missouri became the 24th state to join the Union
1846 – The Smithsonian Institution was chartered by the U.S. Congress
1856 – In Louisiana, a hurricane struck, killing about 400 people
1914 – Austria-Hungary invaded Russia
1921 – Franklin D. Roosevelt was stricken with polio
1945 – The day after the atomic bombing of Nagasaki, Japan announced they would surrender
1948 – *Candid Camera* made its television debut
1977 – The Son of Sam, David Berkowitz, was arrested in Yonkers, New York
1995 – The Los Angeles Dodgers were forced to forfeit a game against the St. Louis Cardinals when fans through hundreds of souvenir baseballs on the field
2000 – The world population reached six billion
2003 – Ekaterina Dmitriev, who was on Earth, and Russian cosmonaut Yuri Malenchenko, who was in space at the time, were married

August 11: Alex Haley 1921, Mike Douglas 1925, Arlene Dahl 1928, Jerry Falwell 1933, Ian McDiarmid 1944, John Conlee 1946, Steve Wozniak 1950, Terry "Hulk Hogan" Bollca 1953, Jim Lee 1964, Joe Rogan 1967, Bubba Crosby 1976, Melky Cabrera 1984

1877 – The two moons of Mars were discovered by Asaph Hall, an American astronomer
1929 – Babe Ruth became the first baseball player to hit 500 home runs in his career
1934 – Alcatraz Federal Prison opened
1941 – The Atlantic Charter was signed by U.S. President Franklin Roosevelt and British Prime Minister Winston Churchill
1962 – Andrian Nikolayev, of the Soviet Union, was launched on a 94-hour flight, becoming the third Russian to go into space

1992 – In Bloomington, Minnesota, the Mall of America opened, becoming the largest shopping mall in the United States
2003 – Charles Taylor, President of Liberia, flew into exile after ceding power to his vice president, Moses Blah

August 12: George IV of England 1762, Diamond Jim Brady 1856, Christy Mathewson 1880, Cecil B. DeMille 1881, Joe Besser 1907, Jane Wyatt 1912, John Derek 1926, Porter Wagoner 1927, Dan Curtis 1928, Buck Owens 1929, William Goldman 1931, Walter Dean Myers 1937, George Hamilton 1939, Jennifer Warren 1941, Mark Knopfler 1949, Bruce Greenwood 1956, Miss Cleo 1962, Sir Mix A Lot 1963, Peter Krause 1965, Rebecca Gayheart 1971, Pete Sampras 1971, Matt Clement 1974, Casey Affleck 1975, Antoine Walker 1976, Plaxico Burress 1977, Cindy Klassen 1979, Dominique Swain 1980

30 BC – Cleopatra committed suicide
1656 – The King Phillip's War came to an end with the killing of Indian chief King Phillip
1833 – Chicago was founded
1851 – Isaac Singer was granted a patent for the sewing machine
1877 – Thomas Edison invented the phonograph and made the first sound recording
1898 – Hawaii was annexed by the United States of America
1898 – The Spanish-American War was ended with the signing of the Peace Protocol
1908 – The first Ford Model T was built
1960 – *Echo I*, the first communications satellite, was launched
1969 – The Boston Celtics were sold for $6 million
1981 – IBM unveiled its first PC
1992 – The North American Free Trade Agreement (NAFTA) was announced between Canada, Mexico, and the United States
1994 – Major League Baseball players went on strike, rather than allow team owners to limit their salaries
2007 – Television talk show host and game show producer Merv Griffin died at the age of 82

August 13: Lucy Stone 1818, Annie Oakley 1860, Bert Lahr 1895, Alfred Hitchcock 1899, Ben Hogan 1912, Fidel Castro 1926, Pat Harrington 1929, Don Ho 1930, Kevin Tighe 1944, Dan Fogelberg 1951, Danny Bonaduce 1959, Corey Patterson 1979, Shani Davis 1982

1521 – Present day Mexico City was captured from the Aztec Indians by Spanish conqueror Hernando Cortez

1792 – French revolutionaries captured and imprisoned the entire French royal family
1913 – Stainless steel was invented by Harry Brearley
1918 – Opha Mae Johnson became the first woman to enlist in the United States Marine Corps
1934 – Al Capp's comic strip *L'il Abner* made its debut in newspapers
1940 – During World War II, the Battle of Britain began
1942 – Disney's *Bambi* opened
1997 – *South Park* debuted on Comedy Central
2004 – The opening ceremonies of the 2004 Olympic Games in Athens, Greece were held

August 14: Doc Holliday 1851, Alice Ghostly 1926, Earl Weaver 1930, Trevor Bannister 1936, David Crosby 1941, Jimmy Johnson 1943, Steve Martin 1945, Susan St. James 1946, Danielle Steel 1947, Gary Larson 1950, Bob Backlund 1950, Mark Fidrych 1954, Rusty Wallace 1956, Jackee Harry 1956, Earvin "Magic" Johnson 1959, Susan Olsen 1961, Brannon Braga 1964, Halle Berry 1968, Catherine Bell 1968, Chucky Atkins 1974, Mike Vrabel 1975, Juan Pierre 1977, Mila Kunis 1983, Clay Buchholz 1984

1842 – The Second Seminole War ended, with the Seminole Indians leaving Florida for Oklahoma
1848 – The Oregon Territory was established
1873 – *Field and Stream* magazine was first published (left)
1896 – Gold was discovered in Canada's Yukon Territory
1908 – The first beauty contest was held in Folkestone, England
1917 – China declared war on Germany and Austria during World War I
1935 – The United States Congress passed the Social Security Act into law
1941 – U.S. President Franklin Roosevelt and British Prime Minister Winston Churchill issued the Atlantic Charter

1945 – It was announced by U.S. President Harry Truman that Japan had surrendered unconditionally, thus ending World War II

1953 – The whiffle ball was invented

1995 – Shannon Faulkner became the first female cadet in the history of The Citadel, South Carolina's state military college

1997 – Timothy McVeigh was formally sentenced to death for the Oklahoma City bombing

2005 – A Cypriot plane crashed into the side of a hill in Greece killing all 121 people on board, including 48 children

August 15: Napoleon Bonaparte 1769, Sir Walter Scott 1771, Charles Comiskey 1859, Florence Harding 1860, Julia Child 1912, Rose Marie 1923, Mike Connors 1925, Abby Dalton 1932, Bobby Helms 1933, Vernon Jordan 1935, Linda Ellerbee 1944, Gene Upshaw 1945, Tony Robinson 1946, Tess Harper 1950, Tom Kelly 1950, Princess Anne of Great Britain 1950, Debi Mazar 1964, Debra Messing 1968, Ben Affleck 1972, Natasha Henstridge 1974, Carl Edwards 1979, Oliver Perez 1981, Joe Jonas 1989

1057 – Macbeth, the King of Scotland, was killed by the son of King Duncan

1824 – Freed American slaves formed the country of Liberia

1914 – The Panama Canal was officially opened

1935 – Will Rogers was killed in an airplane crash

1939 – *The Wizard of Oz* premiered in Hollywood

1944 – The Allied forces of World War II landed in southern France

1945 – Japan surrendered ending World War II, the date becoming known as Victory in Japan (or VJ) Day

1947 – India became independent from Britain and was divided into the countries of India and Pakistan

1948 – CBS-TV debuted its first nightly news broadcast with anchorman Douglas Edwards

1961 – Workers began construction of the Berlin Wall

1969 – The Woodstock Music and Art Festival began

1987 – $100 million in damage was done in the Chicago area when 13 ½ inches of rain fell

1998 – A car bomb in Omagh, Northern Ireland, killed 29 people and injured 370 others

2001 – Astronomers announced the discovery of the first solar system outside our own, after they discovered two planets orbiting a star in the Big Dipper

August 16: T.E. Lawrence (of Arabia) 1888, Menachem Begin 1913, Fess Parker 1925, Lois Nettleton 1929, Robert Culp 1930, Frank Gifford 1930,

Eydie Gorme 1931, Julie Newmar 1933, Stuart Roosa 1933, Lesley Ann Warren 1946, Richard Hunt 1951, Reginald Vel Johnson 1952, Kathie Lee Gifford 1953, James Cameron 1954, Angela Bassett 1958, Madonna 1958, Laura Innes 1959, Timothy Hutton 1960, Steve Carrell 1962, Vanessa Carlton 1980, Cam Gigandet 1982

1812 – Detroit fell to Indian and British troops in the War of 1812
1906 – 1,500 people died in an earthquake in Valparaiso, Chile
1920 – The only fatality to occur in Major League Baseball history happened, when Ray Chapman of the Cleveland Indians was hit in the head with a fastball from Carl Mays of the New York Yankees
1948 – Baseball legend Babe Ruth died at the age of 53
1954 – The first issue of *Sports Illustrated* was published
1960 – Cyprus was granted independence by Britain
1977 – King of rock-and-roll Elvis Presley died at the age of 42 in Memphis, Tennessee at his Graceland mansion

August 17: Davy Crockett 1786, Samuel Goldwyn 1882, Mae West 1893, Maureen O'Hara 1921, Robert De Niro 1943, Butch Hobson 1951, John Romita Jr. 1956, Belinda Carlisle 1958, Sean Penn 1960, Donnie Wahlberg 1969, Jorge Posada 1971, Dustin Pedroia 1983, Jim Courrier 1986

1790 – The capital city of the United States moved to Philadelphia from New York City
1815 – Napoleon began serving his exile when he arrived at the island of St. Helena
1896 – The Klondike gold rush was set off by George Carmack discovering gold on Rabbit Creek in Alaska, later called Bonanza Creek
1903 – Joseph Pulitzer donated a million dollars to Columbia University, starting the Pulitzer Prizes in his name
1943 – The Allied conquest of Sicily was completed as American and British forces entered Messina
1961 – The Communist East German government completed the construction of the Berlin Wall
1969 – Hurricane Camille hit the Mississippi Gulf Coast killing 248 people
1976 – Alex Haley's novel *Roots* was first published
1998 – President Bill Clinton admitted to having an improper relationship with Monica Lewinsky, a White House intern
1999 – More than 15,000 people were killed in an earthquake in Turkey
2002 – In Santa Rosa, California, the Charles M. Schulz Museum opened to the public

2008 – Michael Phelps won his eighth Olympic gold medal in the same Olympics, setting a new record

August 18: Meriwether Lewis 1774, Caspar Weinberger 1917, Shelley Winters 1920, Rosalynn Carter 1927, Roman Polanski 1933, Robert Redford 1937, Martin Mull 1943, Elayne Boosler 1952, Patrick Swayze 1952, Denis Leary 1957, Madeleine Stowe 1958, Bob Woodruff 1961, Edward Norton 1969, Christian Slater 1969, Malcolm-Jamal Warner 1970, Jeremy Shockey 1980

1227 – The Mongol conqueror Genghis Khan died
1900 – Ex-Secretary of State Caleb Powers was found guilty of conspiracy to kill Kentucky Governor William Goebel
1940 – Canada and the United States established a joint defense plan against possible enemy attacks during World War II
1966 – The first pictures of Earth taken from moon orbit were sent back to the United States
1983 – Twenty-two people were killed and over $1 billion in damage was caused when hurricane Alicia hit the Texas coast
1990 – The first shots were fired by the United States in the Persian Gulf Crisis when a U.S. frigate fired rounds across the bow of an Iraqi oil tanker
1992 – Basketball legend Larry Bird, after 13 years with the Boston Celtics, announced his retirement

August 19: Orville Wright 1871, Coco Chanel 1883, Malcolm Forbes 1919, Gene Roddenberry 1921, Willie Shoemaker 1931, Diana Muldaur 1938, Jill St. John 1940, Eddy Raven 1944, Bill Clinton 1946, Tipper Gore 1948, Gerald McRaney 1948, Jonathan Frakes 1952, Mary Matalin 1953, Peter Gallagher 1955, Adam Arkin 1956, Gary Chapman 1957, Ron Darling 1960, John Stamos 1963, Lee Ann Womack 1966, Matthew Perry 1969, Fat joe 1970, Lindsey Jacobellis 1985

1812 – Old Ironsides, the *USS Constitution*, won the 1812 naval battle against the British frigate *Guerriere* east of Nova Scotia
1934 – The first All-American Soap Box Derby was held in Dayton, Ohio
1960 - Francis Gary Powers, an American U-2 pilot, was convicted of espionage in Moscow
1960 – Russia launched *Sputnik V* into space, which included two dogs named Belka and Strelka, as well as 40 mice and 2 rats, these being the first animals in space to be brought back to Earth safely
1977 - Comedian Groucho Marx died at the age of 86
1981 - The final episode of *Charlie's Angels* aired on ABC-TV

August 20: Emily Bronte 1818, Benjamin Harrison 1833, Van Johnson 1916, Jim Reeves 1924, Don King 1931, George Mitchell 1933, Isaac Hayes 1942, Connie Chung 1946, Michael Jeter 1952, Rudy Gatlin 1952, Peter Horton 1953, Al Roker 1954, Don Stark 1954, Todd Helton 1973, Banjamin Barnes 1981, Demi Lovato 1982

1641 – Scotland and Britain signed the Treaty of Pacification
1878 – The American Bar Association was formed
1914 – German forces occupied Brussels, Belgium, during World War I
1939 – The National Bowling Association was founded in Detroit
1940 – France fell to the Germans during World War II
1977 – Deep space probe Voyager 2 was launched by the United States
1989 – Jose and Kitty Menendez were shot to death by their sons Lyle and Erik
1989 – In London, a pleasure boat sank in the Thames River killing 51 people
1998 – United States military forces attacked a terrorist camp in Afghanistan and a chemical plant in Sudan due to their connection with terrorist Osama bin Laden

August 21: Philip II of France 1165, Alfonso VI of Portugal 1643, William IV of England 1765, Count Basie 1904, Friz Freling 1906, Christopher Robin Milne 1920, Jack Weston 1924, Princess Margaret of Great Britain 1930, Wilt Chamberlain 1936, Kenny Rogers 1938, Clarence Williams III 1939, Peter Weir 1944, Harry Smith 1951, Archie Griffin 1954, Kim Cattrall 1956, Jim McMahon 1959, Carrie-Ann Moss 1967, Sergey Brin 1973, Paul Menard 1980, B.J. Upton 1984, Hayden Panettiere 1989

1680 – Pueblo Indians captured Santa Fe from the Spanish during the Pueblo Revolt
1831 – Nat Turner, a former slave, led a violent insurrection in Virginia
1858 – The Lincoln-Douglas debates began
1942 – During World War II, the Battle of Stalingrad began
1959 – Hawaii became the 50th state
1988 – An earthquake on the Nepal-India border killed over 1,000 people
1989 – *Voyager 2*, a U.S. space probe, flew close to the Neptune moon called Triton
1993 – NASA lost contact with the *Mars Observer* spacecraft

August 22: Ned Hanlon 1857, Dorothy Parker 1893, Ray Bradbury 1920, Norman Schwarzkopf 1934, Carl "Yaz" Yastrzemski 1939, Valerie Harper 1940, Bill Parcells 1941, Cindy Williams 1947, Paul Molitor 1956, Collin Raye 1960, Adewale Akinnuoye-Agbaje 1967, Howie Dorough 1973

1485 – The War of the Roses ended at the Battle of Bosworth Field with the death of England's King Richard III

1642 – The English Civil War began when Charles I called Parliament and its soldiers, "Traitors"

1770 – Australia was claimed by England when Captain James Cook landed there

1775 – The American colonies were proclaimed to be in a state of open rebellion by England's King George III

1846 – The United States annexed New Mexico

1851 – The first America's Cup was won by the yacht America

1864 – The Red Cross was formed with the signing of the first Geneva Convention

1901 – The Cadillac Company was founded in Detroit, named after the 18th century French explorer Antoine de la Mothe Cadillac

1902 – Theodore Roosevelt became the first American President to ride in an automobile

1932 – The BBC began its first TV broadcast in England

1966 – Peppermint Patty made her first appearance in a *Peanuts* comic strip

1989 – Nolan Ryan became the first major league pitcher to strike out 5,000 batters

1989 – It was discovered that the planet Neptune has rings

2007 – The Texas Rangers baseball team defeated the Baltimore Orioles, 30-3, scoring the most runs by a team in a modern day Major League game

August 23: Ivan VI of Russia 1740, Louis XVI of France 1754, Gene Kelly 1912, Barbara Eden 1934, Ronnie Cox 1938, Richard Sanders 1940, Shelley Long 1949, Rick Springfield 1949, James Van Praagh 1958, Ed Gale 1963, Kenny Wallace 1963, Jeremy Schaap 1969, River Phoenix 1970, Jay Mohr 1970, Aaron Douglas 1971, Casey Blake 1973, Mark Bellhorn 1974, Kobe Bryant 1978, Rex Grossman 1980, Natalie Coughlin 1982

1305 – William Wallace, Scottish patriot, was executed on orders from English King Edward I

1914 – Japan declared war on Germany during World War I

1926 – Silent-film star Rudolph Valentino died at the age of 31

1939 – Nazi Germany and the Soviet Union signed a non-aggression treaty

1940 – During World War II, Germany started bombing London

1959 – In the *Peanuts* comic strip, Sally debuted as the infant sister of Charlie Brown

1962 – The first live broadcast between the United States and Europe occurred via the Telstar satellite

1979 – Soviet ballet dancer Alexander Godunov defected while the Bolshoi Ballet was on tour in New York City

1984 – South Fork Ranch, the home of the fictitious Ewing clan of the CBS-TV show, *Dallas*, was sold

1990 _ East Germany and West Germany announced they would reunite on October 3rd

1992 – Hurricane Andrew hit the Bahamas with 120 mile per hour winds

1998 – *That '70's Show* first aired on FOX-TV

August 24: Alexander II of Scotland 1198, Harry Hooper 1887, Dennis James 1917, Yasser Arafat 1929, Kenny Baker 1934, Vince McMahon 1945, Joe Regalbuto 1949, Mike Huckabee 1955, Steve Guttenberg 1958, Cal Ripken, Jr. 1960, Craig Kilborn 1962, Marlee Matlin 1965, Reggie Miller 1965, Dave Chappelle 1973, Carmine Giovinazzo 1973, Jennifer Lien 1974, Rafael Furcal 1978, Rupert Grint 1988

79 AD – Mount Vesuvius erupted, killing approximately 20,000 people and burying the cities of Pompeii, Stabiae and Herculaneum

410 – The Visigoths took over Rome

1456 – The printing of the Gutenberg Bible was completed

1814 – Washington, DC, was invaded by British forces that set fire to the White House and Capitol Building

1932 – Amelia Earhart became the first woman to fly across the United States non-stop

1979 – *The Facts of Life* premiered on NBC-TV

1981 – Mark David Chapman was sentenced to 20 years to life in prison for the murder of John Lennon

1989 – Pete Rose, the manager of the Cincinnati Reds, was banned from baseball for life after being accused of betting on baseball

1989 – The U.S. space probe, *Voyager 2*, sent back photographs of Neptune

1992 – Hurricane Andrew hit southern Florida causing 55 deaths in the Bahamas, Florida, and Louisiana

2006 – The International Astronomers Union decided that Pluto would no longer be considered a planet, but would fit into a new category called a dwarf planet

August 25: Allen Pinkerton 1819, Ruby Keeler 1909, Van Johnson 1916, Mel Ferrer 1917, Leonard Bernstein 1918, George C. Wallace 1919, Monty

Hall 1923, Althea Gibson 1927, Sean Connery 1930, Regis Philbin 1931, Tom Skerritt 1933, Rollie Fingers 1946, Anne Archer 1947, Gene Simmons 1949, Elvis Costello 1954, Tim Burton 1958, Billy Ray Cyrus 1961, Ally Walker 1961, Joanne Whalley 1964, Blair Underwood 1964, Albert Belle 1966, Rachael Ray 1968, Jo Dee Messina 1969, Claudia Schiffer 1971, Marvin Harrison 1972, Kel Mitchell 1978, Rachel Bilson 1981, Blake Lively 1987

1814 – The United States Library of Congress was destroyed by British forces
1825 – Uruguay declared independence from Brazil
1875 – Captain Matthew Webb swam from Dover, England, to Calais, France, making him the first person to swim the English Channel
1916 – The National Park Service was established as part of the U.S. Department of the Interior
1921 – The United States signed a peace treaty with Germany
1944 – Paris, France, was liberated by Allied forces, ending four years of German occupation
1944 – Romania declared war on Germany
1981 – The U.S. *Voyager 2* space probe sent back pictures and data about Saturn
1984 – Author Truman Capote was found dead in his home at the age of 59
1985 – Samantha Smith, the schoolgirl whose letter to Soviet leader Yuri Andropov resulted in her peace tour of the Soviet Union, was killed with her father in an airplane crash in Maine
1991 – Belarus declared independence from the Soviet Union

August 26: Sir Robert Walpole 1676, Jim Davis 1915, Irving R. Levine 1922, Geraldine Ferraro 1935, Tom Ridge 1945, Michael Jeter 1952, Branford Marsalis 1960, Chris Burke 1965, Jamal Lewis 1979, Macaulay Culkin 1980, Chris Pine 1980

55 B.C. – Britain was invaded by Roman forces under Julius Caesar
1498 – Michelangelo was commissioned to carve the Pieta
1839 – The ship *Amistad* was captured off the coast of Long Island
1862 – During the American Civil War, the Second Battle of Bull Run began
1914 – During World War I, Germany defeated Russia in the Battle of Tannenberg
1920 – The 19th Amendment top the Constitution was ratified, giving women the right to vote

1939 – The first televised Major League Baseball games were shown, a double-header between the Cincinnati Reds and the Brooklyn Dodgers
1947 – Don Bankhead became the first black pitcher in Major League Baseball
1974 – Charles Lindberg died at the age of 72
1978 – Pope John Paul I became pope

August 27: Confucius 551 B.C., Hannibal Hamlin 1809, Charles G. Dawes 1865, Lyndon B. Johnson 1908, Mother Theresa 1910, Martha Ray 1916, G.W. Bailey 1945, Buddy Bell 1951, Paul Reubens 1952, Chandra Wilson 1969, Jim Thome 1970, Sarah Chalke 1976

1859 – The first successful oil well was drilled in the United States, in Titusville, Pennsylvania
1889 – Boxer Jack Dempsey suffered the first defeat of his career in a bout against George LaBlanche
1912 – The Edgar Rice Burroughs book *Tarzan of the Apes* was published for the first time
1945 – American troops landed in Japan after the surrender of the Japanese government at the end of World War II
1962 – American space probe *Mariner 2* was launched on its was to Venus
1999 – The final crew of the Russian space station Mir left the station to return to Earth
2001 – Work began on the World War II Memorial in Washington, DC

August 28: Leo Nikolayevich Tolstoy 1828, Lucy Hayes 1831, Charles Boyer 1899, Jack Kirby 1917, Nancy Kulp 1921, Donald O'Connor 1925, Roxie Roker 1929, William S. Cohen 1940, David Soul 1943, Daniel Stern 1957, Scott Hamilton 1958, Emma Samms 1961, Shania Twain 1965, Billy Boyd 1968, Jason Priestley 1969, Jack Black 1969, Janet Evans 1971, LeAnn Rimes 1982

1845 – *Scientific American* magazine was first published
1883 – Slavery was banned by the British Parliament throughout the British Empire
1916 – Italy declared war against Germany during World War I
1963 – Dr. Martin Luther King, Jr., gave his "I Have a Dream" speech at a civil rights rally in Washington, DC
1988 – At an air show in Ramstein, West Germany, three jets collided and then plunged into a crowd, killing 70 people
1996 – The divorce of Britain's Prince Charles and Princess Diana was finalized, ending their 15-year marriage

August 29: John Locke 1632, Oliver Wendell Holmes 1809, Barry Sullivan 1912, Ingrid Bergman 1915, George Montgomery 1916, Isabel Sanford 1917, Sir Richard Attenborough 1923, Elliott Gould 1938, Robin Leach 1941, Deborah Van Valkenburgh 1952, Michael Jackson 1958, Rebecca DeMornay 1962, Ed Rogers 1978

1533 – The Incan Empire ended when Atahualpa, the last Incan King of Peru, was murdered on orders from Spanish conqueror Francisco Pizarro
1907 – The Quebec Bridge collapsed, killing 75 workers
1965 – Gemini 5, carrying astronauts Gordon Cooper and Pete Conrad, splashed down in the Atlantic Ocean after eight days in space
1967 – The final episode of *The Fugitive* aired
1990 – Iraqi President Saddam Hussein, in a television interview, declared that America could not defeat Iraq
2005 – Hurricane Katrina caused huge amounts of destruction on much of the Gulf Coast and nearly destroyed New Orleans, Louisiana

August 30: Mary Wollstonecraft Shelley 1797, Shirley Booth 1907, Fred MacMurray 1908, Ted Williams 1918, Bill Daily 1928, John Phillips 1935, Ben Jones 1941, Jean-Claude Killy 1943, Robert Parish 1953, Michael Chiklis 1963, Michael Michele 1966, Cameron Diaz 1972, Shaun Alexander 1977, Cliff Lee 1978, Andy Roddick 1982

30 B.C. – Cleopatra, the seventh queen of Egypt, committed suicide
1835 – Melbourne, Australia was founded
1836 – Houston, Texas was founded
1862 – The Confederates defeated Union forces at the second Battle of Bull Run
1905 – Ty Cobb made his Major League batting debut with the Detroit Tigers
1941 – During World War II, the Battle of Leningrad began
1967 – Thurgood Marshall became the first black man to serve on the United States Supreme Court
1983 – Guion S. Bluford Jr. became the first African-America to travel to space
1984 – The Space Shuttle *Discovery* took off on its first trip to space
1991 – The Soviet republic of Azerbaijan declared its independence
1993 – On CBS-TV, *The Late Show with David Letterman* premiered

August 31: Gaius Caligula 12 AD, Maria Montessori 1870, Arthur Godfrey 1903, Buddy Hackett 1924, James Coburn 1928, Frank Robinson 1935,

Itzhak Perlman 1945, Richard Gere 1949, Edwin Moses 1958, Hideo Nomo 1968, Deborah Gibson 1970, Padraig Harrington 1971

1422 – Nine month old Henry VI became King of England

1803 – Lewis and Clark start from Pittsburgh on their famous expedition

1888 – The first of Jack the Ripper's known victims, Mary Ann Nichols, was murdered

1897 – Thomas Edison received a patent for a movie projector known as a Kinetoscope

1940 – Lawrence Olivier and Vivian Leigh were married

1959 – Sandy Koufax set a National League record by striking out 18 hitters

1964 – California officially became the most populated state in America

1969 – Boxer Rocky Marciano died in an airplane crash in Iowa

1985 – The Night Stalker killer, Richard Ramirez, was captured by residents in Los Angeles

1988 – A Delta Boeing 727 crashed during takeoff at Dallas-Fort Worth International Airport in Texas

1989 – Great Britain's Princess Anne and Mark Phillips announced that they were separating after 16 years of marriage

1991 – Uzbekistan and Kirghiziz declared their independence from the Soviet Union

1997 – Princess Diana of Wales died at the age of 36 in a car crash in Paris, along with millionaire Dodi Al-Fayed

2006 – Stolen two years earlier, the famous painting *The Scream* by Edvard Munch was recovered during a raid by Norwegian police (see image at left)

September

September 1: Edgar Rice Burroughs 1875, Richard Farnsworth 1920, Rocky Marciano 1923, Gene Colan 1926, Boxcar Willie 1931, Ann Richards 1933, Conway Twitty 1933, Lily Tomlin 1939, Barry Gibb 1946, Dr. Phil 1950, Billy Blanks 1955, Gloria Estefan 1957, Tim Hardaway 1966, Ricardo Chavira 1971, Jason Taylor 1974, Clinton Portis 1981

1807 – Former U.S. Vice President Aaron Burr was found innocent of treason
1897 – The first section of Boston's subway system was opened
1905 – Saskatchewan and Alberta became the ninth and tenth provinces of Canada
1906 – Jack Coombs of the American League's Philadelphia Athletics pitched 24 innings against the Boston Red Sox
1923 – About 100,000 people were killed when an earthquake hit Tokyo and Yokohama, Japan
1939 – World War II began when Germany invaded Poland
1945 – The United States received official word of Japan's formal surrender that ended World War II
1969 – Colonel Moammar Gadhafi seized power in Libya after the government was overthrown
1970 – The last episode of *I Dream of Jeannie* aired on NBC-TV
1972 – America's Bobby Fischer beat Russia's Boris Spassky to become world chess champion
1979 – The U.S. *Pioneer 11* became the first spacecraft to visit Saturn
1982 – J.R. Richard returned to Major League Baseball after a two-year absence following a near-fatal stroke
1983 – A Korean Air Lines Boeing 747 was shot down when it entered Soviet airspace, killing 269 people
1985 – The *Titanic* was found at the bottom of the ocean by Dr. Robert Ballard and Jean Louis Michel in a joint U.S. and French expedition

1995 – Sony's Playstation was released in the United States

September 2: Liliuokalani of Hawaii 1838, Peter Ueberroth 1937, Walt Simonson 1946, Billy Preston 1946, Terry Bradshaw 1948, Christa McAuliffe 1948, Nate "Tiny" Archibald 1948, Mark Harmon 1951, Jimmy Connors 1952, Eric Dickerson 1960, Keanu Reeves 1964, Lennox Lewis 1965, Salma Hayek 1966, Cynthia Watros 1968

1666 – The Great Fire of London broke out, which burned for three days destroying 10,000 buildings, including St. Paul's Cathedral
1789 – The U.S. Treasury Department was established
1864 – During the U.S. Civil War, Union forces led by General William T. Sherman occupied Atlanta
1901 – Theodore Roosevelt, then Vice-President, said, "Speak softly and carry a big stick" in a speech at the Minnesota State Fair
1935 – A hurricane hit the Florida Keys killing 423 people
1969 – Ho Chi Minh, president of North Vietnam, died
1969 – NBC-TV canceled *Star Trek*
1992 – The United States and Russia agreed to a joint venture to build a space station
1998 – 229 people were killed when a Swissair jetliner crashed into the Atlantic near Peggy's Cove, Nova Scotia
2005 – Actor Bob Denver died at the age of 70

September 3: Sarah Orne Jewitt 1849, Ferdinand Porsche 1875, Alan Ladd 1913, Kitty Carlisle-Hart 1914, Mort Walker 1923, Eileen Brennan 1935, Charlie Sheen 1965, Luis Gonzalez 1967, Shaun White 1986

1189 – Richard the Lion-Heart was crowned King of England
1658 – Oliver Cromwell died
1783 The Revolutionary War between the United States and Great Britain officially ended with the Treaty of Paris
1895 – The first professional football game was played in Latrobe, Pennsylvania
1935 – Sir Malcolm Campbell became the first person to drive an automobile over 300 miles per hour
1939 – British Prime Minister Neville Chamberlain, in a radio broadcast, announced that Britain and France had declared war on Germany
1943 – Italy was invaded by the Allied forces during World War II
1970 – Vince Lombardi died of cancer at the age of 57
1976 – The U.S. spacecraft *Viking 2* landed on Mars
2005 – Chief Justice William Rehnquist died at the age of 80
2006 – 36-year old tennis great Andre Agassi retired after a 21-year career

September 4: Alexander III of Scotland 1241, Ivan The Terrible 1530, Henry Ford II 1917, Paul Harvey 1918, Dick York 1928, Ken Harrelson 1941, Jennifer Salt 1944, Tom Watson 1949, Lawrence-Hilton Jacobs 1953, Paul Smith 1953, Khandi Alexander 1957, Damon Wayans 1960, Mike Piazza 1968, Ione Skye 1971, Beyonce 1981

476 – Romulus Augustulus, the last emperor of the Western Roman Empire, was deposed when Odoacer proclaimed himself King of Italy
1886 – Geronimo, and the Apache Indians he led, surrendered to the U.S. Army in Skeleton Canyon in Arizona
1917 – The American forces in France suffered its first fatalities in World War I
1950 – The *Beatle Bailey* comic strip was first published
1957 – The Ford Motor Company began selling the Edsel
1967 – *Gilligan's Island* aired its last episode on CBS-TV
1972 – Swimmer Mark Spitz won his seventh Olympic gold medal in the 400-meter medley relay event at Munich, Germany
1993 – Jim Abbott, a one-handed pitcher for the New York Yankees, pitched a no-hitter
1998 – Google was founded by Larry Page and Sergey Brin, students at Stanford University
2006 – Steve Irwin, also known as the Crocodile Hunter, was killed by a stingray while filming off the coast of Australia

September 5: Louis VIII of France 1187, Louis XIV of France 1638, Johann Christian Bach 1735, Jesse James 1847, Napoleon "Nap" Lajoie 1874, Darryl F. Zanuck 1902, Bob Newhart 1929, Bill Mazeroski 1936, William Devane 1939, George Lazenby 1939, Raquel Welch 1940, Loudon Wainwright III 1946, Freddie Mercury 1946, Michael Keaton 1951, Kristian Alfonso 1963, Dweezil Zappa 1969, Tina Yothers 1973, Rose McGowan 1973, Skandar Keynes 1991

1666 – The Great Fire London ended after three days, destroying 10,000 buildings including St. Paul's Cathedral and, miraculously, killing just 16 people
1698 – Russia's Peter the Great imposed a tax on beards
1774 – The First Continental Congress met in Philadelphia
1836 – Sam Houston was elected as the first President of the Republic of Texas
1877 – Sioux chief Crazy Horse was killed
1905 – The Treaty of Portsmouth was signed by Russia and Japan to end the Russo-Japanese War

1930 – Charles Creighton and James Hagris completed the drive from New York City to Los Angeles and back to New York City, all in reverse gear

1960 – Cassius Clay of Louisville, Kentucky won the gold medal in light heavyweight boxing at the Olympic Games in Rome

1975 – A Secret Service agent foiled an assassination attempt against President Gerald R. Ford

1977 – The United States launched *Voyager I*

1989 – Chris Evert retired from professional tennis after a 19-year career

1997 – Mother Teresa died in Calcutta, India, at the age of 87

September 6: Ivan V of Russia 1666, Marquis de Lafayette 1757, Jane Addams 1860, Joseph P. Kennedy 1888, Vince DiMaggio 1912, JoAnne Worley 1937, Sergio Aragones 1937, Swoosie Kurtz 1944, Larry Lucchino 1945, Jane Curtin 1947, Jeff Foxworthy 1958, Michael Winslow 1960, Elizabeth Vargas 1962, Rosie Perez 1964, Foxy Brown 1979, Ramiele Malubay 1987

1620 – The Pilgrims left on the Mayflower from Plymouth, England to settle in the New World

1628 – The Puritans settled in what would become Salem, Massachusetts

1847 – Henry David Thoreau left Walden Pond and moved in with Ralph Waldo Emerson and his family in Concord, Massachusetts

1901 – President William McKinley was shot and mortally wounded (he died eight days later) by Leon Czolgosz (choll-gosh)

1939 – South Africa declared war on Germany

1952 – Canada's first television station, CBFT-TV, opened in Montreal

1959 – The first Barbie doll was sold by Mattel Toy Corporation

1975 – Martina Navratilova requested political asylum while in New York for the U.S. Open Tennis Tournament

1991   The city of Leningrad in Russia was renamed St. Petersburg, as it had once been known prior to 1924

1995 – Cal Ripken played his 2,131st consecutive game setting a new record previously held by Lou Gehrig

1997 – The funeral service of Princess Diana was held at Westminster Abbey

September 7: Elizabeth I of England 1533, Anna Mary Robertson "Grandma" Moses 1860, Thomas A. Hendricks 1819, Peter Lawford 1923, Buddy Holly 1936, Gloria Gaynor 1949, Susan Blakely 1950, Julie Kavner 1951, Corbin Bernsen 1954, Michael Feinstein 1956, Tom Everett Scott 1970, Mark Prior 1980

1812 – Napoleon defeated the Russian army of Alexander I at the battle of Borodino

1822 – Brazil declared its independence from Portugal

1896 – The first automobile race to be held on a racetrack occurred

1921 – The first Miss America Pageant was held

1930 – The cartoon *Blondie* made its first appearance in the comic strips

1966 – The final episode of *The Dick Van Dyke Show* was aired on CBS-TV

1971 – *The Beverly Hillbillies* was seen for the final time on CBS-TV

1979 – ESPN, the first all-sports cable network, began broadcasting

1998 – Mark McGwire set a new major league baseball record for most homeruns hit in a single season when he hit his 62nd

2008 – The United States government took over the two largest mortgage companies in the country, Fannie Mae and Freddie Mac

September 8: Richard I "the Lion-Heart" of England 1157, Joshua Chamberlain 1828, Charles Guiteau 1841, Buck Leonard 1907, Sid Caesar 1922, Peter Sellers 1925, Patsy Cline 1932, Archie Goodwin 1937, Sam Nunn 1937, Maurice Cheeks 1956, Heather Thomas 1957, Latrell Sprewell 1970, David Arquette 1971, Lisa Kennedy 1972, Elena Likhovtseva 1975, Gil Meche 1978, Pink 1979, Jonathan Taylor Thomas 1981

1504 – Michelangelo's *David* was first unveiled in Florence, Italy

1565 – A Spanish expedition established the first permanent European settlement in North America at present-day St. Augustine, Florida

1664 – The Dutch surrendered New Amsterdam to the British, who then renamed it New York

1831 – William IV was crowned King of Great Britain

1900 – Galveston, Texas was hit by a hurricane that killed about 6,000 people

1921 – The first Miss America was crowned

1944 – The first V2 rocket hit London

1952 – The Ernest Hemingway novel *The Old Man and the Sea* was published

1966 – The first episode of *Star Trek* aired on NBC-TV

1972 – The British comedy *Are You Being Served?* debuted on BBC-TV

1974 – President Gerald Ford granted an unconditional pardon to former President Richard Nixon

1974 – Evel Knievel's attempt to jump the Snake River Canyon failed when his rocket cycle deployed the parachute too early

1986 – *The Oprah Winfrey Show* first aired

1994 – 132 people were killed when a USAir Boeing 737 crashed as it was approaching Pittsburgh International Airport

September 9: Thomas Hutchinson 1711, William Bligh 1754, Leo Tolstoy 1828, Frank Chance 1877, Colonel Harland Sanders 1890, Frankie Frisch 1898, Phyllis A. Whitney 1903, Jimmy "the Greek" Snyder 1923, B.B. King 1925, Cliff Robertson 1925, Topol 1935, Otis Redding 1941, Billy Preston 1946, Garry Maddox 1949, Joe Thiesman 1949, Tom Wopat 1951, Angela Cartwright 1952, Hugh Grant 1960, Adam Sandler 1966, Chip Esten 1965, Rachel Hunter 1969, Henry Thomas 1971, Mike Hampton 1972, Goran Visnjic 1972, Kazuhisa Ishii 1973, Michael Buble 1975, Kyle Snyder 1977, Michelle Williams 1980, Edwin Jackson 1983, J.R. Smith 1985, Michael Bowden 1986

1087 – William I of England, known better as William the Conqueror, died at the age of 59 as a result of internal injuries he suffered two weeks before
1543 – Nine-month old Mary Stuart was crowned Mary, Queen of Scots
1776 – The United States of America officially adopts this new name
1791 – Washington, DC was first named, in honor of George Washington
1836 – Abraham Lincoln received his license to practice law
1839 – The first glass-plate photograph was taken by John Herschel
1850 – California became the 31st state in the Union
1926 – NBC was formed as a radio network
1956 – Elvis Presley appeared on *The Ed Sullivan Show* for the first time, although there was a guest host that night
1965 – Sandy Koufax of the Los Angeles Dodgers pitched the eighth perfect game in Major League Baseball history
1976 – Communist Chinese leader Mao Tse-tung died at the age of 82
1979 – Tracy Austin, at 16, became the youngest player to win the U.S. Open women's tennis title
2008 – The television show *Fringe* first aired on FOX-TV

September 10: Pope Julius III 1487, Ian Fleming 1888, Fay Wray 1907, Robert Wise 1914, Rin Tin Tin 1918, Arnold Palmer 1929, Roger Maris 1934, Charles Kuralt 1934, "Superstar" Billy Graham 1943, Jose Feliciano 1945, Margaret Trudeau 1948, Bill O'Reilly 1949, Joe Perry (Aerosmith) 1950, Greg Valentine 1951, Amy Irving 1953, Chris Columbus 1958, Colin Firth 1960, Randy Johnson 1963, John E. Sununu 1964, Guy Ritchie 1968, Ben Wallace 1974, Travis Rice 1982

1608 – John Smith was elected president of the Jamestown, Virginia colony council

1846 – Elias Howe was granted a patent for the sewing machine
1939 – Canada declared war on Germany
1955 – *Gunsmoke* premiered on CBS-TV
1963 – Twenty black students entered public schools in Alabama at the end of a standoff between federal authorities and Alabama governor George C. Wallace
1977 – The last execution by Guillotine was performed in France
2003 – Anna Lindh, the foreign minister of Sweden, was stabbed to death while shopping

September 11: O. Henry (William Sidney Porter) 1862, D.H. Lawrence 1885, Bear Bryant 1913, Ferdinand Marcos 1917, Tom Landry 1924, Cathryn Damon 1930, Robert Crippen 1937, Brian DePalma 1940, Lola Falana 1943, Amy Madigan 1951, Tommy Shaw 1952, Jeff Sluman 1957, Roxann Dawson 1958, Kristy McNichol 1962, Ellis Burks 1964, Moby 1965, Harry Connick, Jr. 1967, Ludacris 1977, Jacoby Ellsbury 1983, Chikezie 1985

1297 – Scotsman William Wallace defeated the English forces of Sir Hugh de Cressingham at the Battle of Stirling Bridge
1609 – Henry Hudson landed on Manhattan Island
1789 – Alexander Hamilton was appointed by President George Washington to be the first secretary of the treasury
1918 – The Boston Red Sox won their last World Series until 2004
1921 – Actor Fatty Arbuckle was arrested for rape
1926 – An assassination attempt on Benito Mussolini failed
1936 – Boulder Dam, now the Hoover Dam, in Nevada was dedicated by President Franklin D. Roosevelt
1940 – Buckingham Palace was damaged during a German air raid
1941 – Ground was broken for the building of the Pentagon
1945 – Mike the Headless Chicken was decapitated and survived another 18 months
1967 – *The Carol Burnett Show* premiered on CBS-TV
1970 – The last *Get Smart* episode aired on CBS-TV
1971 – Former Soviet leader Nikita Khrushchev died at the age of 77 from a heart attack
1974 – *Little House on the Prairie* made its television debut
1985 – Pete Rose of the Cincinnati Reds achieved career hit number 4,192 to break the record held by Ty Cobb
2001 – Terrorists attacked the World Trade Center and the Pentagon by crashing airplanes into them, killing about 3,000 people
2003 – Actor John Ritter died

2007 – Russia tested the largest conventional weapon ever built, known as the Father of all Bombs

September 12: Francis I of France 1494, Henry Hudson c. 1575, Richard Gatling 1818, Maurice Chevalier 1888, Alfred A. Knopf 1892, Margaret Hamilton 1902, Jesse Owens 1913, George Jones 1931, Sir Ian Holm 1931, Henry Waxman 1939, Linda Gray 1940, Barry White 1944, Peter Scolari 1954, Ricky Rudd 1956, Rachel Ward 1957, Amy Yasbeck 1962, James Frey 1969, Paul Walker 1973, Benjamin McKenzie 1978, Ruben Studdard 1978, Yao Ming 1980, Jennifer Hudson 1981, Carly Smithson 1983, Emmy Rossum 1985

490 BC – Athens defeated Persia in the Battle of Marathon
1609 – English explorer Henry Hudson first sailed down what is now known as the Hudson River
1846 – Elizabeth Barrett and Robert Browning eloped
1940 – Cave paintings were discovered in Lascaux, France
1944 – U.S. Army troops entered Germany, near Trier, for the first time during World War II
1953 – U.S. Senator John F. Kennedy married Jacqueline Lee Bouvier
1959 – *Bonanza* aired its first episode on NBC-TV
1963 – The last episode of *Leave it to Beaver* aired
1979 – Carl Yastrzemski of the Boston Red Sox became the first American League player to get 3,000 career hits and 400 career home runs
1983 – Austrian-born actor Arnold Schwarzenegger became a United States citizen
1984 – Michael Jordan signed a seven-year contract to play basketball for the Chicago Bulls
1992 – Dr. Mae Jemison became the first African-American woman in space
1994 – A man was killed when he crashed a stolen, single-engine Cessna onto the South Lawn of the White House
1995 – Kareem Abdul-Jabbar's All-Star Basketball Team defeated the Harlem Globetrotters, 91-85, ending the Globetrotters' 24-year, 8,829-game winning streak
2003 – Country music legend Johnny Cash died at the age of 71
2005 – Hong Kong Disneyland opened

September 13: Walter Reed 1851, John J. Pershing 1860, Claudette Colbert 1903, Bill Monroe 1911, Roald Dahl 1916, Mel Tormé 1925, Barbara Bain 1934, Fred Silverman 1937, Richard Kiel 1939, Bela Karolyi 1942, Jacqueline Bisset 1944, Peter Cetera 1944, Frank Marshall 1946, Nell Carter 1948, Jean Smart 1951, Randy Jones 1952, Bernie Williams

1968, Goran Ivanisevic 1971, Fiona Apple 1977, Ben Savage 1980, Daisuke Matsuzaka 1980, Sean Williams 1986, Mitch Holleman 1995

122 – Construction on Hadrian's Wall began
1503 – Michelangelo began his work on the statue *David*
1759 – The French were defeated by the British on the Plains of Abraham in the final French and Indian War
1814 – Francis Scott Key wrote *The Star-Spangled Banner*
1943 – Chiang Kai-shek became the ruler of China
1948 – Margaret Chase Smith of Maine became the first woman elected to both houses of Congress when she was elected to the Senate
1949 – The Ladies Professional Golf Association of America was formed
1959 – The Soviet Union's Luna 2 became the first space probe to reach the moon
1965 – Willie Mays became the fifth person in MLB history to hit 500 home runs
1969 – *Scooby-Doo, Where Are You?* first aired on television
1970 – The first New York City Marathon took place
1977 – The first diesel automobiles were introduced by General Motors
1977 – The ABC television series *Soap* first aired
1979 – The ABC television sitcom *Benson*, a spin-off of *Soap*, first aired
1985 – Nintendo released Super Mario Brothers
1990 – *Law and Order* premiered on NBC-TV
1993 – *Late Night with Conan O'Brien* premiered on NBC-TV
1995 – *The Drew Carey Show* debuted on ABC-TV
1996 – Tupac Shakur died six days after being shot four times in a drive-by shooting
2008 – Hurricane Ike struck coastal Texas, causing massive damage, especially to Galveston Island

September 14: Ivan Pavlov 1849, Margaret Sanger 1879, Clayton Moore 1914, Robert McCloskey 1914, Walter Koenig 1936, Larry Brown 1940, John "Bowser" Bauman 1947, Sam Neill 1947, Mary Crosby 1959, Faith Ford 1964, Kimberly Williams 1971, Nas 1973, Chad Bradford 1974, Amy Winehouse 1983, Adam Lamberg 1984

1847 – Winfield Scott led the capture of Mexico City during the Mexican-American War
1899 – The first fatal car accident occurred
1901 – President William McKinley died of gunshot wounds he had received 8 days earlier
1901 – Vice-President Theodore Roosevelt was sworn in as President, following the death of President McKinley

1940 – The Selective Service Act was passed by the U.S. Congress providing the first peacetime draft in the United States
1948 – The United Nations headquarters in New York City broke ground
1959 – The Soviet space probe *Luna 2* crashed into the Moon, thus becoming the first man-made object to reach the Moon
1972 – *The Waltons* premiered on CBS-TV
1978 – *Mork & Mindy* premiered on ABC-TV
1982 – Princess Grace of Monaco died at the age of 52 because of injuries she suffered the day before in a car crash
1984 – Joe Kittinger became the first person to fly a balloon solo across the Atlantic Ocean
1989 – The *MTV Music Awards* was held for the first time
1990 – Ken Griffey and Ken Griffey Jr. became the first father and son to hit back-to-back home runs in a Major League Baseball game
1994 – The Major League Baseball season was canceled due to a strike
1999 – Disney World closed down for the first time in its 28-year history, due to an approaching hurricane

September 15: Marco Polo 1254, James Fenimore Cooper 1789, William Howard Taft 1857, Agatha Christie 1890, Jean Renoir 1894, Roy Acuff 1903, Fay Wray 1907, Jackie Cooper 1922, Norm Crosby 1927, Gaylord Perry 1938, Merlin Olsen 1940, Oliver Stone 1946, Tommy Lee Jones 1946, Pete Carroll 1951, Dan Marino 1961, Amy Davidson 1979, Dave Annable 1979, Prince Harry of Wales 1984, Heidi Montag 1986

668 – Eastern Roman Emperor Constans II was assassinated in his bath in Syracuse, Italy
1656 – England and France signed a peace treaty
1789 – The U.S. Department of Public Affairs (later the Department of State) was established
1821 – Costa Rica, El Salvador, Guatemala, Honduras and Nicaragua all declared their independence from Spain
1862 – During the American Civil War, Confederate forces captured Harpers Ferry, Virginia
1916 – Tanks were used for the very first time in battle, at the Battle of the Somme during World War I
1928 – Alexander Fleming discovered penicillin
1935 – Nazi Germany adopted a new flag, featuring a swastika
1944 – Franklin D. Roosevelt and Winston Churchill met in Quebec
1949 – *The Lone Ranger* debuted on ABC-TV
1959 – Soviet Premier Nikita Khrushchev arrived in the United States to begin a 13-day visit, the first Soviet leader to visit the U.S.
1963 – A church bombing killed four young girls in Birmingham, Alabama

1965 – *Lost in Space* premiered on CBS-TV
1965 – *Green Acres* debuted on CBS-TV
1971 – Greenpeace was founded
1982 – The first issue of *USA Today* was published
1986 – *L.A. Law* premiered on NBC-TV
2006 – The UPN television network ceased broadcasting
2008 – Lehman Brothers filed chapter 11 bankruptcy, the largest filing in U.S. history

September 16: Henry V of England 1387, Louis XIV of France 1638, J.C. Penney 1875, Allen Funt 1914, Lauren Bacall 1924, B.B. King 1925, Peter Falk 1927, Susan Ruttan 1948, Ed Begley, Jr. 1949, Susan Ruttan 1950, Robin Yount 1955, Mickey Rourke 1956, David Copperfield 1956, Orel Hershiser 1958, Jennifer Tilly 1958, Tim Raines 1959, Richard Marx 1963, Molly Shannon 1964, Marc Anthony 1968, Alexis Bledel 1981, Brandon Moss 1983, Nick Jonas 1992

1620 – The Mayflower departed from Plymouth, England with 102 passengers (see image to left)
1630 – The village of Shawmut changed its name to Boston
1887 – The very first game of softball was played, in Chicago

1908 – General Motors was founded
1919 – The American Legion was incorporated
1920 – A horse wagon carrying a bomb exploded on Wall Street, killing 38 people
1949 – The first Road Runner and Wile E. Coyote short aired
1953 – The St. Louis Browns baseball team was given permission to move to Baltimore, where they became the Baltimore Orioles
1964 – *Bewitched* first aired on television
1968 – *The Andy Griffith Show* was seen for the final time on CBS
1972 – *The Bob Newhart Show* premiered on CBS-TV
1993 – *Frasier* made its debut on NBC-TV
1994 – Exxon Corporation was ordered by federal jury to pay $5 billion in damages as a result of the 1989 Exxon Valdez oil spill
2004 – Hurricane Ivan hit Pensacola, Florida

2007 – Fantasy author Robert Jordan died at the age of 58

September 17: Charles III (the Simple) of France 879, Pope Paul V 1550, John Rutledge 1739, Konstantin Tsiolkovsky 1857, Rube Foster 1879, William Carlos Williams 1883, Earl Webb 1897, Harold Bennett 1899, Warren Burger 1907, Hank Williams, Sr. 1923, George Blanda 1927, Roddy McDowall 1928, Edgar Mitchell 1930, Thomas Stafford 1930, Anne Bancroft 1931, Orlando Cepeda 1937, Paul Benedict 1938, Phil Jackson 1945, Bruce Spence 1945, John Ritter 1948, Jeff MacNelly 1948, Roger Stern 1950, Cassandra "Elvira" Peterson 1951, Rita Rudner 1956, Amy Roloff 1964, Rasheed Wallace 1974, Jimmie Johnson 1975, Alexander Ovechkin 1985, Molly Roloff 1993

1778 – The United States signed its first treaty with a Native American tribe, the Delaware Nation

1787 – The Constitution of the United States of America was signed (see above)
1796 – President George Washington's Farewell Address was read before the United States Congress
1862 – The Battle of Antietam was held during the American Civil War, resulting in over 23,000 Americans killed
1900 – William Jennings Bryan accepted the Democratic nomination for President
1908 – An airplane crashed in Virginia, killing one person, the first person ever killed in a plane crash, and injuring pilot Orville Wright

1920 – The National Football League was organized in Canton, Ohio
1953 – Ernie Banks became the first black baseball player to wear a Chicago Cubs uniform
1956 – Television was first broadcast in Australia
1962 – U.S. space officials announced the selection of Neil Armstrong and eight others as new astronauts
1963 – *The Fugitive* premiered on ABC-TV
1965 – *Hogan's Heroes* debuted on CBS-TV
1966 – *Mission Impossible* premiered on CBS-TV
1972 – The first episode of *M*A*S*H* aired on CBS-TV
1976 – NASA unveiled the space shuttle *Enterprise*
1978 – The original *Battlestar Galactica* debuted on ABC-TV
1983 – Vanessa Williams became the first black woman to be crowned Miss America
1983 – Johnny Bench, of the Cincinnati Reds, retired after 16 years as a catcher
1983 – Carl Yastrzemski of the Red Sox set a Major League Baseball record when he started his 3,299th game
1984 – Reggie Jackson of the California Angels became the 13th player to hit his 500th home run
1988 – The 24th Olympic Games opened in Seoul, South Korea
1996 – *Spin City* made its debut on ABC-TV
2008 – A dwarf planet discovered in 2004 was officially named Haumea, after the Hawaiian goddess of childbirth and fertility

September 18: George Read 1733, Greta Garbo 1905, Eddie "Rochester" Anderson 1905, Leon Askin 1907, Satchel Paige 1908, Mary C. Jane 1909, Jack Warden 1920, Joe Kubert 1926, Robert Blake 1938, Fred Willard 1939, Frankie Avalon 1939, Ken Brett 1948, Anna Deavere Smith 1950, Darryl Stingley 1951, Dennis Johnson 1954, Ryne Sandberg 1959, James Gandolfini 1961, Holly Robinson Peete 1964, Toni Kukoc 1968, Aisha Tyler 1970, Jada Pinkett Smith 1971, Lance Armstrong 1971, Jennifer Tisdale 1981

1544 – Holy Roman Emperor Charles V and French King Francis I signed the Ceasefire of Crepy-en-Laonnois
1759 – The French formally surrendered Quebec to the British
1793 – President George Washington laid the actual cornerstone of the U.S. Capitol Building
1810 – Chile declared its independence from Spain
1850 – The Fugitive Slave Act was declared by the U.S. Congress, allowing slave owners to claim slaves that had escaped into other states

1906 – A typhoon and corresponding tsunami hit Hong Kong, resulting in 10,000 deaths
1927 – CBS began broadcasting on the radio
1955 – *The Ed Sullivan Show* began on CBS-TV
1965 – *I Dream of Jeannie* debuted on NBC-TV
1970 – Singer and guitarist Jimi Hendrix was found dead in his London home
1975 – The FBI captured Patty Hearst
1978 – *WKRP in Cincinnati* premiered on CBS-TV
1983 – The rock group Kiss appeared without their trademark makeup on MTV
1989 – Hurricane Hugo hit Puerto Rico, killing six people

September 19: Henry III of France 1551, Sir William Golding 1911, Duke Snider 1926, James Lipton 1926, William Hickey 1927, Adam West 1928, Paul Williams 1940, Bill Medley 940, Joe Morgan 1943, Cass Elliott 1943, Randolph Mantooth 1945, Jeremy Irons 1948, Twiggy 1949, Joan Lunden 1951, Kevin Hooks 1958, Lita Ford 1958, Trisha Yearwood 1964, Jim Abbott 1967, Jimmy Fallon 1974, Jessica York 1976, Nick Johnson 1978, Danielle Panabaker 1987

1676 – Jamestown, Virginia was burned to the ground during Bacon's Rebellion
1777 – The Battle of Saratoga was won by American soldiers during the Revolutionary War
1778 – The first budget of the United States government was passed
1796 – President George Washington's farewell address was published
1881 – James A. Garfield died of wounds from an assassin, 11 weeks after being shot
1900 – Butch Cassidy and the Sundance Kid robbed their first bank together
1952 – Linus made his first appearance in a *Peanuts* comic strip
1957 – The United States conducted its first underground nuclear test
1959 – Soviet leader Nikita Khrushchev was told he would not be allowed to visit Disneyland due to security reasons
1970 – *The Mary Tyler Moore Show* premiered on CBS-TV
1981 – Simon and Garfunkel reunited for a concert in Central Park in New York City
1994 – *ER* made its television debut

September 20: Prince Arthur of Wales 1486, Upton Sinclair 1878, Red Auerbach 1917, Dr. Joyce Brothers 1928, Anne Meara 1929, Sophia Loren 1934, John W. Henry 1949, Guy LaFleur 1951, Gary Cole 1956, Crispin

Glover 1964, Kristen Johnston 1967, Gunnar Nelson 1967, Matthew Nelson 1967, Victoria Dillard 1969, Jason Bay 1978, Dante Hall 1978

1519 – Ferdinand Magellan began his circumnavigation of the globe

1633 – Galileo went on trial for his teaching of the Sun being the center of the Solar System (see image above)
1881 – Vice-President Chester A. Arthur was sworn in as President of the U.S. one day after the death of President James Garfield
1891 – The first gasoline-powered car was demonstrated in Springfield, Massachusetts
1946 – The first Cannes Film Festival premiered
1967 – The RMS *Queen Elizabeth 2* cruise ship was launched in Scotland
1973 – Jim Croce was killed in a plane crash on his way to Sherman, Texas, for a concert
1973 – Billie Jean King defeated Bobby Riggs in the Battle of the Sexes tennis match in the Astrodome in Houston, Texas
1982 – The NFL Players Strike began, lasting 57 days
1984 – *The Cosby Show* debuted on NBC-TV, while *Who's the Boss* debuted on ABC-TV
1984 – A suicide bomber attacked the U.S. embassy in Beirut, Lebanon, killing 22 people
1995 – The U.S. House of Representatives voted to drop the national speed limit, allowing states to create their own speed limits

1998 – Cal Ripken Jr. of the Baltimore Orioles voluntarily decided not to start a game, ending his 2,632 consecutive game playing streak
1999 – Raisa Gorbachev, wife of former Soviet President Mikhail Gorbachev, died of leukemia

September 21: H.G. Wells 1866, Chuck Jones 1912, Larry Hagman 1931, Fannie Flagg 1944, Stephen King 1947, Bill Murray 1950, Sidney Moncrief 1957, Dave Coulier 1959, David James Elliott 1960, Nancy Travis 1961, Cecil Fielder 1969, Faith Hill 1967, Ricki Lake 1968, Alfonso Ribeiro 1971, Luke Wilson 1971, Jon Kitna 1972, Nicole Richie 1981, Maggie Grace 1983

1893 – Frank Duryea took what is believed to be the first gasoline-powered automobile for a test drive
1897 – The New York Sun ran the "Yes, Virginia, there is a Santa Clause" editorial
1937 – J.R.R. Tolkien's *The Hobbit* was first published
1938 – A hurricane struck parts of New York and New England killing more than 600 people
1948 – Milton Berle debuted as the host of *The Texaco Star Theater* on NBC-TV
1957 – *Perry Mason*, the television series, made its debut on CBS-TV
1970 – *NFL Monday Night Football* made its debut on ABC-TV
1973 – Henry Kissinger was confirmed by the U.S. Senate to become 56th Secretary of State
1981 – The U.S. Senate confirmed Sandra Day O'Connor to be the first female justice on the United States Supreme Court
1989 – Hurricane Hugo hit Charleston, South Carolina, causing $8 billion in damage
1994 – *Touched by an Angel* premiered on CBS-TV
1998 – *Will and Grace* debuted on NBC-TV
1998 – *The King of Queens* debuted on CBS-TV
2008 – Yankee Stadium closed after 85 years

September 22: Anne of Cleves 1515, Michael Faraday 1791, John Houseman 1902, Bob Lemon 1920, Tommy Lasorda 1927, Eugene Roche 1928, Shari Belafonte-Harper 1954, Debby Boone 1956, Joan Jett 1958, Tai Babilonia 1959, Vince Coleman 1961, Catherine Oxenberg 1961, Scott Baio 1961, Bonnie Hunt 1964, Billie Piper 1982, Laura Vandervoort 1984, Tom Felton 1987

1776 – During the Revolutionary War, Nathan Hale was hanged as a British spy

1862 – President Abraham Lincoln issued the preliminary Emancipation Proclamation
1896 – Queen Victoria of England surpassed her grandfather, King George III, as the longest-ruling monarch in British history
1951 – The first live sporting event was televised on NBC when Duke played the University of Pittsburgh in football
1961 – President John F. Kennedy signed a congressional act that established the Peace Corps
1966 – The U.S. lunar probe *Surveyor 2* crashed into the moon
1969 – Willie Mays hit his 600th career home run
1975 – Sara Jane Moore attempted to assassinate President Gerald Ford
1976 – *Charlie's Angels* made its debut on ABC-TV
1980 – A border conflict between Iran and Iraq developed into a full-scale war
1982 – The first episode of *Family Ties* began airing
1989 – Hurricane Hugo hit the South Carolina coast
1994 – The first episode of *Friends* debuted on NBC-TV
2004 – The pilot episode of *Lost* debuted on television

September 23: Caesar Augustus 63 B.C., Walter Pidgeon 1897, Ray Charles 1930, Ben E. King 1938, Julio Iglesias 1943, Bruce Springsteen 1949, Peter David 1956, Jason Alexander 1959, Chi McBride 1961, Jermaine Dupri 1972, Ricky Davis 1979, Matt Kemp 1984, Joba Chamberlain 1985

1122 – Pope Calixtus II and Holy Roman Emperor Henry V signed the Concordat of Worms
1779 – John Paul Jones, commander of the American warship *Bon Homme*, was quoted as saying "I have not yet begun to fight!"
1780 – During the American Revolution, British Major John Andre was arrested by American soldiers for being a spy, which will lead to the exposing of Benedict Arnold's treason
1806 – Lewis and Clark returned to St. Louis, having completed their famous trek to the Pacific
1845 – The Knickerbocker Base Ball Club of New York was formed, the first baseball team in America
1846 – Astronomer Johann Gottfried Galle discovered the planet Neptune
1939 – Sigmund Freud died in London at the age of 83
1962 – *The Jetsons* premiered on ABC-TV, the network's first color program
1988 – *Whose Line Is It Anyway?* debuted in Great Britain
1995 – *JAG* debuted on NBC-TV
2002 – The first version of Mozilla Firefox was released to the public

September 24: Sir Arthur Guinness 1725, John Marshall 1755, F. Scott Fitzgerald 1896, Jim McKay 1921, Anthony Newley 1931, Jim Henson 1936, Linda McCartney 1941, Mike Berry 1942, Mean Joe Green 1946, Phil Hartman 1948, Kevin Sorbo 1958, Steve Whitmire 1959, Rafael Palmeiro 1964, Kevin Millar 1973, Eddie George 1973, Paul Hamm 1982, Morgan Hamm 1982

1664 – The Netherlands surrendered New Amsterdam to England
1890 – The Church of Jesus Christ of Latter-day Saints proclaimed that polygamy was wrong
1906 – President Theodore Roosevelt announced that Devil's Tower was to be the nation's first national monument
1948 – The Honda Motor Company was founded
1957 – The Brooklyn Dodgers played their last game at Ebbets Field
1968 – *60 Minutes* premiered on CBS-TV
1968 – *The Mod Squad* premiered on ABC-TV
1976 – Patricia Hearst was sentenced to 7 years in prison for her role in a 1974 bank robbery
1977 – *The Love Boat* debuted on ABC-TV
1985 – *Growing Pains* debuted on ABC-TV
1991 – Dr. Seuss, Theodor Geisel, died at the age of 87
1992 – The Sci-Fi Channel began broadcasting
2001 – *Crossing Jordan* premiered on NBC-TV
2005 – Hurricane Rita hit Beaumont, Texas, causing massive damage

September 25: William Faulkner 1897, Phil Rizzuto 1918, Barbara Walters 1931, Juliet Prowse 1936, Michael Douglas 1944, Cheryl Tiegs 1947, Mimi Kennedy 1949, Anson Williams 1949, Mark Hamill 1951, Christopher Reeve 1952, Heather Locklear 1961, Scottie Pippen 1965, Will Smith 1968, Catherine Zeta-Jones 1969, Bridgette Wilson 1973, Matt Hasselbeck 1975, Joel Pineiro 1978, Chris Owen 1980, Rocco Baldelli 1981, Van Hansis 1981, Jansen Panetierre 1994

1493 – Christopher Columbus left Spain with 17 ships on his second voyage to the Western Hemisphere
1513 – The Pacific Ocean was discovered by Spanish explorer Vasco Nunez de Balboa when he crossed the Panama
1775 – Ethan Allen was captured by the British during the American Revolution
1882 – The first Major League double header was played, between the Worcester Ruby Legs and Providence Grays

1890 – The Sequoia National Park was established as a U.S. National Park in Central California

1957 – 300 U.S. Army troops stood guard as nine black students were escorted to class at Central High School in Little Rock, Alabama

1973 – The three crewmen of Skylab II landed in the Pacific Ocean after spending 59 days on board

1978 – 144 people were killed when a private plane and a Pacific Southwest Airlines Boeing 727 collided over San Diego

1981 – Sandra Day O'Connor became the first female justice of the U.S. Supreme Court

1995 – Ross Perot announced that he would form the Independence Party

1997 – NBC sportscaster Marv Albert pled guilty to assault and battery of a lover, and was fired by NBC hours later

2001 – Michael Jordan announced that he would return to the NBA as a player for the Washington Wizards

2005 – Actor Don Adams, best known as Maxwell Smart on TV's *Get Smart*, died at the age of 82

2006 – *Heroes* debuted on NBC-TV

September 26: Johnny Appleseed 1774, T.S. Eliot 1888, George Gershwin 1898, Jack LaLanne 1914, Marty Robbins 1925, Winnie Mandela 1934, Donna Douglas 1939, Kent McCord 1942, Christine Todd Whitman 1946, Lynn Anderson 1947, Olivia Newton-John 1948, Kevin Kennedy 1954, Carlene Carter 1955, Linda Hamilton 1956, Rich Gedman 1959, Melissa Sue Anderson 1962, Larry Izzo 1974, Serena Williams 1981

1580 – Sir Francis Drake finished his circumnavigation of the world

1777 – Philadelphia was occupied by the British during the American Revolution

1789 – Thomas Jefferson was appointed America's first Secretary of State

1789 – John Jay was appointed the first Chief Justice of the Supreme Court

1789 – Samuel Osgood was appointed the first Postmaster-General

1789 – Edmund Jennings Randolph was appointed the first Attorney General

1901 – Leon Czolgosz was sentenced to death for the assassination of President William McKinley

1960 – The first televised debate between presidential candidates Richard M. Nixon and John F. Kennedy took place in Chicago

1962 – *The Beverly Hillbillies* premiered on CBS-TV

1964 – *Gilligan's Island* premiered on CBS-TV

1969 – *The Brady Bunch* premiered on ABC-TV

1985 – The first orca whale born in captivity and survive was born at SeaWorld and named Kalina, although she was also known as Baby Shamu

1991 – Four men and four women began their two-year stay inside the Biosphere II

1993 – The eight people who had stayed in Biosphere II emerged from their sealed off environment

2001 – *Enterprise*, later renamed *Star Trek: Enterprise*, made its debut

2008 – Actor Paul Newman died at the age of 83 after a long battle with cancer

September 27: Louis XIII of France 1601, Johnny Pesky 1919, Jayne Meadows 1920, William Conrad 1920, Wilford Brimley 1934, Dick Schaap 1934, A Martinez 1948, Mike Schmidt 1949, Jim Shooter 1951, Meat Loaf 1951, Shaun Cassidy 1958, Amanda Detmer 1971, Gwyneth Paltrow 1972, Clara Hughes 1972, Jon Garland 1979, Lil Wayne 1982, Avril Lavigne 1984

1066 – William of Normandy, later known as William the Conqueror and William I of England, set sail with his army from France bound for Sussex

1779 – John Adams was elected to negotiate with the British over the American Revolutionary War peace terms

1935 – Child actress Judy Garland signed her first contract with MGM

1935 – The song *Santa Claus Is Coming to Town* was first recorded by Joe Harris

1939 – After 19 days of resistance, Warsaw, Poland, surrendered to the Germans

1954 – *The Tonight Show* made its debut on NBC-TV with Steve Allen as host

1964 – The Warren Commission issued a report on the assassination of John F Kennedy stating that Lee Harvey Oswald was the lone assassin

1964 – The Beach Boys appeared on *The Ed Sullivan Show* for the first time

1976 – *The Muppet Show* premiered on television

1979 – The Department of Education became an official Cabinet position after the final approval from Congress

1983 – Larry Bird signed a seven-year contract with the Boston Celtics worth $15 million

1989 – Columbia Pictures Entertainment agreed to buyout Sony Corporation for $3.4 billion

1995 – The United States government unveiled the redesigned $100 bill

1998 – Mark McGwire of the St. Louis Cardinals set a major league baseball record when he hit his 70th home run of the season

2002 – In Senegal, over 1,000 people were killed when the ocean ferry *MS Joola* capsized
2008 – Zhai Zhigang became the first Chinese person to perform a spacewalk

September 28: Confucius 551 B.C., Ed Sullivan 1902, Al Capp 1909, Brigitte Bardot 1934, Herbert Jefferson Jr. 1946, Janeane Garofalo 1964, Laura Ceron 1964, Moon Unit Zappa 1967, Mira Sorvino 1968, Dustin Penner 1982, Hilary Duff 1987

48 BC – Pompey the Great was assassinated on orders from King Ptolemy of Egypt
1066 – England was invaded by William the Conqueror, who took over the thrown and became King William I
1850 – President Millard Fillmore named Brigham Young the first governor of the Utah territory
1892 – The first night-time football game in the United States took place under electric lights, between Mansfield State Normal School and Wyoming Seminary
1920 – Eight members of the Chicago White Sox were indicted in the Black Sox scandal when they were accused of throwing the World Series
1941 – Ted Williams of the Boston Red Sox became the only person to hit over .400 in a single season
1955 – The World Series was televised in color for the first time
1961 – *Dr. Kildare* premiered on NBC-TV
1961 – *Hazel* premiered on NBC-TV
1974 – First Lady Betty Ford underwent a mastectomy to remove a lump in her breast
1987 – *Star Trek: The Next Generation* debuted on TV
1991 – Marion Barry, the former mayor of the District of Columbia, was sentenced to six months in prison for possession of crack cocaine

September 29: Horatio Nelson 1758, Enrico Fermi 1901, Greer Garson 1904, Gene Autry 1907, Trevor Howard 1913, Stan Berenstain 1923, Jerry Lee Lewis 1935, Larry Linville 1939, Madeline Kahn 1942, Lech Walesa 1943, Mike Post 1944, Bryant Gumbel 1948, Andrew Dice Clay 1957, Jill Whelan 1966, Natasha Gregson Wagner 1970, Alexis Cruz 1974, Zachary Levi 1980

1789 – The U.S. Army was established
1864 – During the American Civil War, the Battle of Chaffin's Farm was fought
1911 – Italy declared war on the Ottoman Empire

1916 – John D. Rockefeller became the world's first billionaire
1954 – Willie Mays of the New York Giants makes *the Catch* at the Polo Grounds in the first game of the World Series
1957 – The New York Giants baseball team played their last game at the Polo Grounds
1960 – *My Three Sons* debuted on ABC-TV
1963 – *My Favorite Martian* premiered on CBS-TV
1978 – Pope John Paul I was found dead after just one month as Pope
1988 – The space shuttle *Discovery* took off from Cape Canaveral in Florida, the first manned space flight since the *Challenger* disaster
2005 – John Roberts was confirmed by the U.S. Senate as Chief Justice of the U.S. Supreme Court

September 30: William Wrigley Jr. 1861, Truman Capote 1924, Robin Roberts 1926, Angie Dickinson 1931, Johnny Mathis 1935, Len Cariou 1939, Victoria Tennant 1953, Barry Williams 1954, Fran Drescher 1957, Marty Stuart 1958, Eric Stoltz 1961, Crystal Bernard 1961, Dave Magadan 1962, Crystal Bernard 1964, Jenna Elfman 1971, Ashley Hamilton 1974, Carlos Guillen 1975, Martina Hingis 1980, Lacy Chabert 1982, T-Pain 1985

1399 – Henry Bolingbroke became the King of England as Henry IV
1868 – Spain's Queen Isabella was deposed and fled to France
1927 – Babe Ruth hit his 60th home run of the season, the most ever in one season and a record not broken until 1961
1935 – The Hoover Dam was dedicated
1946 – An international military tribunal in Nuremberg, Germany, found 22 top Nazi leaders guilty of war crimes
1947 – The World Series was televised for the first time
1955 – Actor James Dean was killed in a car accident at the age of 24
1960 – *The Flintstones* debuted on ABC-TV
1982 – *Cheers* debuted on NBC-TV
1984 – Mike Witt became only the 11th pitcher to throw a perfect game in Major League Baseball
1991 – Haitian President Jean-Bertrand Aristide was overthrown
1992 – George Brett of the Kansas City Royals reached his 3,000th career hit during a game against the California Angels
1993 – An earthquake measuring 6.4 on the Richter scale hit southern India, killing over 10,000 people

October

October 1: Henry III of England 1207, Paul I of Russia 1754, Walter Matthau 1920, James Whitmore 1921, William Rehnquist 1924, Jimmy Carter 1924, Roger Williams 1926, Tom Bosley 1927, George Peppard 1928, Richard Harris 1930, Julie Andrews 1935, Stella Stevens 1936, Rod Carew 1945, Stephen Collins 1947, Randy Quaid 1950, Yvette Freeman 1957, Ted King 1965, Cindy Margolis 1965, Jurnee Smollett 1986

1890 – Yellowstone National Park and Yosemite National Park were both established
1903 – The first modern World Series took place between the Boston Pilgrims (later the Red Sox) and the Pittsburgh Pirates
1908 – The Model T automobile was introduced by Henry Ford
1938 – German forces enter Czechoslovakia and seized control of the Sudetenland
1952 – *This is Your Life* began airing on NBC-TV
1955 – *The Honeymooners* premiered on CBS-TV
1961 – Roger Maris of the New York Yankees hit his 61st home run of the season to pass Babe Ruth's Major League record of 60
1962 – Johnny Carson began hosting the *Tonight Show* on NBC-TV
1971 – Walt Disney World opened in Orlando, Florida, starting with Magic Kingdom theme park and Disney's Contemporary Resort and Polynesian Resort
1979 – The United States handed control of the Canal Zone over to Panama
1982 – EPCOT opened in Walt Disney World
1988 – The Caribbean Beach Resort opened at Walt Disney World

October 2: Richard III of England 1452, Francis Hopkinson 1737, Mahatma Gandhi 1869, Cordell Hull 1871, Groucho Marx 1890, Bud Abbott 1895, Herb Voland 1918, George "Spanky" McFarland 1928, Earl Wilson 1934, Rex Reed 1938, Don McLean 1945, Avery Brooks 1948, Annie Leibovitz 1949, Mike Rutherford 1950, Sting 1951, Glen Wesley 1968, Eddie Guardado 1970, Kelly Ripa 1970, Tiffany 1971, Camilla Belle 1986, Phil Kessel 1987

1187 – Saladin captured Jerusalem after it had been ruled by Crusaders for 88 years
1535 – Jacques Cartier first sighted what is now Montreal
1780 – British officer John Andre was hanged as a U.S. spy during the American Revolutionary War
1835 – The Texas Revolution began with the Battle of Gonzalez
1870 – Rome was made the capital of Italy
1919 – U.S. President Woodrow Wilson suffered a stroke, leaving him partially paralyzed
1950 – Charlie Brown made his debut in the first *Peanuts* comics strip
1959 – *The Twilight Zone* debuted on CBS-TV
1967 – Thurgood Marshall was sworn in as the first African-American member of the United States Supreme Court
1985 – Actor Rock Hudson died from the AIDS virus at the age of 59
2002 – The first of the three-week long Beltway Sniper Attacks began
2005 – The NFL played its first game outside of the United States, when the Cardinals and 49ers played in Mexico City
2005 – The *Ethan Allen* tour boat capsized on Lake George in New York, killing 20 people
2006 – Five girls were killed at a shooting at an Amish School in Nickel Mines, Pennsylvania, before the gunman killed himself

October 3: Fred Clarke 1872, Emily Post 1873, Jean Lefebvre 1922, Harvey Kurtman 1924, Gore Vidal 1925, Glenn Hall 1931, Chubby Checker 1941, Alan Rachins 1942, Roy Horn 1944, Lindsey Buckingham 1949, Dave Winfield 1951, Dennis Eckersley 1954, Stevie Ray Vaughan 1954, Al Sharpton 1954, Hart Bochner 1956, Jack Wagner 1959, Greg Proops 1959, Fred Couples 1959, Tommy Lee 1961, Rob Liefeld 1967, Gwen Stefani 1969, Janel Moloney 1969, Kevin Richardson 1971, Neve Campbell 1973, Talib Kweli 1975, Ashlee Simpson-Wentz 1984

1226 – St. Francis of Assisi died at the age of 44
1863 – President Abraham Lincoln declared that the last Thursday of November would be recognized as Thanksgiving Day

1908 – The *Pravda* newspaper was founded by Leon Trotsky and others
1932 – Iraq gained its independence from Great Britain
1951 – Bobby Thompson of the New York Giants hit a home run in the bottom of the ninth inning against the Brooklyn Dodgers to win the National League pennant, after the Giants were behind by 14 games earlier in the season, the home run being known as the *shot heard 'round the world*
1954 – *Father Knows Best* began airing on CBS-TV
1955 – *Captain Kangaroo* premiered on CBS-TV
1955 – *The Mickey Mouse Club* premiered on ABC-TV
1960 – *The Andy Griffith Show* debuted on CBS-TV
1961 – *The Dick Van Dyke Show* debuted on CBS-TV
1974 – Frank Robinson became the first black Major League Baseball manager when it was announced that he would lead the Cleveland Indians
1985 – The Space Shuttle *Atlantis* was launched on its maiden voyage
1995 – O.J. Simpson was acquitted of the 1994 murder of Nicole Brown Simpson and Ronald L. Goldman
2003 – Roy Horn, of the magical act Siegfried and Roy, was attacked and severely injured by one of their show's tigers
2008 – The $700 billion bailout bill for the struggling United States financial system was signed by President George W. Bush

October 4: Louis X of France 1289, Richard Cromwell 1626, Rutherford B. Hayes 1822, Frederic S. Remington 1861, Buster Keaton 1895, Charlton Heston 1924, Anne Rice 1941, Jackie Collins 1941, Jimy Williams 1943, Tony LaRussa 1944, Patti LaBelle 1944, Clifton Davis 1945, Susan Sarandon 1946, Armand Assante 1949, Bill Fagerbakke 1957, David W. Harper 1961, Jon Secada 1962, A.C. Green 1963, Abraham Benrubi 1969, Jerry Minor 1969, Kurt Thomas 1972, Alicia Silverstone 1976, Kyle Lohse 1978, Rachael Leigh Cook 1979, Jared Weaver 1982, Tony Gwynn Jr. 1982, Kimmie Meissner 1989

1582 – The Gregorian Calendar was implemented by Pope Gregory XIII
1777 – At the Battle of Germantown during the American Revolutionary War, American forces under George Washington were repelled by British forces under William Howe
1830 – Belgium separated from the Netherlands
1940 – Adolf Hitler and Benito Mussolini met in the Alps at Brenner Pass
1943 – During World War II, the United States captured the Solomon Islands
1950 – Snoopy made his debut in the third *Peanuts* comic strip
1957 – The Soviet Union launched *Sputnik I*, the first satellite in space
1957 – *Leave it to Beaver* debuted on CBS-TV

1965 – Pope Paul VI arrived in New York, becoming the first pope to visit the United States or anywhere in the Western Hemisphere
1988 – Televangelist Jim Bakker was indicted for fraud
2001 – Barry Bonds of the San Francisco Giants hit his 70th home run of the season to tie Mark McGwire's Major League record

October 5: Chester A. Arthur 1830, Robert Goddard 1882, Ray Kroc 1902, Larry Fine 1902, Allen Ludden 1918, Bil Keane 1922, Richard Gordon, Jr. 1929, Steve Miller 1943, Jeff Conaway 1949, Karen Allen 1951, Clive Barker 1952, Bernie Mac 1957, Daniel Baldwin 1960, Michael Andretti 1962, Mario Lemieux 1965, Patrick Roy 1965, Rey Sanchez 1967, Grant Hill 1972, Kate Winslet 1975, J.J. Yeley 1976, Enrico Fabris 1981, Nicky Hilton 1983

1813 – Chief Tecumseh of the Shawnee Indians was killed at the Battle of Thames (see image above)
1857 – The city of Anaheim, California, was founded
1892 – The Dalton gang was nearly wiped out while attempting to rob two banks simultaneously in Coffeyville, Kansas
1919 – Enzi Ferrari debuted in his first race
1921 – The World Series was broadcast over the radio for the first time
1930 – Laura Ingalls became the first woman to make a transcontinental airplane flight
1947 – Harry S Truman became the first President to broadcast on TV from the White House
1962 – The Beatles released their first single, *Love Me Do*
1969 – The first episode of *Monty Python's Flying Circus* aired on BBC-TV
1989 – Jim Bakker was convicted of using his television show to defraud his viewers

October 6: Louis-Philippe of France 1773, George Westinghouse Jr. 1846, Alfred Tennyson 1809, Janet Gaynor 1906, Carole Lombard 1908, Bruno Sammartino 1935, Fred Travalena 1942, Britt Ekland 1942, Adam

Kubert 1959, Elisabeth Shue 1963, Amy Jo Johnson 1970, Rebecca Lobo 1973, Ioan Gruffudd 1973, Richard Seymour 1979

1847 – *Jane Eyre* by Charlotte Bronte was first published in London
1927 – *The Jazz Singer* opened in movie theaters, the first talkie
1945 – Billy Sianis and his pet goat were ejected from Wrigley Field during the 1945 World Series Game 4, leading to what many feel was the Curse of the Billy Goat
1979 – Pope John Paul II became the first pontiff to visit the White House
1981 – Egyptian president Anwar Sadat was assassinated at a military rally in Cairo
1996 – Country singers Faith Hill and Tim McGraw were married
2000 – *CSI: Crime Scene Investigation* made its debut on NBC-TV

October 7: Henry A. Wallace 1888, June Allyson 1917, Martha Stewart 1922, Desmond Tutu 1931, Oliver North 1943, John Cougar Mellencamp 1951, Christopher Norris 1953, Yo-Yo Ma 1955, Michael W. Smith 1957, Jayne Torvill 1957, Simon Cowell 1959, Judy Landers 1961, Matt Roloff 1961, Toni Braxton 1968, Priest Holmes 1973, Allison Munn 1974, Taylor Hicks 1976, Rachel McAdams 1976, Charles Woodson 1976, Shawn Ashmore 1979, Aaron Ashmore 1979, Evan Longoria 1985

1777 – During the American Revolution, the Americans defeated the British at the Second Battle of Saratoga, also known as the Battle of Bemis Heights

1849 – Edgar Allen Poe died at the age of 40 (see photograph at right)
1918 – The Georgia Tech football team defeated Cumberland College 222-0
1952 – The television show *American Bandstand* debuted on a local station in Philadelphia
1959 – The Russian space probe *Luna 3* sent back the first photographs ever taken of the back side of the Moon
1982 – *Cats* began its nearly 18-year run on Broadway
1985 – Four Palestinian terrorists hijacked the Italian cruise ship Achille Lauro off the coast of Egypt
1998 – The American television show *Charmed* aired its first episode

218

2001 – Barry Bonds hit his 73rd home run of the season and set a new Major League record

2001 – The United States and Great Britain began bombing Afghanistan, in response to the September 11th attacks

2003 – In California, Arnold Schwarzenegger was elected governor in the recall election of Governor Gray Davis

October 8: Frank Herbert 1920, Rona Barrett 1936, Paul Hogan 1939, David Carradine 1940, Jesse Jackson 1941, R.L. Stine 1943, Chevy Chase 1943, Sarah Purcell 1948, Sigourney Weaver 1949, Michael Dudikoff 1954, Bill Elliott 1955, Stephanie Zimbalist 1956, CeCe Winans 1964, Emily Procter 1968, Matt Damon 1970, Nick Cannon 1980, Angus T. Jones 1993

1871 – The Great Fire of Chicago broke out killing about 250 people and destroying over 17,000 buildings

1918 – During World War I in the Argonne Forest in France, U.S. Corporal Alvin C. York almost single-handedly killed 25 German soldiers, then took 132 more prisoner, while taking 32 German machine guns (see photo to left)

1934 – Bruno Hauptmann was indicted for the murder of the infant son of Charles Lindbergh

1956 – Don Larsen pitched a perfect game in the World Series for the New York Yankees

2001 – President George W. Bush announced the creation of the Department of Homeland Security

2004 – At Alderson Federal Prison Camp, West Virginia, Martha Stewart began her five-month prison sentence

October 9: Charles X of France 1757, Joe Pepitone 1940, John Lennon 1940, Trent Lott 1941, Jackson Browne 1948, Jim Starlin 1949, Robert Wuhl 1951, Sharon Osbourne 1952, Tony Shalhoub 1953, Scott Bakula 1954, John O'Hurley 1954, Linwood Boomer 1956, Annika Sorenstam 1970, Sean Lennon 1975, Brian Roberts 1977, Zachery Ty Bryan 1981, Tyler James Williams 1992

1002 – Leif Erikson landed in North America

1781 – The last major battle of the American Revolution took place in Yorktown, Virginia

1812 – During the War of 1812, American forces captured two British brigs, the *Detroit* and the *Caledonia*

1872 – Aaron Montgomery started his mail order business with the delivery of the first mail order catalog

1888 – The public was admitted to the Washington Monument for the first time

1940 – St. Paul's Cathedral in London was bombed by the Nazis

1974 – Oskar Schindler, who is credited with saving the lives of about 1,200 Jews during the Holocaust, died in Frankfurt, Germany at the age of 66

1985 – The hijackers of the Achille Lauro cruise liner surrendered after the ship arrived in Port Said, Egypt

October 10: Helen Hayes 1900, James Clavell 1924, Peter Coyote 1942, Ben Vereen 1946, David Lee Roth 1955, Tanya Tucker 1958, Bradley Whitford 1959, Julia Sweeney 1961, Brett Favre 1969, Dale Earnhardt Jr. 1974, Pat Burrell 1976, Mya 1979, Troy Tulowitzki 1984

1845 – The United States Naval Academy opened in Annapolis, Maryland

1938 – Nazi Germany completed its annexation of Czechoslovakia's Sudetenland

1943 – Chaing Kai-shek took the oath of office as the President of China

1965 – The Red Baron made his first appearance in the *Peanuts* comic strip

1973 – Vice-President Spiro Agnew resigned after being charged with federal income tax evasion

1986 – An estimated 1,500 people were killed when an earthquake measuring 7.5 on the Richter scale struck San Salvador, El Salvador

2004 – Actor Christopher Reeve died at the age of 52

October 11: Eleanor Roosevelt 1884, Dottie West 1932, Daryl Hall 1946, David Morse 1953, Steve Young 1961, Joan Cusack 1962, Sean Patrick Flanery 1965, Luke Perry 1966, Jane Krakowski 1968, Orlando Hernandez 1969, MC Lyte 1971, Jason Ellis 1971, Dmitri Young 1973, Ty Wigginton 1977, Michelle Wie 1989

1776 – During the American Revolution, the first naval battle of Lake Champlain was fought

1809 – Meriwether Lewis died under mysterious circumstances (perhaps by suicide) along the Natchez Trace in Tennessee at an inn called Grinder's Stand
1890 – The Daughters of the American Revolution was founded in Washington, DC
1956 – The Muppets made their debut on *The Steve Allen Show*
1975 – *Saturday Night Live* was broadcast for the first time, with guest host George Carlin
1983 – The last hand-cranked telephones in the United States went out of service when the 440 telephone customers in Bryant Pond, Maine, were switched to direct-dial service
1984 – American Kathryn Sullivan became the first female astronaut to perform a space walk
2006 – New York Yankees pitcher Cory Lidle was killed when an airplane he was piloting crashed into a New York City apartment building

October 12: Edward VI of England 1537, Joe Cronin 1906, Dick Gregory 1932, Luciano Pavarotti 1935, Tony Kubek 1936, Chris Wallace 1947, Susan Anton 1950, Adam Rich 1968, Martie Seidel (Dixie Chicks) 1969, Kirk Cameron 1970, Bode Miller 1977, Josh Hutcherson 1992

1492 – Christopher Columbus sighted Watling Island in the Bahamas, thinking he had found Asia

1692 – The Salem Witch Trials came to an end (see above)

1918 – A massive forest fire in Minnesota resulted in the deaths of 423 people
1933 – Bank robber John Dillinger escaped from a jail in Allen County, Ohio
1933 – The U.S. Department of Justice purchased Alcatraz Island from the U.S. Army
1938 – Filming began on *The Wizard of Oz*
1960 – Soviet premier Nikita Khrushchev pounded a shoe on his desk during a dispute at a United Nations General Assembly
1964 – The Soviet Union launched *Voskhod 1* into orbit around the Earth, the first space flight to have a multi-person crew
1999 – In Pakistan, Pervez Musharraf seized power in a bloodless coup that toppled Prime Minister Nawaz Sharif
2000 – In Yemen, the *USS Cole* experienced a large explosion, which turned out to be a terrorist attack that has been linked to Osama bin Laden

October 13: Leon Leonwood "L.L." Bean 1872, Nipsey Russell 1924, Lenny Bruce 1925, Margaret Thatcher 1925, Eddie Mathews 1931, Paul Simon 1941, Demond Wilson 1946, Lacy J. Dalton 1946, Sammy Hagar 1947, John Ford Coley 1948, Marie Osmond 1959, Doc Rivers 1961, Jerry Rice 1962, Kelly Preston 1962, Kate Walsh 1967, Trevor Hoffman 1967, Don Orsillo 1968, Nancy Kerrigan 1969, Sacha Baron Cohen 1971, Summer Sanders 1972, Brian Dawkins 1973, Paul Pierce 1977, Ashanti 1980

54 AD – The Roman emperor Claudius I died after being poisoned by his wife, Agrippina, and Nero became emperor
1773 – The Whirlpool Galaxy was discovered by Charles Messier
1775 – The U.S. Continental Congress ordered the construction of a naval fleet
1792 – The cornerstone of the White House was laid
1960 – The World Series ended on a homerun for the first time, when Bill Mazeroski's homerun allowed the Pirates to beat the Yankees
1971 – The first World Series night game was played at Three Rivers Stadium in Pittsburgh, with the Pirates facing the Baltimore Orioles
1977 – Four Palestinians hijacked a Lufthansa airliner to Somalia
1998 – The NBA cancelled regular season games due to a work stoppage for the first time in its history

October 14: James II of England 1633, William Penn 1644, Dwight David Eisenhower 1890, Lillian Gish 1893, E.E. Cummings 1894, Oscar Charleston 1896, C. Everett Koop 1916, Roger Moore 1927, Ralph Lauren 1939, Tommy Harper 1940, Al Oliver 1946, Charlie Joiner 1947, Harry

Anderson 1952, Greg Evigan 1953, Arleen Sorkin 1956, Thomas Dolby 1958, Lori Petty 1963, Joe Girardi 1964, Jim Rome 1964, Steve Coogan 1965, Natalie Maines (Dixie Chicks) 1974, Usher 1978, Boof Bonser 1981

1066 – The Battle of Hastings occurred in England, in which William the Conqueror defeated England's King Harold II
1568 – Mary Queen of Scots went on trial in England
1912 – Theodore Roosevelt was shot while campaigning in Milwaukee, Wisconsin. Roosevelt's wound in the chest was not serious and he continued with his planned speech. William Schrenk was captured at the scene of the shooting.
1926 – The book *Winnie-the-Pooh*, by A.A. Milne, was first published
1944 – German Field Marshal Erwin Rommel committed suicide rather than face execution after being accused of conspiring against Adolf Hitler
1954 – Cecil B. DeMille's *The Ten Commandments*, starring Charlton Heston, began filming in Egypt
1962 – The Cuban Missile Crisis began
1964 – Dr. Martin Luther King, Jr. was awarded the Nobel Peace Prize for his non-violent resistance to racial prejudice in America
1968 – The first live telecast to come from a manned U.S. spacecraft was transmitted from *Apollo 7*
1987 – Jessica McClure, 18 months old, fell down an abandoned well in Midland, Texas
1998 – The FBI charged Eric Robert Rudolph with 6 bombings including the 1996 Olympic bombing in Atlanta

October 15: Virgil 70 BC, Friedrich Nietzsche 1844, Edith Wilson 1872, Mario Puzo 1920, Lee Iacocca 1924, Linda Lavin 1937, Penny Marshall 1942, Jim Palmer 1945, Richard Carpenter 1946, Larry Miller 1953, Tito Jackson 1953, Jere Burns 1954, Tanya Roberts 1955, Sarah Ferguson 1959, Emeril Lagasse 1959

1815 – Napoleon Bonaparte began his exile on the remote island of St. Helena in the Atlantic Ocean
1860 – 11-year-old Grace Bedell wrote a letter to presidential candidate Abraham Lincoln, stating that Lincoln would look better if he would grow a beard
1878 – The Edison Electric Light company began its operation
1900 – Mark Twain returned to the United States after an absence of 9 years
1917 – Dancer Mata Hari, a German spy, was executed by a French firing squad

1946 – Hermann Goering, a Nazi war criminal and founder of the Gestapo, poisoned himself just hours before his scheduled execution
1951 – *I Love Lucy* made its debut on CBS-TV
1966 – The Black Panther Party was created
1981 – The Wave, also known as a stadium wave, was first performed by an audience in Oakland, California at an Oakland A's playoff baseball game against the Yankees
1989 – Wayne Gretsky became the all-time leading point scorer in the NHL
2001 – NASA's *Galileo* spacecraft passed within 112 miles of Jupiter's moon Io

October 16: James II of Scotland 1430, Noah Webster 1758, Paul Hamilton 1762, Oscar Wilde 1854, Eugene O'Neill 1888, Angela Lansbury 1925, Tom Monaghan 1937, Barry Corbin 1940, Tim McCarver 1941, Suzanne Somers 1946, Leo Mazzone 1948, Tim Robbins 1958, Flea of the Red Hot Chili Peppers 1962, Randall Batinkoff 1968, Juan Gonzalez 1969, Wendy Wilson 1969, Kordell Stewart 1972, Paul Kariya 1974, Kellie Martin 1975, John Mayer 1977, Jeremy Jackson 1980

1775 – During the American Revolution, Portland, Maine was burned by the British
1781 – Troops under George Washington captured Yorktown, Virginia during the American Revolution
1793 – During the French Revolution, Queen Marie Antoinette was beheaded
1859 – Abolitionist John Brown led a raid on Harper's Ferry, Virginia
1875 – Brigham Young University was founded in Provo, Utah
1901 – President Theodore Roosevelt incited controversy by inviting black leader Booker T. Washington to the White House
1923 – Walt Disney contracted with M.J. Winkler to distribute the Alice Comedies; this event is recognized as the start of the Disney Company
1987 – Rescuers finally freed Jessica McClure from the abandoned well that she had fallen into in Midland, Texas, after being stuck for 58 hours
1995 – The Million Man March occurred in Washington, DC
2001 – The TV show *Smallville* debuted on the WB

October 17: Richard M. Johnson 1780, James Rudolph Garfield 1865, Jean Arthur 1900, Irene Ryan 1902, Pope John Paul I 1912, Arthur Miller 1915, Rita Hayworth 1918, Montgomery Clift 1920, Tom Poston 1927, Evel Knievel 1938, Earl Thomas Conley 1941, Jim Seals 1941, Gary Puckett 1942, Michael McKean 1947, George Wendt 1948, Margot Kidder 1948, Robert Jordan 1948, Bill Hudson 1949, Howard Rollins 1950, Mae

Jemison 1956, Alan Jackson 1958, Norm MacDonald 1963, Ziggy Marley 1968, Nancy Sullivan 1969, Ernie Els 1969, Chris Kirkpatrick ('N Sync) 1971, Eminem 1972

1346 – King David II of Scotland was captured by King Edward III of England, and would soon begin his eleven year imprisonment in the Tower of London
1777 – American troops defeated British forces in Saratoga, New York
1888 – The first issue of *National Geographic Magazine* was released at newsstands
1917 – The Radio Corporation of America (RCA) was formed
1931 – Al Capone was convicted on income tax evasion and was sentenced to 11 years in prison
1945 – Colonel Juan Peron became the dictator of Argentina after staging a coup in Buenos Aires
1947 – 10,000 acres of Acadia National Park in Maine burned in a forest fire
1979 – Mother Teresa of India was awarded the Nobel Peace Prize
1989 – An earthquake measuring 7.1 on the Richter scale hit the San Francisco Bay area in California, causing 67 deaths and over $7 billion in damages
2006 – The United States population reached 300 million
2007 – The Dali Lama was awarded the U.S. Congressional Medal of Honor

October 18: Pope Pius II 1405, Pierre Trudeau 1919, Chuck Berry 1926, George C. Scott 1927, Keith Jackson 1928, Peter Boyle 1935, Mike Ditka 1939, Lee Harvey Oswald 1939, Pam Dawber 1951, Thomas Hearns 1958, Jean-Claude Van Damme 1960, Erin Moran 1961, Wynton Marsalis 1961, Doug Mirabelli 1970, Alex Cora 1975, Josh Gracin 1980, David Murphy 1981, Zac Efron 1987

1767 – The Mason-Dixon Line was agreed upon
1842 – Samuel Morse laid his first telegraph cable
1851 – Herman Melville's novel *Moby Dick* was first published
1867 – The United States acquired Alaska from Russia
1898 – The United States took possession of Puerto Rico
1925 – The Grand Ole Opry opened in Nashville
1931 – Inventor Thomas Alva Edison died at the age of 84
1977 – A German Special Forces team stormed a hijacked Lufthansa airliner and killed all four hijackers while freeing 86 hostages
1977 – Reggie Jackson tied Babe Ruth's record by hitting three homeruns in a single World Series game

1991 – Azerbaijan declared its independence from the Soviet Union

October 19: Charles Merrill (founder of Merrill-Lynch) 1885, Robert Reed 1932, Michael Gambon 1940, Divine 1945, John Lithgow 1945, Philip Pullman 1946, Evander Holyfield 1962, Ty Pennington 1965, Amy Carter 1967, John Edward 1969, Chris Kattan 1970, Keith Foulke 1972, Joe McEwing 1972, Michael Young 1976

1216 – King John of England died and was succeeded by his 9-year old son, Henry III
1469 – Ferdinand of Aragon married Isabella of Castile, the marriage uniting all the dominions of Spain
1781 – British General Lord Cornwallis surrendered to General George Washington at Yorktown, Virginia in the last battle of the American Revolution
1789 – John Jay was sworn in a the first Chief Justice of the U.S. Supreme Court
1812 – Napoleon Bonaparte's French forces began their retreat out of Russia after a month of chasing the retreating Russian army
1977 – The *Concorde* made its first landing in New York City
1983 – The U.S. Senate approved a bill establishing a national holiday in honor of Martin Luther King Jr.
2005 – Saddam Hussein went on trial in Iraq for crimes against humanity

October 20: Christopher Wren 1632, Henry Temple 1784, Bela Lugosi 1882, Margaret Dumont 1889, Grandpa Jones 1913, Mickey Mantle 1931, William Christopher 1932, Jerry Orbach 1935, Juan Marichal 1937, Earl Hindman 1942, Tom Petty 1953, Keith Hernandez 1953, Eric Scott 1958, Viggo Mortensen 1958, Snoop Dog 1971, Michael Johns 1978, Jennifer Freeman 1985

1740 – Maria Theresa became the ruler of Austria, Hungary and Bohemia with the death of her father, Holy Roman Emperor Charles VI
1803 – The U.S. Senate approved the Louisiana Purchase
1818 – The United States and Great Britain established the boundary between the U.S. and Canada to be the 49th parallel
1944 – Allied forces invaded the Philippines
1955 – J.R.R. Tolkien's *The Return of the King*, the final installment of *The Lord of the Rings* trilogy, was published
1968 – Jackie Lee Bouvier Kennedy married Aristotle Onassis
1976 – More than 70 people were killed when the Norwegian tanker *Frosta* collided with the ferryboat *George Prince* on the Mississippi River

1977 – A plane carrying the musical group Lynyrd Skynyrd crashed in Mississippi, killing lead singer Ronnie Van Zant, guitarist Steve Gaines, and four others

1979 – The John F. Kennedy Library in Boston was dedicated

1991 – The Oakland Hills Firestorm resulted in 25 deaths, over three thousand homes destroyed and over two billion dollars in damages

October 21: Alfred Nobel 1833, Dizzy Gillespie 1917, Whitey Ford 1928, Benjamin Netanyahu 1949, Patti Davis 1952, Carrie Fisher 1956, George Bell 1959, Ken Watanabe 1959, Jeremy Miller 1976, Will Estes 1977, Joey Harrington 1978, Gabe Gross 1979, Kim Kardashian 1980, Andy Marte 1983

1797 – The U.S. Navy frigate *Constitution*, or *Old Ironsides*, was launched in Boston harbor

1805 – The Battle of Trafalgar occurred off the coast of Spain, in which the British defeated the French and Spanish fleets

1854 – Florence Nightingale and 38 other nurses were sent to help in the Crimean War (see image to right)

1861 – Union forces suffered a defeat in the second battle of the American Civil War, the Battle of Ball's Bluff

1879 – Thomas Edison invented the light bulb

1917 – The first U.S. soldiers entered combat during World War I near Nancy, France

1945   Women in France were allowed to vote for the first time

1959 – The Guggenheim Museum was opened to the public in New York

1967 – Thousands of demonstrators marched in Washington, DC, in opposition to the Vietnam War

1980 – The Philadelphia Phillies won their first World Series

1988 – Former Philippine President Ferdinand E. Marcos and his wife, Imelda, were indicted in New York on fraud and racketeering charges

1991 – Jesse Turner, an American hostage in Lebanon, was released after nearly five years of being imprisoned

October 22: John V of Portugal 1689, Daniel Boone 1734, Bill Carrigan 1883, Curly Howard 1903, Jimmy Foxx 1907, Joan Fontaine 1917, Derek Jacobi 1938, Christopher Lloyd 1938, Annette Funicello 1942, Pedro Morales 1942, Catherine Deneuve 1943, Jeff Goldblum 1952, Brian Boitano 1963, Otis Smith 1965, Valeria Golino 1966, Shaggy 1968, Shelby Lynne 1968, Spike Jonze 1969, Ichiro Suzuki 1973, Jeff McInnis 1974, Michael Fishman 1980, Robinson Cano 1982, Zachary Hanson 1985, Jonathan Lipnicki 1990

1746 – The College of New Jersey (later Princeton) received its charter
1784 – Russia established a colony on Kodiak Island, Alaska
1836 – Sam Houston was inaugurated as the first constitutionally elected President of the Republic of Texas (see image to right)
1883 – The Metropolitan Opera House in New York City first opened
1934 – Charles *Pretty Boy* Floyd, the notorious bank robber, was shot and killed by Federal agents in East Liverpool, Ohio
1939 – The first televised pro football game took place between Brooklyn and Philadelphia
1957 – The first U.S. soldiers in the Vietnam War were killed

1966 – The Supremes became the first all-female singing group to have the number one selling album, *The Supremes A' Go-Go*
1968 – *Apollo 7* splashed down in the Atlantic Ocean after orbiting the Earth 163 times
1975 – The Soviet Union's unmanned *Venera 9* landed on the surface of Venus and became the first to send surface pictures of Venus back to Earth
1976 – Red Dye #4 was banned in the United States
2008 – India launched its first unmanned lunar mission, *Chandrayaan-1*

October 23: Peter II of Russia 1715, Adlai Stevenson I 1835, Johnny Carson 1925, Chi-Chi Rodriguez 1935, Pelé 1940, Michael Crichton 1942,

Dwight Yoakam 1954, Sam Raimi 1959, Weird Al Yankovic 1959, Doug Flutie 1962, Gordon Korman 1963, Al Leiter 1965, Ryan Reynolds 1976

42 B.C. – Marcus Junius Brutus committed suicide after his defeat at the Battle of Philippi
1910 – Blanche S. Scott became the first woman to make a public solo airplane flight
1915 – Approximately 25,000 women demanded the right to vote with a march in New York City
1929 – In the United States, the Dow Jones Industrial Average plunged, starting the stock-market crash that began the Great Depression
1983 – A U.S. Marine compound at Beirut International Airport was blown up by a Shiite suicide bomber, killing 241 Americans
1993 – Joe Carter of the Toronto Blue Jays became only the second player to end the World Series with a homerun
2001 – Apple sold the first iPod

October 24: James Sherman 1855, Bob Kane 1915, Bill Wyman 1936, David Nelson 1936, F. Murray Abraham 1939, Kevin Kline 1947, Johnny Kassir 1957, B.D. Wong 1962, Jacqueline McKenzie 1967, Corey Dillon 1974, Monica 1980, Keyshia Cole 1981, Brian Vickers 1983

1537 – Jane Seymour, the third wife of England's King Henry VIII, died after giving birth to the future King Edward VI
1901 – Daredevil Annie Edson Taylor became the first person to go over Niagara Falls in a wooden barrel, receiving only minor cuts and offering the sage advice, "Don't try it"
1929 – In the United States, investors dumped more than 13 million shares in the stock market, on a day that would become known as Black Thursday
1931 – The George Washington Bridge opened for traffic between New York and New Jersey
1945 – The United Nations was formally established less than a month after the end of World War II
1962 – During the Cuban Missile Crisis, U.S. military forces went on the highest alert in the postwar era in preparation for a possible full-scale war with the Soviet Union
1989 – Reverend Jim Bakker was sentenced to 45 years in prison and fined $500,000 for his conviction on 24 counts of fraud
2003 – In London, the last commercial supersonic *Concorde* flight landed
2005 – Rosa Parks died at age 92

October 25: Pablo Picasso 1881, Smokey Joe Wood 1889, Minnie Pearl 1912, Billy Barty 1924, Marion Ross 1928, Helen Reddy 1942, Ivan Koloff

1942, Brian Kerwin 1949, Nancy Cartwright 1959, Tracy Nelson 1963, Michael Boatman 1964, Pedro Martinez 1971, Ciara 1985, Conchita Campbell 1995

1400 – Writer Geoffrey Chaucer died at the age of 57
1415 – England won the Battle of Agincourt over France during the Hundred Years' War
1760 – George III took the British throne after the death of King George II, his grandfather
1812 – During the War of 1812, the U.S. frigate *United States* captured thee British vessel *Macedonian*
1854 – The Charge of the Light Brigade took place during the Crimean War
1917 – The Bolsheviks under Vladimir Ilyich Lenin seized power in Russia
1920 – King Alexander of Greece died from blood poisoning after he was bitten by his pet monkey
1955 – The microwave oven was introduced by the Tappan Company
1962 – American author John Steinbeck was awarded the Nobel Prize in literature
1971 – The PBS children's show *The Electric Company* aired its first episode
1983 – The United States invaded the island country of Grenada
1999 – Golfer Payne Stewart and five others were killed when their Learjet crashed in South Dakota

October 26: Charles W. Post 1854, Benjamin Guggenheim 1865, Judy Johnson 1899, Jackie Coogan 1914, Francois Mitterand 1916, Bob Hoskins 1942, Pat Sajak 1946, Hillary Clinton 1947, Jaclyn Smith 1947, Lauren Tewes 1954, James Pickens Jr. 1954, Rita Wilson 1956, Cary Elwes 1962, Kelly Rowan 1965, Keith Urban 1967, Francisco Liriano 1983, Sasha Cohen 1984, Amanda Overmyer 1984

899 – Alfred the Great, King of the West Saxons, died at the approximate age of 50
1776 – Benjamin Franklin left America for France on a diplomatic mission
1825 – The Erie Canal opened in upstate New York
1861 – The Pony Express stopped running
1881 – The Gunfight at the OK Corral took place in Tombstone, Arizona
1970 – *Doonesbury*, the comic strip by Gary Trudeau, premiered in 28 newspapers
1977 – The experimental space shuttle *Enterprise* successfully landed at Edwards Air Force Base in California
1982 – *St. Elsewhere* premiered on NBC-TV

2000 – Playstation 2 was released in North America

October 27: James Cook 1728, Theodore Roosevelt 1858, Emily Post 1872, Patsy Dougherty 1876, Nanette Fabray 1922, Ralph Kiner 1922, Ruby Dee 1924, Warren Christopher 1925, John Cleese 1939, John Gotti 1940, Lee Greenwood 1942, Ted Wass 1952, Peter Firth 1953, Robert Picardo 1953, Peter Firth 1953, Simon LeBon 1958, Marla Maples 1963, Brad Radke 1972, Kelly Osbourne 1984

1858 – Roland Macy opened Macy's Department Store in New York City
1904 – The New York subway system officially opened
1954 – Marilyn Monroe and Joe DiMaggio were divorced
1954 – The first Walt Disney television show *Disneyland* premiered on ABC
1966 – *It's the Great Pumpkin, Charlie Brown* first aired on CBS-TV
2002 – The Anaheim Angels won their first World Series
2002 – Emmitt Smith of the Dallas Cowboys became the all-time leading rusher in the NFL when he extended his career yardage to 16,743
2004 – The Boston Red Sox won the World Series for the first time since 1918
2006 – The St. Louis Cardinals won the World Series over the Detroit Tigers

October 28: Elsa Lanchester 1902, Jonas Salk 1914, Jack Soo 1917, Bowie Kuhn 1926, Charlie Daniels 1936, Dennis Franz 1944, Telma Hopkins 1948, Bruce Jenner 1949, Annie Potts 1952, Bill Gates 1955, Paul Wylie 1964, Jamie Gertz 1965, Andy Richter 1966, Julia Roberts 1967, Brad Paisley 1972, Joaquin Phoenix 1974, Jeremy Bonderman 1982

1636 – Harvard College was founded
1793 – Eli Whitney applied for a patent for his cotton gin
1886 – A ceremony was held to dedicate the Statue of Liberty, with President Grover Cleveland present
1901 – Booker T. Washington, a prominent black leader, visited the White House, prompting racial riots in New Orleans, where 34 people were killed
1922 – Benito Mussolini took control of the Italian government and introduced Fascism to Italy
1936 – The Statue of Liberty was rededicated by President Franklin D. Roosevelt on its 50th anniversary
1940 – During World War II, Italy invaded Greece
1965 – The Gateway Arch along the waterfront in St. Louis, Missouri, was completed

2007 – The Boston Red Sox won the World Series by sweeping the Colorado Rockies, four games to none

October 29: Henry III of the Holy Roman Empire 1017, Connie Mack 1940, Bob Ross 1942, Richard Dreyfuss 1947, Kate Jackson 1948, Scott Jaeck 1954, Dan Castellaneta 1957, Randy Jackson 1961, Joely Fisher 1967, Winona Ryder 1971, Gabrielle Union 1972, Eric Messier 1973, Travis Henry 1978, Amanda Beard 1981, Eric Staal 1984

1618 – Sir Walter Raleigh was beheaded under a sentence for conspiracy against King James I
1863 – The International Committee of the Red Cross was founded
1901 – Leon Czolgosz, the assassin of President William McKinley, was executed by electrocution
1911 – American newspaperman Joseph Pulitzer died
1929 – America's Great Depression began with the crash of the Wall Street stock market
1945 – The first ballpoint pens to be made commercially went on sale at Gimbels Department Store in New York at the price of $12.50 each
1960 – Muhammad Ali won his first professional fight
1991 – The U.S. *Galileo* spacecraft became the first to visit an asteroid
1995 – Jerry Rice of the San Francisco 49ers became the NFL's career leader in receiving yards with 14,040 yards
1998 – John Glenn became the oldest person to go to space, at the age of 77
2007 – Argentina elected its first female president, Crinstina Fernandez de Kirchner

October 30: John Adams 1735, Charles Atlas 1893, Ruth Gordon 1896, Bill Terry 1898, Juan Marichal 1937, Henry Winkler 1945, Harry Hamlin 1951, Shanna Reed 1955, Kevin Pollak 1958, Diego Maradona 1960, Gavin Rossdale 1967, Jason Bartlett 1979, Ivanka Trump 1981, Trent Edwards 1983

1817 – The independent government of Venezuela was established by Simon Bolivar
1831 – Escaped slave Nat Turner was apprehended in Southampton County, Virginia, several weeks after leading the bloodiest slave uprising in American history
1864 – Helena, Montana was founded following the finding of gold at Last Chance Gulch
1900 – The population of the United States was announced to be over 76 million

1938 – Orson Welles' *The War of the Worlds* aired on CBS radio, causing widespread panic when many people thought the Martians really were invading
1945 – Jackie Robinson signed a contract with the Brooklyn Dodgers, the first black person to sign with a Major League Baseball team
1985 – Space Shuttle *Challenger* lifted off on its final successful mission
1988 – Kraft Foods was bought by Philip Morris
2001 – Michael Jordan returned to the NBA with the Washington Wizards after a 3 ½ year retirement

October 31: Pope Clement XIV 1705, John Keats 1795, Chiang Kai-Shek 1887, Dale Evans 1912, Dick Francis 1920, Barbara Bel Geddes 1922, Michael Collins 1930, Dan Rather 1931, Michael Landon 1936, Tom Paxton 1937, David Ogden Stiers 1942, Sally Kirkland 1944, Deidre Hall 1948, John Candy 1950, Jane Pauley 1950, Dave Trembley 1951, Ken Wahl 1954, Brian Stokes Mitchell 1957, Peter Jackson 1961, Fred McGriff 1963, Rob Schneider 1964, Mike O'Malley 1966, Vanilla Ice 1967, Willow Smith 2000

1517 – Martin Luther posted the 95 Theses on the door of the Wittenberg Palace Church
1864 – Nevada became the 36th state
1926 – Magician Harry Houdini died of gangrene and peritonitis resulting from a ruptured appendix (see earlier photo of Houdini at right)
1941 – Mount Rushmore was completed after 14 years of work
1955 – Britain's Princess Margaret announced she would not marry Royal Air Force Captain Peter Townsend
1984 – Indian Prime Minister Indira Gandhi was assassinated near her residence by two Sikh security guards
1993 – Actor River Phoenix died at the age of 23 after collapsing outside The Viper Room in Hollywood
1999 – EgyptAir Flight 990 crashed off the coast of Nantucket, killing all 217 people aboard
2008 – A gunman took eleven fifth graders hostage at an elementary school in Stockton Springs, Maine, before giving himself up

November

November 1: Stephen Crane 1871, Gary Player 1935, Bill Anderson 1937, Robert Foxworth 1941, Marcia Wallace 1942, David Foster 1949, Lyle Lovett 1957, Rachel Ticotin 1958, Fernando Valenzuela 1960, Anthony Kiedis 1962, Dana Plato 1964, Sophie B. Hawkins 1967, Jenny McCarthy 1972, Bo Bice 1975, Coco Crisp 1979

1512 – Michelangelo's paintings on the ceiling of the Sistine Chapel were first exhibited to the public
1604 – William Shakespeare's play *Othello* was performed for the first time
1611 – William Shakespeare's play *The Tempest* was performed for the first time
1765 – The Stamp Act went into effect in the American colonies
1800 – President John Adams became the first president to live in the White House
1861 – General George McClellan was made the general-in-chief of the Union armies by President Lincoln, replacing General Winfield Scott
1864 – The U.S. Post Office started selling money orders
1870 – The U.S. Weather Bureau (later the National Weather Service) made its first weather forecast
1894 – Russian Tsar Alexander III died and Nicholas II became the new Tsar
1922 – The last sultan of the Ottoman Empire, Mehmed VI, abdicated his throne
1950 – Two Puerto Rican nationalists tried to assassinate United States President Harry Truman
1950 – Charles Cooper became the first black man to play in the NBA

1982 – Honda became the first motor company to manufacture automobiles in the United States

November 2: Edward V of England 1470, Marie Antoinette 1755, Daniel Boone 1734, James K. Polk 1795, Warren G. Harding 1865, Burt Lancaster 1913, Joseph Brennan 1934, Abdullah the Butcher 1936, Pat Buchanan 1938, Stefanie Powers 1942, k.d. lang 1961, Sam Horn 1963, David Schwimmer 1966, Nelly 1974, Sydney Ponson 1976

1083 – Matilda of Flanders, Queen of England and wife of William the Conqueror, died at the age of 51 in Normandy
1889 – North and South Dakota were admitted into the United States as the 39th and 40th states
1920 – The first commercial radio station in America, KDKA of Pittsburgh, began regular broadcasting
1948 – Harry Truman defeated Thomas Dewey for President, despite the headline of the Chicago Tribune, which read "Dewey Defeats Truman"
1992 – Magic Johnson played in his last game in the NBA
1997 – Violet Palmer became the first woman to referee an NBA basketball game
2000 – The first crew arrived at the International Space Station
2001 – The movie *Monsters, Inc.* premiered

November 3: William Cullen Bryant 1794, Leopold III of Belgium 1901, Bob Feller 1918, Charles Bronson 1921, Ken Berry 1933, Michael Dukakis 1933, Steve Landesberg 1945, Shadoe Stevens 1946, Mike Evans 1949, Larry Holmes 1949, Dwight Evans 1951, Roseanne Barr 1952, Kate Capshaw 1953, Dennis Miller 1953, Adam Ant 1954, Kathy Kinney 1954, Phil Simms 1956, Dolph Lundgren 1957, Karch Kiraly 1960, Evgeni Plushenko 1982, Elizabeth Smart 1987

1507 – Leonardo DaVinci was commissioned to paint the *Mona Lisa*
1783 – The American Continental Army was disbanded following their victory in the American Revolutionary War
1796 – John Adams was elected the 2nd President of the United States
1911 – Chevrolet officially entered the automobile market, finding itself in competition with Ford's Model T
1913 – The U.S Government implemented the first income tax
1957 – *Sputnik 2* was launched into space by the Soviet Union, the first to send a dog, Laika, into space
1975 – *Good Morning America* premiered on ABC-TV
1978 – *Diff'rent Strokes* first aired on NBC-TV
1998 – Bob Kane, the creator of Batman, died at the age of 83

1998 – Minnesota elected Jesse "the Body" Ventura, a former pro wrestler, as its governor

November 4: Edward V of England 1470, William III of England 1650, Will Rogers 1879, Walter Cronkite 1916, Art Carney 1918, Doris Roberts 1930, Loretta Swit 1937, Laura Bush 1946, Markie Post 1950, Kathy Griffin 1960, Jeff Probst 1962, Ralph Macchio 1962, Sean "Diddy" Combs 1969, Matthew McConaughey 1969

1501 – Catherine of Aragon and Prince Arthur Tudor met for the first time
1791 – In the Battle of Wabash, the Western Confederacy of American Indians won a major victory over the United States
1842 – Abraham Lincoln married Mary Todd
1918 – During World War I, Austria-Hungary surrendered to Italy
1922 – In Egypt, in the Valley of the Kings, Howard Carter discovered the entry of the lost tomb of King Tut
1924 – Nellie T. Ross of Wyoming was elected America's first woman governor
1979 – Iranian militants seized the U.S. embassy in Tehran and took 63 Americans hostage
1995 – Israeli Prime Minister Yitzhak Rabin, 73 years old, was assassinated
1995 – Morrie Schwartz, the subject of the book *Tuesdays with Morrie*, died of ALS at the age of 78
2001 – Hurricane Michelle hit Cuba destroying crops and thousands of homes
2003 – The most powerful solar flare ever observed occurred
2008 – A plane crash in Mexico City killed Mexican Secretary of the Interior, Juan Camilo Mourino and 12 others
2008 – The United States elected its first African-American President, Barack Obama

November 5: Charles II of England 1630, Roy Rogers 1912, Natalie Schafer 1912, Vivien Leigh 1913, Ike Turner 1931, Elke Sommer 1940, Art Garfunkel 1941, Sam Shepard 1943, Armin Shimermin 1949, Bill Walton 1952, Jon-Erik Hexum 1958, Bryan Adams 1959, Tatum O'Neal 1963, Tim Blake Nelson 1964, Famke Janssen 1965, Javy Lopez 1970, Corin Nemec 1971, Johnny Damon 1973, Kevin Jonas 1987

1605 – The Gunpowder Plot attempted by Guy Fawkes failed, when he was captured before he could blow up the English Parliament
1872 – Susan B. Anthony was fined $100 for attempting to vote in the presidential election

1895 – George B. Selden received the first U.S. patent for an automobile

1935 – The game Monopoly was first introduced to the public

1940 – Franklin D. Roosevelt won an unprecedented third term in office

1946 – John F. Kennedy was elected to the U.S. House of Representatives at the age of 29

1963 – Archaeologists found the remains of a Viking settlement at L'Anse aux Meadows, Newfoundland

1974 – Ella T. Grasso was elected governor of Connecticut, the first woman in the United States to win a governorship without succeeding her husband

1977 – George W. Bush and Laura Welch were married

1990 – Disney's Yacht Club Resort opened at Walt Disney World

1994 – Former President Ronald Reagan announced that he had Alzheimer's disease

1994 – George Foreman, 45, became boxing's oldest heavyweight champion when he knocked out Michael Moorer in the 10th round

1998 – Scientists published a genetic study that showed strong evidence that Thomas Jefferson fathered at least one child of his slave, Sally Hemings

2006 – Former Iraqi dictator Saddam Hussein was sentenced to death for crimes against humanity

2007 – China sent its first lunar satellite into orbit around the Moon

November 6: John Philip Sousa 1854, James Naismith 1861, Walter Johnson 1887, Edsel Ford 1893, Mike Nichols 1931, Sally Field 1946, Glenn Frey 1948, Maria Shriver 1955, Lori Singer 1957, Peter DeLuise 1966, Ethan Hawke 1970, Rebecca Romijn 1972, Emma Stone 1988

1860 – Abraham Lincoln was elected to be the sixteenth President of the United States

1861 – Jefferson Davis was elected as the President of the Confederate States of America

1900 – President William McKinley was re-elected, along with his vice-presidential candidate, Theodore Roosevelt

1935 – Edwin H. Armstrong announced his development of FM broadcasting

1947 – *Meet the Press* debuted on NBC-TV

1990 – About 20% of the Universal Studios backlot in southern California was destroyed in an arson fire

1991 – Kuwait celebrated the dousing of the last of the oil fires ignited by Iraq during the Persian Gulf War

November 7: Marie Curie 1867, Leon Trotsky 1879, Billy Graham 1918, Joe Niekro 1944, Christopher Knight 1957, Keith Lockhart 1959, Dana Plato 1964, Christopher Daniel Barnes 1972, Yunjin Kim 1973, Kris Benson 1974

1874 – The Republican Party of the United States was first symbolized as an elephant in a cartoon by Thomas Nast in Harper's Weekly
1893 – The state of Colorado granted women the right to vote
1908 – Butch Cassidy and the Sundance were reportedly killed in Bolivia
1917 – Russia's Bolshevik Revolution took place
1944 – President Franklin D. Roosevelt became the first person to win a fourth term as president
1962 – Former First Lady Eleanor Roosevelt died at the age of 78
1965 – The Pillsbury Dough Boy debuted in television commercials
1973 – New Jersey became the first state to permit girls to play Little League baseball
1991 – Magic Johnson announced that he had tested positive for the virus that causes AIDS, and that he was retiring from basketball
1991 – Actor Paul Reubens, a.k.a. Pee Wee Herman, pled no contest to charges of indecent exposure
2000 – Hillary Clinton became the first former First Lady elected to public office when she was elected to the U.S. Senate
2008 – A school in Haiti collapsed, killing at least 88 people, many of them children

November 8: Charles X of Sweden 1622, Edmond Halley 1656, Milton Bradley 1836, Bram Stoker 1847, Hermann Rorschach 1884, Margaret Mitchell 1900, Norman Lloyd 1914, Darla Hood 1931, Morley Safer 1931, Esther Rolle 1933, Bonnie Raitt 1949, Mary Hart 1951, Jerry Remy 1952, Alfre Woodard 1953, Leif Garrett 1961, Courtney Thorne-Smith 1968, Tom Anderson 1970, Tara Reid 1975, Bucky Covington 1977, Jack Osbourne 1985

1887 – Doc Holliday died at the age of 35
1889 – Montana became the 41st U.S. state
1895 – Wilhelm Roentgen took the first X-ray pictures
1954 – The American League approved the transfer of the Philadelphia Athletics baseball team to Kansas City
1965 – The soap opera *Days of Our Lives* first aired on NBC-TV
1966 – Edward W. Brooke of Massachusetts became the first African-American elected to the U.S. Senate by popular vote
1966 – Actor Ronald Reagan was elected governor of California

2000 – In Florida, a statewide recount began to decide the winner of the 2000 U.S. presidential election
2004 – During the War in Iraq, 10,000 U.S. forces and a small number of Iraqi soldiers participated in the Siege of Fallujah

November 9: Edward VII of England 1841, Claude Rains 1889, Spiro T. Agnew 1918, Carl Sagan 1934, Bob Gibson 1935, Mary Travers 1936, Robert David Hall 1947, Lou Ferrigno 1951, Bill Mantlo 1951, Tony Slattery 1959, David Duval 1971, Eric Dane 1972, Nick Lachey 1973, Sisqo 1978, Adam Dunn 1979, Nikki Blonsky 1988

1862 – General Ambrose Burnside replaced George McClellan as commander of the Union armies during the Civil War
1872 – A fire destroyed about 800 buildings in Boston
1906 – Theodore Roosevelt left on the first foreign trip by a U.S. President, when he started on a trip to check on the progress of the Panama Canal
1921 – Albert Einstein was awarded the Nobel Prize in Physics
1965 – The great Northeast blackout occurred as several states and parts of Canada were hit by a series of power failures lasting up to 13 ½ hours
1967 – The first issue of *Rolling Stone Magazine* was published
1967 – The unmanned *Apollo 4* spacecraft was launched atop the first Saturn V rocket
1989 – Communist East Germany opened its borders, allowing its citizens to travel freely to West Germany
1990 – Mary Robinson was elected the first female President of Ireland
2006 – Newsman Ed Bradley died at the age of 65

November 10: Martin Luther 1483, George II of Great Britain 1683, Johnny Marks 1909, Roy Scheider 1935, Tim Rice 1944, Alaina Reed 1946, Jack Scalia 1951, Bob Stanley 1954, Sinbad 1956, MacKenzie Phillips 1959, Neil Gaiman 1960, Kenny Rogers (MLB) 1964, Tracy Morgan 1968, Ellen Pompeo 1969, Shawn Green 1972, Brittany Murphy 1977, Eve 1978, Donte Stallworth 1980, Kendrick Perkins 1984, Josh Peck 1986

1775 – The United States Marines was organized
1871 – Henry M. Stanley, journalist and explorer, found David Livingstone, a missing Scottish missionary, in central Africa
1917 – 41 suffragists were arrested in front of the White House
1928 – Michinomiya Hirohito took the throne as Emperor of Japan
1969 – *Sesame Street* made its TV debut
1982 – Soviet leader Leonid Brezhnev died of a heart attack at age 75

1993 – The U.S. House of Representatives passed the Brady Bill, which called for a five-day waiting period for handgun purchases
1996 – Dan Marino of the Miami Dolphins became the first quarterback in NFL history to pass for more than 50,000 yards
2006 – Actor Jack Palance died at the age of 87

November 11: Abigail Adams 1744, Fyodor Dostoyevsky 1821, George Patton 1885, Rabbit Maranville 1891, Pie Traynor 1899, Kurt Vonnegut, Jr. 1922, Jonathan Winters 1925, Barbara Boxer 1940, Fuzzy Zoeller 1951, Demi Moore 1962, Philip McKeon 1964, Calista Flockhart 1964, Jose Offerman 1968, Adam Beach 1972, Leonardo DiCaprio 1974

1620 – The Mayflower Compact was signed by the 41 men on the Mayflower when they landed in what is now Provincetown Harbor near Cape Cod
1831 – Nat Turner, a slave and educated minister, was hanged in Virginia, after inciting a violent slave uprising
1851 – The telescope was patented by Alvan Clark
1889 – Washington became the 42nd state
1918 – World War I came to an end when the Allies and Germany signed an armistice
1921 – The Tomb of the Unknowns was dedicated at Arlington Cemetery in Virginia by President Warren Harding
1926 – U.S. Route 66 was established
1940 – The Jeep made its debut
1942 – During World War II, Germany completed its occupation of France
1946 – The New York Knickerbockers (now the Knicks) played their first basketball game at Madison Square Garden
1952 – The first video recorder was demonstrated by John Mullin and Wayne Johnson in Beverly Hills
2006 – Playstation 3 was released in Japan

November 12: Elizabeth Cady Stanton 1815, Auguste Rodin 1840, Kim Hunter 1922, Grace Kelly 1929, Charles Manson 1934, Wallace Shawn 1943, Al Michaels 1944, Megan Mullally 1958, Nadia Comaneci 1961, Sammy Sosa 1968, Tonya Harding 1970, Craig Parker 1970, Lourdes Benedicto 1974, Anne Hathaway 1982, Omarion 1984

1920 – Judge Kennesaw Mountain Landis was elected the first commissioner of Major League Baseball
1927 – Joseph Stalin became the undisputed ruler of the Soviet Union
1940 – Walt Disney released *Fantasia*

1942 – During World War II, the naval battle of Guadalcanal began between Japanese and American forces
1946 – The first drive-up banking facility opened at the Exchange National Bank in Chicago
1980 – The U.S. space probe *Voyager I* came within 77,000 miles of Saturn while transmitting data back to Earth
1982 – Yuri Andropov was elected to succeed the late Leonid Brezhnev as leader of the Soviet Union
2001 – American Airlines flight 587 crashed just minutes after take off from Kennedy Airport in New York, killing all 260 people onboard
2002 – Stan Lee filed a lawsuit against Marvel Entertainment Inc. that claimed the company had cheated him out of millions of dollars in movie profits related to the 2002 movie *Spider-Man*
2007 – Dustin Pedroia of the Boston Red Sox was chosen as the American League Rookie of the Year

November 13: Edward III of England 1312, Robert Louis Stevenson 1850, Buck O'Neill 1911, Richard Mulligan 1932, Garry Marshall 1934, Joe Mantegna 1947, Tracy Scoggins 1953, Chris Noth 1954, Whoopi Goldberg 1955, Vinny Testaverde 1963, Steve Zahn 1967, Jimmy Kimmel 1967, Ron Artest 1979

1002 – English King Ethelred ordered the killing of all Danes in England, known now as the St. Brice's Day Massacre
1775 – Montreal was captured by United States forces during the American Revolutionary War
1789 – Benjamin Franklin wrote a letter to a friend in which he said, "In this world nothing can be said to be certain, except death and taxes"
1927 – The Holland Tunnel opened to the public, providing access between New York City and New Jersey beneath the Hudson River
1956 – The U.S. Supreme Court struck down laws calling for racial segregation on public buses
1971 – The U.S. spacecraft *Mariner 9* became the first spacecraft to orbit another planet, Mars
1977 – The comic strip *Li'l Abner* by Al Capp appeared in newspapers for the last time
1982 – The Vietnam Veterans Memorial was dedicated in Washington, DC
1995 – Greg Maddox became the first Major League pitcher to win four consecutive Cy Young Awards

November 14: William III of England 1650, Robert Fulton 1765, Claude Monet 1840, Mamie Eisenhower 1896, Joseph McCarthy 1909, Brian Keith 1921, Boutros Boutros-Ghali 1922, McLean Stevenson 1929, Fred Haise

1933, King Hussein of Jordan 1935, Prince Charles 1948, Condeleezza Rice 1954, Yanni 1954, Ray McKinnon 1957, D.B. Sweeney 1961, Laura San Giacomo 1961, Patrick Warburton 1964, Curt Schilling 1966, Lawyer Milloy 1973, Xavier Nady 1978

1851 – Herman Melville's novel *Moby Dick* was first published
1881 – Charles Guiteau's trial began for the assassination of President James Garfield
1922 – The BBC began Broadcasting on the radio in Great Britain
1969 – NASA launched *Apollo 12*, the second manned mission to the Moon
1970 – Southern Airways Flight 932 crashed in the mountains near Huntington, West Virginia, killing 75 people, including members of the football team at Marshall University
1973 – Britain's Princess Anne married a commoner, Captain Mark Phillips, in Westminster Abbey
1998 – Carmen Electra and Dennis Rodman were married in Las Vegas

November 15: John I of France 1316, William Pitt 1708, Georgia O'Keeffe 1887, Bill Melendez 1916, Joseph Wapner 1919, John Orchard 1928, Edward Asner 1929, Yaphet Kotto 1937, Sam Waterston 1940, "Macho Man" Randy Savage 1945, Beverly D'Angelo 1954, Kevin Eubanks 1957, Chad Kroeger 1974, Craig Hanson 1983

1777 – The Continental Congress approved the Articles of Confederation, a precursor to the U.S. Constitution
1864 – During the American Civil War, Union General William Tecumseh Sherman had Atlanta, Georgia burned to the ground, thus starting Sherman's March to the Sea
1920 – The League of Nations met for the first time in Geneva, Switzerland
1926 – The National Broadcasting Co. (NBC) debuted with a radio network of 24 stations
1939 – Construction on the Jefferson Memorial began in Washington, DC, with President Franklin D. Roosevelt laying the cornerstone
1969 – In Washington, DC, a quarter of a million people protested against the Vietnam War
1988 – The Soviet Union Shuttle *Buran* was launched on its only flight
1992 – Richard Petty drove in the final race of his 35-year career
2005 – In Amiens, France, Isabelle Dinoire became the first person to undergo a partial face transplant

November 16: Roman Emperor Tiberius 42 B.C., Burgess Meredith 1908, Daws Butler 1916, David Leisure 1950, Robin McKinley 1952, Terry

LaBonte 1956, Marg Helgenberger 1958, Dwight Gooden 1964, Lisa Bonet 1967, Martha Plimpton 1970, Julio Lugo 1975, Oksana Baiul 1977, Maggie Gyllenhaal 1977, Noah Gray-Cabey 1995

1776 – During the American Revolution, Hessian soldiers captured Fort Washington from the Americans
1907 – Oklahoma became the 46th state
1940 – In occupied Poland, the Nazis closed off the Warsaw Ghetto
1945 – In what became known as Operation Paperclip, the United States secretly admitted 88 German scientists and engineers into the U.S. so they could work for the U.S. rocket program
1952 – In the *Peanuts* comic strip, Lucy first held a football for Charlie Brown
1966 – Dr. Samuel H. Sheppard was acquitted in his second trial of charges he had murdered his pregnant wife, Marilyn, in 1954
1973 – NASA launched *Skylab 4* with a 3-person crew on an 84-day mission
1982 – The NFL strike came to an end after 57 days

November 17: Louis XVIII of France 1755, Shelby Foote 1916, Rock Hudson 1925, Peter Cook 1937, Gordon Lightfoot 1938, Martin Scorsese 1942, Danny DeVito 1944, Lauren Hutton 1944, Lorne Michaels 1944, Tom Seaver 1944, Howard Dean 1948, Stephen Root 1951, Mary Elizabeth Mastrantonio 1958, William Moses 1959, RuPaul 1960, Daisy Fuentes 1966, Sophie Marceau 1966, Leonard Roberts 1972, Brandon Call 1976, Isaac Hanson 1980, Nick Markakis 1982, Christopher Paolini 1983

1493 – Christopher Columbus landed in Puerto Rico
1558 – Elizabeth I (see image to left) became Queen of England upon the death of her half-sister, Queen Mary I
1603 – Sir Walter Raleigh went on trial for treason
1796 – Catherine the Great of Russia died at the age of 67
1800 – The U.S. Congress met in Washington, DC for the first time in the half completed Capitol Building
1863 – During the American Civil War, the Siege of Knoxville began

1869 – The Suez Canal opened with an elaborate ceremony

1913 – The steamship *Louise* became the first ship to travel through the Panama Canal

1970 – The Soviet Union landed the first remote controlled roving robot on the Moon

1973 – President Richard Nixon proclaimed that he was "not a crook"

1997 – Mario Lemieux was voted into the NHL Hall of Fame

2004 – K-Mart announced it was buying Sears

2006 – Playstation 3 was released in the United Sates and Canada

November 18: Louis Daguerre 1789, Imogene Coca 1908, Arthur Peterson 1912, Alan Shepard 1923, Mickey Mouse 1928, Brenda Vaccaro 1939, Linda Evans 1942, Susan Sullivan 1944, Jameson Parker 1950, Kevin Nealon 1953, Elizabeth Perkins 1960, Jamie Moyer 1962, Tom Gordon 1967, Owen Wilson 1968, Gary Sheffield 1968, Sam Cassell 1969, David Ortiz 1975, Jason Williams 1975

1307 – William Tell shot an apple off his son's head with an arrow, according to legend

1493 – Christopher Columbus first spied Puerto Rico

1928 – The first successful sound-synchronized animated cartoon premiered in New York, Walt Disney's *Steamboat Willie*, starring Mickey Mouse

1978 – In Jonestown, Guyana, Reverend Jim Jones persuaded his followers to commit suicide by drinking a death potion in which 914 cult members were left dead, including over 200 children

1983 – *A Christmas Story* was first released in movie theaters

1985 – The comic strip *Calvin and Hobbes* was first published

1985 – Elmo first appeared on *Sesame Street*

1991 – Shiite Muslim kidnappers in Lebanon freed Anglican Church envoy Terry Waite and Thomas Sutherland

1999 – 12 people were killed and 28 injured when a huge bonfire under construction collapsed at Texas A&M

2001 – Nintendo released the GameCube home video game console in the United States

2006 – Tom Cruise and Katie Holmes were married in a castle in Italy

November 19: Charles I of England 1600, James A. Garfield 1831, Tommy Dorsey 1905, Indira Gandhi 1917, Roy Campanella 1921, Joe Morgan (Baseball Manager) 1930, Larry King 1933, Dick Cavett 1936, Ted Turner 1938, Garrick Utley 1939, Dan Haggerty 1941, Calvin Klein 1942, Bob Boone 1947, Ahmad Rashad 1949, Robert Beltran 1953, Kathleen Quinlan 1954, Ann Curry 1956, Michael Wilbon 1958, Allison Janney 1960,

Meg Ryan 1961, Jodie Foster 1962, Terry Farrell 1963, Gail Devers 1966, Jason Scott Lee 1966, Kerri Strug 1977, Jeff Bailey 1978, Ryan Howard 1979, Larry Johnson 1979

1861 – Julia Ward Howe wrote "The Battle Hymn of the Republic"
1863 – Abraham Lincoln delivered the Gettysburg Address
1950 – General Dwight D. Eisenhower became the supreme commander of the NATO-Europe forces
1954 – Sammy Davis Jr. was involved in a serious auto accident which led to the loss of sight in his left eye
1959 – The Ford Motor Company announced they were discontinuing the unpopular Edsel
1969 – *Apollo 12* astronauts Charles Conrad and Alan Bean made mankind's second landing on the moon
1971 – Walt Disney World's Fort Wilderness Resort and Campground opened
1985 – Soviet Union leader Mikhail Gorbachev and American President Ronald Reagan met for the first time
1990 – Milli Vanilli was stripped of their Grammy Award when it was found out that they were not the real singers on their album
1990 – Disney's Beach Club Resort opened at Walt Disney World
1998 – The U.S. House of Representatives began impeachment proceedings against President Bill Clinton

November 20: Kenesaw Mountain Landis 1866, Edwin Hubble 1889, Alistair Cooke 1908, Robert Byrd 1917, Robert Kennedy 1925, Franklin Cover 1928, Richard Dawson 1932, Dick Smothers 1939, Joe Biden 1942, Veronica Hamel 1943, Duane Allman 1946, Joe Walsh 1947, Richard Masur 1948, Bo Derek 1956, Mark Gastineau 1956, Sean Young 1959, Ming-Na 1963, J.D. Drew 1975, Josh Turner 1977

1620 – Peregrine White was born aboard the Mayflower in Massachusetts Bay, the first white child born in New England
1818 – Simon Bolivar formally declared Venezuela independent of Spain
1945 – 24 Nazi leaders went before an international war crimes tribunal in Nuremberg, Germany
1947 – Britain's Princess Elizabeth, later Elizabeth II, married Philip Mountbatten, Duke of Edinburgh in Westminster Abbey
1962 – The Cuban Missile Crisis ended when the Soviet Union removed its missiles and bombers from Cuba
1973 – *A Charlie Brown Thanksgiving* first aired on CBS-TV
1985 – Microsoft Windows 1.0 was released

1990 – Saddam Hussein ordered another 250,000 Iraqi troops into the country of Kuwait
1992 – A fire seriously damaged Windsor Castle in England
2001 – The Justice Department headquarters building was renamed the Robert F. Kennedy building by President George W. Bush

November 21: Voltaire 1694, Josiah Bartlett 1729, Stan Musial 1920, Christopher Tolkien 1924, Laurence Luckinbill 1934, Marlo Thomas 1938, Harold Ramis 1944, Goldie Hawn 1945, Steven Curtis Chapman 1961, Nicollette Sheridan 1963, Reggie Lewis 1965, Troy Aikman 1966, Ken Griffey Jr. 1969, Michael Strahan 1971, Rain Phoenix 1972, Chris Moneymaker 1975, Hank Blalock 1980, Jena Malone 1984

1620 – The Mayflower reached what is now Provincetown, Massachusetts
1783 – The first successful flight was made in a hot air balloon in Paris
1789 – North Carolina became the 12th state when it voted to ratify the Constitution
1877 – Thomas A. Edison announced the invention of his phonograph
1899 – US Vice-President Garret Hobart died of heart failure at the age of 55
1900 – A tornado in Tennessee took the lives of 50 people
1934 – The New York Yankees purchased the contract of Joe DiMaggio from San Francisco of the Pacific Coast League
2002 – NATO invited Latvia, Estonia, Lithuania, Bulgaria, Romania, Slovakia and Slovenia to become members

November 22: George Eliot 1819, John N. Garner 1868, Percival P. Baxter 1876, Charles de Gualle 1890, Rodney Dangerfield 1921, Robert Vaughn 1932, Roy Thomas 1940, Billie Jean King 1943, Greg Luzinski 1950, Richard Kind 1956, Jamie Lee Curtis 1958, Mariel Hemingway 1961, Brian Robbins 1963, Boris Becker 1967, Jay Payton 1972, Scarlett Johansson 1984

1718 – Blackbeard the Pirate was killed off the coast of North Carolina
1917 – The National Hockey League was formed
1943 – U.S. President Franklin Roosevelt, British Prime Minister Winston Churchill and Chinese leader Chiang Kai-shek met in Cairo to discuss the measures for defeating Japan
1963 – President John F. Kennedy was assassinated in Dallas, Texas
1986 – Mike Tyson became the youngest to wear the world heavyweight-boxing crown at only 20 years and 4 months old

1990 – President George H.W. Bush, his wife, Barbara, and other congressional leaders shared Thanksgiving dinner with U.S. troops in Saudi Arabia
1994 – Disney's All-Star Music Resort opened at Walt Disney World
1995 – *Toy Story* was released, the first motion picture created completely using computer-generated images

November 23: Franklin Pierce 1804, Billy the Kid 1859, Boris Karloff 1887, Harpo Marx 1888, Michael Gough 1917, Luis Tiant 1940, Steve Landesberg 1945, Bruce Hornsby 1954, Robin Roberts 1960, Maxwell Caulfield 1961, Jerry Kelly 1966, Dave McCarty 1969, Jonathan Papelbon 1980, Miley Cyrus 1992

1814 – Vice-President Elbridge Gerry died at the age of 70, the second of James Madison's vice-presidents to die in office
1863 – During the American Civil War, the Battle of Chattanooga began
1889 – The first jukebox made its debut in San Francisco
1890 – Princess Wilhelmina became Queen of the Netherlands at the age of 10 when her father William III died
1906 – Joseph Smith, leader of the Church of Jesus Christ of Latter-day Saints, was convicted of polygamy
1936 – *Life* magazine was first published
1961 – The Dominican Republic changed the name of its capital from Ciudad Trujillo to Santo Domingo
1963 – *Doctor Who* debuted on BBC-TV
1969 – The first ground-to-space news conference took place between reporters and astronauts aboard *Apollo 12*
1971 – The People's Republic of China was seated in the United Nations Security Council
1990 – Author Roald Dahl died in England at the age of 74
2005 – Jessica Simpson and Nick Lachey announced they were ending their three year marriage
2007 – A cruise liner, the MS *Explorer*, sank near Antarctica after striking an iceberg with over 150 people aboard

November 24: Zachary Taylor 1784, Henri de Toulouse-Lautrec 1864, Scott Joplin 1868, Alben W. Barkley 1877, Dale Carnegie 1888, Joe Medwick 1911, Irwin Allen 1916, William F. Buckley, Jr. 1925, Oscar Robertson 1938, Paul Tagliabue 1940, Billy Connolly 1942, Marlin Fitzwater 1942, Ted Bundy 1946, Dwight Schultz 1947, Denise Crosby 1957, Brad Sherwood 1964, Garrett Dillahunt 1974, Katherine Heigl 1978

1859 – Charles Darwin published *On the Origin of Species* (see photo of Darwin at left)

1871 – The National Rifle Association was incorporated in the United States

1917 – A bomb exploded at a police headquarters in Milwaukee, Wisconsin, killing nine police officers and one civilian

1932 – The FBI Crime Lab officially opened

1963 – Jack Ruby shot and killed Lee Harvey Oswald live on national television

1969 – *Apollo 12* landed safely in the Pacific Ocean bringing an end to the second manned mission to the moon

1971 – A hijacker named D.B. Cooper parachuted from a Northwest Orient Airlines plane over Washington State with $200,000 in stolen money, never to be seen again

2005 – Pitcher Josh Beckett was traded from the Florida Marlins to the Boston Red Sox

2005 – Actor Pat Morita died at the age of 73

November 25: Andrew Carnegie 1835, Pope John XXIII 1881, Joe DiMaggio 1914, Ricardo Montalban 1920, Jeffrey Hunter 1926, Joe Gibbs 1940, Percy Sledge 1941, Tracey Walter 1942, Ben Stein 1944, John Larroquette 1947, Bucky Dent 1951, Amy Grant 1960, John F. Kennedy, Jr. 1960, Cris Carter 1965, Jill Hennessy 1968, Christina Applegate 1971, Donovan McNabb 1976, Barbara Bush 1981, Jenna Bush 1981

1034 – King Malcolm II of Scotland died, leaving the throne to Duncan, the son of his second daughter, rather than Macbeth, son of his oldest daughter

1120 – The only legitimate heir of King Henry I of England died when the vessel *White Ship* sank

1783 – During the American Revolutionary War, the British evacuated New York
1867 – Alfred Nobel patented dynamite
1885 – Vice-President Thomas A. Hendricks died at the age of 66
1957 – President Dwight D. Eisenhower suffered a stroke
1963 – President John F. Kennedy was buried at Arlington National Cemetery

November 26: John Harvard 1607, Bat Masterson 1853, Hugh Duffy 1866, Lefty Gomez 1908, Charles M. Schulz 1922, Robert Goulet 1933, Rich Little 1938, Tina Turner 1939, Wayland Flowers 1939, Bruce Paltrow 1943, John McVie 1945, Art Shell 1946, Dale Jarrett 1956, Harold Reynolds 1960, Chuck Finley 1962, Garcelle Beauvais 1966, Chris Osgood 1972, Natasha Bedingfield 1981, Chris Hughes 1983

1716 – The first lion to be exhibited in America went on display in Boston
1789 – Thanksgiving was observed as a national holiday for the first time, as part of a recommendation by George Washington
1842 – The University of Notre Dame was founded
1861 – West Virginia was created out of Virginia over a dispute over slavery
1917 – The National Hockey League was founded, beginning with five teams
1922 – In Egypt, Howard Carter entered the tomb of King Tutankhamen
1940 – The Nazis forced 500,000 Jews of Warsaw, Poland to live within a walled ghetto
1941 – President Franklin D. Roosevelt signed a bill establishing the fourth Thursday in November as Thanksgiving Day, as opposed to the last Thursday, which had been established years earlier by Abraham Lincoln
1942 – The motion picture *Casablanca* had its world premiere at the Hollywood Theater in New York City
1950 – China entered the Korean conflict forcing UN forces to retreat
1965 – France became the third country to enter space when it launched its first satellite, the *Diamant-A*
1998 – Hulk Hogan announced that he was retiring from pro wrestling and would run for president in 2000

November 27: Anders Celsius 1701, Buffalo Bob Smith 1917, Bruce Lee 1940, Eddie Rabbit 1941, Jimi Hendrix 1942, Bill Nye the Science Guy 1955, Caroline Kennedy 1957, Mike Scioscia 1958, Robin Givens 1964, Nick Van Exel 1971, Larry Allen 1971, Twista 1973, Jaleel White 1976, Jimmy Rollins 1978

1924 – The first Macy's Thanksgiving Day Parade was held and was so successful it was made an annual event

1934 – Bank robber Baby Face Nelson was killed in a shootout with the FBI in Chicago

1947 – Ted Williams, who won baseball's Triple Crown, was edged out in the voting for MVP by one point, by Joe DiMaggio, who had a 56-game hitting streak during the season

1950 – Shortstop Lou Boudreau, formerly of the Cleveland Indians, signed a two-year contract with the Boston Red Sox for $150,000

1970 – Pope Paul VI, visiting the Philippines, was attacked at the Manila airport by a Bolivian painter disguised as a priest

1973 – The U.S. Senate voted to confirm Gerald R. Ford as Vice-President of the United States after the resignation of Spiro T. Agnew

1983 – A Columbian Avianca Airlines Boeing 747 crashed in Madrid, causing the deaths of 187 people

1983 – Stores across America were flooded with people trying to buy the latest toy craze, the Cabbage Patch Kids dolls

1989 – A bomb blew up a Columbian jetliner just after it took off from the Bogota International Airport, killing all 107 people aboard

2005 – The first partial human face transplant was performed

November 28: Randy Newman 1943, Paul Shaffer 1949, Alexander Godunov 1949, Ed Harris 1950, Jerry Ordway 1957, Dave Righetti 1958, Judd Nelson 1959, Jon Stewart 1962, Matt Williams 1965, Anna Nicole Smith 1967, Chamillionaire 1979, Scarlett Pomers 1988

1520 – Portuguese navigator Ferdinand Magellan reached the Pacific Ocean after passing through the South American strait, later the Straits of Magellan

1582 – William Shakespeare and Anne Hathaway were married

1925 – *The Grand Ole Opry* made its radio debut

1943 – U.S. President Franklin D. Roosevelt, British Prime Minister Winston Churchill and Soviet Leader Joseph Stalin met in Tehran, Iran to map out strategy concerning World War II (see photo on next page)

1963 – President Lyndon Johnson announced that Cape Canaveral would be renamed Cape Kennedy

1964 – The United States launched the space probe *Mariner IV* from Cape Kennedy on a course set for Mars

1979 – An Air New Zealand DC-10 flying to the South Pole crashed in Antarctica killing all 257 people aboard

1988 – Rich Gedman became the highest paid catcher in the American League when he signed a one-year contract with the Boston Red Sox worth $1.2 million

1989 – Romanian gymnast Nadia Comaneci arrived in New York after escaping her homeland through Hungary
1990 – Margaret Thatcher resigned as Prime Minister of Great Britain
1994 – Jeffrey Dahmer, a convicted serial killer, was clubbed to death in a Wisconsin prison by a fellow inmate
2007 – The Christmas special *Shrek the Halls* first aired on ABC-TV

November 29: Christian Doppler 1803, Louisa May Alcott 1832, Nellie Taylor Ross 1876, C.S. Lewis 1898, Madeline L'Engle 1918, Vin Scully 1927, Diane Ladd 1932, Chuck Mangione 1940, Garry Shandling 1949, Jerry Lawler 1949, Howie Mandel 1955, Andrew McCarthy 1962, Kim Delaney 1964, Don Cheadle 1964, Jonathan Knight 1968, Mariano Rivera 1969, Gena Lee Nolin 1971

1777 – San Jose, California was founded, originally called el Pueblos de San Jose Guadalupe
1890 – The first Army-Navy football game was played, with Navy winning, 24-0
1929 – The first airplane flight over the South Pole was made by U.S. Navy Lt. Comdr. Richard E. Byrd

1934 – In the first nationally broadcast NFL game, the Chicago Bears defeated the Detroit Lions, 19-16

1961 – The *Mercury-Atlas 5* spacecraft was launched by the United States with Enos the chimp on board

1963 – President Lyndon Johnson named a commission headed by Earl Warren to investigate the assassination of President John F. Kennedy

1971 – The Professional Golf Championship was held at Walt Disney World for the first time

1975 – Bill Gates adopted the name Microsoft for the company he and Paul Allen had formed

1976 – The New York Yankees signed free-agent Reggie Jackson to a five-year contract worth $3.5 million

1981 – Actress Natalie Wood drowned in a boating accident off Santa Catalina Island, California, at the age 43

1986- Actor Cary Grant died at the age of 82

1992 – Dennis Byrd of the New York Jets was paralyzed after a neck injury in a game against the Kansas City Chiefs

2004 – Ken Jennings' winning streak on *Jeopardy* came to an end after 74 victories and $2,520,700 in winnings

November 30: Jonathan Swift 1667, Mark Twain 1835, Winston Churchill 1874, Lucy Maude "L.M." Montgomery 1874, Efren Zimbalist, Jr. 1918, Richard Crenna 1926, Dick Clark 1929, G. Gordon Liddy 1930, Bill Walsh 1931, Ridley Scott 1937, Robert Guillaume 1937, Linda Bove (Linda on Sesame Street) 1945, Chris Claremont 1950, Mandy Patinkin 1952, Keith Giffen 1952, June Pointer 1954, Joe Kerrigan 1954, Billy Idol 1955, Colin Mochrie 1957, Bo Jackson 1962, Ben Stiller 1965, Des'ree 1928, Ivan Rodriguez 1971, Ray Durham 1971, Mindy McCready 1975, Clay Aiken 1978, Rich Hardin 1981, Kaley Cuoco 1985

1016 – English King Edmund II died

1782 – The United States and Britain signed preliminary peace articles in Paris, ending the Revolutionary War

1804 – The formal impeachment trial of Supreme Court Justice Samuel Chase began in the U.S. Senate

1900 – A German engineer patented a front-wheel drive automobile

1900 – British poet and playwright Oscar Wilde died at the age of 46 in poverty, while in exile in Paris

1936 – London's Crystal Palace was burned to the ground

1939 – The Russo-Finnish War began when Soviet troops invaded Finland

1940 – Actress and comedian Lucille Ball and Cuban musician Desi Arnaz were married

1954 – In Sylacauga, Alabama, Elizabeth Hodges was injured when a meteorite crashed through the roof of her house

1989 – PLO leader Yasser Arafat was refused a visa to enter the United States in order to address the United Nations General Assembly in New York City

2000 – Pitcher Mike Mussina signed a contract with the New York Yankees for six-years worth $88.5 million

2007 – A man walked into the Presidential campaign headquarters in New Hampshire of Hillary Clinton with a bomb and took several hostages for five hours before being arrested

December

December 1: Louis VI (the Fat) of France 1081, Madame Marie Tussaud 1761, Mary Martin 1913, David Doyle 1925, Woody Allen 1935, Lou Rawls 1935, Lee Trevino 1939, Richard Pryor 1940, Bette Midler 1945, George Foster 1948, Treat Williams 1951, Bob Goen 1954, Charlene Tilton 1958, Carol Alt 1960, Joe Quesada 1962, Larry Walker 1966, Matthew Laborteaux 1966, Sarah Silverman 1970, Ryan Malone 1979, Ashley Monique Clark 1988

1822 – Pedro I was crowned the first emperor of Brazil
1835 – Hans Christian Andersen published his first book (see photo at left)
1878 – President Rutherford B. Hayes had the first telephone installed in the White House
1885 – Dr. Pepper was first served
1913 – The first drive-in automobile service station opened, in Pittsburgh
1913 – Ford Motor Company started using the first moving assembly line
1917 – Father Edward Flanagan opened Boy's Town in Nebraska
1919 – Lady Astor was sworn in as the first female member of the British Parliament

1929 – BINGO was invented
1952 – The first sex change operation was reported
1955 – Rosa Parks was arrested for refusing to move to the back of the bus
1956 – Cincinatti Reds outfielder Frank Robinson was chosen unanimously as the National League Rookie-of-the-Year
1956 – Chicago White Sox shortstop Luis Aparicio was announced to be the American League Rookie-of-the-Year, beating out Indian Rocky Colavito and Oriole Tito Francona
1959 – 12 countries, including the U.S. and USSR, signed a treaty that set aside Antarctica as a scientific preserve, which would be free from military activity
1964 – The Houston Colt 45's changed their name to the Houston Astros
1974 – A Boeing 727 crashed at Washington DC's Dulles International Airport, killing all 92 people onboard
1982 – The first permanent artificial heart was implanted in Barney Clark
1989 – National Lampoon's Christmas Vacation was first released in movie theaters
1990 – British and French workers digging the Channel Tunnel finally met under the English Channel
1991 – Ukrainians voted overwhelmingly for independence from the Soviet Union
1998 – Exxon announced that it was buying Mobil for $73.7 billion creating the largest company in the world to date
2004 – Tom Brokaw anchored his last broadcast of the NBC Nightly News before starting his retirement
2008 – President-elect Barack Obama announced his selection of former First Lady Hillary Clinton as his Secretary of State

December 2 John Breckinridge 1760, Pedro II of Brazil 1825, Georges Seurat 1859, Charles Ringling 1863, Ray Walston 1914, Alexander Haig 1924, Jonathan Frid 1924, Julie Harris 1925, Edwin Meese III 1931, Cathy Lee Crosby 1948, Stone Phillips 1954, Tracy Austin 1962, Lucy Liu 1968, Monica Seles 1973, Nelly Furtado 1978, Britney Spears 1981

1804 – Napoleon Bonaparte was crowned Emperor of France
1823 – The Monroe Doctrine was issued, proclaiming an opposition to European colonization of the New World
1848 – Franz Josef I became the Emperor of Austria
1859 – John Brown, a militant abolitionist, was hanged for his raid on Harper's Ferry the previous October
1867 – British author Charles Dickens gave his first public reading in the United States

1901 – King Camp Gillette announced he was going to market razors with disposable blades
1927 – The Ford Motor Company unveiled the Model A automobile
1939 – La Guardia Airport opened in New York City
1942 – The first sustained nuclear reaction occurred at the top-secret Chicago Pile-1, led by Enrico Fermi
1971 – The United Arab Emirates was formed
1988 – Benazir Bhutto was sworn in as the first female President of Pakistan
1993 – The space shuttle *Endeavor* blasted off on a mission to fix the Hubble Space Telescope
2001 – Enron filed for bankruptcy

December 3: Charles VI of France 1368, George McClellan 1826, Joseph Conrad 1857, Andy Williams 1927, Jaye P. Morgan 1931, Bobby Allison 1937, Ozzy Osbourne 1948, Heather Menzies 1949, Mel Smith 1952, Steven Culp 1955, Daryl Hannah 1960, Mike Ramsey 1960, Julianne Moore 1960, Katarina Witt 1965, Brendan Fraser 1968, Paul Byrd 1970, Bruno Campos 1973, Holly Marie Combs 1973, Anna Chlumsky 1980, Brian Bonsall 1981

1818 – Illinois became the 21st state
1828 – Andrew Jackson was elected President of the United States
1904 – Jupiter's moon Himalia was discovered
1917 – The Quebec Bridge opened to traffic
1931 – Alka Seltzer was sold for the first time
1944 – The Greek Civil War began
1950 – Paul Harvey began his national radio broadcasts
1973 – *Pioneer 10* sent back the first close-up images of Jupiter
1979 – At a Who concert in Cincinnati, 11 fans are trampled to death in a stampede for good seats
1988 – Barry Sanders of Oklahoma State University won the Heisman Trophy
1999 – Tori Murden became the first woman to row across the Atlantic Ocean alone, taking 81 days
1999 – NASA lost radio contact with the unmanned Mars Polar Lander as it entered Mars' atmosphere
2003 – Mike Lowell signed a 4-year, $32 million contract with the Florida Marlins
2005 – The Philadelphia Phillies baseball team signed veteran closer Tom Gordon

December 4: John Cotton 1585, Lillian Russell 1861, Jesse Burkett 1868, Wink Martindale 1934, Victor French 1934, Max Baer Jr. 1937, Donnelly Rhodes 1937, Dennis Wilson 1944, Jeff Bridges 1949, Patricia Wettig 1951, Marisa Tomei 1964, Chelsea Noble 1964, Jay-Z 1969, Tyra Banks 1973, Kristina Groves 1976, Kyle Lohse 1978, Lila McCann 1981

1783 – General George Washington said farewell to his officers at Fraunces Tavern in New York
1791 – The world's first Sunday newspaper, *The Observer*, was first published
1875 – Boss Tweed escaped jail and fled to Cuba
1918 – President Woodrow Wilson became the first president to travel to Europe while in office, when he left for the Versailles Peace Conference
1921 – The manslaughter trial of silent film comedian Fatty Arbuckle ended in a hung jury (see photo at right)
1943 – Baseball Commissioner Kenesaw Mountain Landis announced that any club was free to employ black players
1967 – Bert Lahr, best known for his role as the Cowardly Lion in *The Wizard of Oz*, died of pneumonia at the age of 72
1980 – Rock group Led Zeppelin announced it was disbanding
1965 – The United States launched *Gemini 7* with astronauts Frank Borman and Jim Lovell on board
1991 – Associated Press correspondent Terry Anderson was

released after nearly seven years as a hostage in Lebanon
1997 – The NBA suspended Latrell Sprewell of the Golden State Warriors for one year for choking and threatening to kill his coach
1998 – *Unity*, the second module of the International Space Station, was launched

December 5: Martin Van Buren 1782, George Armstrong Custer 1839, Rose Wilder Lane 1886, Fritz Lang 1890, Philip K. Wrigley 1894, Walt Disney 1901, Strom Thurmond 1902, Otto Preminger 1906, Little Richard 1932, Jose Carreras 1946, Jim Messina 1947, Jim Plunkett 1947, Morgan Brittany 1951, Andy Kim 1952, Larry Zbyszko 1953, Art Monk 1957, Carrie

Hamilton 1963, Doctor Dre 1963, Margaret Cho 1968, Cliff Floyd 1972, Amy Acker 1976, Frankie Muniz 1985

1766 – James Christie, founder of the famous auction house, held his first sale in London
1831 – Former United States President John Quincy Adams took his seat in the House of Representatives
1848 – President James Polk triggered the Gold Rush of '49 by confirming the fact that gold had been discovered in California
1908 – At the University of Pittsburgh, numbers were first worn on football uniforms by college football players
1932 – German physicist Albert Einstein was granted a U.S. visa
1933 – Prohibition in the United States ended
1945 – A squadron of U.S. Navy bombers, known as Flight 19, disappeared in the Bermuda Triangle
1974 – The first episode of *Monty Python's Flying Circus* debuted on BBC-2
1978 – U.S. space probe *Pioneer I* sent back the first close-up pictures of Venus
1978 – Pete Rose, after 16-years with the Cincinnati Reds, signed with the Philadelphia Phillies
1988 – Jim Bakker was indicted by a federal grand jury in North Carolina on fraud and conspiracy charges
1990 – The Toronto Blue Jays traded first baseman Fred McGriff and shortstop Tony Fernandez to the San Diego Padres for second baseman Roberto Alomar and outfielder Joe Carter
2007 – *The Golden Compass* was released in movie theaters
2007 – A gunman opened fire at the Westroads Mall in Omaha, Nebraska, killing eight people and then himself

December 6: Ferdinand IV of Castile 1285, King Henry VI of England 1421, William II of the Netherlands 1792, Ira Gershwin 1896, Agnes Moorehead 1900, James Naughton 1945, Larry Bowa 1945, JoBeth Williams 1948, Sonia Manzano 1950, Kin Shriner 1953, Wil Shriner 1953, Janine Turner 1962, Jose Contreras 1971, Richard Krajicek 1971, Ryan White 1971, Kevin Cash 1977, Elian Gonzalez 1993

1492 – Columbus discovered Haiti and the Dominican Republic
1768 – Encyclopedia Britannica was first published
1790 – The U.S. Congress moved from New York to Philadelphia
1849 – Harriet Tubman escaped from slavery
1865 – The 13th Amendment to the Constitution was ratified, abolishing slavery in the United States

1877 – The *Washington Post* newspaper was first published
1877 – Thomas Edison demonstrated the first gramophone, with a recording of himself reciting "Mary Had a Little Lamb"
1883 – *Ladies' Home Journal* was published for the first time

1884 – The construction of the Washington Monument was completed after 34 years of work (see photo of partially completed monument at right)
1889 – Jefferson Davis died in New Orleans at the age of 81
1917 – Almost two-thousand people were killed in a munitions explosion in Halifax, Nova Scotia
1923 – President Calvin Coolidge became the first President to give a presidential address that was broadcast on the radio
1957 – America's first attempt at putting a satellite into orbit failed when a Vanguard rocket blew up on the launch pad at Cape Canaveral
1964 – The *Rudolph the Red-Noses Reindeer* Christmas special first aired on NBC-TV
1973 – Gerald R. Ford was sworn in as the Vice-President of the United States after Spiro Agnew resigned
1976 – The Milwaukee Brewers traded George Scott and Bernie Carbo to the Boston Red Sox for Cecil Cooper
1998 – Astronauts aboard the space shuttle *Endeavour* connected the first two pieces of the *International Space Station*
1989 – The Boston Red Sox signed closer Jeff Reardon
2001 – The Canadian province of Newfoundland officially became known as Newfoundland and Labrador
2005 – The Los Angeles Dodgers hired former Red Sox manager Grady Little as their new manager

December 7: Richard Sears 1863, Willa Cather 1873, Eli Wallach 1915, Ted Knight 1923, Ellen Burstyn 1932, Harry Chapin 1942, Peter Tomarkin 1942, Johnny Bench 1947, Susan Collins 1952, Priscilla Barnes 1955, Larry Bird 1956, C. Thomas Howell 1966, Tino Martinez 1967, Hermann Maier 1972, Terrell Owens 1973, Frankie J 1977, Sara Bareilles 1979, Aaron Carter 1987

1787 – Delaware became the first state of the United States, when it became the first state to vote to ratify the Constitution
1796 – John Adams was elected to be the second President of the United States

1836 – Martin Van Buren was elected the eighth President of the United States
1917 – The United States declared war on Austria-Hungary
1939 – Lou Gehrig was voted into the Baseball Hall of Fame
1941 – Pearl Harbor, Hawaii was attacked by 200 Japanese warplanes, sending the United States into World War II
1941 – Canada declared war on Finland, Hungary Romania, and Japan
1972 – *Apollo 17* was launched, the last manned mission to the Moon
1987 – Soviet leader Mikhail Gorbachev set foot on American soil for the first time
1988 – An estimated 25,000 people were killed when a major earthquake hit northern Armenia in the Soviet Union
1995 – A probe sent from the *Galileo* spacecraft entered into Jupiter's atmosphere
1996 – The space shuttle *Columbia* returned from the longest-ever shuttle flight of 17 days, 15 hours and 54 minutes
1998 – U.S. Attorney General Janet Reno declined to seek an independent counsel investigation of President Clinton over 1996 campaign financing
2003 – Maine received over a foot of snow and the mountains of Maine got almost 3 feet of snow
2005 – The Texas Rangers traded Alfonso Soriano to the Washington Nationals
2005 – *The Chronicles of Narnia: The Lion, the Witch and the Wardrobe* was released in movie theaters

December 8: Horace 65 BC, Mary Queen of Scots 1542, Queen Christina of Sweden 1626, Francis I of the Holy Roman Empire 1708, Eli Whitney 1765, Kenneth Roberts 1885, James Thurber 1894, Frank Faylen 1905, Sammy Davis, Jr. 1925, Maximillian Schell 1930, Flip Wilson 1933, David Carradine 1936, James MacArthur 1937, Jim Morrison 1943, Gregg Allman 1947, Kim Basinger 1953, Teri Hatcher 1964, Sinead O'Connor 1966, Matthew Laborteaux 1966, Jeff George 1967, Mike Mussina 1968, Kevin Harvick 1975, Dominic Monaghan 1976, Reed Johnson 1976, Ryan Newman 1977, Ian Somerhalder 1978, Vernon Wells 1978, Dwight Howard 1985, AnnaSophia Robb 1993

1776 – George Washington's retreating army in the American Revolution crossed the Delaware River from New Jersey to Pennsylvania
1941 – The United States declared war on Japan the day after the Japanese attack on Pearl Harbor
1941 – China and the Netherlands declared war on Japan

1952 – On the show *I Love Lucy*, a pregnancy was acknowledged in a TV show for the first time
1976 – The Eagles released the album *Hotel California*
1980 – John Lennon was shot and killed
1994 – In Los Angeles, 12 alternate jurors were chosen for the O.J. Simpson murder trial
1999 – In Memphis, a jury found that Rev. Martin Luther King Jr. had been the victim of a vast murder conspiracy, not a lone assassin

December 9: John Milton 1608, Clarence Birdseye 1886, Emmett Kelly 1898, Margaret Hamilton 1902, Douglas Fairbanks, Jr. 1909, Broderick Crawford 1911, Tip O'Neill 1912, Kirk Douglas 1918, Redd Foxx 1922, Dick Van Patten 1928, Morton Downey Jr. 1933, Judi Dench 1934, Deacon Jones 1938, Beau Bridges 1941, Dick Butkus 1942, Tom Kite 1949, Michael Dorn 1952, John Malkovich 1953, Donny Osmond 1957, Juan Samuel 1960, Joe Lando 1961, Felicity Huffman 1962, Allison Smith 1969, David Keith 1970, Jesse Metcalfe 1978

1793 – Noah Webster started the first daily newspaper in New York City, the *American Minerva*
1851 – The first YMCA in North America was established, in Montreal
1872 – P.B.S. Pinchback became the first African-America governor of a state, in Louisiana
1941 – China declared war on Germany and Italy
1941 – The first U.S. bombing mission occurred during World War II as they bombed the Philippines
1945 – General George Patton was fatally injured in a car crash in Germany
1965 – *A Charlie Brown Christmas* first aired on CBS-TV
1990 – Lech Walesa won Poland's first direct presidential election in the country's history
1992 – Britain's Prince Charles and Princess Diana announced their separation
1993 – Astronauts aboard the space shuttle *Endeavor* completed repairs to the Hubble Space Telescope

December 10: James I of Scotland 1394, Emily Dickinson 1830, Chet Huntley 1911, Dorothy Lamour 1914, Dan Blocker 1928, Mako 1933, Gloria Loring 1946, Susan Dey 1952, Clive Anderson 1952, Mike McShane 1957, Kenneth Branagh 1960, Nia Peeples 1961, Michael Clarke Duncan 1963, Joe Polo 1982, Patrick Flueger 1983, Raven-Symone 1985

1541 – Thomas Culpepper and Francis Dereham were executed for each having an affair with the fifth wife of England's King Henry VIII, Catherine Howard

1817 – Mississippi became the 20th state

1864 – General William T. Sherman's Union troops reached Savannah, Georgia in their *March to the Sea* (see photo to left)

1869 – Wyoming granted women the right to vote

1898 – The Treaty of Paris was signed, officially ending the Spanish-American War

1901 – The first Nobel prizes were awarded

1906 – President Theodore Roosevelt won the Nobel Peace Prize, the first American to be awarded any Nobel Prize

1936 – Great Britain's King Edward VII abdicated the throne so he could marry an American divorcee

1941 – British Navy ships *HMS Prince of Wales* and *HMS Repulse* are sunk by the Japanese Navy torpedo bombers

1953 – Albert Schweitzer was awarded the Nobel Peace Prize

1964 – Martin Luther King Jr. received the Nobel Peace Prize, the youngest person ever

1965 – The Grateful Dead play their first concert

1983 – Poland's Lech Walesa was awarded the Nobel Peace Prize

1988 – A massive earthquake in Armenia killed 100,000 people

2005 – Comedian Richard Pryor died at the age of 65

2005 – Country music stars Garth Brooks and Trisha Yearwood were married

December 11: Pope Leo X 1475, George Mason 1725, Fiorello La Guardia 1882, Rita Moreno 1931, Ron Carey 1935, Donna Mills 1943, John Kerry 1943, Brenda Lee 1944, Teri Garr 1944, Lynda Day George 1946, Christina Onassis 1950, Bess Armstrong 1953, Jermaine Jackson

1954, Gary Dourdain 1966, Mo'Nique 1968, Mos Def 1973, Rider Strong 1979

1719 – The first recorded sighting of the Aurora Borealis occurred in New England
1789 – The University of North Carolina received its charter
1792 – Louis XVI of France was put on trial for treason (see image to right)
1816 – Indiana became the 19th U.S. state
1928 – In Buenos Aires, police thwarted an attempt on the life of President-elect Herbert Hoover
1936 – Edward VIII's abdication as King of Great Britain became official
1941 – Germany and Italy declared war on the United States, bringing the U.S. into the war in Europe
1951 – Joe DiMaggio announced his retirement from Major League Baseball

1972 – Astronauts aboard *Apollo 17* landed on the moon in the last lunar mission of the twentieth century
1981 – Muhammad Ali fought his last fight
1992 – *The Muppet Christmas Carol* was released in movie theaters

December 12: John Jay 1745, William L. Marcy 1786, William Lloyd Garrison 1805, Caroline Ingalls 1839, Edvard Munch 1863, Edward G. Robinson 1893, Patrick O'Brian 1914, Frank Sinatra 1915, Bob Barker 1923, Ed Koch 1924, Connie Francis 1938, Dionne Warwick 1940, Grover Washington Jr. 1943, Tom Wilkinson 1948, Cathy Rigby 1952, Sheila E. 1957, Sheree J. Wilson 1958, Tracy Austin 1962, Sabu 1964, Jennifer Connelly 1970, Hank Williams III 1972, Mayim Bialik 1975, Orlando Hudson 1977, Garrett Atkins 1979

1787 – Pennsylvania became the 2nd state
1800 – Washington, DC, was established as the Capital of the United States
1870 – Joseph P. Rainey became the first black U.S. Congressman
1901 – Guglielmo Marconi received the first transatlantic radio signal
1911 – Delhi replaced Calcutta as the capital of India
1917 – Father Edward Flanagan started Boys Town
1941 – Great Britain declared war on Bulgaria

1941 – Hungary and Romania both declared war on the United States
1941 – India declared war on Japan
1963 – Kenya declared its independence from Great Britain
1975 – Sara Jane Moore pled guilty to a charge of trying to kill President Gerald Ford in San Francisco the previous September
1979 – The country of Rhodesia changed its name to Zimbabwe
1985 – Arrow Air Flight 1285 crashed following takeoff from Newfoundland, killing 256 people, including 248 U.S. Army airmen
2000 – The Texas Rangers signed Alex Rodriguez to a record breaking 10-year, $252 million contract
2001 – In Beverly Hills, actress Winona Ryder was arrested at Saks Fifth Avenue for shoplifting and possessing pharmaceutical drugs without a prescription

December 13: Eric XIV of Sweden 1533, Henry IV of France 1553, Mary Todd Lincoln 1818, Van Heflin 1910, George Shultz 1920, Larry Doby 1923, Dick Van Dyke 1925, Christopher Plummer 1929, Robert Prosky 1930, John Davidson 1941, Fergie Jenkins 1943, Ted Nugent 1948, Randy Owen 1949, Wendy Malick 1950, John Anderson 1954, Steve Buscemi 1957, Lynn-Holly Johnson 1958, Jamie Foxx 1967, Christie Clark 1973, Jeffrey Pierce 1974, Taylor Swift 1989

1577 – Sir Francis Drake left on his three-year voyage around the world, embarking from Plymouth, England
1636 – The Massachusetts Bay Colony organized three militia regiments to defend against the Pequot Indians, which is recognized today as the founding of the U.S. National Guard
1642 – New Zealand was discovered by Dutch navigator Abel Tasman
1769 – Dartmouth College in New Hampshire received its charter
1862 – At the Battle of Fredericksburg, an estimated 11,000 Northern soldiers were killed or wounded when Union forces were defeated by Confederates under General Robert E. Lee
1947 – The Maine Turnpike opened
1978 – The Philadelphia Mint began producing the Susan B. Anthony U.S. dollar
2000 – Al Gore conceded the Presidential election to George W. Bush, after weeks of controversy
2000 – The Texas 7 escaped from prison and began a robbery spree in which a police officer was shot and killed
2003 – Sadaam Hussein was captured by U.S. troops
2007 – In Major League Baseball, the Mitchell Report was released, a report that fingered many baseball players of using performance

enhancing drugs, including Roger Clemens, Barry Bonds, Andy Pettitte, Miguel Cabrera and Eric Gagne

December 14: Nostradamus 1503, Tycho Brahe 1546, George VI of Great Britain 1895, Margaret Chase Smith 1897, Morey Amsterdam 1908, Shirley Jackson 1919, Charlie Rich 1932, Lee Remick 1935, Hal Williams 1938, Patty Duke 1946, Dee Wallace-Stone 1948, Bill Buckner 1949, Cynthia Gibb 1963, Craig Biggio 1965, Scott Hatteberg 1969, Michael Stoyanov 1970, Billy Koch 1974, Josh Fogg 1976, Sophie Monk 1979, Vanessa Hudgens 1988

1542 – Princess Mary Stuart became Mary Queen of Scots at the age of less than one week old, upon the death of her father, King James V
1782 – The Montgolfier brothers launched their first balloon
1799 – George Washington, died at the age of 67
1819 – Alabama became the 22nd state
1903 – The Wright Brothers made their first attempt to fly, unsuccessfully, at Kitty Hawk, North Carolina
1911 – Norwegian explorer Roald Amundsen became the first man to reach the South Pole
1915 – Jack Johnson became the first black world heavyweight champion in boxing
1946 – The U.N. General Assembly voted to establish the United Nation's headquarters in New York City
1947 – NASCAR was founded in Daytona Beach, Florida
1959 – The *Motown* recording label was founded in Detroit, Michigan
1962 – NASA's *Mariner 2* became the first spacecraft to fly past Venus
1984 – Howard Cosell retired from the NFL's Monday Night Football
1999 – Charles M. Schulz announced he was retiring from the *Peanuts* comic strip
2003 – Pop Century Resort opened at Walt Disney World
2006 – The Boston Red Sox signed Japanese pitcher Daisuke Matsuzaka to a $52 million 6-year deal

December 15: Nero 37 AD, Gustave Eiffel 1832, Charles Duryea 1831, J. Paul Getty 1892, Tim Conway 1933, Art Howe 1946, Don Johnson 1949, J.M. DeMatteis 1953, Mo Vaughn 1967, Garrett Wang 1968, Rodney Harrison 1972, Adam Brody 1979

1791 – The first ten amendments to the Constitution, known as the Bill of Rights, went into effect following ratification by the state of Virginia
1815 – Jane Austen's "Emma" was published
1877 – Thomas Edison patented the phonograph
1890 – American Sioux Indian Chief Sitting Bull was killed in Grand River, South Dakota
1891 – James Naismith introduced the game of basketball to his students
1916 – During World War I, the French defeated the Germans in the Battle of Verdun
1939 – The movie *Gone with the Wind* premiered
1961 – Former Nazi official Adolf Eichmann was sentenced to death by an Israeli court
1965 – Two U.S. manned spacecraft, *Gemini 6* and *Gemini 7*, performed the first space rendezvous, coming within 2 feet of each other
1965 – The movie *The Sound of Music* was released
1966 – Walt Disney died at the age of 65
1970 – The Soviet probe *Venera 7* became the first spacecraft to land softly on the surface of Venus, where it was destroyed after just 23 minutes due to extreme heat and pressure
2001 – The Leaning Tower of Pisa reopened after 11 years of fortifying it, while being careful not to straighten it

December 16: Catherine of Aragon 1485, Ludwig Van Beethoven 1770, Jane Austen 1775, Leopold I of Belgium 1790, Noel Coward 1899, Margaret Mead 1901, Arthur C. Clarke 1917, Liv Ullmann 1938, Lesley Stahl 1941, Steven Bochco 1943, Terence Knox 1946, Ben Cross 1947, Billy Gibbons 1949, Sam Robards 1961, William "Refrigerator" Perry 1962, Billy Ripken 1964, Miranda Otto 1967, Anna Popplewell 1988

1653 – Oliver Cromwell became Lord Protector of England, Scotland and Ireland

1773 – The Boston Tea Party occurred (see image above)

1776 – George, a goose who had lived for 49 years, died

1809 – Napoleon Bonaparte was divorced from the Empress Josephine by an act of the French Senate

1835 – In New York, 530 buildings were destroyed by fire

1901 – *The Tale of Peter Rabbit*, by Beatrix Potter, appeared in print for the first time

1916 – Gregory Rasputin, the monk who had wielded powerful influence over the Russian court, was murdered by a group of noblemen

1944 – During World War II, the Battle of the Bulge began in Belgium

1985 – Two mob leaders were shot dead in New York City and John Gotti assumed the leadership of the Gambino family

1991 – The Republic of Kazakhstan gained its independence

1998 – The United States and Great Britain fired hundreds of missiles on Iraq in response to Saddam Hussein's refusal to comply with U.N. weapons inspectors

2000 – President-elect George W. Bush selected Colin Powell to be the first African-American secretary of state

2005 – Actor John Spencer, best known for playing Leo McGarry on the television show *West Wing*, died of a heart attack at the age of 58

December 17: Maria I of Portugal 1734, Alexander I of Yugoslavia 1888, Arthur Fiedler 1894, George Lindsey 1935, Cal Ripken Sr. 1935, Chris Matthews 1945, Eugene Levy 1946, Bill Pullman 1953, Tracy Byrd 1966, Sean Patrick Thomas 1970, Milla Jovovich 1975, Eric Bedard 1976, Chase Utley 1978, Jin Sun-Yu 1988

1538 – Pope Paul III excommunicated England's King Henry VIII
1777 – France recognized American independence
1830 – South American patriot Simon Bolivar died in Colombia

1903 – The Wright Brothers completed the first successful flight of a motor powered airplane in Kitty Hawk, North Carolina (see photo above)
1967 – The Prime Minister of Australia, Harold Holt, disappeared while swimming in the ocean on the coast of Portsea, never to be seen again
1969 – SALT I talks began
1975 – Lynette Fromme was sentenced to life in prison for her attempt on the life of President Gerald Ford
1983 – A bomb exploded at Harrods Department Store in London, killing seven people
1989 – *The Simpsons* debuted on FOX-TV
1991 – In the NBA, Cleveland beats Miami, 148-80, the most lopsided score ever
2003 – *The Lord of the Rings: The Return of the King*, the final installment the trilogy, was released

December 18: Queen Christina of Sweden 1626, Charles Wesley 1707, Franz Ferdinand 1863, Joseph Stalin 1878, Ty Cobb 1886, Edwin Armstrong 1890, George Stevens 1904, Betty Grable 1916, Ossie Davis 1917, Roger E. Mosley 1938, Keith Richards 1943, Steven Spielberg 1947, Leonard Maltin 1950, Ray Liotta 1955, Ron White 1956, Brian Orser 1961, Brad Pitt 1963, Charles Oakley 1963, Stone Cold Steve Austin 1964, Rachel Griffiths 1968, Casper Van Dien 1968, DMX 1970, Arantxa Sanchez Vicario 1971, Katie Holmes 1978, Christina Aguilera 1980, Ben Watson 1980

1620 – The *Mayflower* landed in present-day Plymouth, Massachusetts
1642 – Abel Tasman became the first European to set foot in New Zealand
1787 – New Jersey became the third state
1865 – When Georgia voted to ratify the Thirteenth Amendment to the Constitution, it went into effect, ending slavery in the United States
1898 – A new automobile speed record was set at 39 mph
1915 – President Woodrow Wilson, widowed a year earlier, married Edith Bolling Galt at her Washington home
1932 – In the first NFL Championship, the Chicago Bears defeated the Portsmouth Spartans (later known as the Detroit Lions), 9-0
1936 – Su-Lin, the first giant panda to come to the U.S. from China, arrived in San Francisco
1956 – *To Tell the Truth* debuted on CBS-TV
1956 – Japan was admitted to the United Nations
1966 – Saturn's moon Epimethius was discovered
1979 – The sound barrier was broken on land for the first time by Stanley Barrett when he drove 739.6 mph
1984 – Christopher Guest and Jamie Lee Curtis were married
1997 – Comedian Chris Farley was found dead in his Chicago apartment at the age of 33
1998 – The U.S. House of Representatives began the debate on the four articles of impeachment concerning President Bill Clinton

December 19: Philip V of Spain 1683, William Parry 1790, Leonid Brezhnev 1906, Little Jimmy Dickens 1925, Robert B. Sherman 1925, Cicely Tyson 1933, Al Kaline 1934, Tim Reid 1944, Richard Leakey 1944, Robert Urich 1946, Kevin McHale 1957, Mike Lookinland 1960, Reggie White 1961, Jennifer Beals 1963, Jessica Steen 1965, Alberto Tomba 1966, Eric Weinrich 1966, Criss Angel 1967, Kristy Swanson 1969, Warren Sapp 1972, Alyssa Milano 1972, Jake Plummer 1974, Jake Gyllenhaal 1980, Maurice Williams 1982

1154 – Henry II was crowned King of England
1606 – Three ships left England, bound for the New World, carrying settlers that would eventually start Jamestown, Virginia, the first of the original thirteen American colonies
1732 – Benjamin Franklin began publishing *Poor Richard's Almanac*
1777 – General George Washington led his army of about 11,000 men to Valley Forge, Pennsylvania, to camp for the winter

1843 – *A Christmas Carol* by Charles Dickens was first published (although some sources claim it was December 17) (see image at right)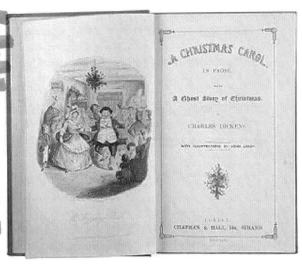

1848 – Author Emily Bronte died of tuberculosis at the age of 30

1910 – Edward Douglass White was sworn in as the 9th Chief Justice of the Supreme Court

1918 – Robert Ripley began his *Believe It or Not* column in *The New York Globe*

1941 – Adolf Hitler became the Supreme Commander in Chief of the German armies

1963 – Zanzibar became independent from Great Britain

1972 – The last manned mission to the moon in the twentieth century, *Apollo 17* splashed down in the Pacific

1974 – Nelson Rockefeller was sworn in as Vice-President of the United States, after Gerald Ford became President, following the resignation of Richard Nixon

1997 – The film *Titanic* debuted in the United States

1998 – President Bill Clinton was impeached on two charges of perjury and obstruction of justice by the House of Representatives

2003 – Images for the new design for the Freedom Tower at the World Trade Center site were released

December 20: Samuel Mudd 1833, Harvey Firestone 1868, Branch Rickey 1881, Irene Dunn 1898, Gabby Hertnett 1900, Morrie Schwartz 1916, George Roy Hill 1922, Kim Young-sam 1927, John Hillerman 1932, Kathryn Joosten 1939, Peter Criss 1945, John Spencer 1946, Oscar Gamble 1949, Cecil Cooper 1949, Jenny Agutter 1952, Michael Badalucco 1954, Joel Gretsch 1963, Chris Robinson 1966, Nicole DeBoer 1970, Aubrey Huff 1976, James Shields 1981, David Wright 1982, David Cook 1982, JoJo 1990

1192 – Richard the Lion-Heart of England was captured and held for ransom by Leopold V of Austria, while returning home from the Crusades

1699 – Peter the Great ordered that the Russian New Year be changed from September 1 to January 1

1790 – The first successful cotton mill in the United States began operating at Pawtucket, Rhode Island

1803 – The Louisiana Purchase was officially turned over to the United States from France at a special ceremony in New Orleans

1860 – South Carolina seceded from the Union, the first state to do so

1864 – Confederate forces evacuated Savannah, Georgia as Union General William T. Sherman continued his March to the Sea

1879 – Thomas Edison demonstrated his light bulb

1928 – Mail delivery by dog sled began in Lewiston, Maine

1938 – Vladimir Kosma Zworykin patented the iconoscope television system

1942 – The Japanese bombed Calcutta

1946 – The movie *It's A Wonderful Life* debuted

1968 – Author John Steinbeck died at the age of 66

1973 – Spanish Prime Minister Luis Carrero Blanco was assassinated in Madrid by a car bomb

1989 – General Noriega, Panama's former dictator, was overthrown by a United States invasion force invited by the new civilian government

1991 – The movie *JFK* opened in the US

1998 – In Houston, Texas, a 27-year-old woman gave birth to the only known living set of octuplets

2002 – Trent Lott resigned as the Majority Leader of the United States Senate

2007 – Queen Elizabeth II became the oldest ever monarch in the United Kingdom, passing Queen Victoria who lived to be 81 years, 7 months, and 29 days

December 21: Thomas Beckett 1118, Roger Williams 1603, Benjamin Disraeli 1804, Willie Lincoln 1850, Herman Joseph Muller 1890, Josh Gibson 1911, Donald Regan 1918, Paul Winchell 1922, Joe Paterno 1926, Phil Donahue 1935, Jane Fonda 1937, Frank Zappa 1940, Samuel L. Jackson 1948, Jeffrey Katzenberg 1950, Joaquin Andujar 1952, Chris Evert 1954, Jane Kaczmarek 1955, Tom Henke 1957, Ray Romano 1957, Florence Griffith Joyner 1959, Andy Dick 1965, Kiefer Sutherland 1966, Khrystyne Haje 1968, LaTroy Hawkins 1972, Dustin Hermanson 1972

1891 – The first basketball game was played

1898 – Scientists Pierre and Marie Curie discovered the radioactive element radium

1913 – The first crossword puzzle appeared in the *New York World*

1937 – Walt Disney premiered the first, full-length, animated feature, *Snow White and the Seven Dwarves*
1940 – F. Scott Fitzgerald died at the age of 44
1945 – U.S. General George S. Patton died in Heidelberg, Germany, of injuries from a car accident
1951 – Joe DiMaggio announced his retirement from Major League Baseball
1958 – Charles de Gaulle was elected President of France
1968 – *Apollo 8* was launched on the first manned mission to orbit the moon
1987 – Over 1,500 people were killed when the passenger ferry *Dona Paz* sank after colliding with an oil tanker in the Philippines
1988 – 270 people were killed when Pan Am flight 103 exploded over Lockerbie, Scotland, due to a terrorist attack

December 22: Connie Mack 1862, Peggy Ashcroft 1907, Lady Bird Johnson 1912, Barbara Billingsley 1915, Gene Rayburn 1917, Hector Elizondo 1936, Steve Carlton 1944, Diane Sawyer 1945, Steve Garvey 1948, Robin Gibb 1949, Maurice Gibb 1949, Rick Nielsen (Cheap Trick) 1950, Ralph Fiennes 1962, Steve Kariya 1977, Jordin Sparks 1989

1864 – During the American Civil War, Union General William T. Sherman concluded his March to the Sea by capturing Savannah, Georgia
1885 – Samurai warrior Ito Hirobumi became the first prime minister of Japan
1937 – The Lincoln Tunnel opened in New York City
1944 – British Prime Minister Winston Churchill arrived in Washington for a wartime conference with President Franklin Roosevelt
1956 – Colo, the first gorilla to be born in captivity, was born at the Columbus, Ohio zoo
1961 – James Davis became the first U.S. soldier to die in Vietnam
1984 – New York City resident Bernhard Goetz shot four black youths on a Manhattan subway who were allegedly trying to rob him
1989 – Berlin's Brandenburg Gate re-opened after almost 30 years being closed
1990 – Lech Walesa was sworn in as Poland's first popularly elected president

December 23: John III of Sweden 1537, Alexander I of Russia 1777, Joseph Smith Jr. 1805, Connie Mack 1862, James Gregory 1911, Helmut Schmidt 1918, James Stockdale 1923, Akihito 1933, Frederic Forrest 1936, Avi 1937, Harry Shearer 1943, Wesley Clark 1944, Susan Lucci 1946, Jack Ham 1948, Jim Harbaugh 1963, Eddie Vedder 1964, Slash

(Guns 'n' Roses) 1965, Greg Biffle 1969, Corey Haim 1971, Brad Lidge 1976, Alge Crumpler 1977, Victor Martinez 1978, Estella Warren 1978, Hanley Ramirez 1983

1783 – George Washington returned home to Mount Vernon, after the disbanding of his army following the Revolutionary War
1823 – The poem *A Visit from St. Nicholas* by Clement C. Moore was published
1888 – Following a quarrel with Paul Gauguin, Dutch painter Vincent Van Gogh cut off part of his own earlobe
1893 – The opera *Hansel und Gretel* by Engelbert Humperdinck was performed for the first time
1940 – The Italian ship *Antonietta* was sunk by a German submarine
1954 – The Walt Disney movie *20,000 Leagues Under the Sea* premiered
1954 – The first human kidney transplant was performed
1966 – *How the Grinch Stole Christmas* first aired on television
1970 – The North Tower of the World Trade Center was finished, becoming the tallest building in the world at 1,368 feet
1986 – Dick Rutan and Jeana Yeager became the first people to fly an aircraft, the *Voyager*, non-stop around the world
1997 – Terry Nichols was convicted by a Denver jury on charges of conspiracy and involuntary manslaughter in the 1995 federal building bombing in Oklahoma City, which killed 168 people
2005 – Chad declared war on Sudan

December 24: King John of England 1166, Dr. Benjamin Rush 1745, Kit Carson 1809, James Prescott Joule 1818, George I of Greece 1845, Johnny Gruelle 1880, Michael Curtiz 1886, Harry Warren 1893, Howard Hughes 1905, Ava Gardner 1922, Lee Dorsey 1924, Mary Higgins Clark 1929, Nicholas Meyer 1945, Steve Smith 1945, Clarence Gilyard 1955, Diedrich Bader 1966, Ricky Martin 1971, Stephanie Meyer 1973, Kevin Millwood 1974, Ryan Seacrest 1974, David Ragan 1985

1814 – The War of 1812 between the United States and England was ended with the signing of the Treaty of Ghent in Belgium
1818 – Franz Gruber of Oberndorf, Germany, composed the music for *Silent Night* to words written by Josef Mohr
1851 – A fire devastated the Library of Congress in Washington, DC, destroying about 35,000 volumes, or two-thirds of the collection
1865 – The Ku Klux Klan was formed
1906 – The first radio program was broadcast
1941 – Japan occupied Hong Kong and Wake Island

1943 – President Franklin Roosevelt appointed General Dwight D. Eisenhower supreme commander of Allied forces
1951 – Libya became independent of Italy
1968 – Three astronauts, James A. Lovell, William Anders and Frank Borman, reached the moon and began the first of 10 orbits
1968 – The crew of the *USS Pueblo* was released by North Korea after being held for 11 months on suspicion of spying
1979 – The Soviet Union invaded Afghanistan
1990 – Tom Cruise and Nicole Kidman were married

December 25: Sir Isaac Newton 1642, Clara Barton 1821, Conrad Nicholson Hilton 1887, Humphrey Bogart 1899, Cab Calloway 1907, Anwar Sadat 1918, Rod Serling 1924, Nellie Fox 1927, Mabel King 1932, Rick Berman 1945, Gary Sandy 1945, Larry Csonka 1946, Jimmy Buffett 1946, Gene Lamont 1946, Barbara Mandrell 1948, Sissy Spacek 1949, Manny Trillo 1950, CCH Pounder 1952, Steve Wariner 1954, Annie Lennox 1954, Rickey Henderson 1958, Dido 1971, Hideki Okajima 1975, Alecia Elliot 1982,

800 – Pope Leo III crowned Charlemagne the first Holy Roman Emperor
1066 – William the Conqueror was crowned King of England
1223 – St. Francis of Assisi assembled one of the first Nativity scenes, in Greccio, Italy

1776 – General George Washington and his troops crossed the Delaware River in a surprise attack against Hessian forces at Trenton, New Jersey (see image above)

1818 – *Silent Night* was performed for the first time, at the Church of St. Nikolaus in Oberndorff, Austria

1868 – President Andrew Johnson granted an unconditional pardon to all Civil War Confederate soldiers

1926 – Hirohito became the emperor of Japan after the death of his father Emperor Taisho

1941 – Hong Kong surrendered to the Japanese

1946 – W.C. Fields died at the age of 66

1977 – Charlie Chaplin died at the age of 88

1989 – Former baseball player and manager Billy Martin died in a truck crash in Fenton, New York

1991 – Mikhail Gorbachev resigned as President of the Soviet Union

2006 – Legendary singer James Brown died at the age of 73

December 26: Frederick II of the Holy Roman Empire 1194, Charles Babbage 1791, E. D. E. N. Southworth 1819, George Dewey 1837, Henry Miller 1891, Richard Widmark 1914, Steve Allen 1921, Alan King 1927, Donald Moffat 1930, Carroll Spinney 1933, Phil Spector 1940, Gray Davis 1942, Carlton Fisk 1947, Ozzie Smith 1954, Jim Toomey 1960, Chris Daughtry 1979, Zach Mills 1995

1776 – During the American Revolution, the British are beaten in the Battle of Trenton

1792 – The final trial of Louis XVI began in Paris

1811 – A theater fire in Richmond, Virginia took the life of, among others, Virginia Governor George William Smith

1825 – The Erie Canal opened

1898 – Pierre and Marie Currie announced that they had isolated radium

1908 – Jack Johnson defeated Tommy Burns to become the first African American heavyweight boxing champion

1919 – Babe Ruth was sold to the New York Yankees by the Boston Red Sox

1933 – FM radio was patented

1933 – The Nissan Motor Company was first organized in Tokyo, Japan

1941 – Winston Churchill became the first British Prime Minister to address a joint meeting of the U.S. Congress

1947 – Twenty-six inches of snow fell on New York City in a 16 hour period of time

1972 – Former President of the United States Harry Truman died at the age of 88

1974 – Comedian Jack Benny died at age 80

1985 – Dian Fossey, famous for her work with gorillas, was found murdered in the bedroom of her cabin in Rwanda at the age of 52

1986 – After 35 years on the air, the soap opera *Search for Tomorrow* broadcasts for the last time

1986 – The world population reached five billion

1991 – The Soviet Union was officially dissolved

1996 – Six-year-old beauty queen JonBenet Ramsey was found beaten and strangled in the basement of her family's home in Boulder, Colorado

2002 – The first cloned human baby was born

2006 – Former President of the United States Gerald Ford died at the age of 93, the oldest of any former president

December 27: Anne de Mortimer 1390, Johannes Kepler 1571, Jacob Bernoulli 1654, Pope Pius VI 1717, Louis Pasteur 1822, Sydney Greenstreet 1879, Marlene Dietrich 1901, William Masters 1915, Bruce Hobbs 1920, John Amos 1941, Cokie Roberts 1943, Mick Jones 1944, Gerard Depardieu 1948, David Knopfler 1952, Arthur Kent 1953, Andre Tippett 1959, Maryam d'Abo 1960, Chyna 1969, Wilson Cruz 1973, Masi Oka 1974, Heather O'Rourke 1975, Emilie de Ravin 1981, David Aardsma 1981

537 – The Hagia Sophia was completed

1831 – Charles Darwin set out on a voyage to the Pacific aboard the *HMS Beagle*

1904 – James Barrie's play *Peter Pan* premiered in London

1918 – The Great Poland Uprising against the Germans began

1927 – Leon Trotsky was expelled form the Communist Party

1932 – Radio City Music Hall in New York City opened

1945 – The World Bank was created

1947 – The children's television program *Howdy Doody*, hosted by Buffalo Bob Smith, made its debut on NBC

1978 – Spain became a democracy after forty years as a dictatorship

1979 – *Knots Landing* premiered on CBS-TV

1985 – Dian Fossey, an American naturalist, was found murdered at a research station in Rwanda

2003 – Former Major League Baseball player Ivan Calderon was murdered in Puerto Rico at the age of 41

2007 – Former President of Pakistan, Benazir Butto, was assassinated as she left an election rally in Rawalpindi by a suicide bomber

December 28: Woodrow Wilson 1856, Ted Lyons 1900, Cliff "Charley Weaver" Arquette 1905, Lew Ayres 1908, Billy Williams 1910, Stan Lee 1922, Martin Milner 1927, Terry Sawchuk 1929, Nichelle Nichols 1933, Maggie Smith 1934, Bill Lee 1946, Richard Clayderman 1953, Denzel Washington 1954, Ray Bourque 1960, Adam Vinatieri 1972, Seth Meyers

1973, B.J. Ryan 1975, John Legend 1978, Sienna Miller 1981, Cedric Benson 1982, Quinton Porter 1982, Thomas Dekker 1987, Mackenzie Rosman 1989, David Archuleta 1990

1065 – Westminster Abbey was consecrated under Edward the Confessor
1612 – Galileo became the first person to observe the planet Neptune, although he mistakenly cataloged it as a star
1694 – Queen Mary II of England died after five years of joint rule with her husband, King William III
1832 – John C. Calhoun became the first Vice-President of the United States to resign, stepping down over differences with President Andrew Jackson
1836 – Spain recognized the independence of Mexico
1846 – Iowa became the 29th state
1867 – The United States claimed Midway Island, the first territory claimed outside the continental U.S.
1945 – The U.S. Congress officially recognized the "Pledge of Allegiance"
1973 – The Endangered Species Act was passed in the United States
1981 – Elizabeth Jordan Carr, the first American test-tube baby, was born in Norfolk, Virginia
1981 – Pat Sajak began hosting *Wheel of Fortune*
1984 – *The Edge of Night* aired its final episode after 28 years on television
1992 – Future Football Hall of Famer Joe Montana played in his final game
2000 – Montgomery Ward announced it was going out of business after 128 years
2004 – The dwarf planet Haumea was first discovered
2007 – Nepal became a federal democratic republic, thus abolishing the monarchy

December 29: Empress Elizabeth of Russia 1709, Madame de Pompadaur 1721, Charles Goodyear 1800, Andrew Johnson 1808, Tom Bradley 1917, Inga Swenson 1932, Ed Flanders 1934, Mary Tyler Moore 1936, Barbara Steele 1937, Jon Voight 1938, Ted Danson 1947, Patricia Clarkson 1959, Paula Poundstone 1960, Jude Law 1972, Theo Epstein 1973, Richie Sexson 1974, Jaret Wright 1975, Shizuka Arakawa 1981, Jessica Andrews 1983

1170 – St. Thomas Becket, the Archbishop of Canterbury, was murdered in his Canterbury Cathedral by four knights acting on Henry II's orders and/or wishes
1778 – During the American Revolution, the British captured Savannah, Georgia without firing a shot

1813 – British soldiers burned Buffalo, New York, during the War of 1812
1845 – President James Polk signed legislation making Texas the 28th state in the Union
1851 – The first American YMCA was organized in Boston
1890 – United States soldiers massacred over 400 men, women and children of the Great Sioux Nation, at Wounded Knee, South Dakota
1934 – The first college basketball game at Madison Square Garden was played, featuring Notre Dame against NYU
1940 – During World War II, Germany began dropping incendiary bombs on London
1975 – A bomb exploded at LaGuardia Airport in New York City, killing 11 people and injuring dozens more
1997 – The Guatemalan Civil War ended after 36 years of fighting
2002 – Cincinnati's Riverfront Stadium, later Cinergy Field, was demolished
2003 – Actor Earl Hindman, best known as Wilson on the TV show *Home Improvement*, died of lung cancer

December 30: Titus of the Roman Empire 39 AD, Rudyard Kipling 1865, Hideki Tojo 1884, Bert Parks 1914, Jack Lord 1920, Bo Diddley 1928, Dell Shannon 1934, Sandy Koufax 1935, Jack Riley 1935, Noel Paul Stookey 1937, James Burrows 1940, Michael Nesmith 1942, Fred Ward 1942, Davy Jones 1945, Patti Smith 1946, Meredith Vieira 1953, Suzy Bogguss 1956, Matt Lauer 1957, Tracey Ullman 1959, Ben Johnson 1961, Dan England 1969, Kerry Collins 1972, Tiger Woods 1975, A.J. Pierzynski 1976, Kenyon Martin 1977, Tyrese Gibson 1978, Eliza Dushku 1980, LeBron James 1984, Ryan Sheckler 1989

1460 – At the Battle of Wakefield, in England's War of the Roses, the Duke of York was defeated and killed by the Lancastrians
1862 – The *U.S.S. Monitor* sank off the coast of Cape Hatteras, North Carolina
1922 – The Union of Soviet Socialist Republics, or USSR, was formed
1924 – Edwin Hubble announced the existence of other galaxies
1953 – The first color TV sets went on sale for about $1,175
1980 – *The Wonderful World of Disney* was cancelled by NBC after more than 25 years on the TV
2003 – The U.S. Food and Drug Administration banned the diet supplement ephedra
2006 – Saddam Hussein, the former dictator of Iraq, was executed by hanging for crimes against his own people
2007 – The New England Patriots football team became the second team ever to end a regular season undefeated, with a 16-0 record

December 31: Jacques Cartier 1491, Charles Cornwallis 1738, George C, Marshall 1880, Anthony Hopkins 1937, John Denver 1943, Ben Kingsley 1943, Barbara Carrera 1945, Tim Matheson 1947, Donna Summer 1948, George Thorogood 1951, Jane Badler 1953, Bebe Neuwirth 1958, Val Kilmer 1959, Rick Aguilera 1961, Esteban Loaiza 1971, Brent Barry 1971

1600 – The British East India Company was granted an English Royal Charter by Queen Elizabeth I
1695 – A window tax was imposed in England, causing many shopkeepers to brick up their windows

1775 – The British stopped an attack by Continental Army generals Richard Montgomery and Benedict Arnold at Quebec (see image to left)
1857 – Britain's Queen Victoria decided to make Ottawa the capital of Canada
1879 – Thomas Edison demonstrated incandescent lighting to the public for the first time
1904 – The first Times Square New Years celebration was held, although it was known as Longacre Square at the time
1929 – *Aulde Lang Syne* was performed for the first time by Guy Lombardo
1944 – Hungary declared war on Germany
1946 – President Harry Truman officially declared an end to the hostilities of World War II
1947 – Roy Rogers and Dale Evans were married
1955 – General Motors became the first United States company to make over a billion dollars in one year
1972 – Major League Baseball star Roberto Clemente died in a plane crash off the coast of his native Puerto Rico
1983 – The AT&T Bell System was broken up by the United States Government

1986 – A fire at the Dupont Plaza Hotel in San Juan, Puerto Rico took the lives of 97 people

1991 – The Union of Soviet Socialist Republics was officially dissolved

1991 – The Civil War in El Salvador ended

1995 – The last *Calvin and Hobbes* comic strip was published

1997 – Michael Kennedy, 39-year-old son of the late Senator Robert Kennedy, was killed in a skiing accident on Aspen Mountain in Colorado

1999 – Russian President Boris Yeltsin resigned

1999 – Control of the Panama Canal was handed over to Panama, from the United States

2004 – Tapei 101, the tallest building in the world, officially opened

2007 – The Big Dig construction project in Boston, Massachusetts ended after almost 17 years

Picture Credits

January 1 – Lincoln with his Cabinet at the first reading of the Emancipation Proclamation, painting by Francis Bicknell Carpenter, oil on canvas, 1864.

January 3 – George Washington rallying his troops at the Battle of Princeton, unknown artist.

January 6 – Anne of Cleves, painting by Hans Holbein, c. 1539.

January 15 – Portrait of **Elizabeth I** of England in her coronation robes, 1600-1610, by unknown painter, of the lost original from 1559, National Portrait Gallery, London.

January 19 – A Live Jackass Kicking a Dead Lion, cartoon by Thomas Nast as it appeared in the January 19, 1870 issue of Harper's Weekly.

January 29 – Photo of **Queen Liliukalani** of Hawaii, Hawaii State Archives.

January 30 – Etching of the 1835 Assassination Attempt on President **Andrew Jackson**, public domain.

January 31 – Portait of **General Robert E. Lee**, officer of the Confederate Army, 1863, Library of Congress Prints and Photographs Collection.

February 10 – Portrait of **Catherine Howard**, by Hans Holbien, 16th century.

February 13 – Portrait of **Joan of Arc**, 1450-1500, Centre Historique des Archives Nationales, Paris.

February 15 – Photo of the wreckage of the ***USS Maine***, 1898.

Feburary 19 – Promotional photo of **Mister Rogers' Neighborhood**, Family Communications Inc.

February 20 – Painting of **Edward VI** by William Scrots, c. 1550, Royal Collection.

Feburary 28 – Lithograph of ***USS Princeton***, 1844, N. Currier, Library of Congress, Prints and Photographs Division.

March 5 – The Boston Massacre, lithograph by John Bufford after William L. Champey, c. 1856.

March 7 – Photo of **Alexander Graham Bell**, c. 1914-1919, Library and Archives Canada.

March 18 – Photo of **Franklin and Eleanor Roosevelt**, shortly after their March 1905 wedding, Franklin D. Roosevelt Library.

April 4 – William Henry Harrison campaign poster, cropped, published by N. Courrier, 1835-1856, Library of Congress, Prints and Photographs Collection.

April 5 – Painting of the baptism of Pocahontas in 1613 or 1614, 1840 painting by John Gadsby Chapman, photograph by the architect of the Capitol.

May 14 – **Skylab** launch aboard a Saturn V rocket, May 14, 1973, NASA photo.

May 30 – **Jane Seymour**, third wife of Henry VIII, c. 1536-1537, Hans Holbien painter, Kunsthistorisches Museum.

June 15 – John of England signs the **Magna Carta**, illustration from *Cassell's History of England*, 1902.

June 29 – The Old **Globe Theatre**, by Wenceslas Hollar in 1642 for his *Long View of London*.

July 4 – John Trumbell's ***Declaration of Independence***, 1819, United States Capitol, Washington, DC.

July 13 – **Jean Paul Morat**, *The Death of Morat*, 1793 by Jacques-Louis David.

August 2 – Death of **William Rufus** of England, from Ridpath's Universal History, 1895.

August 14 – ***Field and Stream*** magazine, September 1903 cover.

August 31 – ***The Scream*** by Edvard Munch, 1893.

September 16 – ***Mayflower*** *in Plymouth Harbor* by William Halsall, 1882.

September 17 – *Scene at the* ***Signing of the Consitution of the United States*** by Howard Chandler Christy, April 1940 painting, United States Capitol.

September 20 – ***Galileo*** *Before the Holy Office*, 19th century painting by Joseph-Nicholas Robert-Fleury.

October 5 – ***Death of Tecumseh***, frieze in the Rotunda of the U.S. Capitol.

October 7 – **Edgar Allen Poe**, photograph of a daguerreotype of Edgar Allen Poe taken in 1848 by W.S. Haartshorn, Providence, Rhode Island, Library of Congress, Prints and Photographs Collection.

October 8 – **Alvin York**, photo of Sergeant Alvin York, in public domain as it was taken prior to 1923.

October 12 – *Examination of a Witch*, **Salem Witch Trials**, painted by Thompkins H. Matteson, 1853, from the Collection of the Peabody Essex Museum.

October 21 – **Florence Nightingale**, c. 1860, Library of Congress, Prints and Photographs Division.

October 22 – *Portrait of* ***Sam Houston***, by J. C. Buttre, 1858, from a daguerreotype by B. P. Paige, The Center for American History at the University of Texas, Prints and Photographs Collection.

October 31 – Photo of **Harry Houdini**, c. 1899, Library of Congress, McManus Young Collection.

November 17 – **Elizabeth I** of England, the "Darnley Portrait", unknown artist, National Portrait Gallery, London.

November 28 – **Tehran Conference**, photograph of **Joseph Stalin, Franklin Roosevelt and Winston Churchill**, 1943, U.S. Signal Corp. Photo.

December 1 – **Hans Christian Andersen**, c. 1860s, from *Bibliothek des allgemeinen und praktischen Wissens. Bd. 5*, 1905.

December 4 – **Roscoe "Fatty" Arbuckle**, Library of Congress, George Grantham Bain Collection.

December 6 – Partially completed **Washington Monument**, Matthew Brady photpgraph, c. 1860, Library of Congress, Brady-Handy Photograph Collection.

December 10 – **Sherman's March to the Sea**, photo by George N. Barnard, 1864, Library of Congress, Prints and Photographs Collection.

December 11 – *Portrait of **Louis XVI of France***, by Antoine-Francois Callet, 1786, Musee Carnavalet, Paris, France.

December 16 – **Boston Tea Party**, 1773, lithograph by Sarony & Major, 1846, Archival Research Catalog, National Archives and Records Administration.

December 17 – The first powered-flight by the **Wright Brothers**, December 17, 1903, photo by John T. Daniels.

December 19 – The title page of **A Christmas Carol**: In Prose, Being a Ghost Story of Christmas, by **Charles Dickens**, illustrations by John Leech, London, Chapman & Hall, 1843, first edition, photo by Heritage Auctions, Inc., Dallas, Texas.

December 25 – ***Washington's Crossing of the Delaware River***, by Emanual Leutze, 1851.

December 31 – Arnold's column is shattered in fierce street fighting during the **Battle of Quebec**, 1775, illustration by Allan Daniel, Canadian Military Heritage, Canadian Department of Defense.

Brian Merrill is a math teacher at Searsport District Middle School in Searsport, Maine. He lives in neighboring Belfast with his wife Cara, a middle school English teacher. Brian has a grown stepson, Seth. *On This Date* was his first book, originally published in 2006. Since the original publication, history has continued to happen, both to the world at large (thus the newest version of *On This Date*), and to Brian. In August 2008, he published *From George W. to George W.: The Presidents and their Cabinets*. In December 2008, Brian published *Boston Red Sox Managers*.

Made in the USA
San Bernardino, CA
30 November 2012